The Education-Jobs Gap

The Education-Jobs Gap:

Underemployment
or Economic Democracy

D. W. Livingstone

Garamond Press

Garamond Press Ltd.,
63 Mahogany Court
Aurora, Ontario L4G 6M8

garamond@web.ca
www.garamond.ca

Printed and bound in Canada

National Library of Canada Cataloguing in Publication

Livingstone, D.W., 1943-
    The education-jobs gap

Includes bibliographical references and index.
ISBN 1-55193-017-X

1. Underemployment.   I. Title

HD5709.L58   1999   331.13   C98-931311-5

Garamond Press gratefully acknowledges the support of the Department of Canadian Heritage, Government of Canada, and of the Canadian Studies Bureau of the same department. The Press also acknowledges the Government of Ontario through the Ontario Media Development Corporation's Ontario Book Initiative.

Contents

Tables and Figures

Tables

Figures

Preface

The education-jobs gap refers to the discrepancy between our work-related knowledge and our opportunities to use this knowledge in interesting and fairly compensated work. My basic argument is that our knowledge generally far exceeds our job opportunities. We are wasting large human learning capacities and achievements through our failure to recognize the existence of a massive "knowledge society" in a vast array of current formally organized and informal learning practices. Education systems can always be improved. But it is not inadequate education that is the primary cause of the education-jobs gap. The basic problem is the lack of decent jobs.

Most of this book is devoted to documenting the unprecedented amount of present learning activity, assessing the extensive and multi-faceted "underemployment" of this learning in paid workplaces, and offering an explanation for why this wastage is happening. The pressures in private market-based economies to sell more cheaply than competitors by reducing labour costs and automating production have led to unprecedented numbers of willing workers being made redundant in terms of one or more of the many faces of underemployment. Each of these faces, namely *the talent use gap, structural unemployment, involuntary reduced employment, the credential gap, the performance gap and subjective underemployment*, is carefully scrutinized.

In spite of this widespread underemployment of existing knowledge, we continue to be barraged by the claim that more and better education and training initiatives are the solution to the lack of decent jobs. On the contrary, the viable solution lies not in educational reforms but in *economic reforms*. Organizing paid work through blind obedience to the presumed dictates of globally competitive markets is not the only choice. The basic alternatives to this shareholder-centred capitalism are either a more stakeholder-based version of a capitalist economy or economic democracy. As the last chapter suggests, there are many possible economic reforms, involving democratic redistribution, reorganization and revaluing of different forms of work, that can lead to substantial reductions in underemployment.

Unless the majority understand the real character of the present economic system and its underlying forces, there is little hope of overcoming the systemic injustices against many of the underemployed within it. Capitalism is not an emperor with no clothes. On the contrary, its productivity has served to clothe more people well than any prior economic system. But, from any fair-minded standpoint, the scope of this system's exclusion of qualified people from meaningful work and fulfilling lives is becoming increasingly intolerable. This book offers some conceptual and empirical resources for all who wish to aid in reversing current underemployment trends. Once we comprehend the massive extent of underemployment of human talents, the social forces actively creating underemployment, and the sorts of economic alternatives that can reduce it, we have a solid basis for social action that can make a difference.

Acknowledgements

I owe large debts to many who helped in the creation of the various parts of this study. The Ontario Institute for Studies in Education of the University of Toronto (OISE/UT) and the Social Sciences and Humanities Research Council of Canada (SSHRC) funded the surveys and case studies that provide some of the central empirical sources of evidence. The Department of Sociology and Equity Studies in Education (SESE) at OISE/UT, as well as the Centre for the Study of Education and Work in SESE, provided a supportive environment in which to conduct these heretical inquiries. The students in the Education and Work graduate seminar and in the Learning and Work Thesis Workshop group in SESE have been especially helpful through conducting their own related interviews and their group discussions of the text. I am also grateful to the University of Saskatchewan for inviting me to present the 27th Annual Sorokin Lecture, and to the University of British Columbia for inviting me to participate in its Noted Scholar Program during 1996. Both universities offered ideal venues to try out the ideas more fully developed in the later chapters of the book.

The individuals who have contributed to the completion of this work are far too numerous to list here. Many colleagues commented on parts of the manuscript or provided useful reference material, including Sandra Acker, Paul Anisef, Ari Antikainen, Bob Bowd, Bob Connell, June Corman, Phil Corrigan, Kari Dehli, Tom Dunk, Don Fisher, Isabel Gibb, Andy Hargreaves, Ted Harvey, Richard Hillman, Alf Hunter, Harvey Krahn, Atsushi Makino, Meg Luxton, Uri Levitan, Peter Mayo, Greg MacLeod, Jim McCarter, Roxana Ng, Paul Olson, Norene Pupo, Herman Robers, Kjell Rubenson, Roger Simon, Alison Taylor, Alan Thomas, Dieter Timmermann, Allen Tough and Terry Wotherspoon. Jack Quarter and Wally Seccombe offered especially insightful detailed critiques. I gratefully acknowledge the gen-

eral interviewing assistance of Bob Bowd, Chi-hung Chen, Henry
Chow, Marnina Gonick, Guida Man, Mike Hersh, Patrice Milewski,
Naja Modibo, Paul Raun, Andrew Thornton, and especially Peter
Sawchuk and Megan Terepocki; the general assistance in establish-
ing interview sites by Pramila Aggrawal, Kathryn Church, Sue Cox,
Gerard Kennedy, Barbara Marchant, Jennifer Stephen, and Marilyn
Venn Norman; and the advice of David Northrup of the Institute for
Social Research at York University on the design of the first repre-
sentative sample survey of those in the credential gap. Of course,
without the thousands of interviewees who generously gave of their
time and spoke frankly about their views on education and jobs little of this work would have been possible.

I owe a special thank you to the core staff members of the SSHRC
Research Network on New Approaches to Lifelong Learning (NALL),
Jill Given-King and Reuben Roth, and those of the OISE/UT Biennial
Survey of Educational Issues, Doug Hart, Brenda Mignardi and Kris-
tine Pearson, as well as my research assistants, Matt Adams, Muriel
Fung, Stephanie Livingstone and Peter Sawchuk. All of them have
provided invaluable research support, particularly Doug Hart who
conducted all the computer-based data analyses. My original editor at
Westview Press, Dean Birkencamp and my later editor, Sarah Warner,
have been very supportive throughout the entire process. Tobin Mac-
Intosh provided excellent typesetting and text design services. Peter
Saunders of Garamond Press supported the book concept from the
beginning and persisted to ensure publication in Canada.

My debts to my wife, Angela, are far, far beyond words. I dedicate
this book to our daughters, Phaedra and Stephanie, in the hope that
they and the rest of their generation will not have to live in the education-jobs gap for much longer.

INTRODUCTION

Mapping The Forest of Underemployment[1]

It is difficult to see the forest for the trees, especially when you are deep inside the forest and there are some large trees. Underemployment is such a forest. Underemployment may be defined, in both individual and collective terms, as the extent to which the knowledge and skill levels of members of the potential labour force exceed their opportunities to use these levels of knowledge and skill in paid employment. A primary objective of The Education-Jobs Gap was to identify multiple dimensions of underemployment and offer empirical assessments of their respective extent. All of the identified dimensions of underemployment were found to be substantial and some were found to be increasing. The opposite condition of underqualification – insufficient knowledge and skill for available jobs – was found to be relatively much smaller and diminishing. Underemployment in its multiple forms was anticipated to become one of the major social problems of the 21st century. Since Education Jobs Gap was published in 1998, research on the various dimensions of underemployment has increased but is still preoccupied with a few dimensions while underestimating the extent of the general problem.

The major focus in both research and related policy discussions continues to be either on official unemployment statistics or on mismatches between educational credentials attained and those required for job entry. Concern with unemployment is justifiable since it is consequential for most aspects of human existence. Nevertheless, a preoccupation with official unemployment statistics ignores other serious dimensions of underemployment. A preoccupation with credential mismatches is much more limiting, particularly since credential inflation combined with increasing formal educational attainments often makes "overeducation" appear to be a fairly stable phenomenon, while other aspects of underemployment may in fact be increasing.

As defined in Chapter Two, the major dimensions of underemployment are the talent use gap, unemployment, involuntary reduced employment, the credential gap, the performance gap and subjective underemployment. This expanded conception of underemployment includes both *time-based complete or partial exclusion from employment* and *skill-based underutilization of capabilities in employment*. Employment status is properly understood as a continuum ranging from long-term complete unemployment to long-term full employment. The notion of underemployment can be applied to any of the six dimensions on this continuum. People in long-term unemployment are most severely underemployed but even those most fully employed in long-term jobs may feel underemployed. Several dimensions of underemployment may be experienced simultaneously, even exclusion and underutilization – which may both be quite extreme among involuntary part-time workers in unfulfilling jobs.

The International Labour Office (ILO) had registered underemployment as an integral part of the framework for measuring the labour force since the late 1940s. The ILO's major definitional effort on the subject in 1982 (see ILO, 1998) recognized both time-based insufficient volume of employment or "visible underemployment," and misallocation of labour resources and skills – or "invisible underemployment." ILO reports in the 1990s offered some estimates of total underemployment on national and global scales. But by the end of the decade, the ILO (1998) had decided to focus on more detailed measures of visible underemployment and concluded that measures of invisible underemployment and skill underutilization were beyond its scope.

As Chapter Two notes, research on the multiple dimensions of unrealized capacities of the potential workforce began in earnest in the U.S in the 1960s. The "subemployment" approach focused on the extent of exclusion from employment of inner city youths. The "underemployment" or "overeducation" approach focused on the underutilization of the qualifications of recent university graduates in available jobs. Most of the subsequent research has continued to be preoccupied with more detailed measures of either time-based exclusion (forms of unemployment) or skill-based underutilization (untapped abilities of job holders).

Drawing on the subemployment approach, the US Bureau of Labour Statistics introduced multiple alternative unemployment measures in 1976. These were all time-based indicators of attachment to the active labour force and included the official unemployment rate (those actively seeking employment for different durations), those waiting for recall or start, discouraged workers available for employment but not actively looking because of lack of perceived opportunities, and the unused portion of involuntary part-time workers' labour time. These supplementary measures of unemployment were also taken up by Statistics Canada (Usalcas and Bowlby, 1999). Other statistical agencies and analysts (e.g. European Commission, 1999; Mitchell and Carlson, 2000) have included and tried to estimate the magnitude of different components of the discouraged worker group such as involuntarily retired, designated disabled and others. Still other independent researchers have recently proposed much more expansive exclusionary measures of underemployment to include numbers of homeless, welfare cases and prison populations (Lacharite, 2002).

Researchers interested in skill mismatches have continued to focus on the educational attainments of the employed labour force compared with estimates by either job analysts or job holders themselves of the education required for job entry or job performance (e.g. Borghans and de Grip, 2000). Again, fairly complex typologies of qualifications and extent of use on the job have been developed and applied to estimate patterns of skill underutilization among the employed (see Oosterbeck, 2000; Johnson, Morrow and Johnson, 2000; Handel, forthcoming). But one aspect of skill underutilization continues to be largely ignored – the talent use gap. Just as the involuntary premature exclusion of willing retired people from employment has not often been considered a legitimate form of unemployment, the systemic forms of discrimination against the talents of some youth cohorts through inequitable streaming and other biased processes in schooling are treated as trees in another forest. In system analytic terms, educational equality has three basic aspects: equality of opportunity (input), equality of treatment (throughput) and equality of result (output). There is extensive literature on the subject (e.g. Lucas, 1999; Biddle, 2001) that clearly establishes the existence of systemic discrimination on grounds of class, race and gender in schooling. The "outputs" of schooling are also the "inputs" of the labour market. The anticipatory underemployment of the talents of youth, as indicated by the under-representation of particular social groups in the graduating cohorts from advanced levels of schooling, should be at least as relevant to comprehending underemployment as the unwilling exclusion of retired people. Education Jobs Gap remains quite alone in addressing this phenomenon as an aspect of underemployment.

There is now general recognition in both the time and skill-based approaches that no single measure can comprehend the phenomenon of underemployment. Both approaches have typically generated more complex measures within their own criteria without seriously considering aspects of the other approach

Some efforts have been made to develop more inclusive conceptualizations of underemployment using both time *and* skill criteria. Feldman (1996) proposes five dimensions: involuntary part-time employment and skill-based measures equivalent to the credential gap and the performance gap, as well employment outside one's own field and reduced or less than average wages. Lester and McCain (2001) correctly see unemployment as a special case of underemployment which they generically conceive as a condition of receiving less reward than qualifications might support. They therefore incorporate both time and skill-based criteria but choose to define and estimate the extent of underemployment simply by subjective preferences to move into another's job over one's own. Researchers using the labour utilization framework approach (e.g. Clogg, 1979; Madamba, 1998) have probably given the most sustained attention to a combination of tine and skill-based measures, typically including official unemployment, involuntary part-time employment, and the credential gap, as well as a measure of relatively low wages. Others have also proposed combining time-based measures of degree of exclusion with similar measures of low pay to construct a structural exclusion index (Burke and Shields, 1999; Barrett, 2001). In most of these approaches it is unclear whether wage levels are actually intended to be indicative of exclusion or of skill underutilization. Indeed, much of the research on skill mismatches treats wage rates as a consequence of underemployment rather than a defining feature. The arbitrariness of any chosen wage level and the difficulty of making valid comparisons over time also undermine the usefulness of such measures. All of these approaches ignore at least a few of the dimensions that Education Jobs Gap argues are essential to comprehend underemployment.

So Education Jobs Gap represents a relatively inclusive approach to both time and skill-based dimensions of underemployment. It addresses two time-based measures (general unemployment and involuntary reduced employment) and three skill-based measures (talent use gap, credential gap and performance gap), as well as subjective underemployment – which could reference either time or skill-based criteria or both. Several other researchers have begun to take up this approach to some extent (e.g. Batenburg and deWitte, 2001; van den Meer and Batenburg, 2002).

In sum, there has been increasing focus on several trees in each part of the forest by those located there, but still very limited effort to comprehend and measure the full extent of underemployment as *both* a time-based and skill-base problem which effects two distinct but overlapping populations – the excluded-unemployed and the underutilized-employed.

CURRENT EXTENT OF UNDEREMPLOYMENT

Evidence reported since Education Jobs Gap was published in 1998 suggests that the overall extent of underemployment continues to worsen globally, albeit with some cyclical tendencies and local variations. Brief comments on time-based, skill-based and subjective aspects of underemployment follow.

Official unemployment statistics indicate that global unemployment was a record high of about 180 million people at the end of 2002 and the world employment situation was characterized as "deteriorating dramatically" by the Director-General of the ILO (2003). The official unemployment rate in industrialized countries had risen to about 7 percent, slightly higher in Canada and approaching 6 percent in the U.S. The official U.S. measure excludes some marginal jobseekers and therefore gives slightly lower estimates of unemployment for both countries than the Canadian definition (Sorrentino, 2000). The unemployment rate of active jobseekers continues to fluctuate in relation to capitalist business cycles but remains persistently well above rates of the post-WWII expansionary period. The numbers of discouraged searchers, available but not actively looking in the past week, also tend to fluctuate along with those of active jobseekers. Discouraged searchers probably add between 5 and 15 percent to official unemployment rates in Canada and the U.S. (Usalcas and Bowlby, 1999; U.S. Department of Labor, 2003; National Jobs for All Coalition, 2003). If *all* discouraged workers who want employment but are not looking were included, the official employment rate could increase by as much as 50 percent (Robinson, 1999; get National Jobs for All Coalition, 2003). In particular, those in involuntary early retirement and full-time students wanting to work but not counted in the labour force have also increased greatly in some countries (European Commission, 1999). The concentration of unemployment in "workless households" among the disadvantaged has also been growing continually (Bell, Houston and Heyes, 1997). While careful comparative studies remain to be done, there does appear to be an upward secular trend through the business cycle in total unemployment of those wanting to work in most advanced capitalist countries.

Only a minority of employed workers in most advanced capitalist economies are now content with their current hours of employment; in the U.S. around 40 percent are content but about a third want fewer hours and a quarter want more hours (Reynolds, 2003). Overwork is generally more common than underemployment in work time mismatches in most countries. But part-time workers are much more likely to want more hours than less. Part-time workers have roughly doubled as a proportion of the employed labour force since the mid-1970s and have recently fluctuated with the business cycle at around 20 percent in both the U.S. and Canada (Tilly, 1998; Council of Ministers of Education Canada, 1999). Multiple job holders who want full-time work but can only get it by combining part-time jobs have also increased gradually to over 5 percent of the employed labour force (Bluestone and Rose, 1997). The proportion of part-timers who want more hours has increased in most countries from around 20 percent in the 1980s to a third or greater now (Noreau, 2000; Canadian Labour Congress, 2002; European Commission, 1999). Involuntary part-time employment has grown to around half of the official unemployment rate in the U.S., Canada and many European countries (Marshall, 2001; National Jobs for All Coalition, 2003; European Commission, 1999). In addition, temporary employment has increased to over 10 percent of all jobs in advanced capitalist economies (ILO, 2003) and most of these job holders also want more secure full-time employment. Involuntary reduced employment, including people in part-time jobs who want more hours and those in temporary jobs who want more permanent ones, also exhibits an upward secular trend through recent business cycles.

It is probably fair to say that an accurate estimate of the total time-based underemployment rate of all who want jobs today in most advanced capitalist economies is around double the official unemployment rate and that the proportions of discouraged workers and those in involuntary reduced employment are both continuing to grow. According to most recent estimates, those officially unemployed or experiencing hidden unemployment in these terms in the U.S now make up about 18 percent of the eligible labour force (National Jobs for All Coalition, 2003). If the subemployment approach practice of including those full-time workers earning less than poverty-level wages were also applied, the total numbers suffering from these forms of underemployment would increase to around a third of the entire labour force in the U.S. and Canada (National Jobs for All Coalition, 2003; Burke and Shields, 1999) and also globally (ILO,2003). In addition, the majority of those designated as disabled have now been discovered to suffer from some form of time-based underemployment (Abbas, 2003). In any case, it is clear that the cumulative trend to greater time-based underemployment has been associated with lower wages, less benefits and diminished job security (e.g. Tilly, 1998; Bluestone and Rose, 1997).

Skill-base underemployment is also very widespread and shows no substantial signs of decreasing. The notion of the talent use gap or anticipatory underemployment of youths through under-representation in graduating cohorts from advanced education is based on the assumption that all social groups have youth cohorts with similar distributions of initial talent and learning capacity. The increasing centrality of educational credentials for hiring makes graduation rates by social origins a key indicator of equity in initial entry into the labour market. Using 1988-94 U.S. data for university graduation rates by family origins, we found that the children of professional employees were about 3.5 times as likely to graduate from university as the children of industrial workers (see Table 2.1). Generational analyses found that this ratio had declined in the post-WWII period of educational expansion and then increased somewhat among the cohorts completing university in the mid 1970s onward. Replicating this analysis with 1996-2002 U.S. data,[2] we find that differences in graduation rates by class origins have continued to increase and that the overall ratio in now about 3.75 to 1. Whites have continued to be over-represented in relation to blacks by about 2 to 1, while men are now only marginally over-represented compared to women. When generalized across the class structure, these measures of under-representation suggest a very large underutilization of talent at the point of entry into the labour force. Similar recent patterns have been found in Canada (Livingstone and Stowe, 2003) Recent increases in tuition fees and the growing need to work while studying have undoubtedly reduced the completion chances for those from lower income families even further (e.g. King and Bannon, 2002). The once-controversial claims of a "correspondence principle" referring to the relations of schooling and the relations of production (and most pertinently to the intergenerational persistence of economic status influences on the "outputs" of schooling and the initial "inputs" to the labour market) have been largely confirmed by more recent empirical studies (Bowles and Gintis, 2001).

Credential underemployment, as indicated by formal educational attainments that exceed job *entry* requirements, appears to have become a fairly stable but substantial condition. Surveys since the 1970s in the U.S. (Daly, Buchel and Duncan, 2000), Canada (Livingstone, 2001; Frennette, 2001) and various European countries (Groot, Maassen and van den Brink, 2000; Green, MacIntosh and Vignoles, 1998) have generally found that around 30 percent of the employed labour force have higher educational credentials than required for new entrants to their jobs. Since the educational attainments of the potential labour force have grown very significantly during this period, (e;g. Statistics Canada, 2000) job entry requirements may have increased accordingly. Whether increased entry requirements are primarily a result of credential inflation by employers to select better qualified workers, heightened educational efforts by job seekers who perceive that they are in an "educational arms race" or increases in job performance requirements may be much disputed. The fact that job entry requirements have increased very significantly cannot be disputed. The credential underemployment of recent graduates is typically somewhat higher than those with longer labour market experience and there are some recent indications of apparent increases in this "credential gap" (e.g. Hay, 2002; van den Meer and Batenburg, 2002). Even if there has been major credential inflation, the potential labour force has been able to keep ahead in this game in many countries.

But in stark contrast to the impressive educational attainment gains since the 1960s, particularly in the U.S. and Canada, the best available direct estimates of the *actual* skill requirements to perform jobs indicate only gradual upgrading over this period (Wolff, 2000, Handel, 2000a; Leckie,1996). There have also been only marginal increases in the proportion of the labour force in the high skilled professional and managerial jobs widely heralded as essential to the realization of a "knowledge-based economy" (Lavoie and Roy, 1998; Handel, 2000b). U,S. Bureau of Labor Statistics' estimates project that only about 20 percent of job openings will require a university degree, compared with over a third of new entrants who have one, while the vast majority of new jobs will require only short-term training (Hecker, 2001). Surveys of the utilization of literacy skills on the job have found that more than 20 percent of workers have significantly greater reading skills than their job performance actually requires (Krahn and Lowe, 1998) and that literacy skill underutilization on the job has been increasing in recent youth cohorts (Boothby, 1999). My own recent estimates of performance underemployment rely on job analysts' assessments of required level of education with a 1998 national sample of the Canadian labour force (Livingstone, 2001). According to this measure, over half of the currently employed Canadian labour force have job-related skills and knowledge that exceed the actual performance requirements of their current jobs. This is very similar to the magnitude of the performance gap found in the U.S. and Canada by the previous analyses in Education Jobs Gap (see Table 2.8). Over a third have matching attainments and performance requirements. About 10 percent are underqualified for their current jobs, at least in terms of educational requirements. While there continue to be demonstrable periodic skill shortages in particular specializations (e.g. Cohen and Zaidi, 2002), they should be understood in the context of these larger and persistent skill surpluses. Comparative analyses of European surveys, relying on worker self-assessment measures, have found that the incidence of underemployment based on performance requirements has been increasing while under-education has decreased (Hartog, 2000).

Job holders' self-perceptions of the match between their qualifications and their job requirements have typically been closer than either credential or performance based measures. There appears to be a strong tendency for job holders to think of themselves as adequately qualified to perform their own jobs whether or not more objective measures indicate mismatches. Analyses of the Canadian General Social Survey find that 23 percent of the employed labour force felt overqualified for their jobs in 1989, 22 percent in 1995 and 24 percent in 2000.[3] The 1998 NALL national survey similarly found that 21 percent rated themselves as overqualified, while only 3 percent considered themselves underqualified and 75 percent thought they were adequately qualified. These estimates of the extent of subjective underemployment are very similar to the earlier findings reviewed in Education Jobs Gap. A more recent Canadian national survey has found about 27 percent of workers perceive themselves to be overqualified for their jobs (Lowe and Schellenberg, 2001).

So direct estimates of the underemployment of job holders generally range from self-ratings around 20 percent who see themselves as overqualified for their jobs, to around 30 percent who have greater credentials than required for entry to their jobs and over 50 percent who may have more knowledge and skill, as estimated by formal education, than is needed to perform their jobs. On all measures, the extent of underemployment is generally greater than the extent of underqualification by a ratio of 2:1 or more. More accurate measures of people's employment-related skills and knowledge and the extent of correspondence with available jobs are certainly needed, as well as longitudinal cohort studies. But the weight of empirical evidence continues to strongly suggest that the actual skill development of the currently employed workforce generally exceeds the gradually increasing job requirements. Further analyses of all of the skill-based underemployment measures by occupational group also continue to confirm that blue collar and white collar workers are much more likely than corporate executives, managerial and professional employees to be underemployed, and that visible minorities and recent immigrants also have relatively high rates (Kelly, Howatson-Leo and Clark, 1997; Livingstone, 2001).

Considering all six measures of underemployment, there are some indications of increases over the past five years, some fluctuations related to business cycle changes and other contextual factors, and few indications of secular decline on any of these dimensions. While many researchers persist in focussing selectively on one or more of either the time-based measures or the skill-based measures and analyzing related characteristics such as individual earnings and social attitudes, the forest of underemployment continues to grow. The overall extent of underemployment has increased since Education Jobs Gap was first published.

REVERSING AND EXPANDING THE EDUCATION-EMPLOYMENT OPTIC

The tendency to focus on educational solutions to economic problems remains pervasive. Current major government policy initiatives such as the Bush regime's "No Child Left Behind" campaign in the U.S. and the federal Innovation Strategy in Canada are premised on a need to overcome purportedly widespread skill deficits in the existing workforce to cope with the onset of a knowledge-based economy, while largely ignoring the need for relevant economic reforms. There are always some conditions of underqualification in quickly changing labour markets, but to assume generalized skill deficits from these cases is to focus on a few small trees in the much larger forest of underemployment. Even human capital theorists are becoming more preoccupied with the problem of "overeducation" in relation to returns on investment in education (e.g. Borghans and de Grip, 2000), while some corporate business entities have begun to bewail the economic costs of failing to recognize workers' credentials and other job-related learning (Bloom and Watt, 2002).

Those who comprehend the nature and scope of underemployment recognize that it is fundamentally an economic and political problem, and that political efforts to rectify related social problems through education reforms – however well-intentioned – may even be counter-productive in effect. As Richard Rothstein (2002, p. 25) concluded in his recent Spencer Foundation Address:

> [O]ur national determination to reform only education and then expect all other forms of inequality and oppression to...take care of themselves will doom us to another half century of lack of progress.

As I argue in Chapter 6, we need to reverse the education-employment optic and address economic reforms directly in order to have a chance to reduce the multiple forms of underemployment. The only effective solutions to current underemployment problems are likely to be found in economic reforms that encourage our highly educated labour forces to make fuller use of their skills and knowledge in paid workplaces. The most feasible reforms include *work redistribution* and *workplace democratization.* In light of the increasing polarization of paid employment between those who feel compelled to work over 50 hours per week and those involuntarily working under 30 hours or unemployed or excluded entirely from paid work, one obvious response is to redistribute employment hours among them (see Hayden, 1999). The alternative is to witness the persistence of our current polarization of work time along with chronically high numbers of actively unemployed and discouraged workers. But, if the performance-based measures of mismatch presented in Chapter 3 and above are remotely accurate, even with significant paid work-time redistribution measures, workplace reorganization is also greatly needed to allow many workers to use their skills and knowledge more fully in their jobs. Research completed after Education Jobs Gap, (Lowe, 2000; Livingstone, 2002) further confirms that greater democratization appears to be the most sustainable way of reducing underemployment in the workplace. General recognition of underemployment should encourage employers, labour unions, employees, governments and local community groups to develop collaborative programs to identify more fully the actual local pools of knowledge and skills in their enterprises and communities. Community development initiatives by allied groups to match people's underused skills and knowledge with local economic needs through democratized job redesign, work redistribution, and creation of environmentally sustainable new jobs (e.g. Milani, 2000) have demonstrated a capacity to actually reduce underemployment.

Expanded conceptions of both learning and work are needed to fully contextuate education and employment relations in advanced capitalist societies. "Work" includes both unpaid housework and community volunteer work as well as paid employment. "Learning" includes informal education and self-directed individual and collective informal learning as well as formal schooling and further education courses. Recent research informed by this expanded conception has found that we are now spending as much time collectively in unpaid work as in paid work and that the redivision of paid and unpaid work between men and women is occurring more rapidly than any upgrading of job skill performance requirements. This research has also discovered that informal education and learning are much more substantial than, and foundational for, institutional forms of both job-related and general adult education. Informal learning is widespread and valuable even among the least schooled, and much more closely related to forms of work over which we have greater discretionary control, such as community volunteer work (see Livingstone, 2002). Substantial research analyzing the forms and effects of informal learning, as well as the interrelations of unpaid work and informal learning with education and employment has barely begun (see Livingstone, 2003;). But it is already clear that the rich body of informal learning of knowledge and skills, especially among less affluent, less schooled social groups (Livingstone and Sawchuk, 2003) only accentuates the level of their underemployment in contemporary paid workplaces.

RESPONSES TO CRITICS

My research in this field owes large debts to Ivar Berg (2003 [1970]) who pioneered study of the underutilization of education in jobs, Randall Collins (1979) who initiated critical study of the credential society, labour utilization framework scholars such as Clifford Clogg (1979) who began to connect time-based and skill-based measures of underemployment, and the many later researchers who have continued to document particular dimensions of the problem. Many of these scholars have suffered the slings and arrows of defenders of the faith in educational solutions to economic problems, especially those who persist in the belief that skill deficits are the fundamental problem and greater investment in human capital will bring secular salvation. Education Jobs Gap has been relatively immune to date.

Most of the published reviews of Education Jobs Gap have been very positive (e.g. diFazio,1999; Parker, 1999; Witte, 1999;Wotherspoon, 1999; Phillips, 2000; Hiscott, 2000). Some human capital theory advocates have predictably ignored most of the dimensions of underemployment, dismissed the analysis as overly sociological and reasserted the validity of human capital theory because of some indications of positive social rates of return among the employed labour force (Musgrove, 1999). Even if this were true, the large and devastating negative returns for the excluded warrant at least some consideration.

A few more substantial published criticisms deserve a response. Derek Wilkinson (2001) suggests that the talent use gap does not belong in an analysis of underemployment. He argues that it really denotes a gap between actual and ideal educational attainment rather than education and jobs, and that because I recognize the importance of informal learning for actual job training I am implying that educational certificates are not necessary anyway. But my analysis certainly stresses the instrumental value of credentials for *getting* a job in our society and, as noted above, sees the outputs of school systems as pivotal initial inputs into labour markets. I continue to believe that the very large talent use gap for those first entering the labour market, as well as the involuntary retirement of many willing older workers, should be considered to comprehend the full extent of underemployment. Conversely, Wilkinson then charges me with being too instrumentalist in focusing on the relations of education to jobs. The focus of the book *is* explicitly on this relationship but I do state in several places that education should be valued for many purposes, including general socialization, citizenship, and personal fulfillment, and never simply reduced to job training. He also raises two related scenarios of increasing standardization of jobs while downloading production costs onto self-employed consumers through corporate power, and the prospect of continuing education cutbacks by neo-conservative governments, the latter possibly rationalized by my documentation of surplus skills and widespread informal learning. I agree that an extreme neo-conservative response would be to insist on cutting back on public education in relation to either reduced employment levels or current skill surpluses. But the active labour force in many countries has actually been expanding as more women have entered the labour market and the numbers of contingent workers swell. Also, as documented more fully in the NALL survey (Livingstone, 2002), underemployment has not reduced great popular demand for advanced and further education, and no regime in a liberal democratic state is likely to impose very drastic education cuts on the electorate. Finally, Wilkinson suggests that self-reports of subjective underemployment may exaggerate and those of under-qualification may underestimate the extent of actual mismatches. There are admittedly mixed findings on self-ratings (Kruger and Dunning, 1999; Myles and Fawcett, 1990). But Wilkinson fails to note that the credential and performance-based measures generally produce *higher* levels of skill-based underemployment. The more pertinent point is that unless more of those who are underemployed on such measures come to perceive themselves to be so and mobilize around progressive economic *and* educational reforms, the regressive scenarios feared by Wilkinson are more likely to come true.

Michael Smith (2001) concurs with me that new technology has not distinctively raised skill demands in the labour force, but he nevertheless insists that the supply of skills is not adequate. He concedes that there is no general scarcity of university-educated labour in Canada and that literacy is only one skill among many. He then focuses on some relatively low *usage* scores on literacy skills in Canada compared to the U.S. and some European countries in intermediate occupations to suggest the possibility of some skill shortages. He also notes – and virtually nobody disagrees – the chronic scarcity of skilled trades workers in Canada. But failure to use skills on the job has been demonstrated by many studies to be more probably a consequence of the job structure than the absence of personal skills. Smith focuses on the single tree of relative literacy skills in intermediate occupations to prove a generalization of skill shortages. The weight of recent evidence directly assessing qualifications and job requirements, as noted above, is strongly to the contrary. Finally, Smith takes me to task for largely ignoring pay differentials between college and non-college graduates in the employed labour force as a possible indicator of shortages of more highly skilled labour. He admits that I do discuss earnings trends (pp. 162-170). He also concedes contrary recent patterns for Canada and the U.S. More to the point, as noted above and in Chapter 4, monetary rates of return to skills are mediated by many other contextual factors and over time comparisons are vitiated by use of various correction formulae. This is just as true of higher salaries as of poverty wages. Regardless of any increases in differential rates of monetary return to educational investment among the employed, the forest of underemployment still stands. The rich are becoming obscenely richer while more and more well educated people are becoming relatively impoverished, either through total unemployment or involuntarily partial employment.

My most powerful critic has actually been my original U.S. publisher, Westview Press. Just before Education Jobs Gap was published in hardcover, Rupert Murdoch's News Corporation, one of the few media conglomerates now engulfing our information industries (see McChesney, 1999), bought the company. My editors resigned. Education Jobs Gap received no further advertising and was even removed from the publishers' website. The small hardcover edition virtually sold out within a few months but a commitment to publish a cheaper paperback edition was breached. This dismissal of the book occurred in spite of the fact that most published reviews were very positive and the Canadian edition published by Garamond Press won the prestigious 1999 John Porter Award of the Canadian Sociology and Anthropology Society. I have no direct evidence of the reasons for Westview's actions. They may, for example, have been based on an assessment of the diminishing marketability of the book in a period of marginal declines in the official U.S. unemployment rate. The fact that Education Jobs Gap offers the first fundamental explanation of the entire phenomenon of underemployment in capitalist societies based on the dynamics of inter-firm competition, class struggles and related technological changes may be merely coincidental. After several years of negotiations, I did manage to regain the copyright from Westview. Fortunately the book gained a sufficient audience in Canada to warrant a new Garamond edition and I am delighted that Elliot Werner of Percheron Press has agreed to distribute the second edition in the U.S.

PROSPECTS

Social policy-related research typically ends with a call for further research. By all means, let us continue to study and document learning and work relations through more inclusive, comparative and longitudinal studies. As I have noted, many dimensions of this relationship have barely been recognized to date. My own current research network is actively engaged in national surveys and case studies on the changing nature of work and lifelong learning in Canada in conjunction with an international advisory team (see www.nall.ca). But it is time for concerned citizens and policy advocates to pursue concerted reforms to address underemployment and related social problems. Decent work for all who want it is eminently possible and also an essential means toward peace in our time.

Various policy advisory reports have been generated on relevant policy options, such as overcoming the separation of work and learning (e.g. National Advisory Panel on Skill Development Leave, 1984) and options for redistributing paid employment (e.g. Advisory Group on Working Time and the Distribution of Work, 1994). There should now be *local, regional, national and international forums which bring together all major interest groups to consider implementing economic policy initiatives to address the problem of underemployment.* With our high levels of formal education and underemployment, and the research knowledge now available about our patterns of work and learning, Canadians and Americans are in a strategic position to lead the world in an open, informed debate about the most preferable, feasible economic and educational reforms to address underemployment, nurture development of a knowledge-based economy and continuing lifelong learning, and provide sustainable living conditions for all citizens. Addressing this agenda in many current paid workplaces, to say nothing of wider political levels, will be very difficult. But the documented existence of a workforce that is amply qualified to achieve much more democratically participatory workplaces, and the alternative prospect of increasing underemployment, should stimulate serious continuing efforts in this direction by many people. Joseph Stiglitz (2002, pp. 252, 267) – one of the original theorists of the use of education as a screening mechanism for job entry (Stiglitz, 1975) – has recently concluded on the basis of his experience as chairman of the Clinton administration's Council of Economic Advisors and senior vice-president of the World Bank that:

Development is about transforming societies, improving the lives of the poor, enabling everyone to have a chance at success and access to health and education.... This sort of development...means that there must also be broad participation that goes well beyond the experts and politicians.... I am convinced that such changes, under the right circumstances, can occur in a relatively short span of time.... We cannot, we should not, stand idly by.

None of the evidence that has accumulated since Education Jobs Gap was first published has raised a serious challenge to the basic thesis. The continuing pursuit of education and learning are inherently valuable and essential for the human species; but their continuing pursuit under currently dominant job structures will only serve to accentuate established levels of many aspects of underemployment. Economic reforms achieved through broad participation are now far more necessary than educational changes to address the education-jobs gap. If we do not seize the initiative, if our current education and training ships and our growing fleet of self-declared "learning organizations" do not respond effectively to the massive icebergs of informal learning and underemployment around them, aspirations to realize a much more knowledge-based economy as well as to maintain our countries' current high global rankings may sink into a titanic historical irrelevancy.

NOTES

1. I would like to acknowledge the Social Sciences and Humanities Research Council of Canada for Research Grant 818-1996-1033 which enabled the conduct of the first national survey of informal learning practices, and Doug Hart and Milosh Raykov for their assistance with the review of literature and statistical analyses.
2. In Education Jobs Gap , the U.S. General Social Survey for 1988 through 1994 was used to estimate differential university graduation rates by class origins as well as generation, sex and race. More recent estimates were generated using the GSS for 1996 through 2002 (see Davis and Smith, 2003).
3. Special tabulations from the Canadian General Social Surveys of 1989, 1995 and 2000, general data available from Statistics Canada Web site http://www.statcan.ca/english.

INTRODUCTION TO 1999 EDITION

Reversing The Education-Jobs Optic

T]here is growing evidence of the extent of the under-used capacities of adults.... [Researchers] have documented the extraordinarily high average level of investment of time, effort and money by individuals into private learning projects.... The significance of this capacity for planning, managing and even financing private learning has not been readily appreciated by those who are responsible for promoting work-related learning.

—Organization for Economic Co-operation
and Development, 1993, 30

The current employment situation entails an enormous waste of resources and an unacceptable level of human suffering. It has led to growing social exclusion, rising inequality between and within nations, and a host of social ills. It is thus both morally unacceptable and economically irrational.

—Michael Hansenne, Director-General,
International Labour Office, 1995, 93

Let's begin with two apparently contradictory social facts. First, there are more highly educated people than ever before and their learning efforts continue to grow rapidly. Secondly, there is mass unemployment and underemployment of capable people. The growing gap between the unprecedented extent of collective knowledge of the people and the diminishing number of meaningful, sustaining jobs has become the major social problem of our times. This is the distinguishing character of the current *education-jobs gap*. There are now officially over 35 million unemployed people in the OECD countries, almost quadruple the average of the 1950s and 60s, when people generally spent much less time in learning activities (OECD

1

1994a, 1996a). According to recent International Labour Organization reports, about a third of the global workforce or 1 billion people are unemployed or underemployed, the highest percentage since the Great Depression of the 1930s (ILO 1996). We will examine other less visible statistical dimensions of underemployment later. But behind all these statistics, the personal sense of wasted potential is more anguishing. Listen, for example, to the pleas of two highly qualified U.S. and Canadian university graduates attempting to cope with this situation:

> All I ever wanted was a home of my own and maybe a car and enough money to support a family. I am a hard worker and a fast learner. I have never had a problem getting along with my bosses or the people I worked with in the computer industry. In the past twelve years, I've been laid off four times.... I currently have three part-time jobs because the trend is to replace every worker with two part-time workers. That way, the corporation doesn't have to offer medical benefits. I now work sixty hours a week and still have no medical benefits. I am 34. All I own is my car and my clothes.... I am rapidly becoming disenchanted with corporate America. And there are thousands more like me.[1]

> My life is spiralling out of control. A while ago I just started crying — I don't have a job and I'm crying. So I've got to center myself.... I'm just floundering and I don't even know what I'm doing — walking into walls. And that's probably why I want to go back to school again.... Then at the [university] placement center, I finally went nuts and demanded some postings. One was a receptionist at a driving school but you had to speak Cantonese. I just went home and started crying again. I just give up. I went, "forget this, this is garbage." And that's just the worst feeling. I *never* give up. For my whole life I've had to fight to become what I want. Then, when I graduated, employers told me I was either too good or I didn't have two years experience or some computer language. And now it's not the French I learned anymore, it's Cantonese! My first response was, "Oh, I give up." But then, maybe we have to start learning other languages, stop being so ethnocentric and North American, think about the future and the outside world. I don't know. It's kind of bleak.[2]

Most of the proposed solutions to the education-jobs gap that have gained public attention focus on making the education system and workforce more responsive to the presumed high skill needs of a global "post-industrial or knowledge economy." Countless recent public commissions have addressed the issue of "what work requires of schools."[3] Political leaders continue to insist that educational reforms will provide the solutions to economic problems.[4] This book argues for reversing the common optic or focus on education as the problem.

Paid workplaces in capitalist economies can and should be democratically reorganized to use much of the existing knowledge and expanding learning potential that are now wasted through widespread unemployment and underemployment. It would be unthinkable for humans to spend a lot of effort training an animal and then give it no chance to perform. But that is exactly what we are doing with rapidly growing numbers of people today. We need to scrutinize our notions of work, as well as the actual job structures and performance requirements of contemporary workplaces, as closely as educational system structures and performance standards have already been reviewed in many countries. Paid work reform should now be considered at least as seriously as educational reform has been.

Certainly educational systems, like any other human institution, should always be open to criticism and improvement. But there is no compelling evidence to indicate that deficient educational provisions have contributed significantly to current conditions of mass unemployment, certainly none that is sufficient to warrant the preoccupation with educational reform as the key solution to the present poor employment conditions. This preoccupation is nothing new. In every prior protracted employment downturn since the Industrial Revolution, business, government and educational leaders have pointed to educational reform as a central means of reinvigorating the labour market in their societies (Curti 1935). In fact, impressive cumulative gains in educational attainment levels have been unable to prevent the periodic reoccurrence of serious unemployment crises. Still we hear incessant appeals for educational change to create jobs.

There have very rarely been enough jobs for all the people who want and qualify for them in private market-based economies. The existence of a "reserve army" of potential workers as well as cycles of technologically-induced unemployment have characterized such economies from their inception. Indeed, various forms of unemployment and underemployment have been chronic among highly skilled and knowledgeable workers most of the time since the first major expansion of capitalist industrial production over 200 years ago. With the enclosure of British agricultural lands in the 1790s, vast numbers of skilled farm labourers were thrown into destitution and tramping to try to find seasonal work. By the early 1840s, hand-loom weavers offered the first example of widespread industrial unemployment. The 1842 report of a Manchester doctor document-ed the effects on these distressed weavers:

> His energies naturally give way under the repetition of fruitless efforts to improve his condition; his spirits are broken, and finding that he has no domestic comforts to lose — that he cannot descend lower in the scale of human existence — that his degradation can scarcely be increased — his wretchedness drives him to despair, and he sinks at last into a state of mental apathy or plunges into reckless improvidence.... The sight of his house without furniture, without food, without fire, and his children perhaps crying for bread, will probably have the effect of impelling him to crime or depriving him of reason. (Report by Dr. H. Baron Howard, Princess St., Manchester, January, 1842, 52. Cited in Burnett 1994, 76–77)

Since the mid-19th century working class autobiographers have provided their own graphic accounts of their experiences of unem-ployment and underemployment. Listen, for example, to the voices of highly trained workers describing their futile search for work during subsequent economic depressions. A tramping cooper's apprentice in early 1870s:

> It is a weird experience, this, of wandering through England in search of a job. You keep your heart up as long as you have something in your stomach, but when hunger steals upon you, then you despair. Footsore and listless at the same time you simply lose all interest in the future.... Nothing wearies one more than walking about hunting for employment which is not to be had. It is far harder than real work. The uncertainty, the despair when you reach a place only to discover that your journey is fruitless, are frightful.... You can imagine the feel-ing when, after walking your boots off, a man says to you, as he jin-gles sovereigns in his pocket, "Why don't you work?" That is what happened to me as I scoured the country between London and Liv-erpool, asking all the way for any kind of work to help me along. (G. Haw 1907, 46–47. Cited in Burnett 1994, 120)

A young cabinet-maker searching for work in London, 1931:

> I found it a harassing and nerve-racking ordeal to accommodate myself to the reduced rate of benefit.... I lived in dread of those empty, boring, monotonous days of walking about searching for a job that was never there, and returning to a lodging bereft of warmth and stimulating food. The emptiness of the belly, and the accompanying tension and worry, produced an emptiness of the brain and of the spirit. I walked about looking for work as much to distract myself as to find work. (M. Cohen 1945, 28. Cited in Burnett 1994, 223)

The deep sense of personal frustration and wasted potential among the burgeoning numbers without decent jobs appears to be very much the same at the end of this century as it was during the last one. The main difference is that the voices of women and people of color are now audible within advanced capitalist societies. The vast majority of the unemployed and underemployed still see a decent job as essential to both their subsistence and their dignity.[5] Those post-industrial thinkers who now celebrate the end of work and the emergence of a leisure society are not listening to these voices.

In spite of the historical record, most private corporate and government leaders continue to promote more formal schooling and training programs as the antidote to unemployment. The oversupply of educationally qualified people on the job market has been disguised by employers' inflation of credential requirements, as well as by scantily based imputations of persistent specific skill shortages and general expressions of dissatisfaction with the quality of job entrants.[6] Specific technical skill requirements for many jobs in private market-based economies *are* continually changing. But the need for narrow new technical skills, which can often easily be acquired on the job by those who have an adequate general knowledge base or job experience, should not be confounded with a lack of general knowledge and skill to do the work. Governments' insistence that more and better training can close the education-jobs gap and their creation of more elaborate training programs have typically merely deferred the problem of job creation.[7]

As Chapter One will document, popular demand for all types of organized schooling as well as informal work-related learning activities continue to grow quickly and perhaps irreversibly. The basic recent response of individual job seekers to the scarcity of jobs has been to pursue further education and learning ever more keenly to enhance their competitive chances of actually finding a job. In spite of widespread recent rhetoric about illiteracy related to both basic learning skills and computers, there is little reliable evidence of declining skills and much to support the improving quality of education and learning in most countries.[8] The pyramids of schooling and icebergs of informal learning are both massive.

Reasonable as these learning responses may be for the individual in a highly competitive labour market, they have only served to widen and deepen the education-jobs gap. More and more highly qualified people cannot find any decent jobs. The many faces of underemployment are virtually all increasing. The full scope of underemployment has rarely been systematically identified and measured. Chapter Two provides an empirically grounded overview of the current extent of underemployment in terms of six basic dimensions: *the talent use gap, structural unemployment, involuntary reduced employment, the credential gap, the performance gap and subjective underemployment.* These many faces of underemployment have rarely if ever been examined together.

However pervasive the conditions of underemployment have become, they have continued to be associated with further learning efforts. *A vicious circle of more learning for fewer jobs is now well established.* More education may generally be personally enriching and learning for its own sake should never be discouraged. But more schooling and training have not created more jobs in any direct sense, nor is much formal education even actually required to perform many current and prospective jobs. Now that taxi drivers and waitresses with advanced degrees are no longer a novelty, we should be reaching the limits of the "education as economic salvation" argument.

Most of what has been written about the education-jobs gap has been from the vantage point of experts aligned with or most sympathetic to the competitive interests of private enterprise and upper management. Recent books that explicitly address closing the education-jobs gap tend to accept the rhetoric of a high skill "post-industrial or knowledge economy" quite uncritically and focus mainly on school reorganization options.[9] Again education is problematized more than work, and largely from a management perspective. In contrast, this book will try to reverse the common optic by focussing more on the perspectives of those actually living in this gap: the unemployed and underemployed, as well as supposedly underqualified workers. Chapter Three documents both current personal experiences of underemployment and their relationship with attempts at lifelong learning. As Chapter Three further reveals, the knowledge and learning strategies of people living in the education-jobs gap are much more extensive than those experts who advocate their further training as the way to close the education-jobs gap have ever recognized.

Chapter Four debunks the current myth of the rapid growth of a "knowledge economy" full of "learning enterprises" with ever higher skill needs, and identifies the limits of the human capital theories that provide the main scholarly rationales for continuing to try to close the education-jobs gap through investment in education. Both knowledge economy and human capital theories are seen to be grounded in overly simplistic notions of evolutionary progress. This chapter draws on the most extensive relevant empirical surveys in the U.S. and Canada, and concludes that overall technical skill requirements have only gradually increased in recent decades. Deskilling may be almost as common as upgrading even in high tech industries. Even the vast majority of employees with very limited elementary schooling attest that they are adequately qualified to perform their current jobs (Livingstone, Hart and Davie 1995, 27).

Human capital theorists are highly influential in both business and government circles. They focus on a gross correspondence between levels of economic and educational development, and on relatively higher earnings of individuals with more schooling, to make the case for more education as the key to renewed economic growth. They generally manage either to ignore the aggregate education-jobs gap or regard it as a problem of "overeducation" which is subject to correction by the normal operation of market forces.[10] So far, there are few signs of this correction.

Efficient exploitation of most productive resources **within** private firms has always been an imperative drive for enterprises operating in the context of inter-firm competition. The dominant organizational tendency within the leading enterprises of industrial capitalism over the past two centuries increasingly has been to coordinate all productive resources across more extensive networks (Chandler 1990). Planned coordination of productive resources such as capital investment and research *across* firms is now becoming a feature of networks and consortia of leading large corporations in the richest economies, a form that some analysts have called "collective capitalism" (Lazonick 1991). In the most advanced case of Japan there has also been limited inter-firm coordination of the job training and retraining of the permanent workforce among core firms (Dore and Sako 1989). But the use of most people's work-related knowledge in conjunction with other productive resources remains largely untapped even by leading Japanese firms. The bottom line is that private profit-driven firms do little to discourage a growing oversupply of their most valuable resource, intelligent labour power, as long as they don't have to worry about the costs of the surplus supply beyond their needs; this surplus supply also tends to mute internal demand for workplace reform. More generally, however much collaboration there may be among a limited core of employees within such firms, the consequence is still far too few available good jobs for all the capable people in the labour market.

One of the first widely recognized challenges to the prevailing myth that advanced industrial economies, as currently organized, need larger numbers of highly educated workers was Ivar Berg's (1970) *Education and Jobs: The Great Training Robbery*. Later important works in the same skeptical tradition have documented the inflation of educational credential requirements for job entry (Collins 1979), the growing extent and experience of underemployment on the job (Burris 1983a, b), and the increasing attempts by professional experts to monopolize valuable knowledge (Derber et al. 1990). While the myth has been exposed and some of the dimensions of underemployment analyzed, the underlying dynamics of underemployment remain to be effectively explained.

In modern private market economies with liberal democratic governments, there has been a deep contradiction between the general public availability of technical information relevant to work, and the more restrictive, hierarchical organization of most workplaces. Just think, for example, of the extensive design, production and distribution knowledge available in your local public library about the types of goods or services you work with, and the limited, routinized information bases that define most employees' jobs. Of course, school systems are also very hierarchically organized and waste massive learning potential through such means as premature streaming of youths into dead-end programs. But, in response to popular democratic demand, schools still produce many more graduates than current market-driven economies will profitably use (see Carnoy and Levin 1985).

Knowledge can no longer be effectively controlled by elites. Private corporate and knowledge elites have tried to restrict access to strategic production information through various means, such as long-term patents, arcane professional terminologies and arbitrary entry requirements. Neo-conservative regimes are now trying to cut back and privatize costly schooling provisions. Budget cuts are certainly increasing problems of overcrowding, violence, teacher burnout, student alienation and discriminatory selection in public schools, colleges and universities. But, since work remains central to most peoples' sense of self-worth and useful work-related knowledge remains widely accessible through diverse sources, these restrictions continually prove unsustainable and the social pressures to share more strategic information and decent work with other capable people continue to mount. This conflict between the proliferation of useful knowledge in democratic societies and the efforts of elites to gain private or exclusive control over strategic work-related information through the construction and execution of "expert knowledge" has been *the central educational contradiction of advanced private industrial market economies.*

Chapter Five offers an explanation for this central contradiction drawing on prior Marxist and Weberian conflict theories of relations between education and work. After a critical review of prior conflict theories, I suggest an emergent theory of underemployment based on ongoing negotiations and struggles over conditions of paid work between those in dominant and subordinate social positions, particularly different class and status locations. Race, gender and generational differences are also considered in testing this theory.

The general argument of the book is grounded in a critical review of relevant survey and case study research in the most advanced capitalist economies, the member countries of the Organization for Economic Co-operation and Development (OECD). The main focus is on the most economically powerful G7 countries (Canada, France, Germany, Great Britain, Italy, Japan and the United States), as well as Sweden which has the longest running social democratic institutions. While underemployment is clearly now a universal problem, the G7 countries constitute the leading edge of the global capitalist economy. Special attention is given to the U.S. and Canada which have experienced the highest levels of formal schooling and of many dimensions of underemployment.

The U.S. General Social Surveys between 1972 and 1990 (Davis and Smith 1994) have been used to extend Berg's (1970) analysis of the "performance gap" between formal educational attainments and the actual educational requirements of jobs among the U.S. workforce. Original empirical evidence on all six distinct facets of underemployment is drawn from a unique time series of eight biennial general population surveys conducted in Canada's industrial heartland of Ontario between 1982 and 1996. These surveys dealt with educational attainments, job requirements and attitudes toward related policy issues.[11] A supplementary survey of corporate executives has been conducted in conjunction with each of these general Ontario surveys. These data offer rare comparative insights into continuity and change in the views of corporate executives and all other major social classes on the education-jobs gap over this period.[12]

But the most important sources of evidence are two sets of in-depth life history interviews with unemployed, underemployed, and underqualified people during 1994–95. The first set were conducted in 1994 in Metropolitan Toronto, through some of the sites where these people could most likely be located: university placement offices, adult basic education classes and food banks. The second set were a follow-up to the late 1994 Ontario general population survey, with the respondents who were identified through that survey as underemployed or underqualified in terms of credential requirements for their jobs. This follow-up interview, conducted in March 1995, is the *first known representative survey of both underemployed and underqualified workers*. These profiles and voices provide the most compelling ingredients of the book.

The most pertinent social policy question is not "what work requires of schools?" but "how can work be reformed to permit fuller use of peoples' current education and continuing learning capacities?" The basic thesis of this book is that *most of us continually learn much more work-related knowledge than we ever have a chance to apply in paid workplaces*. The last chapter, therefore, briefly examines past and possible future forms of organization of work and assesses their capacity to overcome the growing education-jobs gap. Although there is a long lineage of books about and growing popular interest in making paid work more democratic, there is very little research that has linked progressive economic alternatives with education and learning. The most suggestive, if largely schematic, contributions have been made by Henry Levin.[13]

Not only currently paid work but subsistence labours, including domestic labour and community volunteer work, are necessary for our continued existence. Rather than thinking about the paid work-schooling link in isolation, we need to consider all the interactive relations between current paid work, unpaid work, schooling and informal learning in order to begin to narrow the education-jobs gap. I identify and assess three very general economic alternatives, *shareholder capitalism, stakeholder capitalism and economic democracy*. These economic alternatives are associated with differing degrees of popular ownership of work organizations, democratic management of the work process, redistribution of paid work (e.g. a shorter normal full-time workweek) and recognition of new forms of legitimate work (e.g. community service work, more housework by men). The more democratic options that define stakeholder capitalism and especially economic democracy offer real practical prospects for reducing underemployment by permitting more people to apply and benefit from their currently economically wasted human knowledge. Genuinely democratic work reforms can draw on both deep popular sentiments of support and a vast reservoir of useful knowledge of unemployed and underemployed people, while also serving to alleviate many other social problems.

More effectively planned future coordination of work-related learning with work reorganization is certainly compatible with the profit-making objectives of leading corporations. We can expect to see increasingly concerted efforts by corporate leaders to harness the formal and informal learning efforts, or "intellectual capital," of their core employees to enhance production. But what about everybody else? It is conceivable that global corporations could narrow the education-jobs gap for core expert employees within their own increasingly productive and interactive learning enterprises, while underemployment continues to proliferate in the world at large. It is also conceivable that community-controlled enterprises that permit many more people to apply their knowledge and skills more fully could continue to grow. Whether elitist or democratic versions of human resource coordination prevail in the application of useful knowledge to meaningful work is likely to be one of the major political struggles that will shape the social character of the next millennium. The battle lines are already visible in most countries. The following chapters try to offer some guides to collective action for those who would choose the more democratic path.

1

The Knowledge Society:
Pyramids and Icebergs of Learning

Miniaturized electronic technology and its major product, information, cannot be controlled.... Access to information has escalated beyond anything that could have been imagined a decade ago.
—Knel-Paz 1995, 267, 269

Despite the spread of democracy and the rise of the working classes in America, the elite among us often are so indifferent to and illiterate about the folklore or folk cultures, that the folk world represents the equivalent of a low-frequency communication that seldom or never reaches their ears. Yet folk culture represents what has been the dominant world culture since humankind began.... If literacy is to be defined realistically, then it must include developing an awareness and appreciation of the activities and daily interests of most people most of the time in contemporary society. The problem of most people is not the lack of knowledge, but the question of how to manage the scope and intensity of information on a daily basis.
—Browne 1992, 127, 179

INTRODUCTION

To live is to learn. Continual social learning is the most distinctive feature of human beings. We are born more helpless than most other species and then constantly socialized by ever more complex and sophisticated communications with other humans throughout our lives. The cumulative body of human knowledge has grown greatly as we have created many new means of collecting raw data, converted the data into useful information and organized information into diverse bodies of knowledge.[1] Public libraries, camera and sound recording equipment, telephones, radio and television, computers, and a multitude of other new information technologies have proliferated over the past century. When the world around us becomes more challenging or uncertain, our first effective response is often to try to learn more about the situation rather than reacting instinctively. In the current context of economic uncertainties and global challenges to various institutionalized forms of social life, and with the spread of computerized digital telecommunications, our efforts in pursuit of knowledge have been increasing exponentially.[2] By virtually every measure, *we are now spending more time acquiring knowledge than ever before in the history of our continually learning species.*

Many discussions of learning focus exclusively on organized activities related to educational institutions. Some discussions of teacher-led education reduce the focus even further by equating education with schooling. Much of the learning that occurs within current educational institutions has been very hierarchically organized, not only in terms of content sequences but also in terms of who has access to advanced forms of knowledge. Certainly many social analysts over the past century have been preoccupied with the general issue of hierarchical, standardized control of expanding forms of information within formal organizations such as schools as well as paid workplaces.[3] In this chapter, I will document both the continuing expansion of these *"educational pyramids"* and their extended reproduction throughout our lives. But I will also consider other forms of learning which occur beyond the realm of organized educational institutions, learning which is less hierarchical and more voluntary and therefore harder to detect, measure or control. Such activities constitute *"icebergs of learning."* The character and extent of people's participation in this informal learning cannot be simply derived from their formal educational statuses. In particular, there is massively more learning occurring among those in the lower levels of the formal educational pyramid than is generally recognized. Many forms of knowledge remain beyond effective hierarchical control as our sources of information continue to proliferate. Also, virtually all forms of human knowledge have tacit practical dimensions as well as recordable cognitive dimensions. Active engagement in informal learning of both recorded and tacit dimensions continues to be an integral part of the reality of the operation of knowledge-based societies and of advanced industrial workplaces. Orwell's Big Brother may be watching ever more, but it is increasingly impossible to attend to all that we know.

THE GENERAL EXPANSION OF LEARNING ACTIVITIES

Three general sorts of learning practices may be distinguished: formal education or schooling, nonformal or further education, and informal learning.[4] *Formal education* has been defined as full-time study within state-certified school systems. Modern formal schooling has been restricted almost exclusively to young people who have been expected to proceed through extensive graded curricula in lockstep fashion prior to achieving complete adult status.[5] *Nonformal or further* education is all other organized educational activities, including further courses or training programs offered by any social institution. It is such organized non-formal educational programs offered mainly to adults on a part-time basis by diverse authorities that have been the primary focus in recent academic and policy maker discussions about "lifelong learning" and a "permanent education culture." *Informal learning* refers to all those individual and collective learning activities that we do beyond the authority or requirements of any educational institution. Any deliberate effort to gain new understanding, knowledge or skill to which we devote a discernible amount of time and recognize as such may be considered to be an informal learning project.

The distinctions among these three types of learning are somewhat arbitrary and becoming increasingly blurred. Self-directed adult learners have found it convenient to continue more of their learning projects in flexibly scheduled part-time school-based programs, and with advanced credit through such means as prior learning assessment. Independent learners can also consider a burgeoning array of standardized packages of learning materials designed and sold by large private corporations to both school systems and individual consumers. Younger students increasingly face the material necessity of combining part-time paid work with part-time studies, often with multiple transitions between school and work rather than a lockstep march from the end of schooling into the permanent workforce. School authorities increasingly recognize the demographic reality that getting more adult informal learners into their classrooms is the only immediate hope for sustaining enrollment numbers now that the post-World War II baby boomers have marched through and birth rates have declined. The expansion of nonformal or further adult education into the realms of both formal schooling and informal learning now appears to be serving a wide variety of interests. But, whatever distinctions may be made among types of learning, our collective devotion to learning activities through formal schooling, further adult education courses and informal learning continues to grow very substantially.

THE CONTINUING GROWTH OF SCHOOLING

The rate of participation in formal schooling has grown almost continuously throughout the past century. Since the end of the post-World War II period of general economic expansion around 1970, enrollment ratios in post-secondary formal education have continued to increase in most advanced industrial countries, even as guarantees of jobs from such education have diminished. The historical patterns for the U.S. are summarized in Table 1.1. From a tiny minority participating in high school in the early years of the century, the majority of youths were graduating from high school by the end of the 1930s Depression. The high school enrolment ratio continued to climb to near universality in the 1990s. Although "stopping out" has become greater since the early 1970s, over two-thirds of each age group are now graduating from high school with their cohort and over 80 percent graduate eventually (Sandia Laboratories 1993). Between 1900 and 1980, the participation rate in college doubled every twenty years, with majority participation of the eligible age group being reached by the early 1970s. The much smaller proportion attaining graduate degrees increased even more rapidly during this period, doubling every decade to include about eight percent of each eligible age cohort by 1970. Since then, college participation rates have continued to grow; by the early 1990s about 30 percent of each age cohort was graduating. College enrollments expressed in relation to the 18 to 21 age group have continued to grow largely because of the increased participation of people well beyond age 21 in undergraduate programs, while post-graduate degree ratios have been fairly stable since 1970.

So, while the U.S. school system has demonstrated the world's highest enrolment levels and very impressive rates of continuing enrolment growth through most of this century, the recent increase in the high school dropout rate and stability of post-graduate degree

Table 1.1 Formal Educational Attainment in the United States, 1900–1990

Year	High school students/ population 14–17 years old (%)	High school graduates/ population 17 years old (%)	College students/ population 18–21 years old (%)	B.A.s or first professional degree/ population 21 years old (%)	M.A.s or second professional degree/ population 25 years old (%)	Ph.D.s/ population 30 years old (%)	Median years of school completed/ population 25 years and older (%)
1900	7.9	6.4	4.0	1.7	.12	.03	—
1910	11.4	8.8	5.1	1.9	.13	.02	—
1920	26.4	16.8	8.9	2.3	.24	.03	—
1930	44.3	29.0	12.4	4.9	.78	.12	—
1940	62.4	50.8	15.6	7.0	1.2	.15	8.6
1950	66.0	59.0	29.6	14.8a	2.4	.27	9.3
1960	87.8	65.1	34.9	14.3	3.3	.42	10.5
1970	92.9	76.5	52.8	21.1	7.8	1.0	12.2
1980	94.1	71.4	66.0	22.8	7.2	.9	12.5
1990	95.5	68.5	86.4	29.6	7.8	.9	12.7

a Data for 1949

Sources: For 1900–1970, Collins (1979, Table 1.1, 4); for 1980, U.S. Bureau of the Census (1982, Table 27, 212); for 1990, U.S. Bureau of the Census (1992, Table 13, 212, 219, 278).

rates suggest that some saturation points in the lockstep model of schooling of each age cohort may have been reached around 1970 in the U.S. While young people clearly stayed in school in increasing numbers during the 1930s Depression to get a high school diploma, getting the college degree that now is likely to count for decent jobs in the U.S. takes a lot longer and is often only affordable by juggling school and paid work. More people are continuing to stay in school longer as well as coming back later to graduate. The popular demand for schooling is not diminishing; on the contrary, it is extending further and further into adulthood. But the upper reaches of the formal schooling pyramid continue to be accessible to only a very small proportion of the population.

While the U.S. has continued to lead the world in school enrolment levels, large continuing increases in enrolment ratios have been a global phenomenon especially in the post-WW II period (Coombs 1985). Table 1.2 summarizes the post-war enrolment patterns for the G7 countries and Sweden, using slightly different indicators than Table 1.1. In 1950, only the U.S. had approached universal participation in elementary and high school; by 1993, all of these countries except Italy, as well as nearly all other OECD countries, had reached this level. All of these countries have experienced much more pronounced increases in tertiary level enrollments, from under 10 percent in comparison to the 20 to 24 age group in 1950 in all countries to at least 6 times the 1950 level by 1993. The biggest increases occurred in the U.S. in the 1960s and in Canada in the 1980s, after the universal high school enrolment threshold had been reached in each country. In recent years, Canada's tertiary enrolment rate has exceeded the U.S. It should be emphasized here that the fact that Canada's tertiary enrolment ratio has now exceeded 100 percent does not mean that all 20 to 24-year-olds are now attending colleges or universities; it does mean that all of those actually attending post-secondary institutions, including people under age 20 and rapidly increasing numbers among those over 24, now exceed the numbers of all those in the 20 to 24 age cohort. Both the U.S. and Canada have historically had much higher tertiary enrolment levels than any other OECD country and continued into the 1990s as the only countries where actual enrolment numbers exceeded half of the 20 to 24 age cohort. But very significant tertiary enrolment ratio increases have continued in all of these other countries, with the possible exception of Japan since 1980.[6]

Table 1.2 Primary-Secondary and Tertiary Enrolment Ratios, Selected OECD Countries, 1950–1993

Country	Year	Primary-Secondary*	Tertiary†
Canada	1950	78	7
	1960	88	13
	1970	86	35
	1980	94	56
	1990	106	96
	1993	114	103
United States	1950	100	6
	1960	98	12
	1970	101	49
	1980	95	56
	1990	99	72
	1993	105	81
France	1950	NA	4
	1960	90	9
	1970	92	20
	1980	95	26
	1990	103	40
	1993	112	50
Sweden	1950	NA	4
	1960	NA	8
	1970	82	21
	1980	92	31
	1990	94	31
	1993	100	36
Germany (FDR)	1950	NA	3
	1960	87	6
	1970	78	13
	1980	95	26
	1989	105	33
Germany (unified)	1993	115	36

(continues)

Table 1.2 (*continued*)

Country	Year	Primary-Secondary*	Tertiary†
Japan	1950	86	5
	1960	91	9
	1970	92	17
	1980	97	30
	1990	99	31
	1993	100	30
United Kingdom	1950	NA	4
	1960	86	7
	1970	88	14
	1980	92	20
	1990	95	28
	1993	105	37
Italy	1950	55	4
	1960	66	5
	1970	81	17
	1980	82	28
	1990	81	30

* Gross elementary and high school enrolment expressed in relation to currently eligible age cohorts for respective countries.
† Total tertiary enrolment expressed in relation to 20–24 age cohort.

Sources: UNESCO (1965, 1975, 1985, 1995); as well as United Nations (1961, Table 5) for 1950 and 1960 figures on 20–24 age cohort; World Bank (1997, Table 7).

Of course, the formal educational attainment profile of the entire adult population changes more slowly. For example, as Table 1.1 also indicates, since the early 1970s when U.S. high school enrolments reached 90 percent of the eligible age group, there have been more marginal increases in the median years of schooling, from 12.2 to 12.7 years. In spite of more rapid recent increases of tertiary participation rates in Canada, the U.S. population still has a slightly higher median level of years of schooling for the entire adult population (Education Support Branch 1994, 22–23).

In all OECD countries, the average renewal rate of the *labour force* based on individuals leaving the school system is between 2 and 3 percent per year (OECD 1994d, 145; Bengtsson 1993). Nevertheless, during the past generation the formal educational attainment profile of the employed U.S. labour force has changed very substantially, as Table 1.3 suggests.[7] Clearly, the portion of the labour force without a high school diploma has been reduced to a small minority during this period, while the percentage who have post-secondary credentials has doubled, to about a third of the labour force.

Table 1.3   Formal Educational Attainments,
Employed U.S. Labour Force, 1972–1994

Attainments	72 %	76 %	80 %	86 %	90 %	94 %
<High school	32	25	18	15	12	10
HS diploma	52	52	58	56	56	54
College certificate	2	3	4	5	7	7
Bachelor degree	10	15	17	17	17	20
Graduate degree	5	6	7	7	9	10

Source: Davis and Smith (1994) [machine readable data file].

A comparable Canadian profile of changes in the formal educational attainment level of the active labour force over the past decade appears in Table 1.4. This table documents changes between 1978 and 1996 in the formal attainments of the labour force in Canada's industrial heartland of Ontario, on the basis of biennial population surveys.[8] During this period, the aggregate educational attainments of the Ontario workforce have also increased very significantly. In 1978, high school dropouts made up nearly half of the labour force. By 1996, only about a quarter had less than a high school diploma, while there had been very substantial gains in the proportions completing high school, college and university programs. Particularly in light of the very rapid development of the community college program in Canada since the late 1960s, more workers now have some kind of post-secondary credential than have only a high school diploma.

While the U.S. and Canadian labour forces remain the most highly schooled in the world, similar trends have occurred in other OECD

Table 1.4   Formal Educational Attainments,
Employed Ontario Labour Force, 1978–1996

Attainments	78 %	80 %	82 %	84 %	86 %	88 %	90 %	92 %	94 %	96 %
<High school	47	42	40	36	33	33	27	26	25	24
HS diploma	29	32	33	34	36	36	38	38	39	36
College certificate	12	12	13	15	16	15	17	18	18	21
University degree	12	13	13	14	15	15	17	18	19	19

Source: OISE Survey of Educational Issues Data Archive.

countries, with high school diplomas rapidly becoming common-place and substantial growth in the proportions with post-secondary credentials.[9] Virtually everywhere, the labour force has continued to become more highly schooled.

The strong popular demand for more access to advanced formal schooling is unlikely to diminish in the foreseeable future. A few indicators of trends in public attitudes in Ontario are probably typical.[10] Between 1979 and the early 1990s, the proportion of the public who rated having a post-secondary education as "very important" more than doubled from about one-third to more than two-thirds. Support for measures to ease access for worthy applicants, such as increased transferability of course credits and prior learning assessment, has become almost unanimous. More specifically with regard to job requirements, the majority who expect that employers will require post-secondary credentials for more jobs in the future increased from about 60 percent in 1986 to 80 percent in 1994. Perhaps most significantly, opposition to post-secondary entry quotas based on the availability of jobs for graduates is rejected by larger majorities in the 1990s than in the 1970s. At the same time, and in a context of mounting budget cuts, the option of increased government funding for education has gained solid majority support both in Canada and in most other OECD countries.[11]

As participation has become more widespread and as government budgets have been more constrained, rhetorical claims about declining quality of schooling have increased. If more people of less ability are staying in school longer, then overall performance levels should be declining. However, the most rigorous and unbiased studies have consistently found that most generally accepted indicators of educational performance have been either stable or gradually improving over the past few decades (Sandia Laboratories 1993; Berliner and Biddle 1995, 1996; Bracey 1997). One conclusion that follows from these findings is that those women and people from lower class and visible minority backgrounds who had previously been excluded from extended participation in schooling are not significantly different in learning capabilities from those white middle class males who had previously predominated. Inequities in the school system persist, an issue I will examine more closely in Chapter Two. But making advanced schooling more accessible to those from disadvantaged groups has not diluted the quality of schooling in any clearly documented way.

The Second Formal System: Vocational Schooling

The extent to which state-sponsored school systems attempt to provide youths with vocation-specific knowledge varies greatly but has also expanded everywhere over time. The accumulated bodies of recorded knowledge of a growing variety of occupations have become incorporated within the advanced curriculum of formal schooling — from medieval theology, law and medical faculties to recent technological specializations in community colleges. Craft guilds and skilled industrial workers have historically resisted forms of incorporation that would entail giving up independent control of apprenticeships. Vocational schooling at the high school level has developed very differently among OECD countries, depending partly on the strength of labour unions and working peoples' political organizations. In countries with stronger unions, adolescent youths have been encouraged to enter vocational training programs based in unionized workplaces and which have typically combined work and study.

The U.S. historically has had relatively weak labour unions. In contrast to its extensive general schooling provisions, the country has offered only limited forms of vocational schooling. For example, Jonathan D. Turner, a progressive Illinois literary professor and farmer, proposed industrial class universities in the United States in 1851. His plan called for mechanics and artisans to have their own universities.[12] He argued that what was going on in universities at that time under the influence of the clergy, lawyers and doctors was irrelevant to the concerns of the working classes. This proposal was then coupled with a land grant plan. It became the basis for the land grant college bill of 1862 which established the institutions which are the major universities in most of the states of the union today. But some funny things happened on the way to the implementation of Turner's plan. The boards of governors of these public universities were dominated by lawyers and a few farmers. So, for instance, the University of Illinois governors, in their wisdom, decided not to establish a mechanics department or initially even a campus in Chicago which had the bulk of the state's working class. Latin was made a requirement for entry. Engineering, which was emerging as the strategic occupation in the design of machine-driven industrial production, became the major focus of study within the mechanics departments of these universities. Very few fledgling mechanics or other youths of working class origins ended up there; they didn't have the Latin for it or the money.

As industrial unions emerged, there were periodic demands for more vocational-technical schooling for working class kids in Chicago and elsewhere (Wrigley 1982). But, generally, U.S. labour unions remained too weak to have significant influence on school programs, and specific vocational training for the majority of youths was left to the discretion of their employers. School-based vocational high school diplomas remain of very little significance in the U.S. today. The community college originated in the U.S. after WWII, with the declared intent of providing more immediately relevant vocational training for the burgeoning numbers of high school graduates than the established universities were prepared to offer. While some of these colleges now provide valuable training in various technical specializations, their other roles have been to "cool out" and serve as feeder schools for the much larger numbers who have continued to aspire to university degrees.[13]

Historically, Canada has also given little attention to secondary vocational programs, particularly any that provided access to more advanced technical studies. However, the development of some terminal secondary vocational programs and many community colleges in the 1960s to accommodate the baby boom also coincided with a significant growth of labour organizations. As Tables 1.3 and 1.4 indicate, these colleges have become a more substantial part of the post-secondary system in Canada than community colleges in the U.S., and with a greater focus on specific vocational-technical programs (Dennison and Jones 1995).

The exceptional lack of attention to secondary level vocational schooling in North America is illustrated by the comparative statistics in Table 1.5. The reorganization of the post-WWII Japanese school system was strongly influenced by U.S. military occupation and politically weakened trade unions. Vocational secondary programs remain a relatively small and "last resort" part of Japanese secondary schooling; but they have been more significant than in North America, and Japanese schools generally tend to have much closer relations with employers (Dore and Sako 1989; Okano 1984). Most European OECD countries, with stronger labour organizations, have comparatively more substantial secondary level systems of vocational schooling. In most cases, particularly Sweden, France, and Italy, there is a major technical or vocational program stream within the public school system which offers post-secondary access. In other instances, notably Germany (and Switzerland) but also the United Kingdom (as well as Austria and Finland), much of the vocational training of youth occurs in a parallel system more reflective of the form of traditional apprenticeship models than formal school-

Table 1.5 Percentage of Relevant Age Group Attaining Different Types of Secondary-Level Qualifications, Selected OECD Countries, 1990

	General Diploma (%)	Vocational Diploma (%)	Other Certification (%)
United States	75	0	0
Canada	73	0	0
Japan	67	25	0
United Kingdom	34	11	46
France	28	39	6
Germany	25	0	102
Sweden	19	60	0
Italy	17	29	12

* Some of these courses are completed by persons who also obtain general diplomas.

Source: OECD (1994b, 141).

ing. The most developed case is Germany, where a large majority of youths engage in training which is usually jointly organized and run by employers and trade unions, as well as spending a day or two per week in formal school settings. The U.K. has probably experienced the strongest general historical resistance from working people to reduced independent control of apprenticeships through incorporation in state-sponsored education systems. But under the pressure of massive youth unemployment in the late 1970s, British governments have rapidly constructed an entire second school system in which about half of all youths over 14 are now engaged in widely varied combinations of mostly short-term classroom instruction and workplace experience.[14]

Those countries that have well-established dual systems of youth education have tended to have lower youth unemployment rates over the past generation (Dore and Sako 1989, 80; OECD 1994d, 134–145). The countries without such systems have been scrambling to provide more effective forms of vocational schooling to their youth populations. North American opinion surveys have indicated that a concern for greater attention to job training and career preparation in high school has become the general public's highest educational priority (Livingstone, Hart and Davie 1985 30–32).[15] As high youth unemployment rates persisted, both the U.S. and Canada have commenced new vocational training initiatives similar to those in the U.K. for those in their late teens, through such varied means as major vocational training legislation, government-sponsored co-op ed programs, formal agreements between private corporations and local school systems (such as the Boston Compact), and even the rejuvenation of some union-linked apprenticeship programs.[16] However, given the higher existing levels and norms of general high school completion in the U.S. and Canada, much of the future expansion of vocational schooling programs here can be anticipated to occur at the post-secondary level, as is already quite evident in the rapid recent growth of Canadian community colleges.

Whatever the level of the school system being targeted and whatever the means, all of these countries have been making more concerted recent efforts to expand or strengthen their vocational schooling provisions, particularly through more extensive partnerships with the private business sector (see Hirsch 1992).

THE ADULT EDUCATION BOOM

Since the 1960s, largely voluntary adult participation in further education courses on a part-time basis, has generally increased even more quickly than formal school enrollments in most OECD countries. In North America, adult participation has grown from very small numbers. According to the best available estimates, summarized in Table 1.6, annual U.S. participation of people over age 17 in further education courses went from minuscule levels to over 10 percent by the early 1980s, and since then has tripled again by 1995. Similarly, only 4 percent of Canadian adults were enrolled in continuing education courses in 1960, but the participation rate grew to 20 percent by the early 1980s and to about a third by the mid 1990s. According to a Canadian national survey in 1989, over a quarter of employed workers had plans to begin an major educational *program* during the next five years (Lowe 1992, 58–59), while a 1986 Ontario survey found that about half of all adults intended to take at least a single *course* in the foreseeable future (Livingstone, Hart and Davie 1995, 6–7).

Table 1.6   Annual Adult Education Course Participation Rates, U.S. and Canada, 17+ Population, 1960–1995

	1960 (%)	1981–83 (%)	1991 (%)	1995 (%)
U.S.	<5	13	32	40
Canada	4	20	28	38

Sources: (U.S.) U.S. Office of Technology Assessment (1983), Merriam and Caffarella (1991), U.S. Department of Education (1996); (Canada) Selman and Dampier (1991), Devereaux (1985), Statistics Canada (1995a, 1996).

A more detailed analysis of recent trends in adult education participation in Ontario (Livingstone 1992) indicates that these increases have occurred across virtually all social groups. Between 1986 and 1992, participation rates of the total adult Ontario population almost doubled from 20 percent to 36 percent. Significant increases were found in all age groups and at all levels of formal educational attainment, especially among younger adults and high school dropouts. Young employed high school dropouts tripled their participation rates. Enthusiasm for adult education is also indicated by the fact that public support for increased government funding of adult literacy and retraining programs has consistently been even stronger than for the formal school system (Livingstone, Hart and Davie 1997).

Many European countries, particularly Scandinavia, have much longer traditions of active participation in and state support for adult recurrent education courses than the U.S. and Canada. Sweden has probably been the world leader in promoting more flexible ways of combining education with work and leisure throughout the adult life-course. Consequently, adult education participation rates have increased greatly. As Albert Tuijnman (1989, 59) observes, on the basis of a unique longitudinal study: "the past three decades have witnessed a nearly exponential growth in the extent to which people in Sweden have taken part in programs of adult recurrent education." By the end of the 1980s, about half of the adult Swedish population was participating annually in further education courses (Tuijnman 1989, 60). Comparable figures for Germany were around 40 percent (German Ministry of Education 1993). British adult education participation rates appear to be somewhat lower but have also been increasing substantially since 1980 (Sargent 1991). Nearly all European governments have recently been expanding provisions for adult education and facilitating participation, especially in vocational retraining courses (OECD 1991; Tuijnman 1992). In Japan as well there has been a recent proliferation of lifelong learning centers where people of all ages can study any subject; the best estimates suggest that over 30 percent of the adult population are now participating in such courses annually (Japanese Ministry of Education 1994; Masatoshi, Koji and Hiroshi 1994). A permanent education culture is rapidly becoming a reality in all of these countries.

Adult Job Training Programs

Comparing adult job training programs across countries is very difficult, both because of differences in the forms of provision and the lack of surveys using similar criteria.[17] Very few comparable surveys are even available within most countries to assess trends in employee participation in training courses over time.[18] But there are strong indications that workplace-based training programs have generally been growing and broadening their functions since at least around

1980. Three roughly comparable U.S. surveys suggest fairly rapid growth. In 1983 only about a quarter of U.S. employees had received any training courses since being hired (OECD 1991b, 147). By 1991, well over half had participated in a training course within the last two years (Knoke and Kalleberg, 1995), and by 1993 over 70 percent of employers claimed to be providing some type of formal job training program to their employees (U.S. Department of Labour 1994). A number of the most comparable and inclusive Canadian surveys suggest that annual participation in employer-sponsored training programs has increased from around 5 percent in the mid 1960s to between 10 and 15 percent in the next two decades and to over 20 percent in the mid 1990s (Betcherman, Leckie and McMullen 1997, 4). Other Canadian studies also indicate that there has been an acceleration of the number of workers taking various training courses since the 1980s (Bennett 1994, 22–5; Crompton 1992, 30–8). In Europe as well, as Tuijnman (1992, 677) summarizes, "the overall picture is one of expansion in continuing vocational education, especially job training." In Japan, over two-thirds of all employees have received some off-the-job training since joining their current enterprise and many new institutions have recently been developed to provide such training (OECD 1991b, 149; Makino 1996).

Certainly employers are spending increasing amounts to fund employee training programs. In the U.S., rapid growth is suggested by recent growth rates of over 10 percent per year in the expenditures on direct training by organizations with over 100 employees (cited in Marschall 1990). Canadian firms have been spending about half as much on training employees as U.S. firms (Bennett 1994; Crompton 1992). In Japanese firms, training budgets have consistently grown faster than wages, generally over 10 percent per year (Dore and Sako 1989, 80). Many European governments have traditionally spent more on training programs than North American and Japanese regimes (OECD 1989). But it should be noted here that there is no simple correlation between employer expenditures on training courses and employee participation in them. In the first place, few firms have kept accurate records of even their direct training expenditures, and there is no international standard as to what counts as a direct cost (OECD 1991b, 145). Japanese data, for example, are relatively minimal estimates, excluding the wages of those engaged in training courses. It appears that Japanese workers themselves spend about six times as much as their employers do on their workplace-related training (Dore and Sako 1989, 143), whereas North American employers have been paying for about two-thirds of their employees work-related courses. (Betcherman 1992; Rubenson and Willms 1993). Nevertheless, the best available international comparisons suggest that Japanese employers spend from two to five times as much on employee training as North American employers do.

By any measure, North American employers appear to be underinvesting in long-term employee training programs relative to employers in most other OECD countries.[19] While the incidence of employer-sponsored training for legislated health and safety provisions, specific job-related computer skills and encouraging employee teamwork have certainly increased (Betcherman, Leckie and McMullen 1997), there remains little short-term incentive for North American employers to invest in broader based and longer term training programs when skill surpluses abound and both current and prospective employees are already making extraordinary efforts to get further education on their own. As Osberg (1993, 39–40) observes:

> Although it may be widely recognized that in the long run Canadian productivity and Canadian jobs depend upon the skill level of the labour force and the quality of training programs, it is pointless to bewail the lack of a 'training culture' in Canadian industry if the maintenance of high unemployment for prolonged periods of time means that it is not rational for employers to invest heavily in training. It should not be particularly surprising that employers do not usually bother with the expense of an *ongoing* training program, when an excess supply of labour means that the skills which they need are readily available on the open labour market.

The most immediate consequence of the distinctive North American combination of very high formal educational attainments, rapidly increased popular demand for adult education and employers' relative reluctance to pay for more ongoing training programs is the greater growth of general certification and general interest courses than substantial job training programs, as has been the case in Ontario adult education programs since the mid 1980s (Livingstone, Hart and Davie 1993, 26–27). In the longer term, this trend portends a North American labour force that is even more highly educated, but without some of the specific technical vocational skills that may be immediately required to do some specific jobs. In any event, with or without increased employer financial support of substantial job-linked training programs, it is likely that more and more adults in all OECD countries will continue to seek further job-related education wherever they can find it.

The Stacked Decks:
Formal and Further Educational Pyramids

Both formal schooling and further adult education programs have tended to assume quite hierarchical patterns of participation. But, even more importantly, these two educational pyramids generally reinforce one another and serve to exclude recognition of other important forms of learning.

In spite of the massive expansion of public schooling, the school system remains very pyramidal with tiny proportions permitted access to its highest levels. For example, as Table 1.1 indicates, the base of the U.S. school pyramid has grown to include virtually all of those in their mid-teens, but less than one percent reach the top. All school systems have streamed and selected students for higher levels by some version of imputed learning ability. As we have seen, many European systems have done this quite early and obviously by directing most students into terminal vocational programs. From the early years of elementary schooling, North American school systems have generally used ability tracks or streams based on intelligence testing to pre-select those deemed capable of higher education (Oakes 1985; Curtis, Livingstone and Smaller 1992). In Japan, mixed-ability grouping has been the dominant practice until the end of compulsory schooling at age 15, when a "slicing system" allocates students to high schools of markedly different prestige and prospects (Dore and Sako 1989, 18).

The exclusion of most people from the upper reaches of the formal educational system has typically been accentuated by adult education programs. Those who have higher levels of formal schooling are more likely to participate in most forms of further education. According to a 1991 national survey, Canadians with university degrees were about ten times as likely to have taken an adult education course in the past year as were those adults with only elementary schooling (Education Support Branch, Human Resources Development Canada 1994, 41). Swedish adults with only elementary schooling may be much more likely to participate in adult education than Canadians (Rubenson and Willms 1993, ix). But even in Sweden, where state initiatives to incorporate educationally marginalized adults have been greatest, a "cycle of accumulation" clearly operates so that prior formal attainments effectively predict later adult education participation (Tuijnman 1991, 275–285). The available time series studies of adult education enrolment by social background indicate that the gap in general participation between those with the most and the least schooling has *not* been narrowing as the general level of adult participation grows (Livingstone, Hart and Davie 1995; Fisher and Rubenson 1992, 9). Similar disparities have been well documented with regard to adult training programs (OECD 1991, 149; Tuijnman 1992, 685; Crompton 1992, 33). The picture of learning that emerges from studies of formal and further educational activities is, therefore, one of *two expanding and mutually reinforcing educational pyramids.*

Scholars' interpretations of general learning practices have tended to reinforce this pyramidal image of the knowledge society. For example, the field of sociology of education has long been dominated by two themes: transmission of prevailing cultural forms of knowledge, and reproduction of social inequality through schooling. The most influential recent contributors to this field are Basil Bernstein and Pierre Bourdieu.[20] Their prominence is probably closely related to the fact that their works convincingly integrate these two themes in systematic, empirically documented accounts of the process of contemporary schooling. The central claim in each case is that because of the "elaborated cultural codes" or "cultural capital" that kids from higher social class origins have acquired in family settings, they tend to be much more successful in school and subsequently in economic life.

Such cultural deficit theories, as well as predecessors that imputed value deficiencies or cultures of poverty to the lower classes[21] have sometimes dealt quite accurately with some of the discriminatory learning conditions faced by lower class children in schools, as well as similar conditions faced by female students and people of color. But their prime intent has been to describe the cultural reproduction of inequality within schools as fixed institutional forms. This makes them inadequate in three ways. First, they tend to ignore or discount the material conditions, such as inadequate food, housing and clothing, that can limit poor people's learning potential. Secondly, they remain descriptions of the status quo rather than real explanations of it. As Schiff and Lewontin (1986, 4) have noted, these cultural explanations do not:

provide an explanation either for the origin of the environmental variation or for its continuance in the face of a claimed social commitment to equality. If people are simply the products of social circumstances, and if we all agree that freedom and equality are our ideals of social construction, then why have we failed to abolish privilege and poverty? Without a deeper analysis, the cultural explanation of inequality is simply a description and not a causal story. Such a deeper analysis, however, soon challenges the basic assumption that our society is indeed devoted to equality and ends by prescribing revolutionary social reorganization, a result not widely welcomed.

But, thirdly and most importantly for understanding the real contours of the knowledge society, such theories deny or denigrate the continuing capacities of working class people as well as others subordinated on grounds of race, gender, age or disability, to create and reproduce cultural forms and meanings for themselves. These forms of knowledge have typically been submerged or effaced within the dominant school culture. As we shall see, the learning cultures of subordinated groups, while often invisible, may be both rich and dynamic.[22]

So prevalent theories of learning effectively ignore much of the knowledge of subordinated groups which is grounded in their own cultural traditions and lived experience. Cultural deficit theories, in common with innate-difference theories,[23] ignore how schooling itself is shaped by political and economic relationships that lead to the production of educational differences. For innate difference theorists the major current problem with schools is not structured and systemic class, gender and race inequalities per se but "declining standards." They claim that democracy in schooling degrades the quality of education. Their solutions involve the restoration of competition and the reconstituting of meritocratic standards of excellence to select the best and the brightest individuals for enriched and advanced education regardless of socio-economic background (Bercuson et al. 1984; Bloom 1987).

For cultural deficit theorists such as Bernstein and Bourdieu, the problem with schools is that they are not providing sufficient supplementary programs and resources to help disadvantaged individuals overcome their relative deprivation. A wide variety of reforms have been proposed, ranging from pre-school Head Start programs to sensitivity training for teachers in the world views of subordinate cultures (Bereiter and Engelmann 1966; Tharp and Gallimore 1989).

Perceptive ethnographic analyses inspired by cultural capital theory recently have documented class differences in schooling that are directly produced through parent-school interactions (Lareau 1989). There is certainly merit in related pre-school reforms that would address such culturally-grounded learning differences (see Beckman and Klenow 1997).

But for both innate difference and cultural deficit theorists, a systematic scrutiny of the enduring structures of political dominance that frame and condition the reproduction of class, gender and racial discrimination in schooling remains safely beyond their terms of inquiry. Some critics, including myself, have attempted to develop alternative perspectives on school-based learning practices that address such power relations (Livingstone 1987; Curtis et al 1992; Kozol 1991; Wexler et al. 1992). But more importantly for the present study, the fixation on school-centered learning of dominant cultural forms under the strong influence of cultural deficit theorists has led to the widespread failure of educational researchers to recognize or respect other cultures of learning that exist largely beyond the realm of the school, or to consider such informal learning cultures in relation to the formal/further education of both youths and adults. For a very large part of the population living in advanced technological societies today, school-centered learning activities may be a relatively small part of their continual pursuit of knowledge. This is probably most true for those whom the schools have marginalized.

I will address the continuing massive waste in schools of the learning potential of youths from subordinate social backgrounds in the discussion of the "talent use gap" in the following chapter. But first we need to appreciate the hidden depths of the knowledge society.

ICEBERGS OF INFORMAL LEARNING

European and American psychological researchers have long recognized that some of children's most important cognitive and moral development occurs in the realm of play (Piaget 1929; Evans 1973; Kohlberg 1981). Recent post-modernist critiques of Eurocentric, patriarchal cultural forms which celebrate social differences have stimulated empirical research into the social construction of subordinated children's gender and ethnic identities in realms where they retain considerable creative control, such as playgrounds and other peer group activities (Thorne 1993). Long ignored theories of cognitive development which take more explicit account of subordinate groups' actual conditions and their socio-historical context, and which recognized the importance of diverse social relations beyond the realm of established educational institutions to the shaping of both childhood and adult social consciousness, have recently been resuscitated (Vygotsky 1978; Moll 1990; Newman and Holzman 1993). Perspectives on linguistic development and symbolic interpretation that emphasize the polyvalent meanings of words and signs from different subcultural vantage points have also been resurgent (Bahktin 1981). One cumulative impact of such contributions is to validate the significance of informal learning in general and among marginalized people in particular.

In addition, as Michael Polyani has reminded us, "we can know more than we can tell" (Polyani 1983). There are at least two different knowledge traditions: a rational or scientific cognitive knowledge which emphasizes recordable theories and articulated descriptions, and a practical knowledge tradition which stresses direct experience and apprenticeship in various spheres (Molander 1992). In reality, our theories and practice constantly interact.

But practical knowledge frequently remains tacit, unable to be described symbolically. This may occur because knowledge has become too deeply habituated/taken for granted, or because it has been silenced, as is the knowledge of a people whose voices have been oppressed. After the Enlightenment, scientific knowledge became pre-eminent in public discussion while the practical tradition was often ignored. By the 1950s, a mechanistic paradigm of technical rationalist knowledge had become so pervasive that it provoked concerted efforts to restore the role of practical human agency in theories of learning. Some of the most significant, sustained contributions focussed on the learning capacities of adults outside standard classroom settings, such as Malcolm Knowles' (1970) work on individual self-directed learning and Paolo Freire's (1970, 1994) initiatives in collective learning through dialogue, which stress the dynamic active and practical engagement of people in the pursuit of knowledge or cultural change. Silenced practical knowledge is regaining voice, as for example in, "My mother couldn't read but she was smart about life. She must have learned a half dozen ways to prepare cabbage" (Eleen 1995, 26). But most of the recent studies of cultural practices inspired by theories developed from the vantage point of subordinated groups have been concerned primarily with general aspects of personal development, such as social identity, consciousness and intelligence, rather than with their learning activities per se.

The most substantial body of empirical research dealing with learning activities beyond organized schooling is the work on adults' self-directed learning projects which was inspired by Knowles and pioneered by my colleague, Allen Tough (1971, 1979). Tough's early studies, since corroborated by many others, found that well over two-thirds of most adults' intentional learning efforts occurred completely outside institutionalized adult education programs or courses, hence the image of the adult learning iceberg (Brookfield 1981; Brockett and Hiemstra 1991).

Informal learning is much more difficult to distinguish and measure than formal or further participation in institution-based educational programs. The basic distinction between informal learning efforts and the ongoing socialization and information processing that occurs continuously throughout our daily lives is that informal learning efforts involve attempts to gain new understanding, knowledge or skill that we deliberately devote our attention to for at least a few hours and which we can recognize as newly acquired knowledge. Whether such learning is initiated incidentally or by premeditation, and whether it occurs in individual or collective contexts, the critical point is that this knowledge has been acquired through our own voluntary efforts.[24] The empirical research studies initiated by Tough in the late 1960s document that *most* adults are regularly involved in deliberate, self-directed learning projects beyond school and training programs. As Tough (1978, 252) summarized the central finding from a wide array of studies in the 1970s:

> The typical learner conducts five quite distinct learning projects in one year. He or she learns five distinct areas of knowledge and skill. The person spends an average of 100 hours per learning effort — a total of 500 hours per year.

The few roughly comparable sample surveys conducted in the U.S. and Canada since the early 1970s on the general frequency of informal learning are summarized in Table 1.7. The findings suggest that, in spite of the substantial expansion of participation in formal and nonformal education, North American adults generally have continued to spend a great deal and perhaps increasing amount of time on informal learning projects (see also Candy 1993). Certainly the proliferation of information technologies and exponential increases in the production of information have created massively greater opportunities for informal learning beyond their own direct experience by people in all walks of life in recent years.

Table 1.7   Estimated Average Annual Frequency of Informal
                 Learning Activities, U.S. and Canada, 1975–1996

Survey	*# of projects*	*hrs./ project*	*total hours/ year*	*% informal learners*
Hiemstra (1975) [N=256; Nebraskans over 55]	3.3	98	325	84
Penland (1976) [N=1501; U.S. national adult population]	3.3	155	514	76
Tough (1978) [estimate based on 1970s case studies]	5	100	500	N/A
Leean and Sisco (1981) [N=93; rural Vermont school dropouts]	4	106	425	98
Livingstone/Hart/Davie (1997) [N=1000; Ontario adult population]	N/A	N/A	600+	86

The body of research on self-directed learning has been prone to various conceptual and methodological criticisms, including: a sampling bias in favour of urban, middle-class, English-speaking North Americans; a focus on individualistic learning processes while ignoring more collective ones; interview formats that may predispose some respondents to gratuitous responses; and arbitrary operationalization of what counts as a learning project (see Brockett and Hiemstra 1991; Candy 1993). However, the important point here is that it is indisputable that a very substantial amount of informal learning is now occurring among people in virtually all walks of life.

In particular, the limited amount of research on the informal learning practices of economically disadvantaged adults with low formal educational attainments suggests that *the vast majority do a significant amount of informal, self-directed learning*. For example, as noted in Table 1.7, the most thorough related research to date, with rural Vermont adults who were school dropouts (Leean and Sisco 1981), found that they engaged in an average of 4 major learning projects per year consuming an average of over 400 hours. Studies of economically disadvantaged urban adults, high school dropouts, functional illiterates and the unemployed have all found similar patterns.[25] As Tough concludes, the differences found in the amount of self-directed learning *within* any group have been much larger than the differences between groups constituted in terms of gender, age, income, class, and even country.[26] Both this cumulative body of research and the most recent general survey and life history studies (Livingstone, Hart and Davie 1997, 88; Antikainen et al. 1996) confirm that, contrary to the pyramidal patterns of participation in schooling and adult education courses, those in *all* social groups continually engage in a great deal of informal learning and that the learning activities of subordinate social groups in informal settings are generally just as substantial as those of more dominant and highly schooled groups.

Members of dominant social groups who have had any substantial exposure to working alongside those in subordinate groups probably have some sense of their comparable learning capacities, even if this is rarely acknowledged. As Paul Martin (1994, A8), Canada's federal finance minister, put it during a period of recent pre-budget consultation with labour representatives:

> There's a hell of a lot more brain power down there where it's happening than any large institution gives them credit for. Some of the wisest people I have met were people I worked with in those [summer] jobs.

Whether or not people in general are becoming significantly more involved in informal learning generally than they were in previous historical period is a question that awaits either oral history studies which carefully document such practices over long time spans or further longitudinal studies. Our own studies of the informal learning activities of people currently living in the education-jobs gap will be presented in Chapter Three. Certainly there has been a growing awareness among adult educators of the general importance of informal learning based not only on printed forms, but in oral folk traditions and in various current popular cultural forms that rely heavily on non-print media of communication (e.g. visual, artistic, graphic, musical, mechanical, body language).[27] However narrowly or broadly such voluntarily initiated learning activities beyond schooling may be construed, it is now clear that these informal efforts constitute the vast majority of most adults' learning activities. Institutional education programs and courses are indeed, as Tough (1971) originally suggested, the tip of the adult learning iceberg.

Informal Learning on the Job

A recent international study of skill formation at work concluded that:

> Learning-by-doing, while the most prevalent kind of work learning, is also the most invisible and the least documented. Visibility increases where skill formation is the product of a mixture of on-the-job and off-the-job training or of off-the-job training alone. There has been a relative paucity of empirical work on skill formation which is work-led rather than training-led. (OECD 1993, 30)

Several recent U.S. and Canadian national surveys have found that over 70 percent of the job training received by employees is informal (U.S. Department of Labour 1996; Ekos Research Associates 1993). The most recent in-depth U.S. study of over 1,000 workers in seven companies across seven states (Center for Workforce Development 1998, 1) again finds this 70 percent figure and concludes that:

> Informal learning was widespread and served to fulfill most learning needs. In general, we noted that informal learning was highly relevant to employee needs and involved knowledge and skills that were attainable and immediately applicable.... Workers constantly learn and develop while executing their day-to-day job responsibilities, acquiring a broad range of knowledge and skills.

The most inclusive prior national-level assessment is probably a 1989 Australian survey, which addressed both formal structured training programs and unstructured training activities such as asking questions of coworkers, self-learning and watching others do the work. This survey found that participation in organized company training programs differed along the hierarchical lines previously discussed, with university graduates much more involved than those with less schooling. But participation in informal training was more equitable. Over two-thirds of those at all levels of formal educational attainment indicated that they had engaged in such informal job-related learning within the last year (OECD 1991b, 142, 149).

The few ethnographic studies that have looked more closely at the workplace as a site of learning have found extensive informal social learning among manual workers about their work practices, styles and local knowledge beyond individual skills (Kusterer 1978; Darrah 1992; Darrah 1995). Much of this informal learning is unrecognized and taken for granted by workers themselves most of the time, almost invariably beyond the comprehension of management, and very often collective rather than individual learning.[28] As a factory machine operator we interviewed said about his job training:

> You always learn from workmates, constantly. You're always having to show somebody something or learn something. You have to ask other guys. There's just too many different things, or else you would be screwing up too much. There actually is a lot to know.... Formal job training is useful, but the stuff you learn on your own with the guys is the most important. How to streamline. Like the way trainers teach you is how it runs technically. But when you get a feel for the job with the help of the guys, you can run it a lot better than how [formal teachers] showed you.[29]

Informal work-related learning is likely to increase in conditions of economic uncertainty and workplace reorganization. The comment of a middle-aged woman service worker we interviewed recently is probably fairly representative:

> The products are all new from what they were before. I've learned something new almost every day in the past year. We're learning all the time. But it is not recognized by management as job retraining.

The recent literature on organizational development is replete with management declarations of the vital importance of using more of employees' knowledge for the good of the firm, which thereby at least implicitly recognizes the significance of workers' informal learning. A prototypical example is a statement by Matsushita, the Japanese transnational electronics corporation:

Business, as we know, is so complex and so difficult, and the survival of enterprises so uncertain in an environment that is always more uncertain, more competitive and more risky, that their existence depends on the mobilization day after day of each ounce of intelligence. The essence of management consists precisely in mobilizing and gathering the intellectual resources of all employees and putting them in the service of the enterprise.[31] [my translation from French]

Such corporate rhetoric apparently has markedly different effects on the job-related informal learning practices of different types of employees'. As Table 1.8 shows, our recent Ontario surveys have found that employed people in general say that they are now spending an average of about four hours a week, or over 200 hours a year, off the job in unpaid learning activities related to their current jobs. Such voluntary job-related learning remains much more likely among the more highly schooled generally, and business owners and professional-managerial employees in particular, than among other workers who have less control over their jobs. However, service and industrial workers appear to devote very similar amounts of time to *general work-related* learning activities as higher status employees do, about 6 hours a week. But they have *much* less inclination to focus these learning efforts on their specific *jobs*.[32]

In this regard, consider the experience of Bob White (1988, 46–47), now Canada's foremost labour leader:

When you're doing repetitive work, day after unchanging day, the sheer monotony gets to you. Like most of the people in the plant, I was a clock watcher, yearning for the five o'clock whistle so I could get the hell out of there. I don't think people who haven't worked in such jobs realize how deadening it is to have no say in your own work and where every day is the same.... At the same time I began attending UAW [United Auto Workers] education classes, learning about the union movement and meeting people who worked in other UAW plants. I lapped up union shoptalk about contracts and bargaining tactics; I hung on every word when people talked union history. I couldn't get enough of it. I became an avid reader of books about the union movement and reports of legendary bargaining marathons and strikes. The more I learned, the more excited I became.

White may well be exceptional in his passionate union interests. However, there is a long and often repressed tradition of independent working class education grounded in the workplace but covering many related social issues. This tradition remains much stronger in highly unionized European countries but White's own auto workers' union has recently rejuvenated it in North America.[33]

Table 1.8 Informal Work-Related Learning by Occupational Class, Ontario Labour Force, 1994–96

Occupation Class	Informal work-related learning (ave. hrs./week) 1996	Unpaid job-related learning (ave. hrs./week) 1994	Difference
Corporate executive	6	7	-1
Small employer	5	6	-1
Self-employed	7	6	+1
Manager	5	5	0
Professional employee	6	5	+1
Supervisor	6	4	+2
Service worker	6	3	+3
Industrial worker	6	1	+5
Total	6	4	+2

Sources: Livingstone, Hart and Davie (1995, 1997).

But, more generally, virtually all working people remain interested in informally learning things beyond their current jobs that offer greater economic security and chances for more fulfilling work, a common quest for "really useful knowledge."[34] Working class autobiographies offer graphic testimony that, since the inception of industrial capitalism, manual workers with little schooling have been keenly interested in such informal work-related learning when their time and energy allowed.[35] The reflections of a recently retired mine labourer underline this point:

It's obvious that I have a thirst for learning. I have spent the last twenty years of my life doing what you would call self-education. It is obvious to me that those talents were there in the high school system and through circumstances I have had to bury them up until I have reached this stage in my life where I can now indulge in them and thoroughly enjoy them.... But the thing I remember when I started work was that I immediately read and studied the collective agreement. That became a source of power and confirmation. It's a question of deciding to submerge yourself into this [trade union] system rather than the post-secondary school system that I didn't have access to anyway.[36]

His learning may have been "buried" and "submerged" for a long time, in the sense of being invisible to those outside his immediate circle, but he remained actively engaged in informal work-related learning activities throughout his working life. Working class women's informal learning has been even more invisible. Much of women's learning of devalued domestic labour tasks has been hidden in the household. For working class women, the endless burdens of domestic labour in earlier times and the double day in contemporary dual-earner households have left even less time or energy for such autobiographical accounts.[37] As previously noted, we will look more closely and systematically at the current informal learning activities of people living in the education-jobs gap in Chapter Three. The main point here is that the vast majority of people of *all* occupational and formal education levels are now engaged in substantial ongoing informal learning activities, and that much of this learning is related in some way to their paid work, if we construe this work in its broadest terms. The "knowledge economy" is much wider and deeper than current popular accounts which focus on the continuing job and product-specific training of managers and professional employees in the "learning enterprise" ever intimate.[38] For many manual workers especially, specific job-related informal learning is only the tip of the iceberg of their general work-related informal learning.

Illiteracy Panics and Really Useful Knowledge

Nowhere is the underestimation of the distribution of knowledge, and the denigration of knowledge grounded in working class culture and in subordinated folk cultures generally, more evident than in corporate business leaders' and traditional academic treatments of the issue of illiteracy. Illiteracy "panics" have been evoked frequently in periods of high unemployment, with the strong implication that it is the increasing ignorance of people in terms of the basic rudiments of reading, writing and counting that are the root of the problem rather than the organization of the economy.[39] During the current generation there has been renewed emphasis on a decline in literacy and the need for increased literacy in reading and writing to restore economic and social advancement. As expressed through national commissions and best-selling books, cultural literacy is considered to require familiarity with a shared array of specific types of information, information which the current generation woefully lacks. For example, E.D. Hirsch has generated a list of 5000 essential and largely traditional names, phrases, dates and concepts that every American needs to know in order to achieve personal fulfillment and job success (Hirsch 1988). To be culturally literate in the U.S. today, we apparently need to know about such historical figures as Emily Post (but not the Wobblies), Cerberus and Tom Thumb (but not Joe Hill), and Sinclair Lewis (but not Upton Sinclair or Jack London). A basic shared heritage of cultural concepts and background information *is* needed for effective communication in any society. But such arbitrary cultural elitism, whether expressed more abstractly in notions like "cultural capital" or more devastatingly in the content of IQ tests, denies the real cultural experiences of most people. As Ray Browne (1992, 179) observes:

> Those who are at a disadvantage in modern forms of communication are not those lacking in a knowledge of canonical literature and history. Instead, estrangement from modern society and the culture it manifests is disproportionately found among those who have cut themselves off from modern forms of communication, from watching television news, from reading a daily newspaper, from going to the movies, from watching television and from being knowledgeable about and participating in spectator sports and other forms of outdoor recreation. These are not the elite forms of culture, not the type that the conventional print-literacy advocate feels are indispensable. But they reflect the kinds of cultural involvements that characterize most people in our time and place.

As Harvey Graff argues most cogently, literacy has been profoundly misunderstood by most analysts on at least three grounds: definitional, conceptual and contextual (Graff 1987). Definitionally, print literacy is the basic ability to read and write, a set of techniques for communicating, decoding and reproducing written or printed materials. Poor performance by working class kids on culturally restricted tests should not be equated with inability to read and write per se; the latter is much more limited.

Secondly, the commonly used conceptual dichotomy between oral and literate cultures is a false one. In biological-historical terms, as Eric Havelock reminds us, we are a species which uses oral speech to communicate and "reading man" remains "a recent historical accident" (Havelock 1976). In much narrower historical terms, the tendency to deny the significance of oral cultures and their interaction with literate Western cultures has been profound. In Graff's (1987, 28) view:

> The exaggerated emphasis on change and discontinuity, in addition to the excesses of radical dichotomization, are principally responsible for the neglect of the important contribution of oral communications and traditions in receiving, conditioning, shaping, and even accepting the penetration of reading and writing — from the time of the Greeks through the Middle Ages, the early modern period, and on to the present.

Furthermore, oral fluency and reading ability are just two among many kinds of literacy. Additional aspects of literacy include conversance with visual and artistic, spatial and graphic, mathematical, and mechanical types of knowledge. Individuals' learning capacities on these diverse dimensions of knowledge are often not very highly correlated. But all may be recognized as valuable both in the workplace and in general life. For example, print literacy has historically had a low priority in working class views of "really useful knowledge."

Thirdly, the meaning and significance of print and other types of literacy vary greatly depending on historically specific material and cultural contexts. Basic literacy in oral cultures is greatly dependent on environmental perceptions and memory while literacy in print-centered cultures is more reliant on abstract reasoning, a difference that was dramatically documented among Soviet peasants undergoing forced industrialization after the 1917 revolution.[40] But there is no simple linear relationship between the development of print literacy, the expansion of schooling and industrialization. For example, Sweden achieved near-universal levels of reading literacy among both men and women during the eighteenth century, primarily under the impetus of the Lutheran state church, without associated formal educational or industrial development. Conversely, industrialization and sustained economic growth have occurred with widely varied levels of basic literacy (Graff 1981).

Even considering print literacy in narrowest terms, there is very little evidence, beyond rhetorical claims and anecdotes, for any cumulative decline of basic literacy in advanced technological societies. On the contrary, the few recent country-level surveys which have directly measured the literacy skills of representative samples of the population have generally found *much higher* levels of reading ability among younger people. According to the most thorough Canadian surveys, the reading abilities of people born since World War II (i.e. under 45 in 1990) are much higher than those of earlier cohorts. While only about a third of those over 55 can read and interpret relatively complex texts, over three quarters of those under 35 can do so. As the aggregate levels of schooling completed have increased, so have the reading abilities at *every* level of completed schooling. Nearly half of the school dropouts under 35 can read at a complex level, compared with only 20 percent of dropouts over age 55 (Boothby 1993, 29–35).

There are still people who cannot read very well in advanced industrial societies. Table 1.9 summarizes the findings from the four of our countries (Sweden, Germany, Canada and the U.S.) which participated in the first International Adult Literacy Survey (IALS), in terms of the proportion in each age cohort with the lowest level of literacy. Generally the proportion of those achieving only the lowest level of literacy have been declining in each new age cohort in each of the countries included in this study. In Sweden, Germany and Canada the proportion with only rudimentary reading skills has dropped to 10 percent or less of the current youth cohort. The notable exception is the U.S. where it appears that there has been little real decrease in the proportion with the lowest level of literacy since the WWII baby boom generation appeared. But even in the U.S., with about a fifth of the current youth cohort still only achieving a low level of literacy, there has been *no literacy decline, and the vast majority of those with low level literacy skills indicate that their reading skills are adequate for their jobs.*

The vast majority of people in all of these countries indicate that they have sufficient literacy skills for their own purposes in work and daily life. In fact, there is clearly an inflation of literacy criteria in these studies (see Statistics Canada 1996, 19), with virtually the entire population of these countries being presumed to have some

Table 1.9 Proportion at the Lowest Literacy Level* by Age and Self-Rating of Their Reading Skills for Their Main Job, OECD Countries, 1994

	Sweden (%)	Germany (%)	Canada (%)	U.S. (%)
Age Group				
16–25	3	5	10	N/A
26–35	4	6	13	22
36–45	7	9	14	23
46–55	7	7	23	21
56–65	12	18	44	29
Total	6	9	18	23
Self-rating of reading skills for main job				
Good/excellent	N/A	79	87	65
Moderate	N/A	17	7	17
Poor	N/A	4	2	18

* Document reading scale, level 1: Reader may be able to locate a piece of information based on a literal match with some distracting information; may also be able to enter personal information onto a form.

Sources: Statistics Canada/OECD (1995, Table 3.11, Figure 4.7a, 38); Statistics Canada (1996, Table 3.10).

level of functional literacy. As the official intergovernmental report itself (Statistics Canada (1996, 21, 79) concludes:

> The IALS findings provide little evidence to support some pundits' dire predictions of a rapid erosion of either educational quality, or the adult skill base…. Those leaving the labour force have been replaced, by and large, by an incoming cohort … who are collectively much better educated and more literate…. The IALS provides a liberating framework…. No longer do we speak of literates versus illiterates — or haves and have-nots. We can now speak about levels of literacy…. If the IALS were to adopt a mantra, it might be "Level 1 is not an absence of literacy activities, but a lower level of them."

So, in spite of continuing media claims of growing illiteracy of young people today, the best available evidence clearly indicates that there are a lot less print illiterates than there used to be.

Low literacy does remain a significant *social* problem.[41] People who cannot read easily may have serious difficulties coping in some print-oriented contexts. Computerization has extended the difficulty by making more workers and consumers dependent on responding to printed commands. But stigmatizing stereotypes that equate print illiteracy with ignorance and incompetence have been much more debilitating than this illiteracy itself, because such attitudes can pervade the most intimate sense of self-esteem of people so labelled, and thereby inhibit learning and work efforts generally. Consider the following frank admission:

> When I asked her to marry me ... it's hard, you know, you find somebody you love and you try, you know you got this problem with reading, and you know that you're going to have to provide for her, and how do you go about telling somebody that you want to marry that you can't read? Right? Man, it's like opening a bottle, putting a stick of dynamite in it, and hoping it don't go off.... Just the idea of telling somebody that I couldn't read. Hard to make it come out right. And then I found out she knew all about it (Cole 1976, 45–46).

He was evidently a better lover, a better potential provider and a better poet than he recognized!

Many people with low print literacy who excel in other areas of knowledge can transcend damaging stereotypes and cope quite well in everyday life even in the most advanced technological societies. Here are a few good examples:

> I can read a little and write, but it hasn't held me back too much, not having much schooling. I've been able to go through life on mother-wit. And I always did have the gift of music. (Johnny Young, grade four dropout and blues musician, as told to Peter Welding in liner notes for Johnny Young and His Chicago Blues Band, 1966)

> Well, I'm not schoolwise, but I'm streetwise and motherwise and housewifewise. I think there are two kinds of intelligence — streetwise and schoolwise. I don't know much facts about things I learned in school, but I know a lot about life on the streets. I guess I someday might be schoolwise if I stick to it long enough. But what I have now,

what I know already, nobody can take away. (Doreen, quoted in Luttrell 1992, 173)

> They can't buffalo or fool me on anything. As far as doing any kind
> of work, I can do any kind of work that anybody can. I'm far enough
> ahead on stuff, outside of reading, it's quite a job for anyone to trick
> me on anything. There ain't a piece of equipment yet that I can't run,
> or I can't tear down and put back together.... But if I could read and
> write right now I know where I could get a mechanic job that pays the
> top price. That's one thing about reading and writing. A lot of people
> hold it against you and it's *quite a job* getting work on account of it.
> (Phil, quoted in Cole 1976, 66, 84) [emphasis added]

Whatever incapacities may be presumed by expert analysts or some
prospective employers, even those with the lowest print literacy are
actively engaged in many facets of the knowledge society.

In contemporary advanced technological societies, *computer literacy* has rapidly emerged to rival printed forms as an important ingre-
dient in communicative fluency. Computer literacy has become a
general public educational priority rivalling basic reading and writing skills (Livingstone, Hart and Davie 1993, 14–15). We now hear
corporate business claims that the schools are not producing sufficiently computer literate graduates and that a greater infusion of
computer-based education programs is imperative for young people
to cope in the new knowledge economy.[42] But, in fact, basic computer literacy has already become very widespread among youths of all
socio-economic backgrounds, with or without school programs.

Our recent Ontario surveys have assessed basic computer literacy
in terms of ability to do word processing and send electronic mail on
a computer. As Table 1.10 shows, those with more schooling do tend
to be more computer literate. But basic computer literacy in these
terms is quite high and increasing rapidly, so that it now includes the
majority (over 60 percent) of the adult population. Younger people
and those with more schooling are generally much more computer
literate. The majority of university graduates and community college
graduates under 65, high school graduates under 50, and high school
dropouts under 30 are likely to be computer literate. While computer use has also been increasing quickly among those over 65, there is
clearly a persistent generation gap in computer literacy between
seniors of all levels of schooling and all younger people.

Table 1.10 Basic Computer Literacy by Age and Schooling, Ontario, 1996

Schooling	Proportion Who Can Use a Computer*				
	Age Group				
	18–29 (%)	30–49 (%)	50–64 (%)	65+ (%)	Row Total
No diploma	58	33	16	12	26
High school diploma	68	58	47	13	55
College certificate	76	72	66	25	69
University degree	100	92	90	31	89
Column Total	71	60	38	14	61

* Can you do things like word-processing or sending electronic mail on a computer?

Source: Livingstone (1997c).

But the education gap in computer literacy has been closing rapidly among younger people. While the ratio of computer literacy between university grads and school dropouts among those aged 50 to 64 is 5 to 1, among those aged 18 to 29 it is less than 2 to 1. Among the youngest age subgroup (18 to 24) in these adult surveys, nearly 90 percent can use a computer and three quarters have taken a computer course. In all age groups, substantially more adults now know how to use a computer than have taken a computer course (Livingstone, Hart and Davie, 1995, 43–44).

But kids generally do know considerably more than most adults about microcomputers. According to the U.S. census, the majority of American computer users are under 18. Some pundits have even declared cyberspace to be largely ruled by children, with most adults seen as "digitally homeless, the true needy" ("Technomania," 1995, 53). Hyperbole aside, Canadian and U.S. children not only "know about Game Boys, television, music videos, VCRs," as the recent Ontario Royal Commission on Learning (1994, Vol. 4, 8) notes, but can use computers effectively as a learning tool from an early age.

Kids from more affluent families are now much more likely to have home computers than those from the poorest families. The affluent and highly schooled are much more likely to use the Internet (Edwards and Hughes 1995). The danger of creating digital diploma mills and producing a computer-based technocratic elite remains a real concern (Noble 1998). Wide open computer centers in poorer communities could surely aid more equitable assess to the information highway. But if home computer purchases were to follow the trend of other household gadgets, including most recently video cassette recorders, the majority of North American households would have them around the turn of the century (Kettle 1995).

In any case, largely through their own informal learning, people of all social backgrounds are already a lot more computer literate than most public discussions of a current literacy shortage presume. The empirical evidence certainly suggests that there are now more people with basic computer literacy than there are jobs which need it. A 1994 national survey found that 70 percent of all employees in Canada were able to use a computer but less than half did so on their job (Lowe 1996).

Computer literacy is spreading rapidly even among workers with very little schooling. For example, one of our recent interviews was with a middle-aged auto assembly line worker who is a high school dropout. We discovered that he is part of an extensive network of informal computer learners who through observation of computer operators at work, trial and error learning, and mutual help over the phone, but very rarely reading any written instructions, have become proficient to the level of software system reconfiguration. As he describes their informal learning process:

> A lot of trial and error. You learn by doing. You make a lot of mistakes but you learn…. It takes balls because you get in there and you go geez should I do that and am I doing it right? But everybody makes mistakes, presidents, kings, queens, Castro, you know, everybody makes mistakes, it doesn't matter who they are…. The biggest thing is people learning from people, and you don't realize it in school when you're younger I guess. All the guys in the network help each other, the trick is to know exactly when a person can be let go to explore by themself. Nine out of ten people use trial an error. I think some people find it easier to remember by doing it, because you make a mistake and you'll remember it next time. When I have a real severe problem with the computer, I'll pick up the book. I ask three or four people and they don't know, better go to the book.[43]

Whether it is capacity to cope with computers, the printed word or any other general form of information that is presumed to be essential to the knowledge society, those who have cared to look carefully at actual conditions have been unable to find clear evidence for either decline or collective deficiency in relation to current job requirements.

CONCLUDING REMARKS

The evidence presented in this chapter clearly demonstrates that the populations of the richest advanced industrial societies have achieved unprecedented levels of formal credentials and these levels have continued to increase rapidly. It is not inevitable, however, that these trends will continue. Participation at lower levels of schooling has reached universality. The proportions of young people enrolling in universities and colleges could decline if the costs continue to increase and the benefits decrease.

But the popular demand for knowledge per se shows few signs of declining and even now is not centered in the pyramids of formal schooling and further education courses for most adults. As the evidence further documents, the levels of informal practical knowledge attained in the workplace and in everyday life by even the least formally educated people have been both very extensive and generally unrecognized or discounted in public debate and job hiring policies. The pyramids of schooling continue to be supported by massive icebergs of informal learning in most spheres of life in our increasingly knowledgeable society. The icebergs are at least as deep as the pyramids are high.

However, as we will see in the next two chapters, it's now "quite a job" indeed to get any decent work even with extensive formal educational credentials.

2

The Many Faces of Underemployment

Without work all life is rotten. But when work is soulless, life stifles and dies.
—Albert Camus, cited in Langmore and Quiggin 1994, 10

The existing organization of work produces a far-reaching and disturbing squandering of human moral, intellectual and economic potential. As one business consultant put it: "We may have created too many dumb jobs for the number of dumb people to fill them." With so many jobs requiring so few skills it is perhaps not surprising that only one-quarter of American jobholders say that they are working at full potential.
—Murphy 1993, 1–2

INTRODUCTION

To what extent can people use their learning abilities and increasing knowledge in contemporary societies? In this chapter, I will assess this question primarily in terms of the relation between people's learning abilities and their opportunities to apply these capacities in paid employment. The primary sources of evidence here are large-scale survey data. Six distinct dimensions of discrepancies between education and jobs are documented here. These are: *the talent use gap; structural unemployment; involuntary reduced employment; the credential gap; the performance gap; and subjective underemployment.* All six dimensions of "underemployment" or "subemployment" have previously been studied, but rarely if ever have they all been examined together. The full extent of the wastage of people's knowledge and skills by the contemporary organization of paid work has therefore usually been seriously underestimated. Voices will be added to the faces of underemployment in the following chapter.

52

THE CONCEPTS OF UNDEREMPLOYMENT AND SUBEMPLOYMENT

The idea that some people are denied the opportunity to use their full capability at work has been around as long as there have been class societies in which rewarded work has been hierarchically organized and gifted children have been born into the lower ranks. Conversely, the existence of mediocrity among the higher ranks has frequently been recognized by those beneath them; a recent expression of this is the "Peter Principle" which identifies a tendency for managers to be promoted until they reach a level beyond their actual competency (Peters and Hull 1969). Of course, in any market-driven economy, paid workplaces are continually changing and there are always mismatches between employers' aggregate demand and requirements for employees on the one hand, and the aggregate supply and qualifications of job seekers on the other. But the notion of wasted ability among large numbers of the labour force has gained much wider popular currency in periods of widespread unemployment, and especially with the persistence of apparent discrepancies between formal educational attainments and commensurate jobs since the 1960s. These conditions have spawned two distinguishable bodies of research, one concerned with "underemployment," the other with "subemployment."

With the rise of student movements and worker's strikes in the late 1960s, liberal politicians began to worry that growing numbers of highly schooled youths were becoming radicalized because they could not get the sorts of rewarding jobs they expected, and associated researchers became concerned about the problem of their "underemployment" (O'Toole 1975). More conservative colleagues chose to describe the same phenomenon as "overeducation" (Freeman 1976). The basic notion was that highly qualified people could only get routine jobs, became bored and alienated, and rejected the established social order. Several dimensions of underemployment were identified, including a *performance gap* between job holders' educational attainments and the actual task requirements of their occupations (Berg 1970; Collins 1979), a *credential gap* between educational attainments and established job entry requirements (Diamond and Bedrosian 1970), and *subjective underemployment* involving both a conscious perception that people's jobs do not allow significant use of their qualifications (B. Burris 1983b) and the development of revolutionary political consciousness as a consequence of objective underemployment (Derber 1978, 1979; V. Burris 1983). Early estimates of the extent of these forms of underemployment suggested that as many as a quarter to a half of recent college graduates (Rumberger 1984) and from a quarter (Carnegie Commission 1973) to as high as 80 percent of the entire workforce (O'Toole 1975) could be effected. This body of research has focussed mostly on highly schooled young people and on those who currently have jobs.

Also in the 1960s, unrest in U.S. inner cities — expressed most loudly in the 1967 riots — provoked closer attention to employment conditions for people in these areas. Secretary of Labour Willard Wirtz used the concept of "subemployment" to estimate the full extent of employment difficulties in the most distressed black urban ghettos (National Advisory Commission on Civil Disorders 1968, 275; Weir 1992, 89–95). The intent was to develop an index of the discrepancy between the numbers of capable workers and the numbers of adequate jobs. Again, several dimensions were identified. The *officially unemployed* include those jobless people actively looking for employment (most of whom are counted in unemployment statistics). Secondly, there are those who are capable and want to work who have given up looking, often now called *discouraged workers*. Thirdly, the *involuntary part-time employed* include those working only part-time although they want to work full-time. Fourthly, there are *full-time workers who have low earnings*.[1] Using these criteria, government surveys found that between a quarter and a half of the adult population in the largest urban ghettos were subemployed in 1966 (Manpower Report of the President 1967, 75). On the basis of such studies, Secretary Wirtz declared that national measures of official unemployment were "utterly irrelevant" to grasp the employment conditions of the inner cities (cited in Weir 1992, 91). Subsequent studies in this tradition have developed a labour utilization framework to deal with the deficiencies of unemployment measures on a national level (Hauser 1974; Clogg 1979; Sheak 1994). The focus of these studies has been more inclusive of all capable workers and has stressed the lack of adequate jobs for workers at all educational levels.

So, while the underemployment tradition has been preoccupied with the inadequacies of their work among job holders and highly schooled young people, the subemployment tradition has emphasized the absence of adequate jobs for all those who want to work. The two traditions do overlap. Underemployment researchers sometimes refer to unemployment as the most severe form of underemployment for highly qualified people (e.g. Derber, 1978). Subemployment researchers using the labour utilization framework refer to underemployment in terms of low income jobs and aggregate level educational attainment-requirement "mismatches" (Clogg 1979, 218–223). The two traditions merely stress different dimensions of the same general phenomenon: the wasted ability in the workforce. The generic problem is the extent to which a society's supply of adequate jobs falls short of the demand for such jobs.

While the subemployment perspective has been somewhat more inclusive and focussed on the most fundamental aspects of unemployment, the term has now fallen into disuse even among those using the labour utilization framework (e.g. Johnson and Herring 1993). In this book, subemployment will only be used occasionally to refer to unemployment and involuntary reduced employment. I will generally use "underemployment" to denote all dimensions of the wasted ability of the eligible workforce, as they apply to either job holders or the unemployed. Six basic enduring dimensions of underemployment may now be identified, including an even more primary one that both prior traditions have ignored. These dimensions are: (1) *the talent use gap*; (2) *structural unemployment*; (3) *involuntary reduced employment*; (4) *the credential gap*; (5) *the performance gap*; and (6) *subjective underemployment*. All six of these dimensions now appear to represent very substantial chronic problems.

THE TALENT USE GAP

In comparison with all other prior modes of production, modern private market-driven society has generated much greater class mobility. Whereas in pre-capitalist class societies the vast majority of people remained in the classes, estates or castes into which they were born, capitalist labour market dynamics have continually provoked substantial upward and downward occupational class mobility, both intra and inter-generationally. In periods of economic expansion, large numbers of working class youths have been able to obtain more prestigious and secure occupations than their parents and achieve a strong sense of upward class mobility. The great expansion of schooling in the context of post WWII economic growth did lead to substantial upward educational and occupational mobility for many from financially poorer, less schooled families, particularly in North

America. Also, in spite of frequent ruminations about the rise of a "cognitive elite," there is little evidence that either inherent intelligence or positions at the top of the educational and occupational hierarchies have become more *intergenerationally* reproducible (Livingstone 1995b). Conversely, in periods of protracted economic slump, large numbers of people are also likely to experience a loss of prestigious and secure employment and a sense of downward mobility. But even in recessionary times, people born at the bottom of the economic ladder now have a much greater chance of climbing the ladder through their own efforts and abilities than was commonly the case in earlier class societies. In comparative historical terms, this relatively extensive amount of occupational mobility is associated with increased concern that upward movements be based on inherent talent and concerted effort rather than on good luck and the favour of ruling classes.

However, the natural talents of large numbers of people continue to be wasted in our school systems, effectively denying equitable job chances to many youths from poorer social backgrounds long before they enter the job market. The "talent use gap" refers specifically to the difference in educational achievements between those of higher and lower social origins. This concept is based on the assumption that children born into different socio-economic groups tend to have very similar distributions of inherent intelligence. These discrepancies became a matter of great concern to educational policy makers and researchers in the late 1950s when the demand for highly qualified workers was expanding quickly while youths from poor families remained seriously underrepresented in higher education. A wide array of national surveys in the early 1960s documented the extent of inequality of educational opportunity by family origins and led to initiatives to overcome both familial and school-based barriers. The most influential survey was the Coleman (1966) report in the U.S. which attributed the major differences in educational achievement to family economic conditions, and stimulated such state intervention policies as Head Start, school meal programs and inter-school bussing.

As economic conditions worsened at the end of the 1960s and the unemployment of inner city youths and general underemployment of highly qualified graduates were seen to provoke riots and political unrest, government policy makers began to lose sight of the talent use gap related to socio-economic origins, as they became more concerned with barriers to employment than barriers to education (Weir 1992).

Relevant education for employment become more pertinent than educational equality per se. Both the women's movement and civil rights organizations by visible minorities have continued to remind policy makers of talent use gaps in education in terms of systemic forms of discrimination based on their ascribed features. But there has also been a resurgence of biological determinist arguments which have attempted to prove that kids from lower class and black race origins are genetically less intelligent and that they experience no serious talent use gap (Jensen 1969; Herrnstein and Murray 1994). While such arguments have been given wide coverage by the mass media, they have been shown to be seriously flawed on both conceptual and methodological grounds (Cameron 1995; Jacoby and Glauberman 1995; Kinchloe et al. 1996). Whatever shifts occur in specific arguments about educational inequality, one irrefutable fact remains. The range of intelligences within any major social group is massively greater than any difference between such groups. As long as this is true, the underrepresentation of lower socio-economic groups in higher education will continue to indicate a serious waste of talent.

The talent use gap may be estimated by the discrepancies between the aggregate formal educational attainment levels of children from family origins in dominant groups and those of children from disadvantaged origins. The cumulative empirical research strongly confirms that selection for higher levels of schooling continues to favour students from higher class social origins whose parents have both more schooling themselves and higher paying occupations. This may well be the most consistently and strongly documented relationship yet studied by social scientists. Female students and students of color also experience persistent forms of discrimination against their participation at higher levels. These forms of educational discrimination tend to interact, so that black females from lower class origins for example are likely to have among the lowest school completion rates. The enduring problem is a massive wastage of the actual educational potential of many youths of high aptitudes regardless of the educational efforts they may make.

The magnitude of the current talent use gap may be illustrated by comparing the formal educational attainments of those with family origins in selected higher and lower occupational classes and of different sex and race attributes. Table 2.1 provides recent estimates for the U.S. in terms of the attainment of university degrees.

By 1994, almost a quarter of the adult population over twenty-five

Table 2.1   Attainment of University Degrees by Father's
                Occupational Class, Sex, Race and Generation,
                U.S. 25+ Population, 1988–1994.

	Father's Occupational Class		*Total Population*
	Professional Employee (%)	*Industrial Worker (%)*	*(%)*
Total population	46	13	23
Generation			
Born pre 1931	33	7	13
Born 1931–50	54	16	26
Born 1951–70	53	15	29
Sex			
Male	52	15	25
Female	42	11	20
Race			
White	47	13	24
Black	31	10	12
Post 1950 age cohort			
White males	58	18	32
White females	52	14	29
Black males	43	10	14
Black females	36	7	11

Source: Davis and Smith (1994).

had attained a university degree; this was true of nearly half of those
from professional family origins but only 13 percent of those whose
fathers were industrial workers, a ratio of *more than three to one.* When
comparisons are made among the last three generations of adults,[2] this
ratio of more than three to one has persisted at the same time as the
general attainments of the entire population have increased greatly.
Similar discrepancies in school attainments by occupational class ori-

gins are found regardless of sex or race. The gender gap in school attainments has been closing in recent generations but young men are still somewhat more likely to have degrees than women are.[3] The race gap remains more substantial, with whites still at least *twice as likely* as blacks, Hispanics and aboriginals to obtain university degrees. The compound effects of discrimination by class origin, race and sex attributes are such that in the most recent age group that has had the time to complete their schooling, nearly 60 percent of white males from professional family origins have obtained a degree, while only 7 percent black females with fathers who were industrial workers have done so, a ratio of *more than eight to one*.[4]

Simple conservative estimates of the absolute magnitude of these discrepancies in the use of inherent learning capacities suggest that at least twice as many current U.S. adults from disadvantaged class and race backgrounds — *well over 20 million people* — could have achieved a university degree if they had received equal opportunities to those from white upper middle class origins.[5] This represents an extraordinary waste of learning capacity.

Such estimates may be disputed on the assumption that the children of the upper middle classes have been "overeducated" in relation to their inherent abilities rather than lower classes being "undereducated." If this were true, one equitable response would be to *reduce* the proportions of kids from upper middle class families going to universities — not a very likely scenario politically! However, as noted in Chapter One there is no compelling evidence that the intellectual quality of either high school or university students has declined significantly as the proportion of the population graduating doubled.

Earlier estimates of the "talent use gap" which have included various assumptions about additional constraints (such as limited motivation through "cultures of poverty" or lack of material incentives) on university attendance by lower class and black youths have sometimes generated smaller numbers (e.g. Wolfle 1971, 104–174). But as the population has grown and the class and race discrepancies have persisted, there should be little doubt that many millions of Americans of lower class and visible minority origins excluded from higher education are quite capable of successfully completing university. As the economist Howard Bowen (1973, 10) concluded in the 1970s:

> All the evidence indicates that millions of students not in higher education are basically as bright and able as those who are. Clearly, sim-

ple morality urges the opening of opportunities to these people as fast as possible. Education should not be shut off on the pretext that too many people have too much of it.

As Table 2.2 shows, comparable Ontario studies also find persistent class discrimination ratios in university completion of *more than three to one* in favour of children from professional families over those from industrial working class households. Similar patterns are supported by Canada-wide analyses based on census data on general educational attainments (see Creese, Guppy and Meissner 1991) and the most recent findings of the National Longitudinal Survey of Children and Youth concerning differential rates of participation in remedial and gifted education programs by socioeconomic status group (Galt and Cernetig 1997). Once again, these class ratios hold across sex and ethnicity differences. The gender gap has been closing here too, but men remain somewhat more likely to obtain degrees, especially in math and science (Statistics Canada 1995c).

Race and ethnic differences in educational attainments may be somewhat more complex in Canada. People of French ancestry have historically experienced some discrimination in English Canada and this is reflected in generally lower educational attainments than those of British ancestry, who have long been the most dominant ethnic group in political and economic terms (Porter 1961). Most visible minorities are now post-WWII non-European immigrants and many of these people were selected because of the imposition of entry criteria that now favour high educational attainments; hence, in aggregate terms, visible minorities now tend to have higher degree attainments than white Canadians (McDade 1988). But aboriginal people and black people of both indigenous and Caribbean or African origins continue to have lower completion rates than other ethnic groups in Canada, as in the U.S.(Li 1988; Dei et al. 1995).

These recent findings translate into a huge loss of educational talent in the U.S. and Canada. By even the most conservative estimates, millions of very capable North Americans who could easily benefit from post-secondary education are still being denied access while many much less capable kids from more affluent families graduate (Curtis, Livingstone, and Smaller 1992).

The loss of educational potential is even greater in Japan and Europe where university graduates from working class origins are much rarer. A large-scale British longitudinal study of intergenera-

Table 2.2 Attainment of University Degrees by Father's Occupational Class, Sex, Ethnicity and Generation, Ontario 25+ Population, 1988–1996.

| | Father's Occupational Class | | Total Population |
	Professional Employee (%)	Industrial Worker (%)	(%)
Total population	42	8	14
Generation			
Born pre 1931	38	4	6
Born 1931–50	45	6	13
Born 1951–70	42	11	19
Sex			
Male	41	10	17
Female	42	6	12
Ethnicity			
British	40	7	14
French	46	5	8
Non-White	63	11	25
Post 1950 age cohort			
British male	39	11	20
British female	41	8	19
French male	46	6	13
French female	47	10	12
Non-White males	64	7	22
Non-White female	58	16	25

Source: OISE Survey of Educational Issues Data Archive.

tional educational selection also found the persistence of similar advantage of upper middle class origins in spite of general increases in university participation (Halsey 1980). Indeed, virtually all empirical studies have found very substantial attainment differences by socio-economic origins, although there may have been some reductions of intergenerational inequality in a few cases (Shavit and Bloss-field 1993).

The reproduction of social inequalities by the school system has been accentuated by adult education programs. As noted in Chapter One, those who have higher levels of formal schooling are more like-ly to participate in most forms of further education. Those from lower class and some visible minority origins are not only much less likely to obtain a university degree. They are also, as a consequence of less formal schooling, much less likely to enroll in further education pro-grams throughout their adult lives. Certainly as those in lower class positions have become more highly schooled, their adult education participation rates have increased greatly (Livingstone, Hart and Davie 1997). But even in Sweden, where state initiatives to incorpo-rate educationally marginalized adults have been greatest, a "cycle of accumulation" still operates so that lower prior formal attainments by those from lower class origins effectively predict later lower adult education participation (Tuijnman 1991). The available time series studies of adult education enrolment by social background indicate that the gap in participation between those with the most and the least schooling has *not* been narrowing as the general level of adult participation grows (Fisher and Rubenson 1992).

Similar inequalities are also well documented with regard to adult job training and retraining programs specifically. Surveys in the G7 countries and Sweden have found that the recent participa-tion rates of highly schooled employees such as professionals and managers range from about two to ten times those with little school-ing, particularly manual workers (OECD 1991, 149; Tuijnman 1992, 685; Crompton 1992, 33). Again, even in Sweden, professional-man-agerial employees are at least twice as likely as manual workers to have taken a training course in the last year (Tuijnman 1992).

So, while overall educational attainments have increased greatly, the class divide and at least some race gaps in talent use to obtain a university degree have been wide and persistent in most advanced industrial countries. The differences focussed on here with regard to the highest level of schooling are merely indicative of the full scope of the talent use gap, which also includes differential completion and dropout rates at lower levels of schooling. It is clear that the capacity for formal learning of many millions of people continues to be wasted during their school years through the discriminatory treatment of lower class and black and aboriginal minority youths.

The upper levels of schooling may again become even more exclusionary of these youths as post-secondary institutions respond to state funding cuts with tuition fee increases. In any case, the gap between learning capacity and job opportunities continues to be set up for many lower class and visible minority youths well before they have a chance to enter the labour market.

STRUCTURAL UNEMPLOYMENT

The recent OECD (1994a, 7) jobs study observes that unemployment is "probably the most widely feared phenomenon of our times." From the official standpoints of most governments, unemployment is now a serious problem because:

> It brings with it unravelling of the social fabric, including a loss of authority of the democratic system, and it risks the resulting disintegration of the international trading system. (29)

Chronic unemployment is the starkest, most humanly devastating form of underemployment. When it occurs, it touches and undermines nearly all parts of society.

In any market-driven economy, there is always a certain amount of "frictional" unemployment as some people retire and others vacate jobs through quitting, firing or promotion, while others enter the labour market and seek such vacancies. Unemployment rates typically go up and down with business cycles related to investors' confidence in commodity and stock markets. But when there is a persistent gap between the excess number of job seekers and the scarce number of job vacancies, this is know as *structural unemployment*. Numerous types of structural unemployment have been distinguished (Standing 1983; Hart 1990). These include technological unemployment in which new machine-based techniques such as computers and other microelectronic devices eliminate jobs; geographical mismatch where it is too difficult and costly for job seekers to move from established communities to where new jobs are being created; demographic shifts such as increased female labour force participation, increasing numbers of young job seekers, high immigration, and increasing numbers of older people who still want to work; institutionalized benefits plan factors that encourage employers to use overtime with existing workers because it is cheaper than hiring additional workers with benefits, and which discourage unemployed people from taking low-paying jobs because of loss of state income support; and capital restructuring unemployment whereby multinational enterprises move labour-intensive operations offshore to the newly industrializing countries with cheaper pools of labour. While it remains difficult to measure the levels of each of these components, it is reasonably clear that chronic structural unemployment has grown in virtually all of the advanced industrial societies since the 1970s and led to an increasing extent of human damage.

In the U.S., for example, annual average unemployment rates during the post-1973 period have generally been at least two percent higher than in the 1947–73 period; the general unemployment rate has usually been over six percent and the rate for blacks and Hispanics about double that (Mishel et al. 1997, 243). But these statistics only begin to hint at the extent of the damage. A recent New York Times (1996, 6) poll found that nearly three-quarters of Americans have been affected by a permanent job layoff, either personally or of someone close to them during the past fifteen years. As the New York Times' (1996, 7–8) team of reporters concluded from their six-month investigative project:

> The job apprehension has intruded everywhere, diluting self-worth, splintering families, fragmenting communities, altering the chemistry of workplaces, roiling political agendas and rubbing salt in the very soul of the country. Dispossessed workers ... are finding themselves on anguished journeys they never imagined, as if being forced to live the American dream of higher possibilities in reverse.

According to official statistics, an average of over 30 million people have been unemployed in the 26 OECD countries since the early 1980s, compared with under 10 million during the 1950s and 1960s (OECD 1994a). These figures certainly indicate widespread and persistent structural unemployment. But they also *seriously* underestimate the full extent of unemployment. To be counted, you have to be actively seeking full-time employment and frequently registering with a government employment office. Many people who desperately want jobs have given up such active pursuit because of the perceived futility in conditions of extensive structural unemployment. Government statistics offices in all these countries now recognize the phenomenon of the "discouraged worker" and are trying to estimate the extent. One of the most extensive, if now somewhat dated, international comparisons is summarized in Table 2.3. These figures suggest that official unemployment rates underestimate the actual extent of unemployment by between 30 percent and 225 percent. In Canada, for example, the responsible federal agency has recently admitted that it has been arbitrarily omitting discouraged workers who had not actively searched for a job in the prior six months and economists at a leading bank have indicated that this exclusion alone has led to underestimating the jobless rate by 40 percent (Carrick 1996). It should also be noted here that in the low conventional unemployment countries of Japan and Sweden, discouraged workers account for a much greater proportion of the labour force than in most other countries. Moreover, in most of these countries, including Japan, Sweden and Germany, the unemployment rates have continued to fluctuate upward (Odrich 1997).

Table 2.3   Alternative Unemployment Indicators, Selected OECD Countries, 1989

	Long-term Unemployment[a] *(%)*	*Conventional Unemployment*[b] *(%)*	*Conventional plus Discouraged*[c] *(%)*
Italy	7.3	7.8	15.8
Canada	3.1	7.5	9.9
United Kingdom	5.2	7.4	9.3
Germany	4.6	5.8	N/A
United States	1.2	5.3	7.9
Japan	1.1	2.2	7.2
Sweden	0.5	1.4	3.8

[a] Total registered unemployed for over 13 weeks, as percent of the full-time civilian labour force.

[b] Total registered unemployed, as a percent of the full time civilian labour force.

[c] Total full-time *and* part-time job seekers *plus* discouraged workers, as a percent of the civilian labour plus discouraged workers.

Source: Sorrentino (1993, 6)

By 1994, according to conventional measures, the unemployed had increased to about 35 million people in OECD countries (OECD 1994a, 9). If we assume, along with the OECD (1994a, 7, 10), that discouraged workers could add over 40 percent to these totals, the number of unemployed people would be at least *50 million people or about 12 per-cent of the readily available labour force in these countries.*

The persistence of structural unemployment is further indicated by compositional changes in the duration of unemployment, and the ages and educational levels of the unemployed. In most of these countries, the proportion who have been unemployed for more than a year has been spiralling upwards since the 1970s and now consti-tutes almost 30 percent of the conventionally measured unem-ployed (OECD 1994a, 12, 14; OECD 1994b, 48).[6] This level varies greatly between countries with only around 10 percent in long term unemployment in the U.S., Canada and Sweden, whereas in most European Common Market countries the proportion is often over 40 percent. North Americans face both greater individual risks of becoming unemployed and better chances of being rehired quickly than most Europeans. But even here long term unemployment has been increasing significantly (Cohen 1991, 42).

Young people under 25 have typically experienced more than dou-ble the rates of unemployment of prime age (25 to 54) workers, as they enter the labour force and move between jobs trying to find a suitable career line. But the differential between unemployment rates for young and prime age workers appears to have narrowed in most OECD countries (OECD 1994b, 42–43; OECD 1994d, 22–32) as prime age workers have experienced higher and more persistent levels of structural unemployment while youth unemployment rates also remain high.

Those with lower levels of formal educational attainment have also generally been more likely to face unemployment. As employers have come to rely more heavily on educational credentials, especially in hiring decisions, those without them have suffered most greatly. Since the 1970s in nearly all OECD countries, unemployment rates for the least schooled members of the labour force have increased relative to those of the more highly schooled; in the U.S between 1970 and 1990, the unemployment rates of male high school dropouts increased from about 1.9 to 2.5 times the rates of those who have high school diplo-mas or more (OECD 1994b, 38–41). This relative worsening of employment prospects for high school dropouts has occurred at the same time as unemployment rates for the increasing proportion of workers with higher educational qualifications have also increased significantly (OECD 1994b, 40–41). For example, a 1994 Canadian survey of food bank users found that over 10 percent were unemployed university graduates and about 40 percent had some post-secondary schooling (Daily Bread Food Bank, 1994); a more recent Canadian survey has found that more than half the people on welfare who are considered employable have post-secondary education and a good work history (Lakey 1996).

So, the increasing incidence of long term unemployment, the increasing likelihood that prime age workers will experience substantial unemployment, and the long-term increases in rates of unemployment for workers at all educational levels and especially those without diplomas, all point to a growing pervasiveness and persistence of structural unemployment.

But even unemployment estimates that attempt to include discouraged workers fail to consider many who want paid work but feel that they have no real chance because of other unfair barriers. These people, who are typically regarded by policy makers as nonparticipants, are now the "hidden unemployed" (Metcalf 1992). Nonlegitimate barriers such as failure to find accessible childcare or other dependent care and discouragement from job search tend to impede the employment and obscure the employability of women, older workers, people with disabilities and ethnic minorities. There are also legislated restrictions on the rights of disabled people and the retired to pursue employment while they receive other state-administered benefits.[7] Consider, for example, a young woman who needs a job but cannot find or afford essential daycare for her children, a paraplegic who cannot get a job without losing supplementary state medical benefits, or a 66 year old who wants to work but believes that no employer will consider him or her. Non-participation rates have also recently increased in most countries for older workers over fifty-five, especially men, often through forced early retirements (OECD 1994b, 33). Through the conflation of the unemployment of many of these people with non-participation of others in their social categories, and by ignoring these unfair barriers to seeking employment, the extent of unemployment among women, ethnic minorities, older people and people with disabilities is seriously underestimated. McLaughlin (1992, 2–4) estimates that including these hidden unemployed could more than double the real level of unemployment in the United Kingdom. If these estimates were applied across the OECD countries, the real level of unemployment might be found to be around *100 million people*.

The most central consequence of unemployment — be it conventional, discouraged or hidden variants — is now, as it was for the 19th century people quoted in the Introduction to this book, *material deprivation*. The vast majority of those who are deprived of paid employment suffer from material hardships which are often associated with psychological stress. The views frequently promoted in some influential circles, claiming that the unemployed are lazy, immoral, undeserving or psychically deficient (see Burnett 1994; Struthers 1983; McBride 1992; Katz 1993) have received precious little support from the array of researchers who have closely studied the lives of the unemployed over the past sixty-five years. As David Fryer (1992, 119) summarizes his recent thorough review of this research literature:

> Unemployed people are not work-shy; the vast majority are highly committed to paid employment. There is poverty in Western industrialized nations today.... Moreover, poverty is particularly concentrated amongst unemployed people. In addition, previously unemployed people when in employment are disproportionately likely to be located in disadvantaged sectors of the labour market with their own associated psychological, social and material hazards: they therefore suffer cumulative labour market disadvantage which may exacerbate the impact of unemployment. Unemployed people do not live "comfortably enough" on benefits. Rather than benefits levels needing to be reduced still further to maintain incentives for paid employment, as some believe, they clearly need to be increased in the interests of better mental health. If much of the psychological distress of unemployment, diminished self-confidence, reduced activity levels and physical health costs of unemployment are due to inadequate, stigmatized and social psychologically corrosive incomes, then "counselling" approaches ... cannot possibly succeed.

Even in the depths of the Great Depression of the 1930s, there was little evidence that the unemployed had actually given up on work, but plenty of documentation of human ingenuity in coping with very hard material deprivation. Eugene Bakke (1940 282) concluded in the most intensive U.S. study:

> The record of the efforts of the unemployed does not give certain evi-

dence that they have lost their self-reliance. Rather it indicates that they have exemplified this quality upon the foundation of the possibilities available to the unemployed and their families. Before assuming that some new effort to get economic security ... indicates a change in the character of people, it is well to ask whether the new effort is not merely a method more effectively adapted to getting, under contemporary circumstances, the increasing economic security people have always struggled for, or to restoring a measure of security which they had lost in the sweep of economic and social change.

As the current period of economic stagnation has persisted, the numbers in serious material hardship have grown to proportions approaching those of the "dirty thirties." But, once again, well grounded studies are finding that poor people commonly adopt an ethic of hard work and family responsibility, while they try to "bend the rules" of the post WWII benefit system to fit the current employment conditions and non-legitimate barriers to paid work (Jordan et. al. 1992). The lack of decent jobs has become fairly obvious. But the urge to work remains very strong even among the most chronically unemployed.

INVOLUNTARY REDUCED EMPLOYMENT

Involuntary reduced employment is work in non-standard or contingent jobs when you really want secure full-time paid work. The normal number of hours worked to earn a full-time wage in the OECD countries has declined throughout the 20th century (OECD 1994b, 88–92). Full-time workers have historically struggled to use productivity gains for reduced weekly working hours and an increased number of paid days off (civic holidays, vacation days, sick days, parental and educational leaves) for recuperative and leisure purposes rather than retaining long hours for high incomes. In Canada, for example, the normal workweek was shortened from 60 hours to around 40 hours between 1900 and 1960 (Advisory Group on Working Time and the Distribution of Work 1994). Since the early 1960s, this trend has continued, but more slowly in North America than in Europe. In 1960, U.S. full-time workers worked significantly less hours than most Europeans, whereas now they work more hours (OECD 1994b, 90). But the major factor contributing to continuing reductions in average annual hours worked per all employed persons since the 1960s has been the growth of part-time employment.

Part-time employment, which averages around 15 hours per week in most countries, is frequently underemployment. As Mishel et al. (1997, 257) observe:

> Part-timers generally have lower pay, less-skilled jobs, poor chances of promotion, less job security, inferior benefits (such as vacation, health insurance, and pension), and lower status overall within their places of employment.

This type of employment has increased rapidly since the 1960s to become a large and permanent proportion of the workforce. As Table 2.4 suggests, by 1990 part-time workers constituted about a quarter of the employed workforce in most Scandinavian countries, over 15 percent in the United Kingdom, Japan, the U.S. and Canada, and more than 10 percent in nearly all other OECD countries. In Canada, for example, by mid-1994 over 17 percent of employees worked part-time; this represented a doubling over two decades and about half of all new jobs created during the 1979–93 period (Advisory Group on Working Time and the Distribution of Work 1994, 31). By late 1995, the proportion had increased to 19 percent (Carey 1996). These figures underestimate the actual number of part-time jobs because growing numbers of people, now about six percent of the labour force in both Canada and the U.S. (Advisory Group on Working Time and the Distribution of Work 1994, 31; Mishel et al. 1997, 263), are combining part-time jobs to become full-time workers.

As Table 2.4 also indicates, European and North American surveys have found that from a quarter to about 90 percent of all part-time workers would prefer a full-time job. A large part of the part-time workforce in most countries is made up of students who combine paid employment with their studies and women who combine paid work with childcare and/or eldercare. Some of these people do prefer to have part-time employment at these stages in their lives. But, whatever their other pursuits, many of these people would prefer to have full-time work (Stratton 1996; Tilly 1996). By the most conservative direct estimates, involuntary part-time employees now constitute about five percent of the active Canadian labour force and four percent of the U.S. labour force. This translates into more than three quarters of a million part-time Canadian workers (Advisory Committee on Working Time and the Distribution of Work 1994, 2) and around four million U.S. part-time workers (Mishel et al. 1997, 258)

Table 2.4   Part-time Employment, Selected Countries, 1989–1990

	Share of Part-time in Total Employment (%)	Part-timers who want full-time work (%)
Sweden	24	10*
United Kingdom	22	94
Japan	18	N/A
United States	18	24
Canada	15	35
Germany	13	92
France	12	32
Italy	6	51

* The 1989 Swedish figures refer to the proportion of *all* employees who would prefer more hours with increased earnings, and therefore probably significantly underestimate the proportions of part-time workers with such preferences.

Sources: OECD (1994b, Tables 6.8 and 6.14, 77, 92–93); U.S. data, Mishel et al. (1997, Table 4.13, 258); part-timers' preferences for Canada, Advisory Committee on Working Time and the Distribution of Work (1994, Figure 2.5, 22).

who would prefer full-time jobs. In European countries such as Germany and the United Kingdom the proportions are apparently much higher. The increase in involuntary part-time employment has not followed a simple linear pattern but an upward cyclical one. As Chris Tilly (1996, 121) observes, on the basis of one of the most thorough recent U.S. studies of part-time jobs:

> The rate of part-time employment rides a roller coaster: it rises and falls with the unemployment rate, but after each recession over the last quarter century, it has remained a little higher.... It is involuntary part-time employment that propels the ups and downs, and recently the upward drift as well.

In addition, temporary full-time jobs on short-term contractual, casual or piecework bases are not only insecure but frequently poorly compensated and provide relatively little chance for workers to use many of their skills. Such jobs have grown very rapidly since the 1960s. In both Canada and the U.S. the proportions of temporary jobs have probably doubled in the past ten years, and now represent over ten percent of the employed labour force (Evenson 1996; Gibb-Clark 1997; Mishel et al. 1997, 266–69). The biggest private employer in North America is now Manpower Services Incorporated, a Milwaukee-based temporary employee agency with over 600,000 workers. Some analysts estimate that if current trends continue, temporary or contingent workers may constitute half of the North American workforce in the near future (Gordon 1993). While this is improbable, it is very likely that a large proportion of those who take such temporary jobs would prefer work that allows them to apply their knowledge and skills on a more sustained and adequately paid basis.

Worktime is also becoming more polarized. A slowdown in the reduction of the normal work week is evident in most OECD countries since the early 1980s (OECD 1994b, 88). This is because continuing increases in part-time work have been partially offset by a substantial increase in overtime work by full-time workers. In Canada, for example, the proportion of the labour force working more than 50 hours a week increased from six percent in 1976 to 8 percent in 1993, including an increase to over 20 percent of all employed men (Advisory Group on Working Time and the Distribution of Work 1994, 17–18). By early 1997, over 20 percent of all employees said they were working past their regularly scheduled hours; about half of this overtime work, especially by women, was being done without pay (Theobald 1997b). This "long hours culture," largely generated by employment insecurity, also results in less jobs of even the involuntary temporary variety available for the growing numbers of unemployed people. Many observers have pointed to the implications of these trends for the development of a more polarized society (e.g. Schor 1991).

THE CREDENTIAL GAP

How closely matched are the educational attainments of job holders with the credentials required for entry into their current jobs? We hear frequent claims of "credential inflation." In light of the rapid post WWII increases in general educational attainments, it is very likely that employers have increased the educational entry requirements for some jobs beyond the levels of knowledge actually needed to perform them. But there have been very few large-scale empirical studies of employers' actual entry requirements. Collins (1979, 5–7) reviewed the findings of the few prior U.S. surveys based on employers' own reports. We have conducted a more recent series of Ontario surveys between 1982 and 1996 based on employees' reports of current entry requirements for their own jobs (see Livingstone 1987).[8] Holzer (1996) has done 1992–94 surveys of employers in four U.S. cities (Atlanta, Boston, Detroit and Los Angeles). The comparable results of these studies are summarized in Table 2.5.

While these surveys deal with quite different populations, they do permit several basic trend inferences. First, while formal schooling was of little significance even for the professions through the mid-nineteenth century, by the 1930s post-secondary credentials had become an important criterion for entry into most professions; by the 1960s this requirement had become almost universal. With the post-WWII expansion of the school system, post-secondary credentials also began to be commonly required for managerial posts, and by the 1980s a college degree had become a standard entry requirement. A high school diploma also became a common entry condition for clerical work after WWI; since then, entry requirements have increased fairly steadily, so that now nearly half of clerical jobs have post-secondary entry requirements, typically a community college certificate. The most dramatic recent increases in entry requirements have been among manual workers. In the 1930s hardly any manual labour jobs required a high school diploma. By the early 1980s, the majority of skilled manual jobs required a diploma for entry, and about a quarter called for some post-secondary certification. Since the early 1980s, there has been a very rapid increase in the use of high school graduation as a screen for entry into most unskilled manual jobs. Holzer's (1996, 54–57) recent surveys of the array of possible hiring criteria and activities finds that about three-quarters of all non-college jobs now use high school diplomas as an initial screen. Even to push a broom in a steel mill, you now need to have a diploma (see Livingstone 1996c). The "credential society" has definitely arrived.

Since the late 1960s, the employment of large numbers of post-secondary graduates in jobs that only require lower educational entry credentials has been widely documented, especially in North America.[9] Their plight has become a regular feature in our newspapers (e.g. Theobald 1997a, C1). Several different measures of attainment-

Table 2.5 Percentage of Employers Requiring Various Minimum Educational Levels for Job Entry by Employees' Occupational Class, 1937–38, 1967, 1982–1996.

Occupational Class	Job entry requirements	1937/38 (U.S.)	1967 (San Francisco)	1982–84 (Ontario)	1988–90 (Ontario)	1992–94 (U.S.)	1994–96 (Ontario)
Professional							
employees	<h.s.	9	10	2	1		0
	h.s.d+	39	15	13	19	86*	10
	post-sec. cred.	52	75	85	80		90
Managers	<h.s.	32	27	6	5		8
	h.s.d+	54	28	26	30	86*	26
	post-sec. cred.	14	44	68	65		66
Clerical							
workers	<h.s.	33	29	16	18		5
	h.s.d+	64	72	60	46	87*	48
	post-sec. cred.	3	0	24	34		47
Skilled							
manual							
workers	<h.s.	89	62	41	25		23
	h.s.d+	11	38	40	51	60*	54
	post-sec. cred.	0	0	19	24		23
Unskilled							
manual							
workers	<h.s.	99	83	76	58		40
	h.s.d+	1	17	19	40	51*	52
	post-sec. cred.	0	0	5	2		8
N		N/A	104	503	529	3200	489

<h.s. = less than high school completion
h.s.d+ = high school diploma+
post-sec. cred. = post-secondary credential

* Combined high school and post-secondary totals for job entry requirements

Sources: Collins (1979, 6) Table 1.2 for the 1937–38 U.S. National Survey and 1967 San Francisco Bay Area Survey; OISE Survey of Educational Issues Data Archive for all Ontario surveys; Holzer (1996, 56) Table 3.6 for 1992–94 U.S. Employment Surveys in Atlanta, Boston, Detroit and Los Angeles.

entry requirement mismatches have been used. Using a measure of surplus education based on differences between years of schooling attained and self-reported years of schooling required for job entry, Duncan and Hoffman (1978) found that over 40 percent of U.S. workers had "surplus education" for their jobs in 1976.[10] Subsequent studies have relied on more conservative estimates of mismatches based on credentials attained and credentials required rather than years of schooling. Canadian surveys suggest that around 20 percent of the entire employed workforce and larger proportions of younger, more highly educated workers are "overqualified" or underemployed in this sense of having a higher credential than their job requires for entry, and that another 20 percent or so are underqualified ((McDowell 1991). Credential underemployment surely became greater with the explosion of post-secondary schooling in the 1960s, but have attainment-entry credential mismatches increased further among the employed workforce since then?

The best available data source to assess recent trends in the relationship between employees' educational attainments and the job entry requirements established by their employers is probably the 1982–96 biennial series of eight general population surveys we have conducted in Ontario (Livingstone, Hart and Davie 1997). These measures are based on respondents' self-reports of both their formal educational attainments and the current job entry credential requirements of their employers. Table 2.6 summarizes changes in the formal educational attainment levels of the active Ontario labour force since 1982, as well as in the educational job entry requirements currently expected by employers and the extent of correspondence or mismatching between employees' credential attainments and current job entry credential requirements, including the proportions of "underemployed" and "underqualified."[11] During this period, aggregate educational credential attainments have increased significantly, with a reduction of high school dropouts from around 40 percent to about a quarter of the workforce, and roughly equal gains in the proportions who have completed either high school, college and university programs. Educational entry requirements have similarly increased, with an even sharper reduction in jobs which do not require a diploma, from over 40 percent to less than a quarter of all jobs; most of this reduction occurred during the 1980s. The proportion of jobs requiring a high school diploma increased rapidly during the 1980s, from about 25 to over 40 percent. During the 1990s, post-secondary credentials have increasingly been

Table 2.6   Formal Educational Attainments, Job Entry
Educational Credential Requirements, and
Attainment-Requirement Matching,
Ontario Labour Force 1982–1996.

	82 (%)	84 (%)	86 (%)	88 (%)	90 (%)	92 (%)	94 (%)	96 (%)
Attainments								
<high school	41	36	33	33	27	26	25	26
h.s. diploma	33	34	36	36	38	38	39	39
college certificate	13	15	16	15	17	18	18	17
university degree	13	14	15	15	17	18	19	18
Entry Requirements								
no diploma	44	35	33	28	24	23	22	23
h.s. diploma	26	33	37	41	42	43	40	38
college certificate	15	16	14	14	17	16	19	18
university degree	15	16	16	17	17	18	20	21
Match								
underemployed	18	22	18	21	22	23	19	21
matched	60	56	59	56	55	56	55	54
underqualified	22	22	23	23	23	21	26	25
N	620	623	642	621	644	580	664	606

Source: OISE Survey of Educational Issues Data Archive.

used as a screening criteria for job entry. Overall, it appears that job entry requirements have been increasing in fairly close correspondence with the increasing educational attainments of the labour force.

But, as Table 2.6 also shows, substantial mismatches persist and there has been little significant general change in the proportions of credentially underemployed, matched and underqualified employees during this 14 year period in Ontario. At least half of the workforce has consistently held educational credentials that match the entry requirements for their jobs. Around 20 percent of the labour force has been underemployed. Slightly more have usually been underqualified. If employers increase entry requirements, it follows that many of those who are already performing the job with lower credentials will instantly become underqualified in these terms. In any case, the recent rapid increases in employers' job entry requirements have kept credential underemployment levels fairly stable, and ensured that around a quarter of a workforce that has increasingly become one of the most highly educated in the world remains credentially underqualified for their jobs.

As suggested above in the discussion of Table 2.5, a major recent change in entry requirements has been experienced by working class employees. Among all industrial workers, the proportion of jobs with no diploma requirement has dropped from over 60 percent to about a third since 1982, while for all service workers the drop has been from over 50 percent to around a quarter. But these drastic aggregate increases in entry requirements for working class jobs are only reflected in marginal increases in the underqualification of the working class, and are hardly noticeable for the labour force as a whole, because of corresponding increases in educational attainments.

As one might expect, credential underqualification is closely related to educational attainment, with over 40 percent of high school dropouts having less schooling than is currently required for entry into their jobs, while very few university graduates are formally underqualified for their jobs. But the converse is not true; more schooling does not necessarily mean higher credential underemployment. School dropouts are very unlikely to be underemployed, but university graduates have comparable rates of credential underemployment (27 percent) to high school graduates (24 percent) while community college graduates have much higher rates (44 percent). These findings are consistent with those of the 1989 Canadian national survey (Lowe 1992). There continues to be a surplus of qualified workers at all credential levels from high school diplomas to university degrees.

The extent of credential-entry requirement mismatch is certainly related to age, with workers under 25 consistently more than twice as likely (about 27 percent) to be underemployed as those over 55 are (around 12 percent). Throughout this period, men have been slightly more likely to hold jobs for which they are formally underqualified (26 percent) than women (20 percent) are. Non-Europeans in general have been somewhat more likely (29 percent) to be underemployed than the general labour force (20 percent). This is consistent with the findings of Canadian case studies (Henry and Ginzberg

1985) and U.S. statistical analyses (Cain 1986) that have found substantial systemic biases against blacks and Hispanics in employers' hiring practices.

More generally, it should be noted here that the most common of all screening factors used by employers is the personal interview and that, regardless of how impressive one's educational credentials may be, employers' hiring decisions may often turn on such subjective factors as physical appearance, perceived motivation or familiarity with the applicant's family (see Holzer 1996). The credential society is not necessarily based on selection by merit.

THE PERFORMANCE GAP

Once you have a job, to what extent are you able to use your achieved level of skill and knowledge in actually performing it? This is the question which has attracted the greatest attention from researchers and generated the greatest controversy. The dispute has centered around the equivalencies between the technical skills required for job task performance and the amount of schooling needed to ensure that these skills have been acquired. The estimation of technical skill requirements for the U.S. and Canada has been done primarily by government job analysts and published in occasional dictionaries of occupational titles. The most commonly used indicator of skill levels in both countries has been the general educational development (GED) scale. The GED scale is intended to embrace those aspects of knowledge which are required of the worker for satisfactory job performance. The different levels of this scale on each of three dimensions (reasoning, mathematical and language development) are defined in Figure 2.1.

Several major attempts have been made in the U.S. to estimate the extent of correspondence between these performance requirements and the skills acquired through schooling. The earliest detailed effort[12] was by Eckhaus (1964) using the first GED ratings of occupations by the Bureau of Employment Security in 1956 and the 1940 and 1950 U.S. censuses. Eckhaus (1964, 186) concluded that: "these numbers seem to show a growing amount of 'unemployed' high school education in the labour force." The most extensive and careful study has been conducted by Ivar Berg (1970). He applied the 1956 and 1966 GED ratings of occupations to the 1950 and 1960 U.S. censuses, and generated five different estimates of the correspondence between educational attain-

Figure 2.1 General Educational Development Scale

1. Applies common sense understanding to carry out *simple* one or two step *instructions*. Performs simple counting. Learns job duties from oral instruction or demonstration.

2. Applies common sense understanding to carry out *detailed* but uninvolved *instructions*. Uses arithmetic with whole numbers. Files and copies data.

3. Applies common sense understanding to carry out *instructions involving several concrete variables*. Makes arithmetic calculations involving fractions. Files and copies data.

4. Applies principles of rational systems (e.g. bookkeeping, electric wiring systems) to *solve practical problems*. Performs algebraic/geometric procedures. Interprets technical manuals.

5. Applies principles of logical or scientific thinking to *define problems* and interpret extensive technical instructions. Applies advanced mathematical techniques. Evaluates technical data and writes reports.

6. Applies principles of logical or scientific thinking to a *wide range of problems* and applies them to a variety of abstract and concrete variables. Applies advanced mathematical techniques. Evaluates technical data and writes reports.

Source: Excerpted from U.S. Department of Labour (1991, 1009–12).

ment and the education jobs required. He concluded that: (1) there was probably an increase in the numbers of "better" educated people only getting "middle" level jobs and a reduction in the numbers of "less" educated people moving up into such jobs; (2) if present trends continued, educational achievements could likely outdistance job demands; and (3) if educational credentials are increasingly devalued through such excess of the supply of educational achievements over demand, those who become isolated through lack of credentials may become a greater social problem than the underemployment of the highly educated (Berg 1970, 58–60). A later study by Val Burris (1983) offered estimates of "overeducation" based on a 1977–78 U.S. national sample survey and essentially the same mid-1960s GED ratings as Berg had used. On the basis of this cross-sectional study, Burris (1983, 458–59) suggested: that the highest levels of overeducation were found among those with middle levels of educational attainment rather than college graduates, and that a trend toward overeducation may be more a consequence of the failure of community college attendees to get commensurate jobs than the underemployment of university graduates.[13]

As Berg (1970, 51) observed: "Nothing is fixed about the relationship of GED and years of schooling.… Different assumptions can yield extraordinarily diverse findings." In recognition of the lack of consensus and in order to avoid charges of exaggerating the amount of overeducation or underemployment, Burris (1983, 457) opted for the highest proposed educational equivalents from all prior conversion schemes. The range of equivalencies used in these studies is indicated by Figure 2.2.

Figure 2.2 GED Level-Years of Schooling Equivalencies: Eckhaus, Berg and Burris Conversion Schemes

GED Level	Years of Schooling			
	Eckhaus	*Berg1*	*Berg5*	*Burris*
1	0–3	0–7	0–11	0–11
2	4–6	8	0–11	0–11
3	7–9	9–11	0–11	12
4	10–11	12	12–15	13–15
5	12–15	13–15	12–15	16
6	16+	16+	16+	17+

Sources: Eckhaus (1964, Table 1, 184); Berg (1970, Table III–3, 44, 50); Burris (1983, 457).

I will not add to the complexity by proposing yet another conversion scheme, but rather apply Eckhaus', Burris' and two of Berg's schemes to the best available U.S. and Canadian data sets to generate alternative measures of the performance gap. However, a few preliminary comparative points can be made. First, there appears to have been some "bottom-end" truncation in the later schemes. Take math skills, for instance: specifically fractions, which are a criterion for GED level 3, and algebra and geometry, which are a criterion for GED level 4. Across North America and throughout most of the past century, fractions have been taught well before the end of grade eight, and algebra and geometry before the end of high school. Berg's grouped version and Burris' scheme ignore these distinctions among lower GED levels and therefore probably overestimate the skills required for many lower level jobs. Certainly some empirical research indicates that to perform the typical factory or office job in advanced industrial societies still actually requires no more than an adequate Grade 8 formal education.[14] At the other extreme, most schemes ignore post-graduate education. This is partly a result of government officials' truncation of the original GED scale from seven to six levels (Berg 1970, 44–45), which had the effect of forcing those with more than 16 years of schooling down from level seven to level six in the revised scale of the 1960s. So, at the same time as later conversion schemes have chosen to truncate the GED scale at the bottom end, they have been forced to conflate differences between undergraduate degrees and graduate education at the top end. This limitation aside, Berg's first scheme probably represents the most accurate array of current equivalencies.

The best available North American time-series data bases to assess levels and trends in educational attainments and performance requirements are the annual national surveys of the National Opinion Research Center (NORC) and the biennial Ontario surveys conducted by the Ontario Institute for Studies in Education at the University of Toronto (OISE/UT).[15] The NORC survey reports from 1972 to 1990 include GED scores for occupations based on 1971 estimates.[16] The 1980 to 1996 OISE/UT survey data on respondents' occupations has been assigned GED codes based on the coding scheme developed by Alf Hunter and his colleagues (Hunter and Manley 1986; Hunter 1988),[17] from the Canadian Classification and Dictionary of Occupations for the 1971 census.

The patterns using each of these four measures, aggregated across all years, are summarized in Table 2.7. The findings for the U.S. and Ontario are very similar. Eckhaus' scheme generates very high estimates of the level of performance underemployment, with very little

Table 2.7   Educational Attainment-Job Performance Requirement
Matching, United States 1972–1990 and
Ontario 1980–1996.

	Eckhaus	*Berg1*	*Berg5*	*Burris*
	United States 1972–90			
Underemployed	76	56	39	24
Matched	18	29	51	36
Underqualified	6	15	10	40
(N=15269)				
	Ontario 1980–96			
Underemployed	70	56	36	24
Matched	25	30	50	35
Underqualified	4	14	14	41
(N=3667)				

Sources: Davis and Smith (1994) and OISE Survey of Educational Issues
Data Archive.

matching and hardly any underqualified workers; this scheme, which
was originally applied to 1940 data, probably overestimates the extent
of present underemployment. On the other hand, Burris' scheme, by
his own admission produces overly conservative estimates of underemployment, and also suggests that a plurality of people are underqualified to do the jobs they are actually performing — which is, to say
the least, counter-intuitive. Berg's schemes both produce more plausible results. He asserted a preference for his grouped schemes (his versions 3 and 5) as "the conceptually most attractive versions" (Berg
1970, 59), while I have already indicated that I think his first scheme is
based on the most accurate equivalencies. In any event, it is safe to say
on the basis of these analyses that the actual level of performance
underemployment in both the U.S. and Ontario in recent times has
involved between a quarter and three-quarters of the employed labour
force, and more likely has been between 40 and 60 percent.

I have also conducted trend analyses for both the U.S. and Ontario
surveys using all four measures. The general trends are similar for all
measures. The results using Berg1 are presented in Table 2.8. The

extent of performance underemployment appears to have increased during the periods of these surveys. According to the Berg1 measure, there was a gradual increase from 46 percent to over 60 percent of the employed U.S. labour force being underemployed between 1972 and 1990; the comparable figures for Ontario suggest an increase from 44 percent underemployment to just under 60 percent between 1980 and 1996, a slightly shorter but more recent period. According to this measure, performance underemployment has now become a majority condition for the North American labour force.

Age differences in the performance gap are quite pronounced, with nearly two-thirds of workers between 18 and 24 being underemployed compared to one-third of those over 55. People with higher educational attainments are also now more likely to be underemployed, but even high school dropouts frequently still have more education than their jobs actually need. So, while Berg's 1950–60 analysis found that it was those with the least schooling who experienced the largest performance gap, and Burris' 1977–78 analysis discovered the greatest discrepancies between attainments and performance requirements for those with community college levels, performance underemployment is now most common among university graduates. In conjunction with the increasing performance underemployment trends summarized in Table 2.8, these age and education differences certainly suggest that the educational attainments of the employed labour force recently have been increasing more quickly than the actual performance requirements of most jobs.

While performance underemployment is now substantial among most occupational classes, it appears to be highest among those who hold the jobs that are generally regarded as the least skilled. Visible minority employees exhibit somewhat higher levels of performance underemployment than those from white majority ethnic backgrounds. Women are slightly more likely than men to have higher educational qualifications than their jobs actually need. I will examine all of these differences more closely in Chapter Five.

GED-based measures have several limitations that I will examine more closely in Chapter Four in assessing the empirical evidence for the skill upgrading of the labour force in relation to post-industrial and human capital theories of knowledge-work linkages. But other studies, not based on GED measures, have similarly found that, since the early 1970s, almost a third of the employed North American workforce have had work-related skills that they could use in their jobs but

Table 2.8 Trends in Performance Underemployment Levels, U.S. 1972–1990 and Ontario 1980–1996 (using Berg1)

United States (%)	72	73	74	75	76	77	78	80	82	83	84	85	86	87	88	89	90
Underemployed	46	49	53	51	57	52	55	55	59	57	59	56	57	58	59	59	62
Matched	31	31	23	31	26	30	30	31	31	29	29	31	30	28	28	29	29
Underqualified	23	20	19	18	17	18	15	14	11	14	12	13	13	14	13	13	12

(N=768–1166)

Ontario (%)	80	82	84	86	88	90	92	94	96
Underemployed	44	43	50	51	52	54	58	55	57
Matched	29	34	28	33	31	30	31	32	27
Underqualified	27	23	22	16	17	16	10	13	16

(N=526–715)

Sources: Davis and Smith (1994) and OISE Survey of Educational Issues Data Archive.

have not been permitted to do so; this actual underuse appears to have grown to include over 40 percent of the entire workforce in the 1990s. Lawrence Thomas' (1956) study of the U.S. Army General Classification Test scores of over 80,000 men in more than 200 occupations, as well as Berg's later analyses found that:

> Americans of diverse educational achievements perform productive functions adequately and perhaps well in all but a few professional occupations. (Berg 1970, 41)

In spite of much rhetoric about skill deficiencies of the current workforce, there is still little evidence of any general and persistent technical skill deficit among employed workers. A recent survey by the National Center on the Educational Quality of the Workforce (1995) has found that U.S. employers consider over 80 percent of their employees to be fully technically proficient in their current jobs, and that most employers are more concerned with prospective employees' attitudes than their industry-based skills or prior school performance.

The basic point is that the performance gap between educational attainments and actual technical job skill requirements in North America is extensive and increasing on all available measures.

SUBJECTIVE UNDEREMPLOYMENT

The final dimension, *subjective underemployment*, is the most elusive one. People's sense of whether or not their knowledge and skills are being well used in their present employment situation has many facets. Three aspects have been most frequently identified: *perceptions of the fit* of your qualifications to the job; *feelings of opportunity* to use your knowledge and skills on the job; and *sense of entitlement* to a better job. These three aspects are conceptually distinct and do not necessarily correspond empirically. For example, I may not think of myself as overqualified for my current job in terms of the training required to obtain it, but I probably have obtained at least some additional skills that I might like to use if my job conditions were different. Even if I feel perfectly qualified for and fairly satisfied with the skill demands of my current job, I might still see a number of better jobs that I feel I deserve.

Several empirical studies over the past three decades have attempted to estimate levels of subjective underemployment on all three of these aspects. A 1989 Canada-wide survey found that 23 percent of all workers saw themselves as overqualified for their jobs. Nearly a third of all employed university graduates had jobs that they felt did not require a degree, over 40 percent of those with college certificates had jobs that they thought required less formal schooling, and about a third of the workers with high school diplomas also had jobs that did not believe require such credentials; conversely, about a third of those workers with either high school diplomas or less formal schooling held jobs for which they had become formally "underqualified"; that is, formal entry requirements had been increased to a higher credential since they entered the job (Lowe 1992, 58–59).

Earlier U.S. surveys suggested a growth of people's sense that they were not able to fully use their skills in the workplace, with an increase from 27 percent in 1969 to over 36 percent in 1977 (Staines and Quinn, 1979).

The most detailed early study of job entitlement beliefs was Derber's (1978) survey of young unemployed workers in the suburbs of Boston in mid-1977. He found that the majority of these unemployed workers, and especially those with college degrees, felt that their school efforts entitled them to a very good job. A survey of recent high school and university graduates conducted in Edmonton, Alberta, in 1985 (Lowe et al. 1986) also found majority support for a more general question about entitlement to a good job if one has worked hard in school, but with lower support from university graduates.

In our recent Ontario surveys, respondents have been asked about all three of these aspects of subjective underemployment. The results are summarized in Table 2.9. Many hired employees in industrial market economies have probably always had a sense that their employers did not fully appreciate the extent of their work-related skills and knowledge. But they were not keen to display unused capacities in order to avoid greater exploitation of their labour power.[19] Now, as living labour is being incessantly squeezed out of most meaningful forms of paid work, workers may be somewhat more disposed to consciously declare such unused capacities both to themselves and to employers, in order to obtain/retain any decent job. In any case, our most recent surveys have found that around 20 percent of the workforce currently identify themselves as being overqualified for their current jobs, essentially the same level found

Table 2.9 Aspects of Subjective Underemployment,
Ontario Labour Force, 1986–1996

A. *"In terms of your schooling, do you feel you are overqualified, adequately qualified, or underqualified for your current job?"*

	1994 (%)	1996 (%)
Overqualified	21	25
Adequately qualified	72	70
Underqualified	5	3
Can't say	2	1

B. *"Do you have some skills from your experience and training that you would like to be using in your work, but can't use on your present job?"*

	1994 (%)	1996 (%)
Yes	40	41
No	56	55
Can't say	4	4

C. *"With the level of schooling I have, I am entitled to a better job than I have been able to get."*

	1986 (%)	1988 (%)	1990 (%)	1994 (%)	1996 (%)
Agree	32	34	36	35	33
Disagree	44	44	44	43	48
Can't say	24	22	20	22	20
N	647	629	650	745	691

Source: OISE Survey of Educational Issues Data Archive.

in the 1989 Canadian national survey (Lowe 1992). But perhaps the more notable finding here is that over 90 percent of employees in Ontario consider themselves to be at least adequately qualified for their current jobs, while only five percent or less do not. Few respondents are generally likely to declare inadequacy in such a survey. But there is an overwhelming tendency here for the vast majority to declare that their skills at least match those needed to do their jobs. This popular sentiment is consistent with the earlier argument by Thomas (1956) and Berg (1970) that people with most levels of educational achievement are capable of doing most jobs.

When asked for their *general* perceptions about the current relationship between education and job requirements, respondents are most likely to say that people have more education than the jobs require. Over 40 percent of the employed workforce think that people generally have more education than jobs require, about a quarter feel that most people have the right amount, and another quarter feel that most people have too little education (Livingstone, Hart and Davie 1997, 76). Overall, little general popular credence seems to be given to the claim that the workforce is undereducated. In fact, respondents are about twice as likely to perceive that people in general have more education than the jobs require than to think that they, themselves, have more education than their own jobs require.

A generation after Staines and Quinn's (1979) U.S. readings of people's feelings of opportunity to use their knowledge and skills on the job, we have found marginally higher levels of a sense of wasted skills. Specifically, about 40 percent of the employed Ontario workforce now say they have skills from their experience and training that they would like to use in their work but can't use in their present job. This perception of wastage of their skills in the workplace is greater among more highly schooled and younger respondents. But even among the oldest workers with more than elementary schooling, about a third think that some of their education is now being wasted.[20]

Our question on personal entitlement to a better job in the Ontario surveys is not directly comparable with entitlement questions in prior surveys. But the finding that around 35 percent have consistently expressed such a sense of entitlement throughout the past decade, coupled with these prior survey findings of higher levels of entitlement on related questions, at least suggests that there has not been a significant increase in sense of entitlement among the general labour force during this period. As in past tough times, when good jobs become scarce, most people are glad to get whatever paid employment they can find (see O'Brien 1986).

Generally, younger workers have stronger perceptions that they are underemployed on all of these aspects. For example, a majority of those aged 18 to 24 express the belief that they are entitled to a better job, compared with only a quarter of those over 55. Women are slightly more likely than men to believe they are entitled to a better job. Visible minorities are more likely to feel entitled to a better job than those from other ethnic backgrounds. People in lower occupational class jobs are most likely to express subjective views of underemployment. I will look more closely at the lived experience of underemployment in Chapter Three, and at relations between these aspects of subjective underemployment and social background factors, particularly class position, in Chapter Five.

INTERRELATIONS OF THE DIMENSIONS OF UNDEREMPLOYMENT

Before examining these dimensions of underemployment in more depth in the following chapters, I will briefly consider their general relationships to each other. I will first summarize the interrelations of the five objective measures: the talent use gap, structural unemployment, involuntary reduced employment, the credential gap and the performance gap. Then, I will assess associations among the three measures of subjective underemployment. Finally, I will review patterns of relations between the objective dimensions and subjective underemployment.

Among the five objective dimensions of underemployment, one would not expect some of them to exhibit very close relationships. The talent use gap, as an inter-generational phenomenon, involves a long time period between class origins and adult class destination. There is no general empirical evidence in data available for the current study that those who have been born into higher class positions and those who have climbed up from lower class origins are significantly different on any current dimensions of underemployment. For example, the performance gap is about the same in statistical terms for current professional employees whether they come from professional family origins or working class backgrounds.[21]

Structural unemployment, of course, involves different people than the other current objective dimensions of underemployment. Among the currently employed, those who are involuntarily employed part-time might be expected to experience higher levels of credential and performance underemployment because, in spite of similar qualifications to those with full-time jobs, they have been unable to obtain these jobs which are generally presumed to be more secure, well-paid and fulfilling. However, the empirical evidence from the Ontario surveys finds no significant differences in the credential gap or performance gap between those in full-time and part-time employment. This suggests that with the increasing availability of people willing to work part-time, employers have also been able to raise the educational entry levels for these less attractive jobs beyond what many part-time jobs really need, without seriously diminishing the supply of applicants.

We would, however, expect to find a fairly strong relationship between credential underemployment and performance underemployment measures. The most complex jobs actually need quite advanced knowledge and skill to perform, so employers must demand at least corresponding levels of education and training for job entry; conversely, employers are typically loath to offer relatively menial jobs to highly qualified applicants because they are unlikely to stay (Bills 1992). Given these tendencies toward matching educational credentials, entry requirements and performance requirements, it is also more likely that those who do get their job with higher credentials than required for *entry* will also be overqualified to actually *perform* it. As Table 2.10 shows, the credential gap and the performance gap are in fact quite strongly correlated. The majority of those who are highly underemployed in terms of the credentials they bring to their job (i.e. have educational attainments that exceed the educational requirements of their jobs by at least two certification levels) are also likely to be highly underemployed in terms of actual performance requirements. However, at the other extreme, the majority of those who are highly underqualified credentially for their current jobs are likely to have educational attainments that at least match their job performance requirements. Less than a third of those who are credentially underqualified are also underqualified in performance terms. So, while credential underemployment and performance underemployment do tend to go together, credential inflation subsequent to one's job entry may frequently alter this correspondence for those with lower levels of educational attainment. Many people who perform their jobs very well on many practical criteria are no longer eligible to apply for comparable jobs because of their lack of these inflated credentials.

Table 2.10 also confirms that, while there are statistically significant positive associations between the three measures of subjective underemployment, they are empirically as well as conceptually dis-

Table 2.10 Interrelations of Dimensions of Underemployment, Employed Ontario Labour Force

	Cred. Gap	Perf. Gap	Feel over-qualified	Entitled better job	Untapped skills
Credential Gap	x				
Performance Gap	.47**	x			
Feel over-qualified	.19*	.26**	x		
Entitled to better job	.06	.15*	.40**	x	
Want to use untapped skills	-.01	.05	.29**	.36**	x

The measures of association presented are Spearman correlation coefficients, which are appropriate for ordinal measures: *=significant at .0001 level; **=.00001 level.

Source: OISE Survey of Educational Issues Data Archive.

tinct. Personal perceptions of overqualification, untapped skills and entitlement to a better job do tend to go together. But many people who may feel underemployed on one of these dimensions do not on others. Subjective underemployment is itself a multi-dimensional phenomenon which has not yet at least coalesced into a very coherent consciousness of wasted skills.

Since the early 1970s, social theorists have pointed to objective underemployment, particularly among college-educated youth, as a cause of growing disaffection and political unrest (e.g. O'Toole 1975). In general, we expect to find some correspondence between peoples' objective conditions and their perceptions of these conditions. But previous empirical research has generally discovered only weak relationships with social disaffection. Val Burris (1983) used his previously mentioned measure of performance underemployment to examine an array of measures of political attitudes with 1977–78 U.S. national survey data. He found some significant effects of underemployment among the highly underemployed, but "no evidence ... of generalized political effects of overeducation, either in the form of increased political leftism or in the form of increased political alienation" (454). Subsequent U.S. studies have continued to find similarly weak objective-subjective relationships (e.g. Jolin 1987; Rachel 1987).

There are certainly significant relations between some objective dimensions of underemployment and subjective perceptions of underemployment. Feelings of entitlement to a better job than they have been able to get are, of course, most pronounced among the unemployed, with well over two-thirds of the currently unemployed in the recent Ontario surveys generally expressing this view (compare Derber 1978, 1979). Those relegated to part-time employment are also now generally about 20 percent more likely than full-timers to feel they are overqualified for their present job, and entitled to a better job.

The relations of the credential gap and performance gap with our Ontario survey measures of subjective underemployment are also summarized in Table 2.10. Those who have higher attainments than their jobs require for performance may be somewhat more likely to think of themselves as overqualified and also feel entitled to a better job. Those who have higher credentials than required for job entry may also be somewhat more likely to think of themselves as overqualified. But credential underemployment is not significantly associated with a greater sense of entitlement to a better job. The desire to use work skills that you cannot apply in your current job exhibits no significant association with either the credential gap or the performance gap; many others besides the objectively underemployed feel that they have untapped work skills. These findings of only weak relations between objective and subjective measures of underemployment are consistent with the findings of the prior U.S. studies.

Further insight into these subjective-objective relations is provided by Table 2.11 which examines the patterns of association between credential underemployment and subjective sense of underqualification. A small majority of those who are highly underemployed in formal entry terms define themselves as overqualified while the rest of this small group see themselves as adequately qualified to actually perform their jobs. The vast majority of those whose credentials match their job's current entry requirement or who have one credential less than now specified for entry, feel that they are at least adequately qualified for their jobs and almost none feel underqualified. At the other extreme, the vast majority of those who are credentially highly

Table 2.11   Formal Attainment-Entry Requirement Match by
Employees' Self-Assessment of Qualifications, Ontario Labour
Force, 1994

		Self-Assessment		
Attainment- *Requirement Match*	*Over-* *qualified*	*Adequately* *Qualified*	*Under-* *qualified*	*Column* *total*
Highly overqualified	55	44	1	4
Over qualified	32	65	3	16
Matched	21	73	5	56
Under qualified	13	82	5	19
Highly underqualified	14	71	15	5
Row total (N=868)	23	72	4	100

Source: OISE Survey of Educational Issues Data Archive.

underqualified (i.e. have two credentials less than their jobs now formally require for entry) also think they are at least adequately qualified to do their jobs, and only a small minority of this minority see
themselves as actually underqualified. Older workers are clearly more
likely to be credentially underqualified, but they are not more likely to
rate themselves as underqualified for jobs they have often performed
for a long time with extensive on-the-job learning. The relationship
between performance underemployment and subjective underqualification is somewhat stronger statistically, largely because a higher
proportion of those who are designated as underqualified on performance measures define themselves as underqualified than do those
who are credentially underqualified. There is fairly strong evidence
here of the credential inflation that earlier analysts have criticized
using more imposed measures of required job skills (see Berg 1970;
Collins 1979). The few recent studies that have looked carefully at
actual educational requirements for current jobs have found that the
majority really need less than a high school diploma.[22] As Chapter
One has documented, around three-quarters of the North American
workforce has at least a high school diploma. As we have seen here,
only a tiny minority of all workers consider themselves to be under-

qualified. So, it is not very likely that a shortage of education is the main problem in the education-jobs gap.

CONCLUDING REMARKS

The talent use gap between those from socially disadvantaged origins and more affluent families, as indicated by the attainment of university degrees, has remained very wide throughout most of the past century of unprecedented expansion of formal schooling. Estimates of the extent of underemployment of initial talent are bound to be speculative because of the array of mediating factors that intervene between time of first school enrolment and entry into the labour market. But conservative estimates suggest that less than half of the people from lower class and some visible minority racial backgrounds who have the capability actually complete university. There are persistent systemic barriers that deny equal educational opportunity to these people on ascriptive grounds and result in underusing the learning talents of millions of people, at least ten to twenty percent of the adult U.S. and Canadian populations in these terms.

Researchers operating largely in the subemployment tradition have estimated that underemployment in the U. S. ranged from 20 to 30 percent of the available labour supply between 1969 and 1992 (Clogg, 1979; Sheak 1994). These estimates include official unemployment rates, discouraged workers and involuntary reduced employment, as well as other more arbitrary criteria which count in some full-time employed workers (i.e. employed at wages beneath the official poverty standard; or employed with schooling that exceeds the occupation-specific mean by more than one standard deviation statistically). If we omit these more arbitrary criteria, the general estimates of subemployment in the U.S. since the early 1970s have varied between 14 and 24 percent, with cyclical fluctuations in official unemployment rates but generally upward trends in both discouraged workers and involuntary temporary employment (Sheak 1994, 27). Total subemployment rates for Canada may be somewhat less accurate but are likely to be even higher given higher official Canadian unemployment rates (see Carrick 1996). These again are conservative estimates because many of those working for wages beneath the official poverty standard surely should be considered as subemployed by any reasonable human standard.

Credential underemployment among the employed workforce

has been consistently estimated at around 20 percent during the current generation. Performance underemployment probably now affects between 40 to 60 percent of the currently employed workforce and has continued to increase during the past 25 years in the U.S. and Canada.

Subjective underemployment may have been slowly increasing during the past 25 years as several objective dimensions of underemployment have become more obvious. But in the most recent attitude surveys only 20 to 40 percent of the entire workforce still express these sentiments about such aspects as perceived over-qualification, untapped skills and entitlement to a better job. Consciousness of underemployment has not coalesced into a coherent viewpoint, at least not yet.

The levels of underemployment on most of these dimensions have been documented to have reached comparable levels in the U.S. and Canada. Since these two countries have the most expanded systems of advanced formal schooling in the world, it is likely that the general extent of underemployment in most other advanced industrial countries is somewhat lower. But the available data presented here on subemployment measures suggest that extensive underemployment on most dimensions probably exists in all countries considered.

An overall estimate of the extent of underemployment cannot simply be additive. In the U.S. and Canada, objective underemployment would affect well over one hundred percent of the workforce! However, it is safe to say that over half of the potential U.S. and Canadian adult workforces have experienced some of the overlapping dimensions of objective underemployment, and that significantly less have a coherent sense of their underemployment.

The massive scale of the underuse of knowledge and skills in current industrial market economies that is revealed by this analysis may still be difficult for most analysts to accept and may well appear incredible to the general reader — in spite of the fact that estimates of similar magnitude have been made by reputable scholars for over a generation now. But all I have done in the foregoing analysis is to apply the array of conventional measures of underemployment to the array of available data bases.

Some critics will undoubtedly be able to find empirical grounds for lower estimates on specific dimensions of underemployment in particular times and places. Others have already suggested discarding underemployment as a social problem because underemployed college graduates have not become massively disaffected politically; and, furthermore, with continued post-secondary educational expansion, the marginal economic utility of more education is diminishing and seen to be leading to:

> "the realization — by the marginal student in the marginal college in the marginal discipline — that a college education confers no specific set of opportunities." (H. Smith 1994, 97)

The relatively stable and limited nature of job entitlement beliefs in a context of increasing subemployment and performance underemployment over the past decade lends some support to the political aspect of this argument. But there is little credible aggregate-level evidence for declining capacity among college students. Objective underemployment, as estimated by various measures, continues to increase. The growing wastage of knowledge and skills in our workplaces should not be dismissed or relativized just because the highly schooled have not taken to the barricades. Rather than presumptively trivializing the problem,[23] interested researchers should be looking more closely at the actual experiences of those currently living in the education-jobs gap. I will do this in the next chapter.

3

Voices from the Gap: Underemployment and Lifelong Learning

*The need to work in modern society is a real need ... which arises out of
the most basic material conditions of modern society, and which cannot
therefore be altered by the methods of indoctrination alone.*

—Sayers 1987, 21

*People usually have more education and skill than the jobs really need —
and they keep seeking more because of competition for jobs.*

—Underemployed store clerk, 1995[1]

*There is no place for me. The economy has dropped me.... Tuition goes
up. Loans go up. Everything goes up except the number of jobs for university graduates.... I should have known that a general arts education
is useless. I'm made to feel like all I can do is read and talk. Maybe it's
my fault ... I don't know anymore. Maybe I should go back to school and
take something like computers.*

—Unemployed university graduate in sociology;
Mohammed 1997, SS3–4

*Before, we were unemployed and stupid; now we're unemployed and
educated. We're trained, but the result is the same: there is no job. A
bunch of people running around with certificates and no jobs.*

—Displaced, retrained Cape Breton steelworker, 1994;
quoted in deRoche, Riley and Smith 1994, 12–13

INTRODUCTION

This chapter focuses on the experiences of people who have been
living in the education-jobs gap in recent times. This includes those

who are underemployed on any of the six dimensions summarized in Chapter Two, as well as those who have been on the other side of the gap, folks who have been identified as underqualified or under-educated for available jobs. The overriding reality for those on both sides of the gap is, as it was in the "dirty thirties," that there are simply not enough jobs of any sort to go around. There is now a generalized surplus of labour in almost all skill categories in the U.S. and Canada (Sharpe 1993). The question here is how people in these particular statuses are struggling to find security in the present difficult conditions. The basic thesis, contrary to Hubert Smith's (1986) speculation at the end of the prior chapter, is that further education and learning remain prevalent means for trying to cope with job insecurity on *both* sides of the education-jobs gap.

While I have drawn on evidence from several places, the main sources on the least accessible dimensions of underemployment — the credential gap and the performance gap and their subjective effects — are our Ontario studies.[2] Secondary analyses of the 1980–96 biennial series of OISE surveys have been of central importance. During early 1995, we conducted a follow-up in-depth interview with university and college graduate respondents to the 1994 OISE survey who were identified as underemployed, as well as those with high school diplomas or less who were identified as underqualified.

The follow-up to our 1994 Ontario general population survey was selected on the basis of *credential mismatches*.[3] This is probably the first representative in-depth survey of the credentially mismatched. Prior to this survey, during the spring and summer of 1994, our research team had conducted extensive semi-structured interviews with both underemployed and underqualified adults selected from several relevant sites in the Greater Toronto Area, including university placement offices, adult basic education classes and food banks.[4] The following presentation primarily attempts to let those living in the education-jobs gap speak for themselves.

The focus will be on: (1) personal experiences of the five objective dimensions of the education-jobs gap identified in Chapter Two; (2) insiders' general perceptions of the gap between education and employment, and their sense of personal entitlement to a better job; and (3) the role of further adult education and informal learning activities in practical coping strategies and future job plans.

LIVING IN THE GAP

The statistics of Chapter Two only begin to tell the story of the scope of underemployment of people's knowledge and skills in the current job structure of advanced industrial societies. The voices of those actually living in the gap convey much deeper agonies and misgivings, enduring hopes and dreams, and complex coping strategies.

Wasted Talent in School

Various ethnographic studies of working class and black and aboriginal boys and girls have documented how institutionalized school and community relations have continued to reproduce barriers to the full uses of the learning capacities of many young people from these social origins as they prepare to enter the labour force and adult life. But such studies also provide ample evidence of their persistent efforts to resist and overcome these barriers which dominant class and ethnic groups, often in spite of their best intentions, continue to reinforce.[5] These kids' views of school experience are complex combinations of anger, frustration and recrimination for others and themselves, mixed with enduring determination to do the best they can with the hand they've been dealt.

As Gord Wilson, the president of the Ontario Federation of Labour, put it in reflecting back on his own school days:

> In the school yard there was a kind of solidarity among the kids who came from the excluded working class families. And our friendships spilled over into the classroom.... While others mentioned how they "went here ... went there," we all knew we had never been anywhere.... We didn't want to talk about that, so we didn't talk at all. There were also some attitude problems on the part of some teachers. I don't want to make too much of it, but there were several teachers who were always trying to make it up the social ladder, to gain acceptance within the largely well-to-do community of our school's parents. These teachers were much more attentive to some of the kids who came from the higher level of society than to us working class kids.... [W]hen I think back to those kids ... they were expected to do well in school. And they expected it themselves. It was in the air they breathed at home and in school. It was their system. Whereas, with most of us, our parents simply had a great deal of hope that we were going to be higher in life than they had been able to be. But they did-

n't really expect it.... We should have absolutely no shame attached
to what happened to us at school, because ... we did not fail the system, the system failed us (Wilson 1989, 13, 17–18).

A common reaction to these conditions by working class boys
who have had access to manual labour jobs has been to reject the
school's academic curriculum and glorify "street smarts." As Joey,
on of the leading lights in Paul Willis' classic study of British working class boys coming out of comprehensive schools in the mid
1970s, declared:

> I'm more the energetic type, I always think, why fucking walk around
> somewhere, when you can jump over. I'm always fucking jumping
> over fences.... I'm quite satisfied as I am now not taking any leaving
> qualifications, if I'm intelligent enough, it'll fucking show through ...
> or I'll make 'em see that I'm something. I'll make 'em see that I'm
> worth a bit of an investment and perhaps then I'll get on a fucking
> course.... I mean, let's face it, it's fucking easy, it's really fucking easy,
> 'cos all you got to do is learn how to turn a fucking lathe, once you can
> do that, all the measuring and that just becomes fucking routine ...
> anybody can really be an apprentice like (Willis 1977, 94).

But even in this utter rejection of schooling for native wit, Joey holds
out hope for a future training course. A decade later in California, an
Hispanic working class male high school student expresses even more
scathing feelings about his school experiences, but also a much greater
appreciation of the existence of a "credential society":

> Are you asking what we think about school? ... Well, I'll tell you. I
> hate this place. I hate every minute being here. But I want that diplo-
> ma and I want it so I can have a job and a future and not be like those
> dudes you see hanging out on the street corner, drinking their wine
> out of a paper bag and got no future.... You can't even think about
> what you want to [in school]. One minute you have to be sad; then
> serious; you don't have no privacy. (Powers 1985, 133)

In one of the most recent sensitive enthnographies of school life,
Heidi Safia Mirza (1993) has documented how black working class
girls continue to experience and resist various forms of race, gender
and class discrimination in British schools. As Selma, a 16-year-old,
black working class girl reports:

My maths teacher really treats us differently. One day I was stuck on a question, I called him over. He said, "Oh, you know how to do this…." Afterwards this white girl which he likes quite a lot, she was on the same question as me, she did not understand it, then he really did explain it to her and he said, "Selma you can listen now if you want to." Then I said, "Never mind." He never tells her off. She goes and talks to the other pupils but when I get up he starts to shout at me … then I say, "Why don't you tell her." He always picks on mostly all the black girls. (Mirza 1993, 55)

These are among the most self-confident voices of oppressed youth. The culture of silence to which Gord Wilson refers, has led to the labelling of many less assertive kids from disadvantaged backgrounds as incompetent, and subsequently to lifetimes of struggle for subsistence and self-respect. As an illiterate mother describes her school experience:

I come out of school. I was sixteen. They had their meetings. The directors meet. They said I was wasting their school paper. I was wasting pencils. (Kozol 1985, 28)

She is speaking as she accepts eviction from her home on questionable terms which her landlord claims are in her lease, rather than revealing to him that she cannot read and leaving herself vulnerable to further humiliation. As Kozol observes, even the loss of shelter may not be so terrifying as the prospect of loss of self-identity.

Whatever the psychic damage of school-based discrimination, the social costs of wasting people's talents to contribute not only to the economy but to civic society increasingly concern many leaders of disadvantaged groups. In the view of an Ontario local labour movement activist:

So many people, because they have been stifled or not given the opportunities through the educational system, assume that they don't have to take the responsibility or get involved. I've heard so many people, usually working class people, saying "nothing we can do is ever going to change things, you know, the government is always going to have control." They don't realize they put these people in power, and they've always assumed that it's someone else telling them. And I think it's a lot because they were taught that way in school. You don't have any input into what you're going to learn. They now think they don't have any input into how their country is run.[6]

There is substantial evidence in this continuing series of intimate case studies of disadvantaged youths that many have strong positive motivations to contest the systemic nature of the talent use gap with whatever material and psychic resources they can bring to bear on their specific situations. In spite of a stacked deck, few have given up the desire to make a more decent life for themselves.

Chronic Unemployment

As the following quotes from U.S., Canadian and British white, able-bodied, prime working aged men graphically express, the starkest, most humanly devastating form of underemployment is chronic unemployment:

> I was fired without just cause…. It was rough. Of course, I went out almost every day at first and tried to find work…. There was just no work available. There was nothing there at all…. So I went to welfare. Then I really had to swallow my pride. That first day at welfare was quite a day. I've tried to push it out of my mind because they really kind of step on you. I got the feeling that they have an iron hand over you, and you're nothing…. It wasn't long before everything was gone. I had swallowed my pride and I was upset about everything…. We just went without. We didn't eat. That's true. Sometimes for three or four days at a time. And pretty soon you start creating your own problems…. It's hard to even remember how I passed my time…. It's been rough. Human damage, you might say.[7]

> I want to work, to have a job, but there is nothing out there. I don't even bother to go to the employment office anymore. Last year it came to the point where I had the choice of sitting in a cold, dark house or going to the welfare office. I don't have the kind of pride that would let my family starve…. Dignity? I have had no sense of dignity for a long time. I feel as if there isn't room for people like me in this country anymore. I don't want much — just to work and make enough to be self-sufficient. I am good at what I do. I want a job. What has gone wrong?[8]

> What can I give my kids? I just feel empty. I'm ashamed I can't provide them with everything they need. What kind of a father is that? We have no life together, even though we're never apart. I've even stopped

looking for work. Some days, I feel like killing myself. I'm not kidding. If there's no hope for me, what chance will they have? Life won't be worth living. I feel like killing myself and taking them with me.[9]

These voices carry this book's major message. *We all need decent work to lead decent lives.*

Black, aboriginal, female, disabled, young and old voices say the same thing, although they are often muted through other layers of racial, patriarchal, ableist and agist oppression. Listen to a young woman high school dropout:

> [For the past year] I haven't had a job and the hours I spend looking for something just drain me. I spend hours on the phone every day, including weekends. I literally spend all my time looking for a job. I applied to burger places and for positions like dishwashing and waitressing. But people just never call me back.... I can't believe I am 24 right now and everything is pretty much the same as it was when I was in high school. I am a lot wiser, sure, but I'm not ahead at all. People don't really understand how much a search can take out of somebody. Some people are really rude and it's hard having to deal with that constant, "No, no, no." (Dimaris 1997, SS6)

As Lillian Rubin (1994, 247) concludes, on the basis of in-depth interviews with members of a cross-section of American working class families of different racial backgrounds, the pain with which many families — and isolated individuals — are living today and the anger they feel will only be lessened when others in more comfort are *willing to see and reckon with the magnitude of these problems and suffering*. At the root, as Rubin's research graphically illustrates, is the lack of decent jobs.

Only Part-time

Labour leaders have frequently spoken against the rise of part-time employment as a threat to decent jobs. As John Zalusky of the AFL-CIO stated in 1986:

> This nation sorely needs more jobs, not different ways of pulling people into the labour market, or repackaging the 40-hour work week, or redefining the relationships of employee/employer and work. What is being created [by the growth of part-time employment] is a new sub-class of workers. (Cited in Tilly 1996, 168).

While many employers have enthusiastically created part-time jobs as a means of tapping into a cheaper, more flexible labour supply of women and others seeking secondary income, such jobs almost invariably have poorer working conditions and few fringe benefits — and workers with low expectations who are notoriously difficult to organize. As a union staffer who tried unsuccessfully to organize part-time workers at a U.S. insurance company complained:

> [T]he company has inculcated in [the workers'] brains ... [that] you don't deserve any more than you're getting because you're only part-time. And they try to get these folks to compare themselves with 20-hour-a-week waitresses or high school kids working in Burger King for 20 hours a week. (Tilly 1996, 75)

Nevertheless, the dissatisfaction with these conditions by the growing proportion of part-timers who are involuntary is demonstrated by the high incidence of those who take up any kind of full-time job whenever they have the chance (Stratton 1996). Young people who have experienced a regular full-time job are especially bitter about being relegated to more temporary ones. As a male computer programmer in his mid-twenties puts it:

> I worked for a year and a half in programming — then the company closed. That was a horrible day. From that point on, every position I've had was contract.... Contracts are the curse of today's society. There is no stability. People are losing track of their goals. I'd kill to have a house by the time I'm 35, but there is not a chance. We are going down, definitely down. (Van Osch 1997, SS4)

Sentiments of despair over broken dreams are common to many highly qualified involuntary part-time workers, as is clearly expressed in the words of a woman in her late twenties with a bachelor's degree in biology:

> Most of the people I work with in the lab are older than me with superior degrees. They're already vastly underemployed so where does that leave me in the future? I've been doing joe-jobs for years. I've been laid off from part-time jobs that nobody wanted five years ago. For this I spent years in university. None of my friends have real jobs and that includes people with business and law degrees who went through school convinced there would be gold at the end of the

rainbow. My parents didn't raise me to believe, nor did I ever think, that I would end up on a jobless scrap heap. But it's a possibility I find myself thinking about more and more these days. (Maryam Erfani, quoted in Ferguson 1994)

Living in the Credential Gap

Those who have full-time jobs often express satisfaction that they have been able to find or retain them in this context of widespread unemployment and part-time employment. But the condition of being credentially mismatched for your job can also be a preoccupying frustration, especially for those who expected that their educational credentials would bring them something better.

Community college graduates are most likely to experience credential underemployment, generally over 40 percent as noted in Chapter Two. As a young black woman with a community college certificate in travel and tourism, but who is now working long hours as a room attendant, says:

> Whenever I look at my paycheck I would feel down and low. And I know I might be stranded here forever.... I feel embarrassed to tell others what I do for a living. Whenever I say 'I'm a room attendant,' others will lose their interest in me and say 'oh.' That's the end of the conversation.... It's not only about the money. I feel mentally and physically exhausted after cleaning 16 rooms a day in the motel. It's a very stressful experience. You feel you're worthless after all the education and hard work you put in to better yourself. It's rough. (Keung 1997, A10)

As a young white woman university graduate with three degrees and a job as a lifeguard expresses it:

> It's kind of depressing, because after $40,000 worth of education, I'm doing the same job I did in Grade 10. (Theobald 1997a, C1)

Underemployed university graduates are often dismissive of the formal educational requirements of their jobs. They also tend to belittle the practical training involved. A young francophone male with two university degrees, now working as a cook in a pub, says:

> This sort of job doesn't require anything. Nothing I've learned at school has helped in the job. I've learn from my workmates and the boss. In a

couple of shifts you just learn the job.... There's no real need for a high school diploma. But I wouldn't have gotten hired without higher educational credentials, because the mindset is "why should we take a person who has no high school diploma when there are plenty that do." In fact, lots who work here have a university degree.[10]

A young white woman with a bachelor of education degree, working as a telemarketer, observes that:

The only qualifications [to be a telemarketer] is that you have to be fluent in English and have some knowledge of computers. Grade 9 would be plenty. The most important thing is to be able to be patient and polite. I haven't been able to use any of my education in this job.

A young aboriginal woman with a liberal arts degree, who has been working as a nanny, is equally derisive about her job entry requirements:

Basically nothing was required [for job as a nanny]. I'm very critical of that because I could have lied, I mean, I could have been a mass murderer and I'd still get the position. They basically ask you if you had child care experience, so I mean I did basically grow up with my kid sister.... And they liked me because I got my B.A. But they treated me like garbage.

Those people who are experiencing the *underqualification* side of the credential gap often stress the importance of on-the-job-learning for their jobs, while typically denying the need for formal educational credentials and sometimes denigrating the relevance of advanced schooling for this work. As a white male factory worker in his early thirties who dropped out of high school sceptically observed:

At our place which is just your standard manufacturing facility, I mean it's not rocket science, I think a lot of the qualifications for the job are actually manufactured. I mean the Grade 12, is that a real qualification that you need to do the job, or is it really just a barrier to some people? Especially when you look at the older workers with hardly any schooling who've been making the product for 30 years — they're still making it!

Another thirtysomething white male factory worker who didn't complete high school, but whose job now requires a diploma for entry, says:

> It's a dirty job. You have to work hard and learn as you go. You don't really need a diploma, just know how to read and be agreeable and hard working. You could learn the job quickly. I started from the bottom and worked my way up. I used a bit of knowledge that I learned in school shop courses but really learned a lot from my workmates.

Yet another white male factory worker who has recently taken a forced early retirement adds:

> I didn't need grade 9 to work on the line. I've got eyes, ears, strong hands — that's how I learn. It was there in front of you — you either picked it up or you got your butt kicked until you learned it! Some of these people with a B.A. are as brainless as a cockroach, sorry to say. Without a book, they're practically useless.

The one job entry requirement that was widely recognized as important by those lacking the credentials now required for their jobs was literacy. But, as the literacy survey findings cited in Chapter One suggest, even most marginally literate people claim to be able to perform well in jobs that they are now being arbitrarily excluded from because of lack of credentials. An older white female with little schooling, who was recently laid off as a hospital housekeeping supervisor, complains that:

> I was hired on the basis of experience. Now the job requires grade 12. I tried to hide my illiteracy. When it came to doing memos in front of people, I needed to go to the office to look for a dictionary. But I was good at my job. I worked hard on correspondence courses to be able to do the writing. Instead of just laying us off, they should have sent us to learn computer skills. Instead they hired young people and after a few months everyone with a background like us was laid off.

The overall impression left by interviews with those in the credential gap is that *both* the underemployed and the underqualified have found formal educational entry requirements to be only superficially related to many of their jobs. As in the large scale surveys cited in Chapter Two, we have found very few underqualified people who suggest they no longer have the requisite skills to do their jobs adequately, and many credentially underemployed who live everyday with a deep sense that their skills and prior education are being wasted.

Living in the Performance Gap

There is generally a close relationship between credential underemployment and performance underemployment among most of the people we have interviewed in depth. Those who talk about their own performance gap usually emphasize how easy their jobs have been to learn and how little challenge work presents to their ability, beyond their ability to tolerate demeaning work. A thirtysomething white male with a bachelor's degree in English and Psychology, working as coat checker states:

> Coat checking does involve being able to be efficient. It's somewhat physically demanding because generally everybody wants their coat at the end of the night.... You need the ability to keep a cool head. But pretty much any trained chimpanzee could do it. Of course, you need a high level of patience as does anyone who works within the service industry.

A young black woman with a liberal arts degree, working as an admitting clerk at a hospital, says that:

> It's pretty evident that high school is all you need to do this job. It's an easy job, you don't have to think about it. I don't want to say I do it as a robot, but I do go through it with ease, don't find it a challenge.... There can be lots happening sometimes and you do need a good memory. But you sure don't need to be a rocket scientist!

A middle aged white male with a high school diploma, who works on an auto factory assembly line, declares that:

> There isn't that much to learn about the job. It's very simple. There's a write up … it doesn't take a genius to read it.... Anybody can do it. The person I'm working with has a chemical imbalance. Sometimes he doesn't know who he is, where he is. I have to work with the man and I feel sorry for him. He crows like a rooster and then sometimes he acts like a horse, he goes up and down yo-yo moods, but he does the job. It does not affect doing the job. Sometimes you have to tell him whose turn it is, but HE DOES THE JOB! The job itself does not

require education, any above average education is wasted, there's no way that you can use it.

Those who are technically *underqualified* to perform their current jobs on GED criteria generally stress the importance of on-the-job training and basic common sense, but rarely convey any sense of performance difficulties. A middle aged white male service manager with a high school diploma thinks that:

If someone was starting from education into my job today they likely would take college or university management courses, but my training was ongoing on the job. You can still do the job without really being formally trained.

A young black female high school dropout, working as a nurse's aide, says:

You share patients' emotions in this job and sometimes you feel very low. The job is supposed to need Grade 12. But you just need to use common sense and that takes you straight to where you are going. School knowledge can be useful, but this job requires a lot of real world knowledge, "the real McCoy."

A young white male Grade eight dropout, who has been working as a construction labourer and struggling with his low literacy, describes his job performance requirements:

They didn't need nothing. Just show up, that's it. You didn't even have to speak. It didn't matter. You learn everything on the job. There's nothing new.

Neither the underemployed nor the underqualified people we have interviewed have generally found their job performance to be very demanding. Virtually every interview conveys a sense of wasted potential, of knowledge or talents that it has been impossible to use in the jobs these people have been able to obtain. This sentiment is just as strong among the high school dropouts as the university graduates. As one credentially underqualified factory worker puts it, "You never have to use your mind in that plant."

INSIDE VIEWS OF THE EDUCATION-JOBS GAP

Perhaps the most basic questions we can ask about the general social attitudes of those living in the education-jobs gap are how common they think this gap is, and whether they feel entitled to a better job.

General Perceptions of the Gap

How does the overall relationship between education and jobs look as it is viewed from opposite sides of the gap? As Table 3.1 summarizes for the current Ontario labour force, peoples' personal underemployment status does not have very strong effects on their general perception of the education-jobs gap at present. The most common attitude is that people generally have more education than their jobs require; about 40 percent of the general labour force express this view. The rest are about evenly split on this issue between feeling that most people have about the right amount of education or thinking most people have too little education. Regardless of one's personal underemployment status, this pattern appears to hold. Those who are highly underemployed — either in terms of objective attainment-requirement criteria or their self-perceptions of their own status — are not significantly more likely than those who are in matched or underqualified statuses to think that other people generally are underemployed. Conversely, those who are underqualified are at least as likely to believe that most other people are underemployed as to think that others share their own underqualified status. The unemployed also express mixed views but are no more likely than other folks to think that people generally have too little education for the available jobs. Overall, there is relatively little popular support for the notion that much of the workforce is undereducated for current job needs.

In our follow-up in-depth interviews, the most common theme among the credentially underemployed was that there is an oversupply of educated people for current jobs. Most tended to see this perceived general overqualification of job-holders in terms of an arbitrary use of advanced formal educational credentials as a screening device:

> Generally speaking, I think people have more education than the jobs require — based on examples I have seen. There are guys with

Table 3.1   General Perceptions of the Education-Jobs Gap by
Personal Underemployment Status,
Ontario Labour Force, 1994–1996

"Do you think that people generally have more education than their jobs require, the right amount or too little?"

Personal Underemployment Status	More education	Right amount	Too little	Total
Credential gap				
Highly underemployed	48	23	30	4
Underemployed	41	31	28	15
Matched	40	28	32	54
Underqualified	51	29	20	20
Highly underqualified	45	20	35	7
Performance gap				
Highly underemployed	46	24	29	23
Underemployed	39	31	30	33
Matched	46	28	26	29
Underqualified	46	24	30	9
Highly underqualified	57	14	29	6
Self-perception				
Underemployed	52	22	26	22
Matched	44	29	26	70
Underqualified	43	16	40	4
Unemployed	34	34	27	4
Total (N=1235)	44	27	29	100

Source: OISE Survey of Educational Issues Data Archive.

advanced degrees who are parking attendants at Ontario Hydro. I guess the logic is 'gee, look at the labour market. If we can get people with more education to fill these jobs, why not?' (Unemployed middle aged male with a Masters' degree).

I tend to feel that people are overqualified and educational credentials are simply used as a screening mechanism. And I doubt that there are many really underqualified in this situation of low employment. (Unemployed young male lawyer).

Underemployed people at all occupational levels bemoan the lack of suitable jobs for those with post-secondary education.

Everybody is now overqualified for their jobs. There's just not enough jobs. (Underemployed young male professional with a university degree)

People who graduate from college and university are taking any job they can get. Most are menial jobs not related to the programs they graduated from. (Underemployed middle aged female service worker with a college certificate)

But among underqualified school dropouts in our in-depth interviews, there are also strong sentiments that the supply of highly qualified job seekers exceeds the available jobs:

Many people have more qualifications than the jobs need. There just aren't enough jobs. We have to take what's there for survival. Because things are changing, we have to change, too. (Unemployed middle aged male welder with elementary education)

There's definitely more education and fewer jobs — that's the situation right now. Many college graduates come out of school to find nothing there for them and they are underused. There are people who have Masters' degrees working at the local Burger King. (Underqualified middle aged female part-time nurse's aid with Grade 9)

Some of our underemployed interviewees see this situation as the unavoidable consequence of the growing democratic demand for education:

Things in general may average themselves out but in my situation I see lots of people who have too much education for what they are doing. Half of the telemarketers here have university degrees. But you can't stop people from taking education. (Underemployed young female telemarketer with a B.Ed. degree)

But some of the unemployed university graduates are very critical of what they now see as impractical abstract content in general undergraduate programs:

> I think in essence we're an unqualified society. We're seeing with free trade that we're not good enough competitively. We need more reeducation, more retraining. I don't just mean more university education. A general arts degree really doesn't train you for anything, you know.... It's garbage. I mean you have nothing concrete. (Unemployed young female with a B.A. degree)

This theme of a need for more practically oriented education programs is even more common in the views of older underemployed trades workers. The recognition of a generalized overqualification for current jobs is often coupled with an important distinction between the profusion of general formal education and a lack of either advanced technical skills or practical experience:

> Everybody applying to work in a factory now has some kind of degree. I feel that advanced education is a waste of money as far as getting a job is concerned. People with low levels of education are just as smart. Many educated people don't actually know anything in terms of practical skills. They still need to learn their 'trade.' They need to adapt another kind of training program because not everyone can be a doctor or a lawyer. (Underemployed middle aged male industrial worker with a college certificate)

Most of our credentially underqualified interviewees also tended to talk about a general condition of underemployment. But the dominant theme among underqualified employees is the explicit concern that overqualified workers are taking over scarce jobs:

> Because of the unemployment situation, lots of overqualified people are out of work. I've talked to a lot of people. There are engineers working on the assembly line with 2 or 3 degrees. Sitting at GM doing factory stuff, they're taking jobs away from properly qualified people. (Underqualified older male autoplant lead hand without a high school diploma)

> A lot of jobs that don't require a university degree can be done by a high school graduate or less. A lot of degree holders take jobs away from people who couldn't go to university. (Underqualified older female service worker with a high school diploma)

Some small employers and managerial personnel, particularly those who themselves are formally underqualified for their own jobs, are also frank about the lack of need for advanced formal education for most jobs:

> Most workplaces don't actually need the level of education they require. Most people applying to me are university graduates and they do not use their university knowledge. (Middle aged male small employer with a high school diploma)

> Most jobs have limited attributes required to do them and you don't use all your skills. (Older male manager with a high school diploma)

Underqualified interviewees are somewhat more likely than others to talk about underqualification for jobs as the prevalent general condition. But almost invariably they refer to a shortage of specific job training rather than a shortage of general education and knowledge, the need for more practical experience rather than formal educational credentials:

> A *lot* of people need more education. There's been a basic breakdown. We need more qualified technical skills. (Unemployed middle aged female factory worker with Grade 4 education)

> Most people have too little knowledge. Many people are not learning much on the job and not willing to take low paying ones. Even university grads are not well prepared for jobs. Schools can't seem to get on top of what companies require. (Unemployed middle-aged male plasterer with Grade 6 education)

> Lots of people need more training, especially older employees to keep up. Some training just creates human robots for everything. But every day they're coming out with new things. (Unemployed older male factory worker with Grade 9 education)

The perception of education being too general or impractical recurs most often in our interviews with management personnel who are underqualified for their own jobs:

> Their education covers too many things. There are people sending in resumes for any job even though they are not qualified, or they are

overqualified and the jobs are not specific to their individual skills. (Underqualified middle aged male manager with a high school diploma)

Personal experience is really more important than formal schooling. Most employees have simply learned their tasks on the job. (Underqualified middle aged male supervisor with a high school diploma)

In general, there is little tendency among our interviewees to deny the existence of the education-jobs gap. Those on opposite sides of the credential gap are, of course, more likely to focus on and generalize from their own respective conditions of underqualification or underemployment when they talk about the gap. Few of the credentially underemployed seriously consider the notion of too little education for available jobs. There are either too few jobs for all the highly educated, or their general education could be supplemented by more specific job training. On the other hand, the credentially underqualified also reject the notion of too little *general* education. While they are more likely than the underemployed to stress the value of additional specific job training and practical experience, they are more concerned about artificially high formal educational credential requirements excluding them from jobs they know they can do.

The prevailing sense from our respondents is that most people have plenty of formal education in relation to current workplace demands. Younger, more highly schooled workers are more likely to complain about lack of opportunities to apply their formal education, while older, less schooled workers complain about younger job entrants' lack of practical experience. But notions of continual skill upgrading and creative work challenges find little resonance in the comments of these credentially mismatched workers. It is the *waste of education and knowledge in the workplace*, either because of lack of opportunity or lack of practical focus, that is the most common underlying theme. Job shortages and shortcomings, much more so than people's educational deficiencies, generally preoccupy *both* credentially underemployed and underqualified people's perceptions of the education-jobs gap.

Entitlement to a Better Job

As noted in Chapter Two, most empirical research has found the underemployed to be quite similar to the general population in their political consciousness and behavior. The most extensive prior U.S.

and Canadian studies have found very limited radicalizing effects associated with either youth unemployment or underemployment (for example, Baer et al. 1982; V. Burris 1983; Tanner, Lowe and Krahn 1984). Several studies have pointed to the centrality of job entitlement beliefs in young people's economic and political world views. But, as the most extensive Canadian study conducted in the mid-1980s concluded with regard to the political views of highly educated youths, their sense of job entitlement was more pragmatic than radical. Rather than searching for radical solutions, most of these youths still saw job creation as the solution to the unemployment crisis (Lowe et al. 1986, 17). More recent tendencies in job entitlement beliefs have been assessed by the OISE surveys, as summarized in Table 3.2.

Since the mid-1980s, about half of the Ontario labour force has consistently rejected the proposition that their education entitles them to a better job, while only around a third feel they are so entitled. Those who are underemployed on objective credential or performance measures are somewhat more likely than those with matched or underqualified statuses to think they deserve a better job. But even among the highly underemployed, only around half have expressed a sense of entitlement to a better job throughout the past decade.

Of course, most of those who clearly perceive themselves to be underemployed feel they deserve a better job. Younger workers who are highly underemployed on objective credential or performance criteria also express higher entitlement beliefs. For example, in recent years over 60 percent of highly underemployed post-secondary graduates under 30 years of age have agreed that their education entitles them to a better job, as opposed to hardly any of the highly underqualified people under 30.

But the most striking finding is that the majority of those who are underemployed on both objective credential and performance measures have continued to blame themselves for their failure to get a better job. Even among the objectively highly underemployed, around half tend to agree that they have themselves to blame. Even among those who clearly think of themselves as underemployed, almost 40 percent are inclined to accept self-blame. Regardless of feelings of entitlement, the majority of Ontario workers of all ages and educational statuses have expressed agreement in these surveys with the view that it is their own fault if they have not obtained a good job. To the extent that survey instruments can detect such personal senti-

Table 3.2   Sense of Job Entitlement by Education-Job Matching Status, Employed Ontario Labour Force, 1986–1996

	Believe I'm entitled to a better job*					Blame myself for not getting a better job**		
	86 (%)	88 (%)	90 (%)	94 (%)	96 (%)	86 (%)	88 (%)	94 (%)
Credential Gap								
High underempl.	51	53	46	50	48	43	59	58
Underemployed	35	35	43	41	46	58	56	46
Matched	32	32	36	34	33	53	59	48
Underqualified	28	30	26	32	22	63	55	42
High underqual.	23	25	23	23	16	67	68	65
Performance Gap								
High underempl.	49	40	49	43	45	53	53	48
Underemployed	30	33	35	39	36	53	62	44
Matched	24	33	30	33	31	55	56	48
Underqual.	23	34	33	30	26	59	57	60
High underqual.	22	30	27	13	11	73	58	55
Self-perception								
Underemployed				76				38
Match				28				55
Underqualified				30				54
Total	32	34	36	38	33	58	59	51
N	591	591	619	614	610	591	501	614

* "With the level of formal education I have, I am entitled to a better job than I have been able to get."
** "If I have not been able to get a better job, it is mainly my own fault."

Source: OISE Survey of Educational Issues Archive.

ments, the tendency to self-blame among the underemployed does not appear to have diminished as the shortage of attractive jobs has persisted. These findings suggest that only weak job entitlement sentiments may now exist in the overall workforce.

Our in-depth interviews with those on both sides of the credential gap allow a more nuanced assessment of job entitlement beliefs. Our underemployed respondents generally do assert some form of entitlement to a better job, mainly on the basis of having met what they perceive to be their side of the education-job bargain. But their rationales for failure to obtain such jobs are often complex:

> Sure, I deserve better than this. But society also deserves better out of me. Society has invested a lot in me. I am responsible for filling that back into society. I've made lots of mistakes and nobody owes me anything. But there are many larger forces, like institutionalized forms of discrimination, that are major obstacles. (Unemployed middle aged male professional with a Masters' degree and a disability)

> Why shouldn't we have a good job if we go through the system and qualify to do it! I have more to offer. I'm not being challenged. I think I could really *do* something else.... But I probably made the wrong [educational] choices. I didn't pick a concrete option that would make me employable. I do blame myself for not being where I'd like to be.... But equal access to education is not a reality. I think it's determined where you're going to get to by who you are, and what you look like and what your parents did or didn't do. (Young black female part-time admitting clerk with a B.A.)

> I deserve better because I did everything they said. I got my degree, I can speak two languages, I'm learning computers. I mean, I have more basic knowledge than most people. I can do any job that someone tells me. I've never failed at anything before, it's frustrating! ... I can't blame myself because, again, I think I did everything I was told to. I guess I blame the university system and the government for telling you that this is what you need. Maybe I'm just crude, but you don't go to school just to improve yourself, you go to get a job! (Unemployed young female with a B.A.)

A few underemployed graduates do explicitly reject their right to a better job — on the classic liberal grounds of individual responsibility in a free market:

> I deserve any *opportunity* that I can create for myself, that I work for. Am I qualified for a better job — yes I am. Deserve a job, that's anoth-

er issue altogether.... I truly believe most of what happens to an individual is up to an individual, especially in cases like mine where I've had lots of advantages.... Basically, you get what you pay for, and if you haven't paid for it you don't get it. And whether that payment takes the form of training, or motivation, or drive or any of those other things, it's still a form of payment to get what you want. I mean we are in a capitalist, consumerist society. (Underemployed middle aged male waiter with a B.A.)

For underqualified school dropouts, there is little inclination to deny a basic right to a better job in our in-depth interviews, but plenty of personal reasons offered for not being able to get one:

Everybody feels he or she deserves a better job. But I can't blame anybody. I just didn't stay in school for long. (Unemployed middle aged male labourer with elementary schooling)

Everybody deserves a better job, but it requires more qualifications. I don't blame nobody. You can't sit down and feel sorry for yourself. Just get up and do the right thing. You have to keep working. (Underqualified middle aged female part-time nursing aid with Grade 9)

If you're trained, you should be able to have a decent job. But people aren't hiring. I've looked for a long time in a lot of places. You really get tired of it.... I can tell you right now there's a lot of people I see around and I can guarantee you they won't be going far in life. Not enough education, and it's hard for people to get trained. Now it's too late for many; and the economy is terrible now. (Unemployed middle aged male factory worker with some high school)

Some of the underqualified express more fatalistic views about their own limited entitlements:

If you're lucky you will get a better job. It's a tough economic situation and I don't have adequate training or education yet. But, anyways, it depends on one's luck. (Middle aged female electrical assembly temporary worker with some high school)

If I get more education I'll deserve a better job, but I don't deserve it with what I've got now. My parents didn't give me enough education. They made me leave school and go out to work. (Unemployed middle aged female factory worker with some elementary schooling)

In general, a sense of entitlement to a better job appears to be quite widely held among *both* our credentially underemployed and under-qualified interviewees. Regardless of their general perceptions of the extent of the education-jobs gap, most in-depth respondents harbour at least faint hopes that they should be able to get a better job. The tendency to blame oneself primarily for the failure to get a better job seems to be pretty weak in both groups. People on both sides of the education-jobs gap finger bad economic conditions, shortsighted government policies, irrelevant educational programs and other institutional forces. But they typically see themselves as active agents of many of their own present and future education and job choices in the context of such constraints. The choice which is most frequently referred to is getting further education.

UNDEREMPLOYMENT AND LIFELONG LEARNING

If workers experience discrepancies between their formal education and their job requirements, what are their general responses in terms of further learning practices? I will look first at participation in adult education courses, and then at involvement in informal learning activities.

Underemployment and Adult Education

It was often suggested in the early studies in the underemployment tradition that workers might tend to become disenchanted both with further work-related learning and established society in general (e.g. O'Toole 1975). But more recent empirical studies have found that the underemployed have been at least as likely as other employees to be planning further education. Beverly Burris' (1983a, 285) case study of underemployed clerical workers found that:

> The more education already obtained, the more likely was there to be a stress on increased educational attainment as a central life goal…. In some cases, the pursuit of more education becomes a central source of compensatory self-identity, valued as an end in itself; more commonly, however, education is viewed as a means to obtaining a better job.

A later case study of underemployed male college graduates in British Columbia in the late 1980s (Borgen, Amundson and Harder 1988) documented a complex array of responses to the general condition of underemployment, including anger, frustration and sadness; but this study also discovered frequent efforts at retraining for job change, or further education that "I can always use ... in other aspects of my life" (156). Similarly, on the basis of a Canadian national survey, Lowe (1992, 58–59) concludes that:

> Ironically, many individuals possessing higher credentials than required for their particular job believed that they must obtain even more education to compete effectively for a better job.

As for the underqualified, who have lower formal educational attainments and are frequently school dropouts, the prevailing assumption has been that they typically have even lower learning motivation and capacity for continuing education than the underemployed.[11] But, again, empirical studies have uncovered little evidence to support this assumption. The underqualified, just like everybody else, now believe that obtaining a post-secondary formal education is becoming increasingly important to getting along in this society and to qualifying for a future job (Lowe 1992, 89–107; Livingstone, Hart and Davie 1995, 32). A recent New York Times poll (1996, 48) found that over 90 percent of all workers are now interested in getting more training and education to increase their chances of keeping a job. Faith in the power of more education to close the education-jobs gap, or at least compensate for it, appears to be strong on both sides of the gap.

According to the 1989 Canadian survey, further education plans were most common in sales and service jobs where people were most likely to feel overqualified (Lowe 1992, 53–59). Further analysis of OISE Survey data indicates that the underemployed have been slightly more likely than others to have such plans, but that the majority of those who were underqualified also expected to take further courses. Only among the tiny numbers of workers who were highly underqualified on performance criteria and had only elementary schooling was there little expressed interest in further education courses in the mid 1980s (Livingstone, Hart and Davie 1987).

Our preliminary analyses of *actual* participation rates in organized adult education courses, as reported in our series of general Ontario surveys between 1986 and 1992, have found no significant differences in participation rates between credentially underemployed, matched and underqualified workers (Livingstone 1993b). Analysis of the 1994 and 1996 surveys confirms these findings. The credential gap has little effect on participation in further education courses.

However, further analyses of participation by *performance gap status* provides a somewhat different picture. As Table 3.3 summarizes, those whose educational qualifications exceed the actual performance requirements of their jobs are just as likely as those with matched statuses to participate in further education courses. The highly underemployed remain at least as likely as those with matched statuses to have enrolled in a course during the prior year. The participation of young underemployed post-secondary graduates in further education increased especially quickly during the early part of this period (Livingstone 1992). But those who are underqualified for their jobs on performance criteria had lower participation rates than other workers in the mid 1980s. Their participation increased to parity levels by the early 1990s, but appears to have declined again more recently. As noted in Chapter One, there has been a reduction of government provision of general adult education courses during the mid 1990s; the highly underqualified, who are also typically the lowest income workers as well as the least schooled and oldest, have probably borne the brunt of these reductions.

It should be noted here, as Table 3.3 also documents, that the officially unemployed have increased their participation rates in further education programs quite dramatically over the past decade, from less than 10 percent in the mid-1980s to around a third in the 1990s. This may reflect increased government efforts to reallocate social welfare funds, such as unemployment insurance, to provide increased retraining programs for the unemployed, as well as the increased difficulty of qualifying to be counted as officially unemployed and eligible to enter such programs. In any case, the officially unemployed are now participating in further education courses with as high a frequency as any other social group. While many of these courses may be very useful to unemployed workers, a vicious downward spiral of training courses appears to now have been established among the unemployed and marginally employed, whereby previously secure workers take such a course when laid off, then bump other lower level workers from their temporary jobs and into similar courses, only to be bumped themselves in the next round by more highly certified applicants.[12]

So, at both extremes of the education-jobs gap, among highly underemployed post-secondary graduates and unemployed underqualified high school dropouts, the participation rates in adult edu-

Table 3.3   Participation in Adult Education Courses by
                Performance Gap Status, Ontario Labour Force,
                1986–1996

Performance Gap Status	Annual Participation Rates						
	86 (%)	88 (%)	90 (%)	92 (%)	94 (%)	96 (%)	Ave. (%)
High underemployed	32	34	45	38	32	33	36
Underemployed	25	30	34	40	33	32	33
Matched	31	30	34	39	33	36	34
Underqualified	12	22	25	34	32	22	22
High underqualified	12	19	24	34	11	11	16
Unemployed	7	16	28	40	32	39	30
Totals	26	30	34	37	32	31	32
N	590	559	581	526	715	610	3580

Source: OISE Survey of Educational Issues Data Archive.

cation courses are now comparable to or higher than the general
population rates. With the lone exception of the small minority of
the older working poor with very little schooling, there is no sign in
these voluntary participation rates of any growing disenchantment
with educational institutions among either the underemployed or
any other discernible social group.

Our in-depth interviewees' responses to questions about their
future plans and aspirations concerning education and jobs provide further insights into the extent of belief, on both sides of the
education-jobs gap, in the power of education to improve future
life chances.

For the underemployed, the equation between more education
and better jobs is far from certain in light of the underuse of education in their present jobs. But the apparent necessity to respond to
this uncertainty by pursuing yet more formal education also remains
largely unquestioned:

I don't have anything I would call a plan at this point.... There is certainly a thought at the back of my mind that more education would be a goal at some point. Certainly it would be a potential goal at least.... If I am to remain in the field that I am in, I need to learn a lot more about computers, accounting and other things specific to the field, basically improving my qualifications. In today's economy, the employer expects you to have it when you walk in the door. But, to be honest, I've no idea what I want to do with the rest of my life. (Underemployed middle aged male waiter with a B.A.)

I think I will be going back for my doctorate, it seems, the way jobs are.... I'd like to be a professor or open a small business. I'm pretty sure I can get these jobs. It will take a while, but I need more education. It's just one last hurdle! (Underemployed young male part-time cook with a Master's degree)

If a student loan comes through, I'm going to broadcasting school. And I've got to get computer training.... After all my education, I should have an answer, but I just want a job. There's a huge gap between the dream and most of this stuff. It's so far away for me. (Unemployed middle aged male civil servant with multiple degrees)

It is very important for people to get a good education. Some people can't, but there should still be an emphasis on continuing education, because nobody wants to work at MacDonalds' all your life. (Underemployed older female service worker with a college certificate)

Among the underqualified interviewees, there is a virtually unanimous equation between further educational credentials and either a better job or a fuller life:

I'm discouraged because I didn't pass the math test to get into the program I wanted. It takes so long to go through all the upgrading courses and I'm afraid I'll be too old to find a job. But education is so very important. I don't mind going to school the rest of my life because I enjoy learning.... I want to get enough training to open my own business — and get a high school diploma with math when I retire. (Unemployed older female service worker with no formal schooling)

I'd love to get my grade 11, that's my dream.... I'd really like to be an auto mechanic but I'm not able to get it — don't have enough skills in my head, too little education. Education is still my dream. I feel I've been deprived of something. If I had the education, I wouldn't be here today. Education gives you power.... I'm not a smart person, but I'm not a stupid person. (Unemployed middle aged female factory worker with some elementary schooling)

After upgrading, I'm going to an adult high school to get some training credits — unless I score a job, and then training's kaput. I don't think that will happen. I've looked for any kind of a job — not hiring, too much experience, not enough experience, just hired somebody else, et cetera. It gets very depressing. I'm trying hard. That's all you can do. You've got to try somewhere. (Unemployed middle aged factory worker with some high school)

I'd like to do an advanced credit course and take a skill. I've got to get some education. I don't know exactly what now, but I have to see if I can get a better job. Want to learn more about my hobbies, too. I hope I'll be able to get a job if I get some school in — looks like a lot of people hope so! (Underqualified young male factory worker with some high school)

The entire concept of the economy is downsizing. Computers run our operations. It's all changing. What I used to do on a 12 hour shift can be done in 2 hours. Some might say why spend the money to educate more people. But in 10 years we will all need more education because everything is so sophisticated. (Underqualified older male industrial worker with some high school)

You shouldn't tell a person they can't learn. Can't say, hey, you go to high school and that's it. That is wrong. A mind is a terrible thing to waste. (Underqualified older male supervisor with some high school)

So, in spite of their common experience of a superficial connection between their formal educational attainments and the requirements of their current or recent jobs, both underqualified school dropouts and underemployed university graduates continue believe and act as if more education is the personal solution to living in the education-jobs gap. There are undoubtedly many motives associated with the popular demand for and engagement in adult education. But whether the major motivation is seen to be competition for scarce jobs, the desire to be an effective consumer or citizen, assertion of the democratic right to equal educational opportunity, or a more generic quest for knowledge to cope with uncertain times, there is now an almost universal general perception that more education is a fundamental imperative in contemporary society.

Underemployment and Informal Learning

As the discussion in Chapter One has generally documented, informal learning outside of organized courses is at least as extensive as course-based learning in current societies. However, the now well-established tradition of research on self-directed learning has paid virtually no attention to the informal learning practices of the underemployed, and very little attention to the informal learning of the underqualified, however these respective groups may be defined.[13]

Although there have been a few case studies that have touched on the continuing education efforts of underemployed college graduates (B. Burris 1983a; Borgen Amundson and Harder 1988), there are no known prior studies that have focused on the informal learning activities of underemployed post-secondary graduates. But the research cited above regarding their participation in adult education courses at least provides no evidence to infer that they are now any less keen on voluntary learning activities than most other folks.

The very limited amount of prior research on the learning practices of economically disadvantaged adults with low formal educational attainments suggests that the vast majority do a significant amount of informal learning (see Leean and Sisco 1981; Sisco 1983). Studies of economically disadvantaged urban adults, high school dropouts, functional illiterates and the unemployed have all found similar patterns.[14]

As discussed in Chapter One, the 1996 OISE Survey asked all respondents to estimate the amount of time they typically devoted to informal learning activities outside organized coursework. We have analyzed these estimates by underemployment statuses. As with the findings for the general estimates presented in Chapter One, and most other prior comparative studies of informal learning activities, the variations within underemployment statuses are far greater than between statuses. Analyses of the incidence of informal learning by the credential gap have found no significant differences in either the amount of work-related or general interest learning between the underemployed, the matched and the underqualified. Regardless of one's credential gap status, the amount of informal learning people engage in appears to be very similar.

But once again, relations between the *performance gap* and informal

Table 3.4   Estimated Informal Learning Activities by Performance Gap Status, Ontario Labour Force, 1996

	Average Hours per Year*		
	Work-related[1]	*General interest*[2]	*Total*
Performance Gap Status			
Highly underemployed	350	325	675
Underemployed	300	275	575
Matched	300	325	625
Underqualified	400	300	700
Highly Underqualified	225	200	425
Unemployed	300	325	625
Total			
(N=691)	325	300	625

*Weekly estimates have been multiplied by 52 weeks and rounded to the nearest 25 hours.

1 "Not counting coursework, about how many hours in a typical week do you spend trying to learn anything related to your paid or household work, or work you do as a volunteer? Just give your best guess."

2 "Not counting coursework, about how many hours in a typical week do you spend trying to learn anything of general interest to you? Just give your best guess."

Source: Livingstone, Hart and Davie (1997).

learning activities is a bit different. The results in relation to the performance gap are summarized in Table 3.4. Those who are moderately underqualified on performance criteria average more time in work-related informal learning that anybody else, about 400 hours a year. This may reflect their greater need to upgrade their skills for adequate job performance. But the small number who are highly underqualified for their jobs tend to spend less time in both work-related and general interest informal learning activities than any other group; this pattern is very similar to their participation in adult education courses. This group only represents about five percent of the labour force and includes mainly people who are older with very little schooling; they typically have very limited income and very limited time for informal learning beyond their low wage jobs. But even these folks with little schooling and little discretionary time estimate that they devote an average of over 400 hours a year to informal learning.

In the follow-up interviews to the 1994 OISE Survey, conducted in 1995 with credentially mismatched respondents to the initial survey, we pursued extensive questioning about all their organized and informal learning practices over the prior year. The basic findings are summarized in Table 3.5.

Underemployed university/college graduates and underqualified people with high school or less were spending an average of about 13 hours per week, or 680 hours per year, on their various deliberate learning activities. The average amount of time spent on work-related and other general interest courses by both groups was quite simi-

Table 3.5   All Estimated Learning Activities of Credentially Underemployed College Graduates and Underqualified Non-college, Ontario Labour Force, 1994

	Average Hours per Year*				
	Work-related courses	*Other courses*	*Informal work-related*	*Informal other interests*	*Total*
Credential Gap					
Underemployed college	50	30	310	370	760
Underqualified ≤h.s.	30	30	240	240	600
Total					
(N=136)	40	30	310	310	680

*Course time has been estimated by respondents in terms of total contact hours and related homework assignments. Weekly estimates for informal learning activities have been multiplied by 52. All averages have been rounded to nearest 10 hours.

Source: Follow-up interview of credentially mismatched respondents to Tenth OISE Survey of Educational Issues, February-March, 1995.

lar, as was the amount of time devoted to informal work-related learning. The main difference was that underemployed university/college graduates claimed to be spending more time in informal learning related to their general interests.

This finding might be taken to suggest that underqualified people with less schooling have less predisposition or capacity to engage in informal learning activities beyond their work than underemployed university and college graduates do. But this would be to ignore the fact that self-directed learning is often underestimated among working class people because of a tendency to deny a major learning component in some manual activities,[15] just as many professional and managerial class people find it difficult to recognize important manual components in their activities. For example, one of our respondents, who would be classified as functionally illiterate by most standards, spent a good deal of time in the interview resisting the notion that any of her personal activities could constitute a learning project. But she also added that:

> I like meeting people and learning about things and I do a lot of sports and practical things like crocheting. But it's all old stuff, not real learning. (Underqualified middle aged female factory worker with less than four years of elementary schooling)

More fundamentally, as noted in Chapter One, the entire tradition of research on self-directed learning projects is based on a conceptual model of an individually-realized intentional learning process. Particularly in many working class households and communities, a significant amount of important learning occurs without planning, in collective learning processes.[16] Such learning is beyond the scope of conventional measures of learning activities, again serving to underestimate the scale of working class learning. The current study is subject to the same limitations in this regard.[17]

However, at least these results are consistent with and shed a little further light on the general population survey findings that underemployed and underqualified people are spending substantial amounts of time in continuing learning activities in relation to their work and more generally. Both underemployed university/college graduates and underqualified non-college workers spend at least as much time on informal work-related learning as people whose credentials match their jobs. They also spend much more time in informal learning projects than they do in organized course-based learning, generally about *ten times as much time*. Neither underemployment nor underqualification serves to shrink the iceberg of informal learning.

As in prior studies that have compared patterns of informal learning across social groupings, variations in learning time *within* the underemployed college and underqualified school groups is much greater than the differences between them. In particular, there is no systemic difference between the credentially underemployed or underqualified and the rest of the workforce in their work-related continuing learning capacities and interests.[18] Regardless of their work status and in spite of various institutional and material barriers, most folks living in the education-jobs gap continue to engage in quite substantial informal learning activities.

In terms of the more specific content of their learning activities, both underemployed college graduates and underqualified non-college respondents participate in a wide array of work-related courses. School upgrading courses are most common among the credentially underqualified, while the underemployed are frequently involved in courses to develop additional vocational skills such as business administration. But the most common course participation in both groups now is in computer training.

Some of the flavor of the kinds of informal learning that underemployed and underqualified people engage in around their paid workplaces is conveyed by our in-depth respondents' comments:

> Our products are constantly changing. We're reading blueprints, drafting all kinds of new things. I learn something new almost every day. We're learning all the time, but it's not job retraining. (Underemployed middle aged male industrial worker with a community college certificate)

> Once you get into a job, you realize how you start to learn more about business and what goes on. Formal education only has a minor role in the picture. There's a lot more learning to do once you finish school. You learn everyday at work. (Underemployed middle aged female service worker with a university degree)

> Much of my learning in the last year has been in response to the downsizing of our whole plant. They're reorganizing the entire work structure, giving us more accountability. We have to learn new concepts of team participation. But I've also been taking the time to read

up about my rights and options if the next lay-off hits me. (Under-qualified middle aged male factory worker with some high school)

I've spent a lot of time in internal cross-training, with someone else to cover a different job. We always do lots of on-the-job training with new techniques. And I've spent a fair amount of time in learning new computer programs. (Underqualified young male technician with a high school diploma)

Overall, these recent surveys and follow-up interviews indicate that there are no significant differences between matched and mismatched employees in their increased general participation rates in organized adult education courses. The general population survey of informal learning activities and the follow-up interviews with credentially mismatched employees demonstrate that there are also no major differences between underemployed and underqualified employees in the total amount of time they now devote to work-related learning activities. It appears that these mismatched employees are spending at least as much time in informal learning as adult learners generally were in the 1970s, an average of over 600 hours per year compared to the earlier general average of about 500 hours. The condition of underemployment has evidently not discouraged people from continuing both their work-related and general learning activities. As for objectively underqualified workers, most of whom deny they are actually underqualified for their jobs, the evidence suggests that most of them are devoting at least as much effort to continuing work-related learning activities as matched and underemployed workers. The learning efforts of both the underemployed and the underqualified are clearly much more extensive than the dominant rhetoric of corporate and government leaders about the pressing need for those in the education-jobs gap to get more training would suggest.

CONCLUDING REMARKS

As most of the voices in this chapter testify, the education-jobs gap is not a pleasant place to live. It is fairly clear that one of the most common current responses to this situation is to seek more education and training. This mindset is as common among underemployed university and college graduates as it is among underqualified school dropouts. These people live with a deep-seated recognition of the arbitrariness of the formal educational credential requirements set for the jobs they have had. They understand, more intimately than those living within the current comfort of job requirements matched to their educational attainments, that employers are upping the ante for job entry and that the link between entry requirements and educational attainments is being loosened in a buyer's job market.

Those living in the education-jobs gap give no serious indication of giving up on the faith that more education should get them a better job. Indeed, their current situation seems to have provoked in many at least a quiet sense of desperation that somehow they must continue to get more and still more education, training or knowledge in order to achieve any economic security. These sentiments resonate through most of our interviews. Such increasingly common learning efforts among the unemployed and underemployed underline just how wide the gulf between the knowledge base of the general population and the limited knowledge required in most jobs has become.

The conviction of these marginalized people that our current economic system can produce the jobs to which they continue to feel at least ambiguously entitled has definitely been shaken severely. But, in the absence of any economic alternative that seems plausible, most of those living on both sides of the education-jobs gap are actively engaged in trying to revise rather than reject this conviction. As in the 1930s, the waste of human potential is immense and gut-wrenching. Just as during the "dirty thirties," the economic polarization between the haves and have-nots has also increased greatly. The difference is that the promise and pursuit of further education are now playing a much larger role than make-work programs in preoccupying the swelling number of outcasts and misfits of the labour market.

4

Debunking the "Knowledge Economy": The Limits of Human Capital Theory

Our [higher] educational system is not a public service, but an instrument of special privilege; its purpose is not to further the welfare of mankind (sic), but merely to keep America capitalist ... [through] class greed and selfishness based upon economic privilege.
—Upton Sinclair 1923, 18, 478

Earnings greatly understate the social productivity of college graduates (and other educated persons) because they are (allegedly) only partly compensated for their effect on the development and spread of economic knowledge.
—Gary Becker 1964, 209

Science is something more (and less) than the dispassionate pursuit of knowledge. How scientific information is shaped is often predetermined by the prevailing ideological climate. For centuries scientists have paid dearly for maintaining iconoclastic views. Their oppressors have often been other scientists working in tandem with the established powers of society.
—Michael Parenti 1996, 221

INTRODUCTION

If the common response of so many people to conditions of their own underemployment is to seek still more education, there must be some substantial bases for this response. In this chapter, I will look critically at two of these bases: (1) the widespread belief that jobs in the emerging future economy will require vastly increased numbers of highly educated workers; and (2) the relationship between more education and increased earnings which is widely presumed to

133

apply not only to individuals but to societies.

Most of the chapter focuses on the claims of those scholars who have constructed the image of a *"post-industrial economy"* or a *"knowledge economy"* which has become a common article of faith in public discourse. If, as these scholars claim, most of the emergent jobs in private market-driven economies will probably need an advanced education, then pursuing more education while one endures current underemployment is a reasonable response. Most of these prevalent theories of employment-related knowledge development are based at least loosely on notions of evolutionary progress. I will examine the actual knowledge and skill requirements for paid work in advanced private market economies, particularly the U.S. and Canada, and find some of these theories' claims to be illusory.

Investment in formal education has been associated with both higher individual earnings and growing societal wealth. These relationships have been most fully conceptualized and documented by *human capital theory* which stresses the value of peoples' learning capacities as a factor of economic productivity.[1] This perspective is built on the intellectual foundations of neo-classical market theory and the generally optimistic assumptions of the evolutionary progress paradigm. It reflected the post-WWII conditions of simultaneous expansion of employment and education fairly well, even though Berg (1970) and others documented the existence of a significant performance gap in the 1950s. The "learning-earning" link is still valid at the individual level, although with diminishing marginal utility. But it is disintegrating at the aggregate or societal level and this disintegration is occurring beyond the margins of the market returns perspective of human capital theory.

THE EVOLUTIONARY PROGRESS PARADIGM: "POST-INDUSTRIAL"/"KNOWLEDGE ECONOMY" THEORIES

The conservative social historian, Robert Nisbet (1970) has suggested that all theories of social change are based on the metaphor of organic growth and/or the analogy of the life cycle. Certainly the theories of social evolution and continual progress that have been prevalent for most of the past century and a half in western societies have been grounded in organic growth metaphors: from Social Darwinism, to Weber's rationalization/bureaucratization, to Parsons' structural differentiation, to "post-industrial"/"knowledge economy" theories.

There is a rudimentary explanatory mechanism at the root of most evolutionary theories, namely Charles Darwin's notion of random variation/selective survival in a seldom kindly environment. But the biological survival of the fittest has frequently resulted in species extinctions, while modern social evolutionary theories have been mainly optimistic extrapolations of the most positive recent trends.

Optimistic extrapolation is surely the case with "post-industrial"/ "knowledge economy" theories. As promoted most notably by Daniel Bell (1964, 1973) in the U.S., John Porter (1971) in Canada, Alain Touraine (1969) in France and Radovan Richta (1969) in eastern Europe,[2] post-industrial theory anticipated the growing centrality of theoretical knowledge, continuing expansion of tertiary-level occupations, the increasing eminence of a professional and technical class, and a general upgrading of the skills needed for work, as well as greater leisure time. As I have noted elsewhere (Livingstone, 1983, 181), the creation of the future in this largely technocratic mode of thought:

> ... apparently means discovering trends and then using further technical ingenuity to either mute or facilitate them. However sophisticated they become, such approaches are based on a presumption that the future really depends on forces that are beyond human capacity to control in any significant way. The enduring image of the future left by all such writings is one of irreversible technocratic trends remote from whatever social and political capacities ordinary people might retain.

This mode of thought serves to glorify the capacities of technocrats/experts themselves and resonates with increasing attempts by professional experts in many fields to monopolize knowledge that many others are capable of mastering and using (Derber, Schwartz and Magrass 1990; Perkins 1996; Parenti 1996). This is surely one reason why, in spite of demonstrated empirical inadequacies and withering critiques from other researchers, post-industrial/knowledge economy advocates continue to assert the increasing pervasiveness of scientific knowledge and upgraded skills in the workplace.[3]

As we have seen in prior chapters, there is ample empirical warrant for describing contemporary advanced private market societies in terms of people's increasing pursuit of knowledge. But we have also seen that the capacity of paid workplaces to utilize people's knowledge has become increasingly problematic. As a consequence of their presumption of the increasing centrality of scientific/technological knowledge and general skill upgrading of the workplace, post-industrial/knowledge economy theorists have continued to ignore most aspects of underemployment, most notably the performance gap. With increasing underemployment, post-industrial theorists' claims for the workplace have become less credible in relation to most people's experience. I will examine these claims more closely in the following section.

The overly optimistic character of the evolutionary theories of modernization and industrialization of the entire globe along Western society lines that emerged in the immediate post World War II expansionary period has now been shown by the absolute and relative economic impoverishment of much of the "underdeveloped" world, as well as by the reassertion of alternative models of society in some of these regions (Latouche 1993; World Bank 1997). There has been a common intellectual tendency in periods of widespread social malaise for theories of progress to be challenged by theories of decline.

The decline theories that have contested linear progress versions of societal growth in periods of widespread unemployment — from Nietzsche and Spengler through Sorokin to the more diffuse reflections of current post-modernists — usually rely on implicit analogies of the life cycle of birth-growth-decline-death-rebirth. Pitirim Sorokin (1937–41), in his *Social and Cultural Dynamics*, produced at the end of the 1930s Depression, has provided one of the most elaborate taxonomic descriptions of long-term social change based on this life cycle analogy.

Among social theorists of the post-1970 era, optimistic projections of progress have again been challenged, this time by post-modernist eclecticism and post-structuralist ambiguity. While much of post-modernist theory celebrates social differences and the subjective identities of subordinated people, the underlying model of societal change is typically some version of decline or death of one form of society, often coupled with the nascent emergence of another.[4] Neither Sorokin nor current post-modernist theorists have suggested an alternative *explanatory* dynamic for societal change in general or education-work relations in particular. Whether the world is deemed to be getting better or worse, most influential theories of social change have continued to be grounded, as Nisbet suggests, in simple analogies of growth and decline, and to regard such trends as largely beyond the control of collective social agency. But even in the present period of pervasive underemployment, revised theories of evolutionary progress tend to prevail in the public spheres of life, as evidenced by popular acceptance of the general view that continual economic growth remains necessary to ensure a healthy society.

The "Knowledge Economy" and Workplace Realities

The emergence of a "post-industrial" workplace dominated by highly educated information service workers has been heralded since the early 1960s (see especially Bell 1964, 1973). The theories of post-industrialism have promoted the belief that the prevalence of information processing over material handling in the mode of production would necessitate skill upgrading and greater creativity and critical thinking of workers. In short, post-industrial/knowledge economy theories generally assume or assert that *workers increasingly require more skill, become more involved in planning their own work, and increasingly constitute a professional class.* We will examine the empirical evidence for each of these three basic claims below.

There have certainly been substantial changes in the composition of the employed workforce over the past generation in nearly all market economies. Most obviously, there has been sectoral decline of manufacturing and relative growth of personal, financial and social service employment. This is the pivot point for most "post-industrial" projections. Other evident compositional shifts have been the relative increase of part-time and temporary jobs, and greater participation of married women in paid employment (see OECD 1994a). But in relation to these compositional shifts, empirical researchers have been at least as likely to posit deskilling, less planning involvement and poorer compensation as their post-industrial opposites. Indeed, for virtually every aspect of contemporary paid work, advocates of degradation theses rather than post-industrial upgrading trends can be easily found in the research literature. Part of the difficulty in assessing levels and changes in actual work requirements has been that our customary ways of thinking about these requirements do not clearly distinguish between the technical tasks involved and the people doing them.

From Adam Smith (1776) to the present, most theorists and researchers of divisions of labour have confounded the *technical division of tasks* and the *social division of workers.* From Smith's famous analysis of the pin factory onward, there has been a widespread presumption that the separation of a work process into distinct steps for productive efficiency, task specialization, naturally leads to a detailed social division of labour among workers. But, as some observers of the more minute divisions of contemporary work within and between occupations have recognized, identified technical tasks can be efficiently allocated among workers in a variety of ways, not necessarily social divisions based on single tasks (e.g. Drucker 1954; Braverman 1974). The fact that surgeons now perform a wide array of manual tasks while factory assembly workers perform only a few is a *social construction* rather than an inherent feature of these forms of work per se. As James Murphy (1993, 23) insightfully observes of relations between technical and social divisions of labour:

> Any concrete account of the division of tasks, of occupations, of castes, presupposes the distinction between the division of functions and the division of persons. The specialization of legal, political, military, educational, and religious functions does not logically entail the social monopoly of these functions by specialists. It is well known that lay people can perform many of these functions for themselves perfectly well. How these functions have been historically appropriated by specialists is a fundamental question for the theory of the division of labour. Just as the technical division of tasks in the factory does not account for the detailed social division of workers, so the technical division of functions in society does not account for the social division of professionals and the laity.

As new machines and routines have been devised for work tasks, work theorists from Smith on have generally assumed that their implementation in a more detailed social division of labour would increase general productive efficiency, as long as workers could be motivated to use them as designed. The factory assembly line of simple technical tasks presented the classic motivational problem here, which industrial design specialists have attempted to resolve through incentives ranging from wage and benefit increases to various consultation processes among workers. This tendency to see the social division of labour as essentially determined by and necessarily adapting to available task techniques has been quite pervasive.[6] But in cases of highly automated production, the detailed division of labour has become so segmented and mind-numbing for line workers that industrial designers have had to resort to technical task recombinations. In the process they illustrate that technologies are actually the *interaction* of technical divisions of tasks and social divisions of workers rather than machine-driven imperatives. In contrast, the post-industrial theorists' solution to the question of changing work requirements has been simply to assume rapidly increasing automation of most manual tasks and their replacement by professional and technical jobs based on theoretical knowledge.

A balanced assessment of the contemporary character of and trends in work requirements should directly consider: (1) the *technical division of labour* in terms of the allocation of simple and complex tasks between jobs; (2) the *social division of labour* in terms of the respective participation of various workers in planning the execution of tasks; and (3) their consequential effects on the *class structure of work*.

Division of Technical Skills

Over the past generation, notably since the publication of Harry Braverman's (1974) "deskilling thesis," there has been a massive amount of research literature arguing for and documenting both deskilling and upgrading trends in the technical skill levels of labour processes in advanced industrial economies (see Wood 1989). Braverman's study represented the first major challenge to the post-industrial upgrading thesis. It generated several waves of empirical case studies, the first documenting deskilling trends, followed by others on worker resistance to deskilling, and then more nuanced studies of negotiations between employers and employees over technical task divisions (V. Smith 1994). Such case studies certainly confirm that upgrading has not been a universal trend.

Aggregate data to determine the actual extent of upgrading and deskilling in the workforce as a whole are difficult to find. A first approximation for the U.S. and Canada is provided by applying the technical skill requirements estimated by government job analysts in dictionaries of occupational titles to large-scale sample surveys. The two most commonly used indicators of skill levels in both countries have been the general educational development (GED), and specific vocational preparation (SVP) scales. As discussed in Chapter Two, the GED scale is intended to embrace those aspects of knowledge which are required of the worker for satisfactory job performance. The different levels of this scale on each of three dimensions (reasoning, mathematical and language development) were defined in Chapter Two (see Figure 2.1).

The major division in this scale is between the first three levels which involve primarily executing concrete tasks and the other three levels which entail more complex problem solving functions. I have applied standard GED ratings of respective U.S. and Canadian occupational classifications to the annual surveys of the National Opinion Research Centre (NORC) between 1972 and 1990, and to the OISE surveys in Ontario between 1980 and 1996.[7] This procedure generates the patterns summarized in Table 4.1.

These findings, based on mid-point splits for each of the six GED

Table 4.1 GED Scores of 4 or more, Employed Workforce, U.S., 1972–1990 and Ontario, 1980–1996 (median scores)

| | % with GED of 4 or more | |
	U.S.	Ontario
1972	51	
1973	52	
1974	53	
1975	51	
1976	51	
1977	49	
1978	52	
1979	–	
1980	55	57
1981	–	–
1982	53	60
1983	58	–
1984	55	60
1985	57	–
1986	59	60
1987	59	–
1988	59	58
1989	60	–
1990	59	62
1992	61	
1994	61	
1996	60	

Sources: Davis and Smith (1994); OISE Survey of Educational Issues Data Archive.

levels,[8] suggest a gradual overall upgrading of the technical skill level required in jobs over the past twenty-five years. The more detailed distributions indicate that very few jobs (less than one percent) have been rated at the lowest skill level throughout this period, while jobs rated at the highest skill level have increased from about three percent to five or six percent. Similar conclusions have been drawn by Howell and Wolff (1991) for the U.S. over the 1960–85 period and by John Myles (1988) for Canada as a whole over the 1961 to 1981 period, based on GED scores and other related measures with census data.

A longer general historical comparison for the U.S. can be constructed by drawing on the earlier aggregate GED estimates produced by Eckhaus (1964) for 1940 and Berg (1970) for 1950 and 1960, as summarized in Table 4.2.

Table 4.2 GED levels, U.S. Employed Labour Force, 1940–1990 (median scores)

GED Level	1940 (%)	1950 (%)	1960 (%)	1972 (%)	1980 (%)	1990 (%)
1	9	7	<1	<1	<1	<1
2	20	27	16	15	13	12
3	43	27	28	33	31	29
4	21	32	32	32	34	34
5	5	6	18	16	17	19
6	2	3	3	3	4	6

Sources: 1940: Eckhaus (1964, Table 3, 185); 1950, 1960: Berg (1970, Table III-1, 46); 1972, 1980, 1990: Davis and Smith (1994).

These general estimates suggest that there may have been a substantial upgrading of technical skill requirements between 1940 and 1960 with a reduction in simple instruction, level one jobs from almost ten percent to less than one percent, while problem solving jobs with skill levels of 4 or greater increased from under 30 percent to over half of all jobs. This is a period that saw first the growth of a war economy which drew massive numbers of rural people from traditional small commodity forms of production work into military and factory employment, followed by rapid post-war growth of public and service sector employment. In contrast, the post-1960 period, the widely heralded era of the new knowledge economy, has experienced less dramatic sectoral shifts, with comparatively stable and gradually increasing required technical skill levels in the overall job structure. Indeed, the most extensive U.S. study finds that the upgrading effects of changes in the industry and occupational composition of employment on technical skill levels appears to have steadily declined during the 1960–85 period (Howell and Wolff 1991, 490–91).

The pattern of gradual upgrading of the U.S. and Canadian labour forces in the post-1960s period is further confirmed by analyses of the SVP scale, which estimates the specific vocational preparation required for each job simply in terms of the amount of time needed to learn the techniques, acquire information and develop facility for average performance. This time estimate includes any relevant vocational education, apprenticeship training, further education courses, on-the-job training and/or essential experience in other jobs.

Table 4.3   SVP Levels, Employed U.S. Labour Force, 1940–1990

SVP Level	1940 (%)	1950 (%)	1972 (%)	1980 (%)	1990 (%)
1. Short demonstration	1	<1	<1	<1	<1
2. Up to 30 days	17	21	4	3	5
3. Up to 3 months	13	8	22	17	15
4. Up to 6 months	23	24	18	19	19
5. Up to 1 year	4	5	9	10	8
6. Up to 2 years	18	14	16	18	18
7. Up to 4 years	21	24	26	26	25
8. Over 4 years	3	4	6	7	10

Sources: 1940, 1950: Eckhaus (1964, Table 4, 186); 1972, 1980, 1990: David and Smith (1994).

Table 4.3 indicates that, compared with the 1940–50 period, there are now very few U.S. jobs in which adequate performance can be achieved with less than a month of specific vocational training; the small proportion of jobs that require more than four years of preparatory training, as well as the proportion needing over a year of training, have increased somewhat since 1950. A small and very gradually increasing majority of the labour force have required more than a year of vocational preparation throughout the 1972–90 period. The SVP scores are very strongly correlated (Spearman=.79, p<.00001) with the GED scores; virtually all jobs with GED scores over 4 require more than a year of training, while very few jobs with lower GED ratings need more than a year of vocational training.

Myles (1988) analysis of the SVP scores of the Canadian labour force based on census data has found similar trends for the 1961–81 period. As Table 4.4 summarizes, jobs requiring less than 30 days of training decreased during this period while jobs needing over two years of training increased.

Table 4.4 SVP Levels, Employed Non-Agricultural Canadian Labour Force, 1961–1981

SVP Level	1961	1971	1981
1. Up to 30 days	21	18	12
2. Up to 3 months	22	29	17
3. Up to 6 months	15	17	18
4. Up to 1 year	15	15	19
5. Up to 2 years	11	11	11
6. Over 2 years	18	20	23

Source: Myles (1988, Table I, 340).

Comparing Tables 4.3 and 4.4 suggests that the Canadian occupational structure may have had somewhat more jobs requiring very little training time than the U.S. In any case, the overall post-1960 pattern of changes in required training time in both economies suggests a gradual decline of low skill jobs and a gradual increase of high skill jobs.

There are numerous limitations to occupational dictionary-based skill ratings. As one of the designers of the GED scale, Sidney Fine (1968, 370) himself has noted: "one should hardly become wedded to the absolute estimates ... the estimates for any given job are only significant relative to estimates for other jobs." More specific problems include selection biases, limited updating of ratings, and limited capacity to consider both skill level changes related to occupational composition as well as those within individual jobs in trend analyses. The number of job titles rated in these occupational dictionaries increased from 4,000 in 1956 to over 23,000 in 1993 (U.S. Department of Labour, 1993). The initial selection of titles was far from inclusive of all types of jobs. While post-1960 versions have become much more inclusive, the selections are still not necessarily representative of all current jobs and the varying inclusiveness makes comparisons over time somewhat suspect. General updating of the job ratings has only been done a few times while the rerating of individual jobs has occurred on a more ad hoc basis. The rating scales are therefore always both somewhat selective and out of date in their applicability to the current workforce. Both the occupational composition of the workforce and the skill levels of individual existing jobs continue to change more rapidly than these rating scales are able to reflect.

In terms of changing skill content *within* specific jobs, Berg's (1970, 47–48) comparison of the first two U.S. general dictionary GED ratings published in 1956 and 1966 found that 54 percent of the original 4,000 job titles retained the same GED level in the later year, 31 percent were rated higher and 15 percent were rated lower. He also noted that this set of titles had been reduced by about a third through consolidation. He suggested that a net upward trend in the skill level of these individual jobs was at least partly an artifact of the grouping itself, in which the GED for the new consolidated title had to be as high as the highest of the old titles. He also speculated that employers may have expanded the scope of some of these jobs in response to the supply of better-educated workers. In any event, this painstaking analysis cannot address what was happening with the other 10,000 individual titles available in the 1966 dictionary, to say nothing of the compositional effects of the distribution of people in these jobs on the overall skill level of the workforce. Other and subsequent assessments using successive editions of these same occupational dictionaries have also found that there have been substantial changes in skill content in both directions within existing jobs. But the net effect is small (Horowitz and Herrnstadt 1966; Spenner 1983).

In contrast to Berg's analysis, my above analyses of GED changes from the 1970s to the present are based on sample surveys that rely on skill ratings of jobs conducted at an early point in this period. These survey results may reflect changes in skill levels related to changes in the distribution of occupations fairly well; but these estimates provide no reading of changes in the skill levels within existing jobs over this period. In this regard, it should also be noted here that Myles (1988, 350–51) supplementary survey analysis found that respondents' self-reports generated significantly more polarized estimates of required training times for the Canadian labour force in the early 1980s than SVP scores did. The safest conclusion is that there is substantially more upgrading *and* deskilling occurring within specific occupations than measures based on invariant GED and SVP scores capture, but no definitive evidence for a dominant upgrading trend within existing jobs.

But the gradual *overall* skill upgrading trend in technical skill requirements of jobs since 1960 suggested by the above tables is corroborated by the most extensive prior reviews of both compositional and within-job effects in other research based on U.S. population surveys and census dictionary job titles (Spenner 1983), as well as by other recent large-scale studies using different data and measures. Cappelli (1995) uses a measure of skill developed by Hay Associates, the world's largest compensation consulting firm, a composite measure which includes "know how" (capabilities, knowledge and techniques needed to do the job, ranked according to complexity); "problem solving" (how well defined and predictable job tasks are); and "accountability" (autonomy in decision making). He analyzes Hay's extensive records for U.S. jobs in manufacturing from 1978 to 1986, and in clerical work from 1978 and 1988. Taking account of both occupational composition and job content changes, he finds a discernible upskilling of most of the remaining production jobs within the declining manufacturing sector, while both upskilling and deskilling are evident within the expanding clerical sector. Howell and Wolff (1991) found similar trends for 1960–85 using census-based data and measures. Applying both conventional GED/SVP scores and other measures of cognitive complexity and routine activity to census data, Myles (1988, 342–345) found the reverse pattern for the Canadian labour force between 1961 and 1981; that is, he found no change in the skill composition of industrial workers' jobs but substantial upgrading of service workers' jobs. In all of these instances, the aggregate trend for the entire labour force was gradual skill upgrading.

Assessments of technical skill requirements should distinguish between *enlargement* of the number of technical tasks to be performed and *enrichment* of the level of technical knowledge needed for the job. Manufacturing jobs have generally become more complex in terms of the array of technical tasks to be performed in a given time. This has occurred through job amalgamation, multi-tasking, multi-crafting and speed-ups in the context of early retirements and lay-offs. But task intensification does not necessarily require higher knowledge. When work organizations downsize, restructure and computerize, the remaining workers are forced to learn a *wider* array of technical tasks rather than higher order, more complex or creative ones. As a skilled trades worker interviewed for our case study of workplace changes in the steel industry (Livingstone 1996, 50) recently observed:

> There's just less guys (sic) to do the job faster. There's also more responsibility because there's less senior guys to talk to when there's a problem.... We're running with seventy percent less men and we're still putting out the same amount of product here. So you tell me that's not efficiency! [The steel company] has become more trades-oriented with the trades doing more labour work too. Trades have really crossed over and are doing more labour work than the art of the trade, because they can get rid of a janitor and you can sweep your own floor.

The Report of the Commission on the Skills of the American Workforce (National Center on Education and the Economy 1990, 3) concluded that:

> 95 percent of American companies still cling to old forms of work organization. Because most American employers organize work in a way that does not require high skills, they report no shortage of people who have such skills and foresee no such shortage.... Most employers we interviewed do not expect their skill requirements to change. Despite the widespread presumption that advancing technology and the evolving service economy will create jobs demanding higher skills, only five percent of employers were concerned about a skills shortage.

The surplus of qualified workers that we have previously documented in Chapters Two and Three is probably an even larger factor in employers' lack of concern about a skills shortage than "old forms of work organization." In any case, there is little evidence of any general and persistent technical skill deficiency among employed workers (see National Center on the Educational Quality of the Workforce 1995) A recent OISE survey (Livingstone, Hart and Davie 1995) found that 95 percent of employees in Ontario consider themselves to be at least adequately qualified for their current jobs. Also, as Chapter Three has documented, underqualified employees are most likely to be involved in further learning activities to upgrade their technical skills and retain their jobs.

The most obvious recent change in the technical division of work has been the rapid, widespread introduction of computer-based technologies. For example, a Canada-wide longitudinal survey has found that the proportion of employees working directly with computer technologies increased from about 15 percent in 1985 to 37 percent in 1991 (Betcherman et al. 1994). A 1994 U.S. survey (National Center on the Educational Quality of the Workforce, 1995) found that over 40 percent of production and non-supervisory employees were using computers in their jobs. But this shift from material production to data processing does not necessarily translate into higher technical skill requirements for jobs. For most employees, more of the general control of the work process has tended to become computer-based rather than human-centered. A variety of sectoral studies of the effects of information technology and new production arrangements have found few gains in either most workers' need for higher order skills or opportunities to exercise discretionary control in task performance (Dawson and Webb 1989; Beirne and Ramsay 1992; Menzies 1996). Again, whatever skill increases may be involved appear to have been far exceeded by rapid increases in the computer literacy of the workforce (Lowe 1996; Livingstone 1997c).

Even in the most advanced "high tech" production firms, recent case studies have found that only low levels of basic skills are required for successful performance of assembly work. The much vaunted training and testing programs of Motorola Corporation have been found to be an expensive way to upgrade hourly employees who never use their new skills because they remain in traditional handwork jobs (Brown, Reich and Stern 1990). In California's Silicon Valley, a case study of four successful high tech companies found that there was no assembly work that actually required more than a solid eighth grade education (Weisman 1993).

Overall, the weight of available empirical evidence suggests that there has indeed been a net upgrading of the technical skill requirements of the North American job structure since the 1940s. But the most substantial gains occurred prior to 1960 and the slight upgrading that is discernible since then reveals the related upgrading claims of most post-industrial/knowledge economy theorists to be quite exaggerated.

Social Division of Labour

At least in the U.S. and Canada since the 1960s, it is evident that this gradual technical upgrading of jobs has been greatly exceeded by the rapid expansion of the educational qualifications of the workforce. Chapter Two provides ample documentation in terms of the performance gap. This condition appears to have provoked both increased disaffection with the inherent technical limitations of their jobs among workers, and heightened concern among corporate leaders and management consultants about enhancing worker commitment to the firm. As James O'Toole (1977, 38, 60), author of the *Work in America* report for the U.S. Secretary of Health, Education and Welfare in 1972 which offered one of the first documented accounts of this disaffection, later observed:

> No industrialized nation has been able to produce an adequate number of jobs that provide the status, and require the skills and educational levels, that their workforces are achieving.... [T]he situation is nearly Malthusian in its proportions: levels of educational attainment have tended to grow in almost geometric progression, while the number of jobs that require highly qualified persons has risen much more slowly.... What is clear from almost every study of job dissatisfaction is that the placing of intelligent and highly qualified workers in dull and unchallenging jobs is a prescription for pathology — for the worker, the employer, and the society.

The most obvious expressions of this disaffection were rebellions by young workers on highly automated assembly lines such as the Lordstown, Ohio, auto plant (Aronowitz 1973). There have been some widely publicised subsequent attempts to redesign the technical division of labour to give workers more integrated sets of tasks, as in Volvo's experiments with whole auto assembly teams at its now closed Uddevalla plant (Berggren 1992, 1994). But a far more frequent response has been to offer workers a more consultative role in decisions about the allocation, evaluation and modification of technical tasks without reversing the detailed technical division of labour. This is what is now commonly called the "high performance workplace." There are multitudes of alternative models available for enhancing worker participation in organizational decision-making, the defining feature being greater voice for workers in some of the firm's affairs. But in North America to date there has been much more advocacy than implementation of such consultative models.

In spite of much management hoopla about corporate cultures, learning organizations and teamwork, surveys of U.S. and Canadian business executives indicate that the vast majority of enterprises have made no major organizational changes in response to the increasing educational calibre of recent graduates (Harris 1991; Betcherman et al. 1994). The most extensive U.S. surveys of actual changes in workplace practices have found that only about a third of private sector firms have made substantial use of any of the most widely heralded innovative consultative practices (i.e. teams, job rotation, quality circles and Total Quality Management), and that such practices do not cluster together in any discernible "high performance" form (Osterman 1994; see also Lawler et al. 1992; Gephart 1995). The most recent national survey (National Center on the Educational Quality of the Workforce 1995, 3) concluded that:

> Despite the considerable attention given to new modes of work organization, the use of high-performance work systems among employees still remains the exception rather than the rule. Only one-quarter of establishments reported using any bench-marking programs to compare practices and performances with other organizations, and only 37 percent reported that they had adopted a formal Total Quality Management (TQM) program. Very few workers engage in practices that have become the hallmarks of high-performance work: only 12 percent of non-managerial workers participate in self-managed teams, and only 17 percent participate in job rotation.

There does appear to be a significant relationship between extensive adoption of any of these "flexible" work practices and the percentage of core employees who receive (company-identified) formal off-the-job training (Osterman 1994, 182–187). But, as we have seen in Chapter Two, such formal training is only the tip of the learning iceberg among workers. The massive extent of work-related learning now occurring on and off the job is historically unprecedented. The actual uses of much of this learning at work remains highly problematic even in the small number of high performance firms.

Whether the new participatory model is called TQM, ISO 9000+ or re-engineering, there has generally been little recombining of technical skills and much emphasis on workers sharing their existing production knowledge for more efficient production, ultimately leading to leaner production systems and less workers performing production tasks. From the vantage point of most North American workers, the vast majority of work organizations, including most high performance ones, actually continue to operate on principles of hierarchical control of technical design and planning knowledge as well as strategic investment and management decisions by small numbers of executives and experts. There is a strictly limited capacity to plan or design the technical division of labour by most subordinates just as in older mass production forms. As means to encourage greater allegiance and productivity, there may be flatter hierarchies, increasing incorporation of subordinate workers into consultation processes such as work teams and quality circles, and broader access to computer-based information systems in a minority of work organizations. But, while lower levels of management and supervisory positions may be eliminated in this process, the surveillance and constraint over most workers' worksite practices has often increased rather than decreased through the centrally controlled manner in which microelectronic technologies usually have been introduced (Parker and Slaughter 1994). Over half of all non-managerial employees now participate in regular meetings to discuss work-related problems (National Center on the Educational Quality of the Workforce 1995, 3). But another recent national survey of worker representation and participation finds that, although the majority of workers feel it is important for them to have a lot of influence on decisions about such matters as scheduling, compensation, training, safety, technology use and work goals, only about a quarter report that they have a lot of involvement; most of those who said they wanted more actual involvement also said they would be unlikely to get it (cited in Gephart, 1995, 43–44).

An estimate of trends in workers' perceptions of their extent of participation in workplace decision-making is provided by the OISE survey series which regularly asked Ontario employees about their extent of involvement in planning and supervisory roles in their jobs between 1980 and 1992. The findings are summarized in Table 4.5.

Managers, professionals, semi-professionals and supervisory employees have perceived little change in their degree of authority. The vast majority of managers have continued to see themselves in controlling roles while nearly all supervisors also identify themselves

Table 4.5   Self-Reported Design or Supervisory Role,
Employed Ontario Labour Force, 1980–1992*

Occupational Class	% reporting design or supervisory role						
	1980	*1982*	*1984*	*1986*	*1988*	*1990*	*1992*
Managers	86	94	88	88	84	89	86
Professional employees	69	74	67	65	74	73	76
Semi-prof. employees	55	56	51	50	60	58	59
Supervisors	89	90	91	93	93	93	91
Service workers	24	29	26	21	45	47	40
Industrial workers	12	19	21	20	31	37	36
Total Labour Force	41	46	43	42	52	56	53
N	477	449	480	494	485	489	416

* The survey question was: "What sort of authority role, if any, do you generally have within the main enterprise or organization in which you are now working?" The response options were: (1) follow established work procedures with constant or frequent supervision by superiors; (2) follow established work procedures with little supervision; (3) no supervisory role over others, but generally required to design major aspects of own work; (4) supervise work of other employees within a work unit; (5) executive control over a branch, division or plant; (6) general control of entire enterprise or organization.

Source: OISE Survey of Educational Issues Data Archive.

in terms of their control of subordinates. Smaller majorities of professional and semi-professional employees continue to consider their jobs in terms of combinations of a significant design role and supervisory leadership of other workers. The most notable changes have been in service and industrial workers' increasing sense of their involvement in design and supervisory roles. The proportions of workers who feel they are closely supervised by superiors have fallen by about half over this period, while those who feel they have a significant design or team leading role has roughly doubled. Sceptical researchers have rightly identified definite limits to the "responsible autonomy" of workers in relation to managerial prerogatives (Friedman 1977) and accurately characterized some worker participation schemes as sophisticated means to enhance management control, or "democratic Taylorism" (Adler 1993). Nevertheless, these workers' shifting perceptions are probably related to actual increases in consultative workplace practices and consequent incremental gains in popular support for notions of workplace democracy. While the technical skills of workers may continue to be significantly underutilized in their jobs, they are increasingly being consulted about the deployment of those technical skills that they are permitted to use.

Looking beyond the North American context, there are important differences among the advanced industrial economies in the predominant models of social organization of the workplace, particularly in terms of their recognition and effective integration of workers' skills and knowledge. One of the sharpest analyses of these differences is William Lazonick's (1991) comparison of the business organization structures and strategies that have prevailed in U.S. "managerial capitalism," in contrast to the previously dominant "proprietary capitalism" of the United Kingdom and the emergent "collective capitalism" of Japan. In simple terms, leading Japanese companies have managed to integrate shop floor operatives, as well as the line and staff specialists in the middle and the managerial generalists at the top of the enterprise, into consensual decision making processes. U.S. companies created "technostructures" of committed managers and specialists with secure career ladders and discretionary work roles, but have refused to seriously consider operative employees as members of the same family. The leaders of British firms have traditionally regarded themselves as exclusive guardians of the firm, while leaving formation of specialist standards to the lower echelons and control of work organization on the shop floor. As Lazonick (1991, 42–43) summarizes the consequences of these models for skill utilization in the workplace:

> Through the organizational commitments inherent in permanent employment, the skills and efforts of male blue-collar workers have been made integral to the organizational capabilities of their companies, thus enabling the Japanese to take the lead in innovative production systems such as just-in-time inventory control, statistical quality control, and flexible manufacturing. Critical to the functioning of these production systems is the willingness of Japanese managers to leave skills and initiative with workers on the shop floor. Indeed, the recent

success of Japanese mass producers in introducing flexible manufacturing systems owes much to the fact that, for decades before the introduction of the new automated technologies, blue-collar workers were granted considerable discretion to monitor and adjust the flow and quality of work on the shop floor. Japanese practice is in marked contrast to the U.S. managerial concern with using technology to take skills and the exercise of initiative *off* the shop floor, a practice which goes back to the late nineteenth century when the success of U.S. mass production was dependent on breaking the power of craft workers and transferring the sole right to plan and coordinate the flow of work ... nor did [Japanese employers] have to resign themselves simply to leaving skills on the shop floor in the hands of autonomous craftsmen, as was the case in Britain.

Lazonick probably exaggerates the extent of utilization of workers' skills in Japan through this more inclusive social division of labour. Certainly there is evidence of substantial underemployment there. "Lifetime" employment in the leading firms has relied heavily on temporary labour in a wide array of less secure statuses, particularly for women and in smaller firms. Permanent employment provisions are now declining as both official unemployment and use of temporary workers mount (Mullaby 1994; Odrich 1997). Moreover, the detailed technical division of labour has remained almost as fragmented and management-controlled as in the U.S. model, even if the divisions have been more flexible. But through an array of integrative institutional structures and strategies, leading Japanese firms were able to increase the social involvement of many workers' skills in job performance (Kamata, 1983, Kamazawa 1996).

Scandinavian and some other continental European countries, notably Germany with its co-determination model, have also developed institutional structures that have enabled more integrative participation by workers in the production and knowledge development decisions of their firms (Maurice et al. 1986). The stronger union movements in these countries have ensured more equitable sharing of the consequent productivity gains rather than ploughing them back into expanded production, so global market share increases have been less spectacular for European firms than in the Japanese case during the 1970s and 80s.

More generally, such comparative analyses suggest that the extent of skill utilization in the workplace is a function of the social bargains that have been struck and continue to be negotiated between employers and employees rather than any immutable trend. The success of this Japanese model in increasing productivity and the consequent "Japanese challenge" in established markets of American firms provoked increasing management receptivity to experiment with new forms of industrial relations in the U.S., just as the post WWII reconstruction and the "American challenge" did previously in Europe (Servan-Schrieber 1971). While the roots of managerial capitalism run deep in North America, even here shifts to new social divisions of labour that require increased worker input have been underway for some time at levels ranging from business organizational strategies to specific job redesign (Kochan and Useem 1992). But, as the U.S. surveys cited above indicate, such shifts to greater worker involvement in production decisions appear to have been very gradual and limited to date.

So what effects have these continuities and changes in the technical and social divisions of labour had on the occupational class structure?

The Changing Class Structure: More Experts, Fewer Workers?

The most explicit prediction made by post-industrial theorists like Bell is that the proportion of expert employees in the class structure is bound to increase rapidly while the proportion of manual workers declines. The first difficulty is determining which jobs count as experts; the second, what class designation to give them. For Bell (1973, 374) "the major class of the emerging new society is primarily a professional class, based on knowledge rather than property," with four different "estates" — the scientific, the technological (applied skills of medicine, economics and medicine), the administrative and the cultural (artistic and religious) — only loosely associated through their common defence of the idea of learning. Classical professionals such as doctors, lawyers and architects, modern professionals such as scientists and engineers, as well as managers with specialized knowledge in any of these areas are widely assumed to be members of this class. But what of the growing numbers of technologists and technicians in these areas? They acquire highly specialized knowledge but are often highly constrained in opportunities to apply it. In support of their central predictions, post-industrial theorists initially claimed these jobs, along with other white-collar service jobs, are part of a "new middle class" (Friedson 1973). Conversely, Marxist theorists typically claimed them to be the "new working class," technical workers

Table 4.6 Class Distribution, Employed U.S. Labour Force, 1960–1990

Class location	1960	1970	1980	1990
Employers	7.9	5.3	4.8	4.7
Petty bourgeoisie	5.5	4.1	4.5	5.1
Managers	7.5	7.6	8.0	8.3
Expert managers	3.9	4.4	5.1	6.0
Professional employees	3.5	4.5	5.5	6.9
Supervisors	13.7	14.9	15.2	14.8
Workers	58.1	59.2	57.0	54.1
Skilled workers	13.5	14.1	12.9	12.8

Source: Wright (1997, 99) based on respective censuses and imputations from a 1980 survey of class locations.

whose specialized knowledge is becoming increasingly strategic to automated production processes (Mallet 1975). Subsequent conceptual and empirical works from both perspectives have been more likely to recognize complexities and contradictions in the class identity of such jobs (Walker 1978; Abercrombie and Urry 1983; Sobel 1989; Carter 1989; Crompton 1993). For my purposes here, technologist/technician jobs will be designated as "semi-professionals," rather than arbitrarily conflating them with professionals or definite working class jobs.

Although occupation-based analyses and class analyses are quite closely related, there are important differences. In class analyses, those whose main livelihood comes from ownership of a business are distinguished from those who are hired employees. Someone who is a carpenter by trade might be hired as a skilled industrial wageworker; but another carpenter may own a construction company; yet another might be a foreperson mainly supervising several other carpenters. Similarly, an engineer could be an owner, a manager or a hired professional employee. Studies of job structures based simply on occupational designations may be helpful for identifying the general division of technical skills. But such studies often conflate employers with employees, and also underestimate the number of employees in some occupations who have important authority roles in the workplace (see Wright 1980). These distinctions are especially significant in relation to rates of increase in the proportions of professional experts in the workforce, given their very small proportions at the beginning of the post-WWII period.

Empirical studies that have attempted to distinguish between the social and technical divisions of labour, including the division between owners of enterprises and wage and salary employees, now provide relevant tests of both post-industrial and Marxist predictions about class trends. Erik Olin Wright, a leading neo-Marxist class theorist, has spearheaded a cross-national series of large-scale surveys to carefully estimate the current class structures of various countries. Based on his own 1980 survey and U.S. census data since 1960, Wright (1997, 91–113) has produced his own assessment of the relative efficacy of post-industrial and traditional Marxist theorists' predictions of trends in the distribution of classes. His basic findings for the 1960–90 period are summarized in Table 4.6.

Wright's main findings are consistent with the *direction* of post-industrial theory predictions. The proportion of professional employees is estimated to have almost doubled over this 30 year period, from 3.5 percent to nearly 7 percent of the employed labour force. Conversely, the proportion of workers is found to have declined since 1970, from 59 to 54 percent; the proportion of skilled workers also declined. Wright (1997, 108, 111) concludes that:

> The specific pattern of sectoral and class shifts for experts and expert managers is consistent with the expectations of those post-industrial theorists who emphasize the increasing importance of knowledge and information in post-industrial economies.... The results ... pose a real challenge to traditional Marxist expectations about the trajectory of development of the class structure of advanced capitalist societies in general and particularly about the process of proletarianization. Contrary to the traditional Marxist expectation, the working class in the United States has declined over the past three decades, and this decline appears, if anything, to be accelerating.... Unless these trends are a temporary detour, it thus appears that the class structure of capitalism continues to become increasingly complex rather than simplified around a single, polarized class antagonism.

Wright has made major contributions to our understanding of comparative class structures, both through his survey work and his conscientious efforts to adjudicate his own and other class theories with careful reference to empirical data. The main limitations of this particular trend adjudication effort are that it is based partly on imputations from a survey at a single point in 1980 and — like many others — it continues to conflate technical and social divisions of labour in identifying some employee class locations. In particular, respondents' self-reports in this survey about the degree of authority and autonomy they exercise in their jobs have been used as primary criteria to identify managers, supervisors and professional employees. This general practice has been seriously criticised even by some of Wright's collaborators (e.g. Clement and Myles 1994, 261–66) and the criticisms have provoked several revisions of his class schema. Nevertheless, Wright has continued to use versions of these self-reports to distinguish employees in contradictory class locations from the working class. However, as Table 4.5 illustrates for the Ontario case, there are increasingly significant numbers of employees in definitely working class jobs — as well as a majority of semi-professional employees — who perceive themselves to have meaningful design and supervisory roles. Their assertion of this view does not automatically convert them into either supervisors or professional experts.

The series of OISE surveys provide estimates of the Ontario class structure between 1980 and 1996 based on measures of ownership status and the technical and social division of labour, but which are not dependent on respondents' self-reports of their workplace authority as Wright's 1980-centered estimates are. The results are summarized in Table 4.7. The pattern is somewhat different than that found by Wright for the U.S. Employers have consistently made up around six or seven percent of the class structure in both cases, but the self-employed have continued to constitute at least twice as high a proportion of the workforce in Ontario. This reflects a greater persistence of small commodity production in agriculture and other crafts, and is consistent with the later industrialization of Canada than the U.S.[10] The smaller proportion of managers in Ontario is also consistent with the fuller development of the managerial capitalist model in the U.S., as documented by Lazonick (1991) and others;[11] the proportion of managers may have increased slightly during this period. The proportion of professional employees appears to have remained roughly constant throughout the period, while semi-professionals may have increased somewhat. The most notable change in Ontario seems to have been the rapid decline of supervisors from 12 percent to 4 percent, in contrast to apparent stability in Wright's U.S. estimates. This is, in fact, a trend predicted by post-industrial theorists as being in

Table 4.7   Class Distribution, Employed Ontario Labour Force, 1980–1996

Class Location	1980	1982	1984	1986	1988	1990	1992	1994	1996
Corporate capitalists	<1	<1	<1	<1	<1	<1	<1	<1	<1
Small employers	7	6	7	5	5	6	8	9	8
Petty bourgeoisie	13	13	10	10	9	12	11	13	14
Managers	5	6	7	6	7	9	7	7	8
Professional employees	8	7	8	11	9	8	11	8	7
Semi-prof. employees	8	8	10	10	9	10	10	11	12
Supervisors	12	11	8	8	8	6	5	4	4
Service workers	23	27	25	25	26	26	27	28	29
Industrial workers	24	21	25	24	27	22	23	20	17
N	604	558	570	587	577	609	518	686	634

Source: OISE Survey of Educational Issues Data Archive.

correspondence with the rise of professional experts who supervise themselves. But perhaps the most striking finding is that the working class has not discernibly decreased. Service worker jobs without supervisory titles and lacking specialized technical knowledge have definitely increased and industrial sector worker jobs have decreased; but both of these components of the working class together continue to comprise nearly half of the class structure. While sampling error cannot be discounted in making such inferences from the OISE surveys, other census-based Canadian analyses corroborate a gradual decline of supervisory employees over the 1961–86 period and a more substantial growth of semi-professional and managerial than professional employees, as well as the decline of industrial workers and an at least partially offsetting increase of service workers (Myles 1988, 343; Clement and Myles 1994, 82).

Leaving aside the larger Canadian petty bourgeoisie and smaller managerial class, the main differences between Wright's U.S. estimates and these Ontario estimates of changes in the class distribution revolve around different measures of the supervisory role. The proportion of employees with official occupational titles of supervisor or foreperson is declining in both Canada and the U.S.[12] Unless one is prepared to assume with Wright that the increasing consultation of workers can turn them into lower level members of the professional-managerial structure, the most reasonable conclusions from these findings are: (1) that definite working class jobs remain around half of the employed workforce in both countries; and (2) that professional jobs may be increasing slowly at the expense of supervisory employees.

Comparative trend analyses of changes in the occupational class distributions using other measures and including additional European countries and Japan (e.g. Esping-Andersen et al. 1993, 38–39; Steven 1983; Savage et. al. 1992) have found similar patterns: continuing working class majorities and expanding semi-professional and professional-managerial class groups, but no country where professional experts constitute as much as ten percent of the class structure. Whatever more sensitive and precise subsequent empirical readings determine in this regard, it is at least clear that working class jobs still occupy around half of the workforce in most advanced private market economies and that, at the current rates of increase of professional experts, they will remain a small minority of the class structure for the foreseeable future. It is also true that, contrary to predictions drawn from classical Marxist theory, there is no discernible current trend toward the proletarianization of the vast majority of the employed workforce into working class jobs (see Marshall 1997).

There have also been suggestions, based on workers' self-reported training requirements, that skill requirements are becoming more polarized within working class jobs themselves. Myles and Clements' 1982–83 Canadian Class Structure Survey (Myles 1988, 351–52) found that both blue-collar and white collar workers' self-reports of required training time for their jobs produced more polarized skill ratings than standard SVP scores; in particular, Myles found that much higher proportions of workers self-reported that their jobs took less than a month to learn than SVP scores indicate.

To assess this posited trend and also any other general trends in relations between class positions and skill requirements, we have analyzed GED scores by class position, as well as by skilled and other (i.e. semi-skilled and unskilled) industrial and service worker jobs, in the OISE surveys from 1980 to 1996. The results are summarized in Table 4.8.

Table 4.8   Class Position by Average GED Score,
             Employed Ontario Labour Force, 1980–1996

Class Location	*1980*	*1990*	*1996*
Corporate capitalists	5.5	4.9	5.3
Small employers	4.5	4.0	3.4
Petty bourgeoisie	4.0	3.8	3.6
Managers	4.7	4.9	4.9
Professional employees	5.1	4.9	5.2
Semi-prof. employees	4.6	4.5	4.6
Supervisor	4.1	4.2	4.4
Service workers	2.9	3.3	3.2
Skilled service	3.4	3.4	3.4
Other service	2.7	3.0	3.1
Industrial workers	2.7	2.8	2.5
Skilled industrial	3.1	3.3	3.3
Other industrial	2.5	2.2	2.1
Total Labour Force	3.7	3.8	3.9
N	595	566	572

Source: OISE Survey of Educational Issues Data Archive.

These findings, based once more on largely invariant GED ratings done in the 1970s, offer little support for any major skill upgrading in relation to the changing occupational class distribution of the entire Ontario labour force. In particular, compositional changes in managerial, professional and semi-professional class positions have generated no significant skill upgrading during this period. Of course, the GED scores probably provide conservative estimates of actual upgrading because of their very limited capability to read skill changes within specific occupations. With regard to the polarization thesis, the range of GED scores (as estimated by standard deviation measures) has remained quite constant within most class positions. An increasing gap between the mean scores of skilled workers and semi/unskilled workers in the *declining* industrial sector offers some support for skill polarization, but the skill difference appears to be closing between skilled and other workers in the *expanding* service sector. An extensive survey-based cluster analysis of 1973–90 current population distributions of employment and quality of jobs in the U.S. has also found little evidence of declining numbers or decreasing skill requirements in the lowest job clusters corresponding to the class positions of semi/unskilled service and industrial workers (Gittleman and Howell 1995). So, there is only limited evidence of skill polarization. However, there is much greater evidence of polarization of some other aspects of job quality, especially wage polarization which is addressed in the following section.

Overall, the changing class structure is probably associated with gradually increasing skill requirements for paid work in most advanced private market economies. Daniel Bell's professional class is increasing, but very slowly. Working class jobs with narrow technical task requirements and very limited social authority continue to constitute the numerically predominant class position.

The so-called "post-industrial era" does not appear to have produced the oft-claimed more interesting and fulfilling paid work for burgeoning numbers of professional experts and other knowledge workers. Certainly the proliferation of information technology has not produced the more pleasurable work for all that advocates like Bell had projected. As Krishan Kumar (1995, 154) concludes his own recent assessment of "post-industrialism":

There is no question of the significance of the new information technology in large areas of social and economic life. This does not amount to the establishment of a new principle of society, or the advent of some "third wave" of social evolution. In most areas, information technology has speeded up processes begun some time ago; it has aided the implementation of certain strategies of management in organizations; it has changed the nature of work for many workers; it has accelerated certain trends in leisure and consumption. But it has not produced a radical shift in the way industrial societies are organized, or in the direction in which they have been moving. The imperatives of profit, power and control seem as predominant now as they have ever been in the history of capitalist industrialism. The difference lies in the greater range and intensity of their applications made possible by the communications revolution; not in any change in the principles themselves.

These trends are much more modest than the visions of a knowledge-based economy initially expressed by post-industrial theorists in the early 1960s projected, and especially modest in comparison with the massive expansion of advanced schooling and adult education.

THE LIMITS OF HUMAN CAPITAL THEORY

The most influential explanation currently on offer to account specifically for education-job relations is *human capital theory*. The core thesis is that peoples' learning capacities are comparable to other natural resources involved in the capitalist production process; when the resource is effectively exploited the results are profitable both for the enterprise and for society as a whole. From its inception in the United States after World War II, human capital theory tended to equate workers' knowledge levels primarily with their levels of formal schooling, to rely on quantitative indices of amount of schooling in estimating individual economic returns to learning, and to infer that more schooling would lead to higher productivity and macroeconomic growth (e.g. Schultz 1963; Becker 1964). Throughout the post-1945 expansionary era, the simultaneous increase of school participation rates and earned incomes in advanced industrial market economies lent evident support to both the *individual and aggregate* dimensions of this perspective and encouraged the popular view that more schooling would inevitably lead to greater economic success.

The *individual* level relationship between educational attainment and income has remained strong in relative terms. Table 4.9 summarizes the strength and stability of this relationship in most of the G7 countries and Sweden, in terms of the greater earnings accruing to those with university degrees in comparison to those with high school diplomas. In all of these countries, university graduates have consistently earned significantly more than high school graduates. Individual investment in higher education has therefore continued to represent a reasonable economic choice as long as the individual economic costs of obtaining it (in terms of tuition fees and deferred income) were not prohibitive.

Table 4.9 Ratio of Earnings of University Graduates versus
High School Graduates, Employed Males,
Selected OECD Countries, 1970s to 1990s

Country	University/High School Earnings Ratio		
	Circa 1970	*Circa 1980*	*Circa 1990*
Canada	1.75	1.70	1.71
France	1.88	2.38	2.42
Germany	N/A	1.25	1 .27
Japan	1.31	1.25	1.28
Sweden	1.44	1.22	1.36
United Kingdom	1.52	1.32	1.53
United States	1.55	1.57	1.89

Source: OECD (1994c, Table 7.A.1).

However, simple earnings ratios do not tell the whole story. As Table 4.10 summarizes for the U.S. case, real wages in constant dollars are lower in the mid 1990s than they were in the early 1970s for all workers except those with advanced degrees. The wages of other college graduates have slowly climbed back to early 1970s levels but those of people without a college degree have continued to fall precipitously. The decline in wages for the non-college workforce may be attributable to many factors, including deunionization, a shift to low wage industries, a falling minimum wage, and import competition. But, as the data in the prior section indicate, this wage decline is unlikely to be related to the declining technical skill of the U.S. workforce. In any case, it is clear that the main cause of the growing wage gap between U.S. college graduates and less educated workers has been the decline of non-college workers' wages rather than any strong growth in the college wage (Mishel, Bernstein and Schmitt 1997, 170).

More generally, while school enrolment rates have continued to increase since the early 1970s, average incomes have stagnated, unemployment rates have fluctuated upwards and underemployment of highly schooled people has been recognized as a social problem. The applicability of human capital theory's *aggregate* or societal-level "returns to learning" claims has been thrown into doubt. The belief

Table 4.10 Change in Real Hourly Wage by Education,
U.S. Labour Force, 1973–1995

Year	<High school	High school	Some college	College	Advanced degree
Hourly wage			*(in 1995 dollars)*		
1973	$10.65	$12.17	$13.45	$17.66	$21.52
1979	10.59	11.86	12.92	16.55	20.34
1989	8.91	10.79	12.53	16.98	22.07
1995	8.16	10.46	11.64	17.26	22.81
Percent change					
1973–79	-0.6%	-2.6%	-3.9%	-6.3%	-5.5%
1979–89	-15.9	-9.0	-3.1	2.6	8.5
1989–95	-8.4	-3.0	-7.1	1.6	3.3
1979–95	-23.0	-11.8	-9.9	4.3	12.1

Source: Mishel, Bernstein and Schmitt (1997, Table 3.18).

that more education brings greater societal economic benefit has been a general article of faith in all post-industrial theories and cornerstone of human capital theories. As noted above, the end of the post-WWII expansionary era in the early 1970s brought serious challenge to this belief. As Table 4.11 summarizes, real increases in average wages and benefits for the U.S. labour force as a whole virtually ceased during the 1970s while the average education and skill levels of the workforce continued to increase. Contrary to the precepts of human capital theory, collective investment in education has grown significantly while compensation growth has stagnated.

During the same period, 1973 to 1995, the real U.S. Gross Domestic Product rose by nearly 40 percent, while real hourly wages of non-supervisory workers declined by about 15 percent; during the 1980s, virtually all of the earnings gains went to the top 20 percent of the workforce, two-thirds accruing to the top one percent of earners (Thurow 1996). Similar trends have been found in Canada (Morisette 1995). By the mid-1990s, the typical U.S. chief executive officer was making well over 100 times as much as the typical factory worker.

Table 4.11 Hourly Compensation, Education and Skill Levels, U.S. Nonfarm Business Sector, 1948–1994

Year	Real Hourly Compensation (1992=100)	Average Years of Schooling	BLS Labour Skill Index* (1987=100)
1948	n/a	9.8	91.0
1959	61.5	10.5	94.7
1973	88.1	12.0	96.4
1979	95.4	12.5	96.5
1989	97.7	13.1	101.2
1994	98.4	13.4	105.0
Annual Growth			
1948–73	n/a	.8%	.2%
1959–73	2.6%	1.0	.1
1973–79	1.3	.7	.0
1979–89	.2	.5	.5
1989–94	.1	.5	.7

*The Bureau of Labour Skill Index is a broad measure of labour skill which reflects changes in the amount and economic value of experience and educational levels.

Source: Mishel, Bernstein and Schmitt (1997, Table B, 25).

This huge wage gap, far larger than in any other advanced industrial economy, had more than doubled since the 1970s (Sklar 1995, 11).[13] But aside from the extraordinary gains of executives, the rising wage differential between college educated and non-college educated employees during the 1980s and 90s in the U.S has been more the result of declining wages for the many than of increasing salaries for the few.

In this context of stagnant wages and continuing general increases in the education and skill levels of the overall workforce, the association between income and conventional measures of skill such as GED and SVP has been modest and declining. As Gittleman and Howell (1995, 423–27) document for the U.S. case in their 1973–90 analysis of six job quality "contours," the majority of "subordinate primary" contour blue collar workers who are unionized have been able to protect their wage levels far better than white collar service workers who have higher cognitive skill requirements in their jobs but who are rarely unionized; the poor, non-union "secondary" service and blue collar jobs that remained around 40 percent of U.S. jobs during the 1980s, and which employed very high proportions of blacks and Hispanics, saw *wage levels and most other aspects of job quality decline while occupants' education levels increased.* Earlier comparative analyses of skill and wage trends during the 1960–85 period found that low skill, high wage jobs were declining in the goods industries while service jobs with low wages but at least moderate skill levels were increasing (Howell and Wolff 1991). The growing weight of empirical evidence makes it clear that, rather than a "skill deficit," most working Americans are now experiencing a "wage deficit" (Sklar 1995, 28; Mishel and Teixeira 1991). The most highly educated work force in the world now works longer for less than do less educated but more unionized workers in other major industrialized countries (OECD 1994d, 22–23).

Human capital theory clearly needs to be retooled. There have been at least three sorts of retooling efforts which focus, respectively, on stressing the relative individual benefits of schooling, enhancing the quality of schooling, and emphasizing the benefits of lifelong learning.

Adherents to the original human capital thesis have attempted to defend it against critiques that it has failed to take account of changing aggregate-level conditions, by focusing quite narrowly on documenting continuing *relative* economic benefits, especially the lower unemployment rates and relatively high earnings of those with higher formal credentials. The declining collective economic rewards for educational investment tends to be regarded as a continuation of only partial compensation through individual incomes and more intangible spin-off benefits for the general enrichment of civil society; so nations that have invested more in schooling are still considered ahead in global competition (Becker 1993, 1996). Recent sociological perspectives, such as Ulrich Beck's (1992) individualization theorem, that stress the disintegration of class commonalities and the rise of competition as the main mode of human interaction, offer some theoretical support for closer attention to individual training and job choices (see Timmerman 1995). But the narrowing of the empirical target to relative individual benefits simply ignores the biggest challenge to human capital theory, the evident societal underemployment of credentialed knowledge.

Secondly, some human capital advocates have suggested that declining or unimproving quality of schooling is now the central problem, and that by raising standards, starting earlier or providing more privatized or specialized forms, both human capital creation and economic growth can be rejuvenated (Beckman and Klenow 1997). Nobody would argue against continuing to try to improve the quality of educational services; but many would disagree that educational quality has in fact declined. Some human capital analysts offer more nuanced relative arguments for school reforms to enhance national productivity and economic competitiveness based on comparative studies of superior student performance in other countries, such as U.S. comparisons with Japan, Taiwan and China (Stevenson and Stigler 1992). But the general assumption is that the post-industrial/ knowledge economy requires a leap in workers' skills and the schools must perform to higher standards to close the gap (e.g. Business Week 1988, 104). The focus is usually on the skills purportedly needed by "high performance" firms, and numerous innovative school reforms have been suggested to make the schools more responsive to these needs and thereby close the gap (e.g. Berryman and Bailey 1992; Marshall and Tucker 1992; Resnick and Wirt 1996).

The claim that declining school quality is serving to depreciate human capital is typically made in terms of young people's falling performance levels on standardized tests. Such historical comparisons are often fraught with fallacy of composition errors of logic. That is, either average scores of entire current youth cohorts are compared with those of more restricted earlier enrolments, or specific bits of knowledge are used to argue an increasing general ignorance thesis. While most of these claims have now been systematically refuted (see especially Sandia Laboratories 1993; Berliner and Biddle 1995, 1996; Mishel et al. 1997, 182–84), they continue to be recycled in evermore selective forms. Of course, the curricula and pedagogies of current educational systems will change, and we can and should continue to try to improve them; raising standards, starting earlier and more relevant curriculum all remain worthy objectives. But rather than bemoaning decline from an idealized past, or becoming fixated on international league tables of current math scores, we should celebrate the fact that much larger and increasing proportions of today's young people are mastering much larger and increasing bodies of school knowledge (see Bracey, 1997). As noted in Chapter One, the recent purported crisis in adult illiteracy has also found little empirical basis. In sum, the evidence does not show any cumulative general decline in the quality of education. What it does show is that people of all ages in advanced industrial market economies are increasingly using their learning capacities more effectively through the institutions of organized education to gain greater amounts of knowledge. If the aggregate quality of schooling has not been shown to decline inter-generationally, this is a significant achievement in light of the massive increases in the proportion of the population participating and particularly the increasing proportions of non-English speaking entrants into the school system. Blaming the quality of the educational system for the breakdown of the aggregate learning-earning connection is like blaming the producer of any form of labour for employers' failure to utilize it. Do we blame the chef for the patron's failure to finish a well-cooked meal?

Thirdly, some popular revisionist approaches to human capital theory no longer focus on schooling but on "human capital externalities," such as lifelong job-related learning among workers (Lucas 1988; Romer 1994). The dynamic centre of human capital creation is now seen to reside either in highly concentrated urban zones where "symbolic analysts" live, work and continually solve, identify and broker production problems (Reich 1991), or in "learning organizations" which create intellectual capital by facilitating collaborative problem solving within their workforces (Senge 1990; Nyhan 1991). The central empirical claim of human capital theory — that greater learning efforts are closely related to higher earning level — is resuscitated by downplaying schooling and emphasizing that effective employees must become continual adult learners in an increasingly globally competitive enterprise environment (OECD 1996d).

The "learning organization" arguments of human capital revisionists like Reich and Senge, although largely rhetorical to date, begin to draw greater attention to aspects of learning previously ignored or taken for granted by human capital theory's earlier fixation on schooling and credentialed knowledge, namely the informal work-related learning of workers and their cumulative bodies of tacit knowledge. In some sense, we all know that substantial informal learning is essential to master a new job. Most employers rely heavily on informal on-the-job training. However, the ethnographic studies and more extensive surveys of work-related learning referred to in Chapter One seriously undermine learning organization revisions of human capital theory, by exposing the lack of sustained relations between continued learning and earning for most workers.

As Chapter One documented, corporate executives, professional employees and service and industrial workers all now spend about the same amount of time in work-related informal learning. Human capital theory assumes that those who are more highly compensated are exercising greater learning capacities. But these results suggest that, at least in terms of informal learning time, the most poorly paid employees are devoting just as much effort to work-related learning in general as the most highly paid employers. The striking occupational class differences in the extent to which people get to use this acquired knowledge in their actual jobs were also noted in Chapter One, especially in terms of the discrepancy between the *general work-related* informal learning and *job-specific* unpaid learning of service and industrial workers. The fact is that large and growing numbers of people do substantial amounts of work-related informal learning throughout their working lives. But many either do not have the opportunity to apply this acquired knowledge in their paid workplaces or, if they can apply it informally, to be recognized and rewarded for doing so. The promoters of learning organizations have got it backwards. The challenge is not to facilitate more collaborative learning but to establish fair incentive structures, especially among service and industrial workers, to use and compensate the extensive amount of informal learning that is already occurring.

Growing proportions of people who have invested many years of their lives in acquiring advanced formal educational qualifications are unable to obtain commensurate jobs, as I have previously documented most clearly in terms of the performance gap. The growing proportions of underemployed youths generally continue to try to realize their extensive educational investments in the job market, and even continue to make more such investments. The prospect of losing these investments through not being able to use them in the job market is again increasing (Krahn 1997). But, more generally, most people find diminishing credibility in human capital advocates' arguments that those with the most formal education are still likely to get good jobs, when they see so few of these to go around.

All of these efforts to repair human capital theory remain in jeopardy because of their failure to account for the growing general gap between peoples' increasing learning efforts and knowledge bases on the one hand, and the diminishing numbers of commensurate jobs to apply their increasing knowledge investments on the other. The evidence presented in prior chapters on the massive extent of both people's learning activities and their underemployment represents a major contradiction for human capital theory. Appeals to an immanent knowledge economy have limited credibility for those living in the education-jobs gap. The "learning for earning" thesis is increasingly reduced to a strategy for relative individual advantage and decreasing marginal returns. Human capital theory appears to have reached its limit as a rationale for increased social investment in education.

CONCLUDING REMARKS

The image of contemporary society inherent in post-industrial/ knowledge economy and human capital theories proves illusory. While an aggregate upgrading of the technical skills needed for job performance is gradually occurring, our collective acquisition of work-related knowledge and credentials is far outpacing this incremental shift. Such underemployment is scarcely recognized in post-industrial and human capital theories, beyond the "frictional adjustment" that is regarded as natural in market economies. What the cumulative findings of increasing technical skill levels, changing cross-national patterns of social divisions of labour and general class distributions point out is that the relations between knowledge and work are not explicable through simple evolutionary growth models.

The organizational structures of the workplace and the strategies used by employers and employees vary quite widely across current industrial market economies. The Japanese model of "collective capitalism" appears to have been relatively effective in utilizing the working knowledge of operative level workers in lifetime contract conditions within leading firms. This leading edge case clearly illustrates that there is nothing inevitable about development of the technical and social divisions of labour. The employment contract can be modified in various ways to include or exclude the knowledge and skills of the non-owning classes. The North American model of "managerial capitalism" is generally regarded as being much more exclusionary of the knowledge and skills of operative workers. While such models may well be gross simplifications of actual conditions, the high levels of performance underemployment documented here among the North American labour force are consistent with this model.

It is becoming increasingly apparent that the connections between knowledge and work are mediated by the individual and collective negotiating powers of those in different class, gender, race and generational groups. For example, the proportion of the U.S. labour force that is unionized has dropped from a peak of over 35 percent in 1945 to less than 15 percent overall and even lower in the private sector by the mid-1990s; the sharpest drop has been since the mid-1970s, demarcated by President Reagan's wholesale firing of striking air controllers in 1981 (Sklar 1995, 30–32). While productivity and profits have recovered to post-WWII highs in the 1990s, the wages of a politically weakened work force have continued to stagnate. The "downsizing of America" in terms of good jobs and future expectations has reached deeply into the previously secure middle classes (New York Times 1996; Ehrenreich 1989; Rubin 1994). The depth of citizen resentment of these conditions is provoking elected politicians to speak out. In the words of David Bonior, U.S. Congress minority whip prior to the 1996 federal election:

> There's something wrong when the stock market reaches record highs driven by corporate profits that are up 14 percent, while the amount corporations are spending on wages and benefits is falling.... If we can't speak out against the growing chasm between the rich and the rest of America for fear that somebody will accuse us of waging class warfare, then we really are lost in the wilderness. (Quoted in Handelman 1996, B3)

The desperate and ultimately successful mid-1997 nationwide walkout of United Parcel Service's workforce of frequently well-educated, largely part-time and poorly paid drivers, loaders and sorters may represent another benchmark in U.S. negotiations over job quality (Herbert 1997). At least some corporate leaders in North America are now willing to speak publicly about the depth of the economic benefits problem. As Courtney Pratt (1997, 3), President of Noranda Metals, declared recently:

> If the business community doesn't come together to define its social responsibility and then to act on that definition, I fear we will not achieve that better society.... We are increasingly becoming a society of haves and have-nots ... and in our streets the plight of the extreme have-nots is increasingly visible to us all ... [and] profoundly disturbing.... [W]e risk being pulled apart — polarized — at a time

when we should be recommitting to each other.

All this is a far cry from the optimistic post-industrial projections of the 1960s, as well as those of many current knowledge economy and human capital theorists. Conflicts of interest between haves and have-nots need to be recognized as a starting point for understanding changes and continuities in the education-jobs gap.

5

Explaining the Gap:
Conflicts Over Knowledge and Work

For the workforce itself, mass literacy was an ambiguous project. No section of the labouring population was wholly illiterate and the skills of literacy and many of the structures of thought educators associated with them had long been used in a variety of employments.... At every point the issue of the existence of rules, who defined and enforced them, and whether they were recorded and transmitted orally or in writing, raised questions of authority and independence.

—Vincent 1989, 105

The future of work in the United States will depend on the relative power and strategic initiatives of corporations, workers, and other groups with influence over the organization of production.

—Gordon, Edwards and Reich 1982, 227.

The company wants us to be subservient, different from salaried workers. The company wants to see us differently. But we're not, we all have our talents and individual priorities.... If I was laid off, there are skills I could fall back on. I've taken some courses and I have my own computer, for example. But it's difficult now because there just aren't many jobs out there.

—Hamilton steelworker, quoted in Livingstone 1996c, 56

INTRODUCTION

Why do they do it? Why do so many people in the face of not being able to use so much of their current skill and knowledge in past or present jobs, persist in seeking even more skill and knowledge, spending unprecedented and still increasing amounts of time and effort in formal schooling, further education courses and informal work-related learning activities? As Chapter Four documents, the answer does not lie in simplistic notions of a technologically driven knowledge-based economy or pervasive upgrading of work requirements; these notions do not accord with workplace realities. Nor is it merely a matter of people investing in all the credentials and skills they can to compete individually on open labour markets for diminishing numbers or proportions of good jobs. There are elements of descriptive accuracy in these notions, but taken as generalizations they become highly misleading, both as statements of fact and in their implication that the present education-jobs gap is inevitable in the future. A more adequate answer lies in understanding the basic social relationships that drive capitalist production systems and related learning practices. These relations are complex, contradictory and dynamic, in contrast to the simple, linear and immutable notions of more schooling for more skilled work and more earnings that underlie much of the present popular and scholarly thinking on the issue of education-work relations.

I will suggest that conflict theories generally offer better insights into both workplace change and differences in people's development and uses of workplace-related knowledge and skill. After critically reviewing contemporary Marxist and Weberian theories of education-work relations, most notably Bowles and Gintis' (1976) correspondence thesis, as well as Carnoy and Levin's (1985) contradictory demands thesis and Randall Collins' (1979) credential society thesis, I will draw on some of these perspectives to propose a more specific conflict theory of the education-jobs gap. This theory focuses primarily on class-based conflicts among employers, professional-managerial salaried employees, wageworkers and the unemployed over knowledge and work requirements in advanced capitalist societies.

CONFLICT THEORIES OF KNOWLEDGE AND WORK

Robert Nisbet's (1970) classic account of theories of social change gave short shrift to another general type of change theory not entirely contained within the "progress or death" mode of thought, namely intergroup conflict theories which recognize the existence of long-term opposing group interests within societies (and global social systems) as forces determining the extent of continuity and change. Certainly the classical conflict theories of the past two centuries have generally regarded group conflicts as a vehicle of evolutionary progress. For example, Karl Marx viewed class struggle as leading irrevocably from capitalism to communism, while Max Weber regarded class, status and party conflicts in the context of unavoidable rationalization/ bureaucratization of society. But the primary focus of such theories has been on identifying different group interests and using them to explain continuity and change in social structures and processes, rather than relying on simpler metaphors of organic growth or decline.

While there have been many types of conflict theories proposed to explain social change in industrial societies (see Connell 1996; Boudon 1997), those that have been most fully developed to account for education-work relations have probably been founded on Marxist or Weberian perspectives, sometimes both.[1] Certainly most subsequent studies of conflicting interests among social groups in the sphere of work rely heavily on enduring insights of Marx and Weber. A brief resume of their respective approaches to conflicting group interests follows.[2]

At the most general level of analysis of the capitalist economy or mode of production, Marx recognized two fundamental groups: wage labourers or proletarians, who do not own any means of production and are compelled to hire out to capitalist enterprise in order to obtain wages for their subsistence; and capitalists or bourgeoisie, who own business enterprises and are obliged to hire wage labourers and organize their co-operative labour process so that the goods and services produced can be sold for sufficient profit to stay in business and expand. Marx saw the exploitative extraction of unpaid labour time from workers in this relationship as the central conflict in capitalism.[3] He also recognized the continuing existence of a third distinct class, the self-employed or petty bourgeoisie, who own their own means of production and work on their own account without employing paid labour. His own case studies, particularly of France in the 1848–51 period, identified other middle and "lumpen" classes. Since Marx died in the 1880s, we have seen the rise of the joint stock company, extended authority hierarchies within enterprises and growing proportions of hired workers employed in public service and distribution of commodities rather than producing them; many neo-Marxist analysts have identified further divisions of labour among middle class employees, most notably managers and professionals.

For Weber, who developed his group distinctions early in the twentieth century partly in critique of Marx, the central animating aspect of social life was not exploitation but the pursuit of power or domination over others. He understood economic power in modern capitalism as the capacity to control and benefit from exchange of goods and services within an increasingly rationally calculated and routinely administered work organization. Economic classes were basically common situations within market exchange relations rather than relations of production. But, like Marx, his basic categories of all class situations were founded in the possession or absence of property. He distinguished four main social class groupings or market positions. These were: large property owners or capitalists, who own sufficient property to have disposition over the products of other people's labour; small property owners or petty bourgeoisie, who only own enough property to dispose of the products of their own labour; propertyless white-collar workers, who tend to have specialized marketable skills; and the manual working class, who tend to have only their general labouring capacity to sell. As Weber himself had anticipated (Weber 1968 [1928], 937), status and life style distinctions prevailed over "naked class situation" in the stable economic times after 1945, and neo-Weberians ignored his property-based class distinctions in developing an array of status-based occupational scales. In the present, more uncertain period, some neo-Weberian reconceptualizations of group conflicts have reclaimed these property distinctions (e.g. Murphy 1988).

The current convergence of neo-Marxist and neo-Weberian class distinctions is evident in the class structure models proposed by prominent social theorists who claim affinity with either or both of these figures (e.g Wright 1985, 1997; Bourdieu 1984). For my immediate purposes, the most important point is that there is support from both perspectives to recognize both ownership of property and social and technical divisions of labour as relevant criteria in making class distinctions. The commonly made distinctions in class analyses of advanced industrial market societies now include most of the following: large and small employers; the self-employed; managers and professional employees; supervisors; skilled/unskilled white collar service workers and blue collar manual workers (see Livingstone and Mangan 1996). I will subsequently argue that such class distinctions are intimately related to different degrees of correspondence between education and work.

The most concerted prior effort to theorize the education-jobs gap may be found in the work of Randall Collins (1979) on the "credential society." He begins with a rejection of the technocratic belief, central to post-industrial theories, that technological change requires constant skill upgrading of growing proportions of jobs and a responsive expansion of formal education. From an explicitly neo-Weberian perspective, Collins develops a status group competition theory which argues that educational credentials are formal cultural currencies that are less closely related to technical skills than to people's relative capacity to control access to occupational power. His basic explanation of the relations between education and occupational status is as follows:

> People are actively concerned with the process of gaining and controlling occupational power and income, not merely (or even primarily) with using skills to maximize production.... The workers with the greatest skills are not the best paid.... That is to say, there is not only productive labour, but there is also political labour.... Political labour is above all a matter of forming social alliances within and sometimes across organizations, and of influencing others' views of the realities of work.... The overall structure of the modern occupational world may be conceived as a range of variations in the possession of "political" resources for controlling the conditions of work and appropriating the fruits of production; hence it can be seen as a range of mixtures of productive work with political work.... Social classes may be distinguished by the amount of property they possess, but ... it is how "positions" are shaped that constitutes the most immediate form of property in the labour market, and it is by the shaping of such positions that income is distributed.... It is property in positions that is crucial in determining most of class organization and class struggle in everyday life. For material and financial property (if we except home ownership) is concentrated within a quite small group, but property in positions shapes class relations throughout the population.... Technological change, within this context ... does not raise the skill requirements of most jobs very much; the great majority of all jobs can be learned through practice by almost any literate person.... How hard people work, and with what dexterity and cleverness, depends on how much other people can require them to do and on how much they can dominate other people.... Schools have been especially important for forming new group structures, ranging from the creation of the gentry class of traditional China to the formation of specialized occupational enclaves in contemporary America. (Collins 1979, 49–50, 53–54, 61).

The major consequence of this status competition is credential inflation. That is, increasing numbers of occupational groups use credentials provided by the formal educational system, credentials which are often far beyond the production requirements of their work, to construct and maintain positions for themselves in the labour market. The empirical analysis focusses on four of the biggest and most important professions in modern society: medicine, law, engineering and teaching, and their comparative success in shaping educational programs to ensure the distinctive cultures and self-conscious organization of their occupational communities. Collins (1979, 181) ends up positing a kind of credential plutocracy in which the most mobilized occupational communities bargain among themselves for ever greater self-regulatory powers, so that "the ongoing process of reform in America, as different private groups enter the bargaining, only serves to make private property interests ever more strongly entrenched."

In typical Weberian fashion, Collins (1979, 72, 203–4) expects increasing fragmentation into more closed occupational castes in the foreseeable future. He has been criticised for attributing an exaggerated power to credentialed groups while cynically reducing the substance of credentialed knowledge, and also largely ignoring noncredentialist bases of power and stratification (Morrow and Torres 1995, 201–204). Others have supplemented Collins' historical analysis of the expansion of the U.S. higher education system by documenting the role of business interests (particularly land speculators) in the decentralized launching of the college system, while refuting his view that multi-ethnic conflict was the driving force of this expansion (Brown 1995). Whatever the limitations, Collins' work remains the most systematic attempt to explain what I have called in prior chapters the performance gap, the discrepancy between people's actual knowledge and the technical or production requirements of their current jobs.

Ironically, however, his emphasis on the position-shaping powers of occupational groups discourages any specific attention to the credential gap per se, the discrepancy between the education acquired by job entrants and required by employers. Indeed, the thrust of Collins' theory is to suggest ever tighter links between occupational communities and required credentials, even as the performance gap between actual and required technical knowledge continues to inflate. He does recognize that in the 1960s "the credential system went into a state of explicit crisis" (Collins 1979, 191), as credentials no longer guaranteed jobs. The only way he can begin to account for this tendency is to appeal beyond the dynamics of the credential system to its "interaction with the struggle for economic position and with the level of economic productivity" (194).[4] But he does little more than allude to the continuing problems of unemployment and underemployment, and the rough and crisis-prone balance between the absorption of surplus labour and the breeding of student disillusion by the educational system, otherwise called "the credential system of occupational placement" (195). To explain most fundamental aspects of underemployment requires recourse to theories that give greater continuing importance to conflicts between employers and current and prospective employees over conditions of work, without denying the power of specialized occupational communities to shape access to and requirements for their own positions in the class structure of work. As I shall discuss below, Weberian theories of occupational status competition need to be complemented by Marxist theories of class struggle.

The general theoretical perspective I propose as useful for explaining the continuity and changes that we are currently experiencing in the employment and learning practices of advanced industrial market societies incorporates some elements of Collins' credential society thesis. But it draws more centrally on the historical materialist or Marxist tradition, shorn of many of its Victorian era presumptions, including: the dogmatic notion of *linear progress toward the communist millennium*, a *Eurocentric* world view which has regarded European civilization as the dynamic core of global life, a persistent anthropomorphist bias particularly in taking human mastery over the physical environment for granted and dismissing the social impact of destructive forces that do not issue directly from creative human action, a *technological determinism* that assumed the inevitability of an increasingly detailed technical division of labour, and a *male chauvinist* bias particularly in the failure to appreciate either the value of household and child-rearing labour or the connection between property relations and the patriarchal dominance of men over women.

The orthodox Marxist tendency to regard all social struggles as either centred in or derived from class relations of production is now obviously inadequate as well. The social movements of oppressed people that have swept the globe during the post-WWII era, including movements for national self-determination, the civil rights of visible minorities, the liberation of women and mobilizations of youths and the elderly for their social rights, as well as the only periodic re-emergence of workers' struggles into the public sphere, provide ample evidence of this fact. The collective identities widely embraced in the late twentieth century — of nation, race and ethnicity, gender and generation, as well as class — have their distinct histories (see Hobsbawm 1994; Mann 1995; Marable 1985; Miles 1996). Each should be studied in its particularity, and increasingly in their interaction (see Hartsock 1983; Sacks 1989; Mohanty 1997).

Most pertinently for the purposes of this book, forms of knowledge and types of skills that are grounded in the subordinated group experiences other than class-based ones, particularly those of race, gender, generation and disability, may be systemically discounted in many negotiations between employers and workers over the value of labour. This devaluing is a consequence of the very limited power representatives of such groups have had to define any of the terms of reference in both the recognition of authentic forms of knowledge and owner-employee relations. For example, it is now well documented that women's ways of knowing as well as major women creators of knowledge have been largely ignored through most of history (Spender 1980), while many of the technical skills most commonly associated with women's work in either paid employment or the household have typically been devalued or invisible in conventional thinking about the concept of skill (Steinberg 1989; Gaskell 1992). As we have seen in Chapter Two, even more debilitating claims about the learning capacities and skill competencies of blacks and other racial minorities have continued to be widely asserted and assumed on the basis of various imputed cultural or genetic inferiorities (Herrnstein and Murray 1994). These false assumptions have had devastating effects on job prospects for racial minorities (Henry and Ginzberg 1985).

Race, gender and age differences in underemployment will be identified in the following analysis wherever these are visible using conventional sources of empirical evidence.[5] However, it follows from the above discussion that many forms of educational and employment discrimination on these grounds are unlikely to be visible in such data bases. Further theoretical development and empirical study are needed to comprehend the depths of conflict over knowledge and work in terms of gender, race, generation and disability-based power relations.

But the recognition of the importance of these multiple oppressions in education-job relations does not provide sufficient warrant to ignore class-based struggles. The primary focus here will be on class-based struggles, precisely because so much recent discussion of education-job relations has discounted or ignored these conflicts which are readily verifiable using conventional sources of evidence.

Any theory is only as good as its empirical accuracy. If historical materialism or any other theory cannot explain empirical reality, it should be discarded. But historical materialism has been discarded prematurely by most North American scholars. The reasons are complex, including most obviously the legacy of the anti-Communist campaign that began in the 1940s. But class-based struggles continue to emerge and we have yet to find a better theory to explain them, so variants of Marxist social theory also continue to reemerge. Sympathetic critics have begun to correct each of the above defects of Marxist social theory and many of these corrections are helpful to the explanation and proposals presented in this book.[6]

Suitably revised Marxist social theory, as other inter-group struggle theories, draws attention to the relations between people themselves as historical actors constructing, reproducing and changing social structures such as economic and educational systems, rather than relying on more abstract metaphors of organic growth, or social closure, for its explanatory power. Most importantly, there is an enduring kernel of truth in Marx's insights into capitalist production dynamics[7] that remains pivotal to understanding learning-work relations, and particularly underemployment, in contemporary market-based societies.

CAPITALIST PRODUCTION DYNAMICS

There are at least three distinguishing assumptions of historical materialist social inquiry.[8] The first assumption is the view that the relationships between the owners of the means of production and the actual producers of goods and services provide *a* primary basis for the continuous construction of historical societies. The second is that in capitalist societies, characterized by the exploitation of hired labour, it is among those dependent on selling their labour power that the primary historical agency for changing the economy or mode of production may be found. The third assumption is that the analysis of these production relations can have strategic political relevance for human emancipation. In simpler terms, production relations are crucial, the "working class" is the main economic change agent, and inquiry is committed to aiding workers' liberation and pursuit of social justice. These are assumptions that, I would argue, can be retained — as long as they are grounded in a contemporary understanding of class relations, and recognition of gender, race/ethnic and generational differences as having their own irreducible forms as well as intimate linkages with class relations.[9]

The historical materialist perspective originated in early nineteenth century Europe when capitalist enterprises based on hired labour were becoming prevalent and working class movements made their first sustained appearance. Theoretical development in the materialist method of critical inquiry continually entails observation and analysis of concrete historical phenomena.[10] It is now well documented that Marx's own continuing application of this method led to substantial modification of fundamental concepts, such as surplus value (Rosdolsky 1977), and of more specific analytic distinctions, such as class differences (Hayes 1993). There is no good reason that such modifications should have ceased with his death. Later conflict theorists, notably Max Weber, have used critiques of Marxist theory and the flowering of historical scholarship to build superior accounts of both the preconditions for the emergence of capitalism and the full set of institutional forms that have ensured its reproduction (see Collins 1980).

But some of Marx's general theoretical points of arrival continue to constitute relevant points of departure for contemporary empirical analyses of capitalist societies in general, and of change and continuity within work and knowledge relations in particular. As Marx saw it, the capitalist mode of production involved three essentially contradictory relationships.[11]

1. Inter-firm competition: private firms must sell their commodities in marketplaces against those of other firms and so must limit their operating costs and expand their markets. Market competition means that losing firms go bust or are taken over while winners expand their market share in a continual process of destructive regeneration. But surviving firms are also compelled to try to avoid unrestrained competitive pressure and sustain capital accumulation through limited co-operation (e.g. information sharing, price leadership, support of government regulation) in a "dance of scorpions."
2. The class struggle between capital and labour: capitalist own-

ers of the means of production attempt to take over more and more of the potential means of producing vendible commodities and to claim more unpaid labour time (surplus value) from workers in the form of profits; workers try to keep for their own consumption and security as much as possible of this value via wage bargains and by limiting and controlling their exertions. The specific coercive or co-operative forms of this extraction process vary over time and space but remain pivotal determinants of social structure. Both the distribution of labour time (e.g. reductions in the standard workweek) and the extent of recognition and compensation of employees' knowledge and skills are intimately related to society's changing class structure.

3. Revolutionizing forces of production: both inter-capitalist competition and class struggle impel capitalists to encourage the continual development of the capacity of our productive forces — that is, the nature transforming relationship between human labour and the means of production — while striving for private control over this process. In marked contrast with pre-capitalist societies, technical knowledge relevant to production becomes more publicly accessible at the same time as entrepreneurs and financiers try to appropriate it temporarily for their own profits. While production of vendible goods and services has therefore generally expanded, the accompanying tendency within private enterprises has been to reduce the amount of labour required to produce a given amount of a commodity by replacing human labour with more cost-efficient and dependable mechanized means of production. So, workers lose established jobs in older industrial sectors (e.g. agriculture) and capitalists must seek to expand commodity production into more realms. Just think, for example, of the contest between free public use versus corporate commercial control of cyberspace such as the Internet.

In relation to this tendency to squeeze labour out of established production processes, Marx also posited a long-term tendency toward a falling average rate of profit. He anticipated that this tendency would lead periodically to a decline in the collective willingness of capitalist owners to reinvest in productive activities. Such unwillingness has indeed occurred, usually coupled with sizeable reductions in the mass demand for durable commodities and with more speculative paper investments. In these accumulation crises, capitalists have typically attempted to counteract the dominant tendency and to start a new round of sustained accumulation of capital. The crises of the late 1800s and the 1930s were mitigated when capitalists regained profitability through major offensives to reorganize the production process to take more surplus value from the labouring classes. Methods included such measures as increasing the intensity of the labour process (through speed-ups and lay-offs), drawing on reserve pools of labour to weaken the organized labour movement and depress wages, widening formal public ownership of stock, harnessing major untried technological innovations, and carving out entirely new commodity markets.

In the 1970s, the world capitalist economy once more encountered an intense accumulation crisis which has led to increasingly extensive efforts at reconstituting production relations around the globe. The most evident signs of this offensive have been increases in corporate takeovers and bankruptcies combined with massive lay-offs, creation of larger contingent reserve labour forces and demands for concessions in collective agreements, plus the rapid introduction of increasingly automated production systems in advanced capitalist core regions, and the reallocation of more labour-intensive processes to cheaper labour areas.

This, in a nutshell, is what Kumar (1995) has alluded to in Chapter Four and what I have elsewhere called the "accelerated continuity thesis" of contemporary capitalist production.[12] What we are seeing is really a familiar story at higher speed. The upheavals of patterns of production have occurred throughout the history of Western industrial capitalism in one key sector after another, in agriculture during the 19th century, in energy generation and transportation in the early 20th century, in manufacturing since the 1960s, and now in the service sector. The basic features of these periodic upheavals have been similar. In short, there has been a persistent tendency toward capital-intensive, labour-displacing forms of technological change to enhance productivity and ensure profits in one sector after another. The recent upheaval in heavy manufacturing industries such as steel, and the rapid expansion of less secure service sector employment are the most current manifestations of the fundamental underlying dynamics of the industrial capitalist mode of production which have prevailed in Western societies for roughly two centuries. This is hyper-industrial capitalism rather than "post-industrial" society.

Empirical assessments of the contemporary global capitalist system of production, and of the most recent economic slump in advanced capitalist societies, in terms of the basic contradictory relationships identified by Marx (i.e. inter-firm competition, competitive negotiations between employers and workers over profits and benefits, and continual revolutionizing of the forces of production) are readily available (e.g. Storper and Walker 1989; Ross and Trachte 1990; Livingstone 1993). The central point for our purposes is that current tendencies in global capitalist production continue to be explicable through these contradictory relationships. Many intellectuals now either ignore or caricature this explanation of the dynamics of industrial capitalism. But it is regularly empirically demonstrated that the underlying logic of industrial capitalism that Marx detected continues to drive changes in production relations of private enterprises within all sectors of the economy, from agricultural seed companies to fast-food outlets and from computer manufacturers to software firms, in an ever-widening array of vendible goods and services.

All productive capitalist enterprises are at least periodically impelled to invest in new technologies and new product lines, and to undertake a related intensive reorganization of their workforces in order to survive. The development of the capitalist labour process has entailed a wide variety of changing employer strategies and tactics in relation to their employees; these initiatives usually have revolved around profitability prospects of particular production processes rather than any primary concern about either controlling or deskilling workers per se.[13] Much of the recent literature heralding a "post-industrial society," or somewhat more modestly arguing that "flexible specialization" production techniques are indicative of a second industrial revolution or that a "post-Fordist regime of accumulation" is imminent, tends to exaggerate both the pervasiveness and distinctive character of recent economic changes.[14]

These changes are best understood as employers' fairly widespread implementation of a new set of technologies with much smaller, recombinable standardized components or modules (especially in microelectronics), along with strategies to motivate workers to use their discretion to operate these devices efficiently. The primary objective is still to ensure the profitable production and marketing of diversified commodities, and the primary consequence for labour is the continual insecurity of employment. Neither the changing sectoral composition of employment from manufacturing to services nor accelerating rates of change in employment conditions and commodity markets should obscure the continuity of these underlying contradictory relations.

From their inception, capitalist enterprises have generated demands for educational change. Inter-capitalist competition is *constantly* destroying firms, forcing enterprise restructuring and provoking movement of capital from one town, sector or technology to the next, all of which necessitates workers' *flexibility* in terms of job switching, geographical mobility and retraining. At the same time, the revolutionizing of productive forces continually alters jobs, divisions of labour and technical skill requisites, so that most workers need a *general industrial literacy*. So, class struggle is persistently grounded in the contradiction that capitalist enterprises are compelled to nurture these general learning capacities of workers in order to enhance productivity, while owners must also appropriate workers' ingenuity and routinize their tacit knowledge in order to remain profitable. Although specialized bodies of knowledge proliferate, they can increasingly only be applied profitably in production processes based on the interdependent labours of workers who widely share a general knowledge base. These general tendencies are now most obvious in the retraining schemes of "mature" manufacturing industries which have reached a condition of overcapacity in relation to available markets for their products.[15]

The central educational idea in Marxist theory is the desirability of a genuinely *polytechnical* education which, for all children over a given age, combines productive labour with instruction and physical education, and which can produce both efficient, versatile workers and "fully developed human beings." Marx detected meagre and contested elements of this form of education coincident with the development of modern industry or "machinofacture." These elements were expressed in educational clauses of the Factory Acts in early nineteenth century England. The volatile and contradictory educational implications of the capitalist form of production were quite evident to Marx (1867, 487–88):

> If Modern Industry, by its very nature, necessitates variation of labour, fluency of function, universal mobility of the labourer, on the other

hand, in its capitalistic form, it reproduces the old division of labour with its ossified particularisations. This absolute contradiction between the technical necessities of Modern Industry, and the social character inherent in its capitalistic form, dispels all fixity and security in the situation of the labourer; it constantly threatens, by taking away the instruments of labour, to snatch from his hands his means of subsistence, and, by suppressing his detail-function, to make him superfluous. This antagonism vents its rage in the creation of that monstrosity, an industrial reserve army, kept in misery in order to be always at the disposal of capital; in the incessant human sacrifices from among the working-class, in the most reckless squandering of labour-power, and in the devastation caused by a social anarchy which turns every economic progress into a social calamity. This is the negative side. But if, on the one hand, variation of work at present imposes itself after the manner of an overpowering natural law, and with the blindly destructive action of a natural law that meets with resistance at all points, Modern Industry, on the other hand, through its catastrophes imposes the necessity of recognising, as a fundamental law of production, variation of work, consequently fitness of the labourer for varied work, consequently the greatest possible development of his varied aptitudes.

The key point here is the squandering of labour power simultaneous with continuing development of people's varied skills and knowledge. This gap between workers' knowledge and workplace utilization has existed since the inception of modern industry in the early 1800s. Unfortunately, while Marx clearly perceived this gap, the most influential neo-Marxist theorists of education-production relations have chosen to emphasize an education-jobs correspondence perspective.

NEO-MARXIST THEORIES OF EDUCATION AND WORK: THE LIMITS OF THE CORRESPONDENCE THESIS[16]

For generations after Marx's death, theoretical writing in the Marxist tradition noted class conflicts over educational provisions, but generally tended to treat them merely as "superstructural" reflections of more fundamental class relations in the production process (e.g. Rubin 1972; Levitas 1974). The significance of Samuel Bowles and Herbert Gintis' (1976) "correspondence thesis" is that it attempted to specify and empirically verify the linkages between educational systems and their economic contexts and, secondly, that much of the subsequent conceptual work in this tradition amounts to a dialogue with this thesis.[17] I will briefly review Bowles and Gintis' basic argument.

Bowles and Gintis began by assuming that education must perform the stabilizing function of affirming dominant social institutions and cultural forms, but that it should also play the personal developmental and egalitarian roles envisaged by Marx. In explicit opposition to the benign assumptions of the functionalist sociology of Talcott Parsons, they attempted to show that schools in capitalist societies, largely because of the absence of a democratic economy, consistently thwart full personal development and serve to legitimate rather than reduce social inequality in the process of performing this stabilizing function (Bowles and Gintis 1988, 236). But this was as close as they came to problematizing underemployment. Drawing mainly on recent empirical research on the division of labour in modern capitalist enterprise and on educational inequalities, Bowles and Gintis posited a general tendency toward correspondence of the social relations of production and education. More precisely, their correspondence principle asserts that in capitalist societies:

> the division of labour in education, as well as its structure of authority and reward, mirror those of the economy. Second, it holds that in any stable society in which a formal educational system has a major role in the personal development of working people, there will tend to emerge a correspondence between the social relations of education and those of the economic system (Bowles and Gintis 1988, 237).

Secondly, through a critical reading of U.S. economic and educational history, they argued that changes in the structure of education have been closely associated with changes in the social organization of production (Bowles and Gintis 1976, 234). Most originally and tentatively, Bowles and Gintis then attempted to identify the general mechanisms that translate economic interests into educational programs. They noted that disjunctions between the incessantly changing system of capitalist production and an educational system internally organized to reproduce a given form of the social relations of economic life have been most evidently and regularly accommodated through the relatively uncoordinated pursuit of interests by many individuals and groups as mediated through decentralized educational decision-making arenas (Bowles and Gintis 1976, 236). But during periods of serious disjuncture between the school system and the economy — the turning points of U.S. educational history — concrete political struggle along class-interest lines has become more apparent. Bowles and Gintis concluded:

> The major actors with independent power in the educational area were, and continue to be, labour and capital. We conclude that the structure and scope of the modern U.S. educational system cannot be explained without reference to both the demands of working people — for literacy, for the possibility of greater occupational mobility, for financial security, for personal growth, for social respect — and to the imperative of the capitalist class to construct an institution which would both enhance the labour power of working people and help to reproduce the conditions for its exploitation (1976, 240).

More specifically, they found that major institutional changes in education have been the culmination of co-ordinated activity of social classes animated by these contradictory objectives (Bowles and Gintis 1976, 178–79). Their path-breaking work has stimulated much of the subsequent critical research on education-work relations.

The criticisms of Bowles and Gintis' work have been very extensive. They were charged with being economic reductionists who see class relations of wage labour as simply reproduced through a mechanistic "capitalogic" applied to educational practices (Gorelick 1977). Their very generalized conception of structural contradictions and class struggle discouraged attention to class formation and class conflict over education (Hogan 1979). Some critics saw their heavy emphasis on the structural forms of social relations in both workplaces and schools as obscuring the roles of actual historical class agencies, especially in the virtual absence of any specification of working-class culture and very limited attention to resistance through working-class politics (Sarup 1978, 1982). Many other critics dismissed their inattention to other specific features of education-work relations (Curtis 1984; Giroux 1981; Gonzales 1982; Katznelson et al. 1982; Livingstone 1983).

In Bowles and Gintis' (1988) most substantial response to their legion of critics, the basic defence of their correspondence thesis is that it is not a comprehensive theory of contemporary schooling but only a theory of the linkage between education and the economy and, secondly, that the correspondence between the social relations of education and those of the economy only asserts itself in the long run. But they also concede that they failed to develop a *theory of educational contestation* comparable to their interpretation of capitalist production as a "contested terrain," partly because of their continuing reliance on the orthodox Marxist base-superstructure model of the economy-education relationship which regarded the latter as determined by the former. They have now rejected this model in favour of a conception of society as a reproductive and contradictory totality which is made up through asymmetric, recursive, constitutive, overlapping "games" played at multiple sites (such as state, family, education, economy, community). Bowles and Gintis (1988, 242) assert that this conception expresses "a perfect duality of structural determination and the contingency of human history upon social practices." However, to add complexity and assert a structure/agency duality is not to resolve the fundamental limitations of their correspondence thesis. As Robert Moore (1988, 61) has observed with respect to both Bowles and Gintis' major critics and their own revisions:

> Although collectively these various tendencies have constructed an approach which is both complex and coherent, it is noticeable that the concern has been virtually exclusively with *developing the complexity of the model* within which the correspondence principle is seen to operate rather than investigate the principle *as such*.

Most seriously, in terms of education-work relations, there has been an empirical failure to establish actual historical correspondences between forms and contents of educational practices and those within the social relations of direct production. The most thorough historiographic study of the development of mass schooling from a Marxist perspective (Simon 1974, 1991) suggests substantial and persistent differences. There is also considerable recent evidence that educational organizations are especially lacking in close internal co-ordination among management structures, teaching activities and other outcomes, and that such "loose coupling" makes the official policies of formal management exceptionally responsive to external pressures without seriously affecting internal social relations (Weick 1976). Moreover, as Bowles and Gintis do recognize, the flow of people between schools and workplaces is mediated in large part through individual transactions in labour markets and via state intervention.

As I have documented in earlier chapters, the chronic overproduction and underemployment of highly educated labour market entrants through these mediations now appears to be an enduring feature of advanced capitalist societies. There is little indication that the correspondence between educational credentials and actual job requirements was very close in the prior post-WWII expansionary period either (Berg 1970). More generally, there is very little empirical evidence that mass schooling has ever served as an effective site of simple working class socialization into the specific work attitudes desired by employers (e.g. Musgrove 1979; Hickox and Moore 1992). Bowles and Gintis' "correspondence in the long-term" therefore appears analogous to the French structural Marxist Louis Althusser's (1971) determination of everything by production relations "in the last instance." The correspondence never comes.

The theoretical battles that have occurred in the wake of Bowles and Gintis initial formulation of their correspondence principle have often taken the form of assertion and counter-assertion without recourse to substantial empirical evidence. As Daniel Liston (1988, 68, 72) has observed:

> Educational Marxists, while critical of a strong paradigm of functionalism, employ facile functionalist "explanations" that either assume the truth of their propositions or are framed in a manner immune to empirical examination.... The arguments surrounding reproduction theory can be characterized as theoretical battles that continually alter the explanatory object and the conceptual framework while using confused, if not illicit, forms of explanation.[18]

The major emphases in these recent neo-Marxist theoretical battles are summarized in Figure 5.1, in terms of the perennial structure/agency and consensus/conflict dualisms of sociological thought.[19]

Bowles and Gintis' (1976) original formulation of the correspondence thesis was a major theoretical challenge to orthodox Marxist notions of schooling as simply a superstructural reflection of capitalist reproduction requirements. But throughout their various revisions (Gintis and Bowles 1981; Bowles and Gintis 1988), they have retained a central emphasis on the structural correspondence and essential unity of education and production relations.

Other neo-Marxist scholars, reacting to the structuralist bias in the reproduction theories of either Althusser or Bowles and Gintis, have drawn on Gramscian hegemony theory to focus on the agendas and actions of ruling class and subordinate class group representatives to establish educational policies and negotiate new "educational settlements" in periods of social crisis (Centre for Contemporary Educational Studies 1981, 1989). The emphasis here tends to be on the reconstruction of ideological consent via strategic initiatives of dominant class alliances.

Figure 5.1   Explanatory Foci of Neo-Marxist Theories of Education-Work Relations

Consensus/Conflict	*Structure*	*Agency*
Consensus-Unity	Correspondence thesis, capitalist reproduction requirements (Bowles and Gintis)	Dominant class hegemony, ideological consent (Centre for Contemporary Cultural Studies)
Conflict-Contradiction	Popular democratic demands counterposed to capitalist reproduction requirements (Carnoy and Levin)	Subordinate group contestation for self-determination (Hogan, Willis)

Another distinct approach explicitly rejects Marxist structural functionalist explanations as well as consensus assumptions, while stressing the conflicting intentional actions of a wider array of class agents, especially the choices of working class youths. Liston (1988, 68–72) terms this the "class-formation approach" and cites authors such as Paul Willis (1977) and David Hogan (1985). These resistance theorists have in common an insistence that working class educational outcomes are not determined either by structural economic requirements, as the correspondence thesis would have it, or by capitalist ideological domination, as hegemony theorists tend to assume; rather, although the deck may be stacked against them, working class people still try to control their own lives, creating cultural meaning and making various educational choices. To date, this approach has focused mainly on documenting the cultural production of the working class through ethnographic and historiographic studies, without intending to offer any systematic and verifiable alternative explanation for general education-society relations or even specifying *any* limits for the school systems that arise in capitalist societies. Hogan (1985, 48) has declared this most boldly:

> The relationship between a particular structure of schooling and a particular structure of capitalism is irreducibly contingent, the outcome of complex conflicts and choices, not of some functionalist imperative.

For our purposes, the most important "alteration of the theoretical object" in reaction to the onesidedness of Bowles and Gintis' account has emphasized the structural contradictions between capitalist production imperatives and working peoples' popular demands for education, particularly as these are mediated by the liberal democratic state (Carnoy and Levin, 1985). In this approach, there is much greater stress on the schools as an arena of social conflict than the correspondence thesis allows. Unfortunately, while conflicting class agents are posited, both social classes and schools tend to be treated as highly structuralist expressions of the assumed contradictory requirements of capital and the democratic state. Nevertheless, the specific formulation of contradictory relations between capitalist reproduction and popular demand for education recuperates Marx's earlier insight about the education-jobs gap, and has provided a conceptual basis for extensive empirical studies of trends in underemployment (e.g. Rumberger 1980, 1984; Levin and Rumberger 1989; Johnston 1993).

In sum, the cumulative impact of critical debate over Bowles and Gintis' structural correspondence thesis within the neo-Marxist tradition of scholarship has been to encourage the elaboration of education-society models of greater conceptual complexity, along with a search for other theoretical foci which put greater emphases on social agency and conflict relations in accounting for substantial recent educational changes. It is probably fair to say that most current interpretive studies in this field are characterized by quite complex *descriptions* of structural factors underlying educational change and by *ad hoc* analyses of political practices involved in particular educational policy issues. As Roger Dale (1992, 207) puts it in a more general assessment of "socially committed" approaches to the sociology of education:

> The 'theoretical' projects ... may be dominated on the one hand by ad hockery and on the other by a restriction to concept development rather than theoretical development.

The key historical materialist insight which is obscured by the complex descriptive perspectives of much recent critical research on education-work relations is that class-based struggles *over* education persist in capitalist societies. At the most abstract level, class struggle in capitalism is the confrontation of two historical actors, capital and labour, each of which respond to *different but mutually conditioned logics*. Working class individuals and organizations continue to create partially autonomous bodies of knowledge through their specific practices, and to contest acceptable forms and contents of state and employer-sponsored education programs on this basis (Sharp et al. 1989; Jackson 1992; Sissons 1990). The "class formation approach" has grasped at this point empirically, but largely through a documentation of the spasmodic resistance of working class youths *within* the informal interstices of effectively reified models of school structures. So has the credential society approach, which stresses the contests for control of occupationally legitimating bodies of knowledge waged by craft unions as well as professional employees (Collins 1979, 131–181).

Working class possession of distinct and autonomous means of education was probably more substantial in the early nineteenth century prior to the creation of state-run systems of elementary schooling (Johnson 1979). The capacity of capitalist owners and their allies to "colonize" the sphere of everyday life and invade working class cultural experience has increased immensely since then (Brosio 1991). But to recognize the dominance of capital's cultural power should not be to deny the effective existence of working class cultural power (see Livingstone 1987). Without romanticising working people's political consciousness, those contemporary empirical studies alive to the potential existence of class struggle over education have found working class political practices to be significant, if often mediated, influences over specific educational programs at both local and national state levels (e.g. Wrigley 1982; Dale et al. 1990; Curtis et al. 1992).

As noted in Chapter One, the most influential general theories of the reproduction of social inequalities through schooling have been the works of Pierre Bourdieu and Basil Bernstein. Both of these eminent scholars have drawn on the Marxist tradition in developing their conceptions. Bourdieu's (1970) notion of "cultural capital" was developed by analogy with Marx's analysis of capital as a social relation, while Basil Bernstein's (1965) notion of restricted and elaborated language codes was inspired by the work of the Marxist psychologist, Vygotsky. A brief critical appreciation of their contributions may be helpful for the development of more conflict-sensitive explanations of education-work relations.

In both Bourdieu and Bernstein, the primary emphasis is placed on the general cultural knowledge, sophisticated vocabularies and precise information about how schools work that children from higher status origins acquire from their families. The possession of these cultural tools leads to their greater success in school relations than working class kids. Such cultural theories offer considerable insights into the discriminatory schooling conditions faced by working class people and the construction of the talent use gap. While a great deal of contemporary learning theory takes a class-blind and individualist perspective, both Bourdieu and Bernstein have developed structurally grounded models of class differences in cultural sensibilities and linked them to differential effects of schooling processes. In Bourdieu's case, as in human capital theories generally, an analogy is made between capital assets and human learning capacities. Children of the affluent classes, who have acquired familiarity with bourgeois cultural forms at home (through exposure to their parents knowledge and manners, 'good' books, museums, etc.) are seen to possess the means of appropriating similarly oriented school knowledge relatively easily. Working class kids, in contrast, find their unfamiliarity with these cultural forms to be a major obstacle to successful school performance. Bernstein makes similar arguments primarily in terms of language codes, with upper middle class children considered to possess more elaborated codes for abstracting and generalizing from school curricular materials. Both scholars, with the aid of teams of colleagues, have done extensive empirical verification and refinement of their models, deepening both their complexity and their insights into the discriminatory cultural processes that operate against the working class in most schools. Both theorists expose the dominance side of cultural reproduction in excruciating detail. At least in this limited sense, their contributions are comparable to those of feminist and anti-racist scholars who have critically exposed the dominant codes and structures of patriarchal and racist cultural forms (Spender 1980; Said 1993).

But Bourdieu and Bernstein have been preoccupied with delineating the cultural reproduction of inequality within fixed institutional forms. Thus, their accounts remain one-dimensional, functionalist descriptions of the status quo rather than real explanations of it (see Curtis, Livingstone and Smaller 1992, 6–25). Bourdieu's and Bernstein's theories of class cultures have ignored a central rule of sociological investigation promulgated by one of the founding fathers of sociology they both build on, Emile Durkheim: to understand any social fact, we must study it through the full range of its variation. They never comprehend the creative cultural practices, independent education and learning activities, or collective cultural agency of the organized working class.

Working class people are always presented as reactive, atomized and marginalized in their perspectives, even in their most recent, empirically grounded works (Bourdieu 1993; Bernstein 1996). For example, as Fowler (1997, 11) observes, Bourdieu has exaggerated the cultural dispossession of the masses and excluded any popular art in his category of consecrated culture, constructing a canonical closure which is too complete and which blinds him to the existence of authorship within these popular art-forms.

The rediscovery of this creative agency, as expressed especially through the working class novel and the historiography of working class life, has been initiated by sympathetic intellectuals operating initially outside established academies and often engaged in adult working class education jobs, most notably Raymond Williams and E.P. Thompson.[20] There are now vibrant areas of study of popular literature, working class historiography and ethnography which are making these subordinated cultural voices more widely heard. Much of this research is being conducted by individual scholars of working class origins who remain in continuing tension with the academies that employ them (Ryan and Shackrey 1984).

The popular education tradition has long been involved outside academic settings in empowering groups of working class and impoverished people through critical reflection on their own local conditions. Paolo Freire's conscientization approach to cultural animation (1970, 1994) is in some ways the reverse of Bourdieu's and Bernstein's preoccupation with structured forms of symbolic dominance. The conscientization focus is on the group's own generative themes and problems, and movement toward resolving action. Besides general critiques of the oppressiveness of "banking education," this approach has paid little attention to documentation of oppositional (or counter-hegemonic) cultural forms among working people, the wider recognition of which could sustain transformative cultural action beyond the small group level. Nevertheless, similar consciousness-raising methods have been effective tools in organizing unorganized workers as well as building the civil rights and women's movements. Some recent progressive adult education programs supported by the local state and focused on unemployed and often dispirited working class people have had similar objectives and achieved impressive results at least on a temporary basis (Lovett 1983; Ward and Taylor 1986). But transformative education and learning initiatives may have more likelihood of survival when they are supported directly by labour unions (see Newman 1993; Martin 1996). My colleagues and I have documented some leading cases elsewhere (Livingstone et al forthcoming).

The basic point is that working class and other subordinated groups continue to exercise their own learning capacities both within and outside dominant class forms of knowledge. The knowledges that they produce and reproduce continue to constitute oppositional forms within the realm of education per se as well as in the broader spheres of individual and collective informal learning, as I have illustrated in Chapter Three.

More broadly, the socialization of the forces of knowledge production (especially through the availability of free voluntary forms such as public libraries, trade union schools, and now electronic information networks) is a major source of autonomous cultural production by subordinate social groups. The increasing availability to working class people of such socialized forces of knowledge production represents a continual challenge to private capitalist efforts (via conglomerate ownership of mass media, commodified information packages) to appropriate the social relations of knowledge production. This opposition between socialized forces and privatized relations of knowledge production is the *fundamental contradiction of knowledge development and education in capitalist societies*. As Davis and Stack (1992, 10–11) express it:

> Knowledge costs almost nothing to duplicate, especially if it appears in digital form. As a greater percentage of goods become knowledge, the nature of production as resource exhaustive, labour-consuming and scarcity-bound becomes obsolete. The new productive forces are resource-conservative, yet generate an abundance. "Ownership" becomes an irrelevant concept if many people can possess the same thing simultaneously. Property rights as we have known them simply get in the way, and hold back development. The holding back takes many forms: ... expensive lawsuits, ultimately paid for by the consumer, over ownership of interfaces; increased surveillance to catch "information pirates"; decreased access to public information as databases are privatised and information is commodified; ... and even the criminalisation of knowledge itself as it is classified as weaponry, lest it get into the wrong minds.

After a secular trend of quantitative expansion of formal schooling since the 1830s, the unprecedented restriction and closure of state-sponsored educational programs and chronic underemployment of highly educated workers are now making the systemic opposition between advanced capitalist societies' capacity to produce knowledge and the private capitalist appropriation of applied forms of knowledge more obvious. At least, the assumption of education as a rational system that universally expands for the social good is coming apart. Consider, for example, the current amalgamation, downsizing and closure of education programs across North America. Consider as well the recent efforts to reprivatize libraries through user fees. There may be demographic warrant for some current downsizing of school systems. But the cumulative popular need and demand for knowledge will not easily be reversed, however "non-correspondent" such popular demand may become with current job provisions of capitalist enterprises and the strong desires of corporate executives.[21]

In retrospect, Bowles and Gintis' correspondence thesis represents a pivotal moment in critical studies of education and work in advanced capitalist societies. Their bold arguments provoked a wide array of reconceptualizations and original descriptive studies of the relations between educational practices and their social contexts. As fiscal pressures on state-sponsored schooling have persisted, and as evident public disputes *and* negotiations over major educational issues have continued, neo-Marxist theorists increasingly have attended to both conflictual and consensual elements in the *interplay* of educational structures and agents.

Ironically, however, neo-Marxist theories of education and work have actually paid very little close empirical attention to the production relations and grounded class analysis they assume to be central to this relationship. Bowles and Gintis basically assumed that the origins of the mass, hierarchically organized form of public schooling were associated with the development of a "Fordist" industrial regime characterized by a mass of low skilled workers directed by an elaborate management structure. As I have noted earlier, neither the "Fordist" production regime nor the "post-industrial/knowledge economy" have been nearly as pervasive as their advocates have asserted. Bowles and Gintis' critics have largely overlooked this failing (see Livingstone 1995c).

More recent neo-Marxist (and post-modernist) theorists of education have sometimes compounded the error by uncritically accepting the notion of an emergent "post-Fordist" era of more flexible and less hierarchical production and by elaborating comparable features of a "post-Fordist" educational system (e.g. Brown 1992; Hickox and Moore 1992; Brown and Lauder 1992; Carter 1997). While these analysts may note the nascent or speculative nature of their analyses, they effectively repeat many of the mistakes of the original correspondence thesis on the basis of even less empirical evidence. This is not to deny that some of the institutional features of both production systems and educational systems described in these accounts indicate significant changes. But such dichotomous "pre/post" analyses tend to obscure the underlying social dynamics in both spheres. Indeed, with rare exceptions (Anyon 1980; Connell et al. 1982; Livingstone 1983; Carnoy and Levin 1985; Shapiro 1990), neo-Marxist research on education has largely ignored the continuity of the basic contradictory relationships in capitalist production discussed above, as well as failing to offer specific analyses of the full array of class forces — grounded in production relations — whose class-based practices impinge on education.

AN EMERGENT THEORY OF THE EDUCATION-JOBS GAP

With regard to the form of capitalist production, an alternative "accelerated continuity thesis" is suggested here, based on contradictory relations in the capitalist production process originally identified by Marx. This thesis argues that the strategies and structures of capital-labour relations in immediate production continue to be more contingent on the productivity/profitability of labour than they are on either capitalist control of labour or imperative and rapid skill upgrading. In view of the otherwise opposed interests of labour and capital, educational systems are likely to assume a polytechnical character rather than a strictly vocational one; they are also likely to remain only loosely related to present capitalist production requirements. In any case, it is increasingly clear that class relations in education are mediated substantially beyond relations in production while class-based demands also interact with other social demands in the politics of education. Class effects in the knowledge production, governance and learning process spheres of education, therefore, cannot be accurately read off or derived from capitalist production relations. The education-jobs gap is likely to be class-specific in each of the several dimensions of underemployment, with variations subject to continuing contestations between major class groups across time and space.

From this general perspective, educational change is hardly an inevitable rational progression expressing the structural imperatives of capitalist production, nor is it merely the contingent expression of particular class conflicts. Rather, educational change is the indeterminate result of confrontations and negotiations between historically specific groups of class-based agents simultaneously constituted in gender and ethnic terms. These confrontations are grounded in different but mutually-conditioned logics and the negotiations are mediated through previously institutionalized educational forms. We continue to make our own histories but in contested contexts not of our own choosing. This is the "contested subordination" perspective on learning-work relations that I propose as both theoretically coherent and empirically verifiable.[22]

In any private market-based economy, the sweep of change is continual. Inter-firm competition, technological innovation, and negotiations between employers and employees over working conditions, benefits and knowledge requirements all lead to incessant shifts in the numbers and types of jobs available. Population growth cycles, modified household needs and new legislative regulations also frequently serve to alter the supply of labour. At the same time, popular demand for general education and specialized training increases cumulatively as people generally seek more knowledge, different skills and added credentials in order to live and work in such a changing society.

So, there are always "mismatches" between employers' aggregate demand and requirements for employees on the one hand, and the aggregate supply and qualifications of job seekers on the other. The accelerating productivity of capitalist enterprises regularly throws workers into unemployment, reproducing the most evident part of the reserve army of labour. In societies with liberal democratic state regimes that acclaim the right to equal educational opportunity, and with labour markets in which both employers and job seekers make mainly individual employment choices, the dominant historical tendency has been for the supply of educationally qualified job seekers to exceed the demand for any given type of job. These same dynamics also generate underqualification of some workers, particularly older employees who have had few incentives to upgrade their skills and credentials.

In capitalist societies, as both Marxist class theorists and some Weber-inspired social closure theorists (e.g. Murphy, 1988) recognize, the principal powers of definition and exclusion have accrued to those with the ownership of substantial private property. These powers generally have been accorded greater protection than other social rights by the legal and coercive sanctions of the state. This "deep structure of closure" (65–70), as Murphy calls it, and the related control of material resources by large capitalist owners and top private and state sector managers, profoundly limits the clear public expression of contending claims of competence, skill or value by those not allied with the interests of property owners. As Murphy (1988, 182) argues, more derivative and contingent forms of social closure such as those attempted by members of occupational specializations, have owed much of their success to their extent of complementarity with this deep structure:

> The success of any credentialed group in carving out a monopoly depends on its success in propagating the claim that its credentials certify the presence of some skill (and that their absence indicates lack of that skill) and that the skill itself is necessary and of value. Such

success is not a matter of intellectual rigor, but rather of ideological struggle, itself founded on the structure of power in society. It is not just a question of the power of that particular credentialed group, but the structure of power in society within which the group can carve out its own position of power.

This is the "dirty truth" that Michael Parenti (1996) speaks of with regard to the oppression of the views of scientists whose research has seriously challenged dimensions of this deep structure of power. Nevertheless, as I have argued above, established power structures should not be reified; they are continually subject to resistance and change, especially in response to the collective actions of well organized subordinate social groups.

Within this context, as neo-Weberian status competition theorists like Collins have illustrated, people in various occupational specialties manage to aggrandize the knowledge required for their own work and justify greater associated earnings than other workers through particularly certified credentials. Also, as Bourdieu and Bernstein have best documented from dominant class standpoints, more general conflicts occur through the schools in every generation over the appropriate cultural content of knowledge. The traditional distinction between "intellectual" and "manual" labour may be better understood in terms of these position-shaping initiatives by mobilized occupational groups, in de facto alliances with capitalist class groups, than as accurate characterizations of deficient actual skills or learning capacities of manual workers; many working class people continue to resist such pejorative distinctions both at school and work (see Willis 1977; Browne 1981; Curtis et al. 1992).

On all of the above grounds, we should expect to find differential underemployment throughout the active labour force, but especially among those with the least economic and political power to define the appropriate requirements for their jobs or prospective jobs. In particular, we should expect to find higher levels of underemployment of their working knowledge among those in lower class positions, as well as among those social groupings whose general subordination in society has put them at a disadvantage in labour market negotiations, especially younger people, ethnic and racial minorities and women.

From this general theoretical perspective on the education-jobs gap, I can generate predictions about class-specific differences in the extent of underemployment on each of the six basic dimensions of

Figure 5.2   Predicted Underemployment by Class Position

Class Location	Dimensions of Underemployment					
	Talent Gap	Struct Unemp	Invol P/T	Cred Gap	Perf Gap	Subj Under
Corporate capitalists	Low	Low	Low	Low	Low	Low
Small employers	Med	Med	Low	Low	Low	Low
Petty bourgeoisie	High	High	Low	Low	Low	Low
Managers	Low	Low	Low	Low	Med	Low
Professional employees	Low	Low	Low	Low	Med	Low
Semi-prof. employees	Med	Med	Med	Med	Med	Med
Supervisors	Med	Med	Med	Med	Med	Med
Service workers						
Skilled service	High	Med	Med	High	High	High
Other service	High	High	High	High	High	High
Industrial workers						
Skilled industrial	High	Med	Med	High	High	High
Other industrial	High	High	High	High	High	High

the education-jobs gap: the talent use gap; structural unemployment; involuntary reduced employment; the credential gap; the performance gap; and subjective underemployment. I will also offer some preliminary empirical tests of the differential patterns across the current class structure and by other social background features. The predictions are summarized in Figure 5.2. The evidence is drawn mainly from the OISE/UT Survey of Educational Issues which provides the most inclusive class-specific data available on all six dimensions of underemployment.[23]

Class and the Talent Use Gap

The *talent use gap* is endemic in any class society. In advanced capitalist societies, in addition to the material advantages provided by affluent class family origins, the position-shaping efforts to promote dominant class cultural distinctions have persistently ensured systemic underrepresentation of lower class youths in advanced education. I have illustrated this condition in Chapter Two in terms of the differential completions of university degrees by those from professional and industrial working class family origins. A more inclusive set of class-specific predictions is offered here. I would generally expect that those from corporate capitalist families would have the highest post-secondary attendance and completion rates followed by those from professional and managerial family origins, these being the families that are typically the most affluent and possessing the most "cultural capital" in relation to current forms of schooling. Small employers because of their less substantial wealth, semi-professionals because of their relatively weak claims to expert knowledge, and supervisors because of their subordinate status to managers, are all able to provide relatively less support for their children to complete university. The children of workers, as well as those of the self-employed or petty bourgeoisie, can provide the least material support for children's advanced education and it is in these class groups that the greatest waste of learning capacity is likely to occur in the schools of advanced capitalism.

As Table 5.1 summarizes, the empirical results from the Ontario samples are generally consistent with these predictions. Since corporate executives are such a tiny part of the population, it is difficult to find enough respondents in a general sample with a parent who is/was an executive to be able to provide a reliable estimate. However, prior contemporary studies strongly suggest that corporate elite families have developed strong traditions of sending most of their children to exclusive private schools and on to the "best" universities (Clement 1975; Cookson and Persell 1985). Over 40 percent of those from professional employee family origins and nearly a third of those from managerial households have completed university. More than a quarter of those whose fathers were small employers have also completed university. Those with semi-professional and supervisory parents have the average university completion rates of the total labour force, around 20 percent. Also as predicted, the lowest university completion rates are found among children of industrial workers and the self-employed, 10 to 15 percent. The only inaccurate prediction involves the children of service workers, who attain university completion rates comparable to those from semi-

Table 5.1 Father's Class by Respondent's Highest Level of Schooling, Ontario Labour Force Over 25, 1988–1996

Father's Class	Respondent's Highest Level of Schooling (% with university degree)
Corporate executive	50+*
Small employer	27
Self-employed	15
Manager	30
Professional employee	43
Semi-prof. employee	21
Supervisor	18
Service worker	20
Industrial worker	10
Total labour force	18
N	2644

*insufficient cases for more reliable estimate

Source: OISE Survey of Educational Issues Data Archive

professional and supervisory families, rather than the lower rates of those from industrial workers' families.

Further analyses by specific age cohorts only slightly modify these class differences. In light of the general expansion of schooling, younger people from most class origins tend to have higher educational attainments. But the talent gap does appear to have narrowed somewhat as the attainments of those from lower class origins have increased more rapidly. Among all age cohorts, the university degree rates for those from professional families range between 40 and 50 percent. Of those from either industrial or service working class origins who are over 55 years of age, less than 5 percent have attained university degrees. Among younger age cohorts, these attainment rates have doubled for those from most lower class origins, including those from industrial working class families. The rates have quadrupled to over 20 percent for the growing numbers from service worker families. The white collar working class has been making exceptional efforts to improve the educational chances of their children.

The educational attainments by different class origins are very similar for both men and women. Ethnic background does have important effects on university degree attainment, as documented in Chapter Two. But the most relevant point for our purposes is that neither sex nor ethnicity alters the basic pattern of inter-generational class differences in educational attainment.

Many would take it to be self-evident that those from more affluent families can better afford to send their children to university, so these kids continue to be more likely to go. Cultural capital theorists also predict the persistence of a similar pattern of class differences in schooling as determined more directly by language codes and cultural beliefs. Whatever the specific class factors involved, the above findings indicate the persistence of at least some systemic class biases against lower class students in current schools. They also suggest some post-WWII decline in the talent use gap as working class people have struggled against these biases (see Curtis, Livingstone and Smaller 1992).

But the magnitude of the continuing class-related talent use gap is still the most striking finding. If we were to assume, for example, that not only over 30 percent of the children of executives, professionals and managers — who constitute about 10 percent of the parental population — were capable of completing university degrees, but also similar proportions of those from other parental class origins, then *about half* of the total adult labour force who have the potential to complete university have not been enabled to do so. While this is only one of many possible measures of the talent use gap, it is clear that this gap remains a primary dimension of the class struggle over education.

Class and Structural Underemployment

Structural unemployment has only been recognized as a major social concern in periods of protracted economic slump, like the 1930s and the period since the 1970s, when there are obviously large numbers of well qualified people who cannot find any paying jobs. Those occupational classes that have been most able to limit access to their jobs via either capital assets (corporate capitalists) or specialized credential criteria (professional and managerial employees) are least likely to experience sustained unemployment. Small employers and the self-employed, with fewer capital assets and typically less capability to restrict entry into their markets than corporate enterprises, may be somewhat more vulnerable to business failure but can usually fall back on other employment in their fields. Semi-professional employees and supervisors with less control of specialized knowledge are more vulnerable to redundancy, replacement and lay-off than professionals and managers. Skilled industrial and service workers who have been successful in retaining or gaining some control over the process of certifying the requisite technical skills of their job or trade may experience higher levels of unemployment than professional and managerial employees but lower than less skilled workers. In each of the above employee class groups, diminished prospects in one's present job can at least sometimes be replaced by downward mobility into a lower class job. Less skilled workers who have very few recognized skills to contribute distinctively to their paid work, or to protect them from replacement by others in the reserve army of labour, face the highest likelihood of unemployment. In periods of high unemployment, employers are especially likely to use these replacement workers to increase the unemployment and weaken the bargaining power of most current wage and salary employees, especially those without strong occupational associations or unions to protect them.

As Table 5.2 shows, the order of average unemployment rates in Ontario during the 1980–96 period is generally as predicted. A few cautions should be noted in interpreting this table. About 40 percent of the unemployed respondents in these samples have not provided information on their occupational class. Many of these are likely to be unskilled workers but they could also be from any other class, including former proprietors. The rates are generally very conservative, including mainly those who qualify for formal unemployment benefits. Beyond these numbers, discouraged workers are most likely to be found among the working class, where unemployment rates are highest. But basically the general pattern is that the owner classes have very low unemployment rates, professional-managerial groups have modest unemployment rates, and workers have much higher rates — about double those of professionals and managers. The most striking finding, even with these conservative measures, is that throughout this period over 5 percent of the working class has consistently been unemployed while owners and managers have avoided unemployment; the traditional reserve army of labour is alive, if not necessarily very well.

The anomalous finding that skilled industrial workers generally have slightly higher unemployment rates than less skilled workers

Table 5.2   Class Position by Average Unemployment Rate,
Ontario Labour Force, 1980–1996

Class Position	Average Unemployment Rate (%)
Corporate executives	0
Small employers	0.3
Self-employed	0.5
Managers	1.4
Professional employees	3.0
Semi-prof. employees	3.8
Supervisors	3.3
Service workers	
Skilled service	4.0
Other service	5.8
Industrial workers	
Skilled industrial	6.8
Other industrial	5.7
Total labour force	6.2
N	5787

Source: OISE Survey of Educational Issues Data Archive.

may be primarily explained by older skilled workers continuing unsuccessfully to seek commensurate paid work after termination from their prior employment, while their less skilled co-workers opt for early permanent retirement or settle for poorer jobs. Among younger cohorts, the unemployment rates for skilled workers are lower than for less skilled workers, as predicted. Generally, younger people in all class positions have the highest unemployment rates while the middle aged have the lowest.

Average unemployment rates are comparable between men and women within all class positions. Within each employee class position there is a notable difference by union status, with unionized employees having about half the average unemployment rates of nonunionized employees. The inverse relationship between educational attainment and unemployment noted in Chapter Two interacts with class position. In particular, owners and managers generally have much lower unemployment rates than their educational attainments alone would predict, while industrial workers with post-secondary credentials have much higher unemployment rates than their education would predict. The general pattern of class differences in unemployment rates persists when each of these other factors is considered. Comparable surveys of the proportions in different employee classes' who have experienced unemployment in the last five years, conducted annually in the United Kingdom since 1983 (Spencer 1996), have found very similar differential unemployment rates between professional-managerial employees and manual and non-manual workers.

Class and Involuntary Reduced Employment

Involuntary reduced employment tends to be higher whenever there is high structural unemployment with many people seeking any kind of paying job, or when large numbers of people who had not previously sought wage labour rapidly enter the labour market (e.g. peasants forced off the land and into urban peripheral employment; married women without prior employment who are seeking to help their households make ends meet). Since business owners decide their own working conditions and measure their work in profits rather than hours, part-time status has less consequence for them than for wage and salary earners; however, the extent to which their firm can provide employment for them is likely to vary inversely by the firm's asset level, with the self-employed most likely to be forced into combining part-time employment in their firm with other means of surviving. Professional and managerial employees' credentialized knowledge control makes it more unlikely that they will be forced to take up part-time work than lower level employees. Managers, and supervisors as well, are also hired to provide coordination and surveillance of extensive labour processes, functions that employers have generally regarded as more effectively handled on a full-time basis. Lower level employees, including semi-professional employees and skilled and unskilled workers, are generally more vulnerable to involuntarily reduced working hours, unless they have collective bargaining agreements that protect their working conditions. But even with unions to protect them, unskilled workers are most vulnerable to be relegated to part-time jobs.

Readily available data sources permit only limited tests of these predictions. The primary sources used here are the OISE Ontario surveys, and Tilley's (1996, 67–68) reanalyses of the 1992 Current

Population Surveys for selected U.S. industries. Neither of these sources provide fully adequate measures. The Ontario surveys do not distinguish voluntary from involuntary part-time employment measures but they do permit a detailed class analysis. The U.S. survey distinguishes involuntary part-time employment but only in a few sectors, mainly the retail industry, and identifies only a limited number of class positions. But in combination the results permit some inferences. The major findings are summarized in Table 5.3.

Most of the findings are consistent with the predictions. Among

Table 5.3   Class Position by Part-time Employment, Ontario Labour Force, 1980–1996 and Involuntary Part-time Employment, U.S. Retail Industry, 1992

Class Position	Ontario Average Part-time Employment 1980–1996 (1) (%)	U.S. Retail Involuntary Part-time Employment 1992 (2) (%)
Corporate executives	7*	
Small employers	19	
Self-employed	31	
Managers	4	2
Professional employees	14	7
Semi-prof. employees	27	
Supervisors	9	9
Service workers		15
Skilled service	24	
Other service	37	
Industrial workers		
Skilled industrial	6	4
Other industrial	13	
Total labour force	21	9
N	5202	11447

Sources: (1) OISE Survey of Educational Issues Data Archive; (2) Current Population Survey tapes as reported in Tilley (1996, Table 4.2).

owners, the incidence of actual part-time employment is related to capital asset level, with very few corporate executives claiming this status; almost a third of the self-employed do so, which is a higher incidence than among most employee class groups. Managers and supervisors both have very low levels of part-time or involuntary employment, while professional employees have somewhat higher levels, but lower than most other white collar employees, including semi-professionals and service workers. Skilled workers generally have lower levels of part-time or involuntary employment than other workers, as predicted. There is, however, a very large difference between the incidence of part-time employment in the industrial and service sectors. Indeed, the incidence of part-time employment among skilled industrial workers is lower than predicted, as low as it is among corporate executives and managers. A basic sectoral explanation for this difference may be that manufacturing industries generally operate on either continuous or full shift production schedules, while many service sector firms try to adjust their schedules more frequently to customer demand and rely on more contingent labour forces with large numbers of part-time lower level employees. But, as suggested above more generally, differential levels of unionization in these two sectors is also likely to be a major factor.

Another recent Canada-wide survey of worktime preferences by standard occupational categories (Drolet and Morisette 1997) allows only a few employee class comparisons. But the general patterns are consistent with the predictions about involuntary part-time employment. That is, the lower the incidence of full-time employment, the greater the desire for more worktime. Only about 15 percent of professionals and managers express a desire to work more hours than they do now. Other employees in the industrial/manufacturing sector are much more likely than professionals and managers to want more worktime, and the desire for more worktime is highest in the service sectors.

There are other important differences in involuntary reduced employment that interact with these class differences. Younger workers are both more likely to have only part-time employment and to desire more worktime. Over a third of those aged 18 to 24 are working part-time, as opposed to around 20 percent of all other age groups up to 65. About half of those aged 15 to 24 want more work hours, compared to only 15 percent of those over 45. There are major sex differences in the actual incidence of part-time employment, with only 10 percent of

men but over a third of women in this status. But there is no significant sex difference in the desire for more worktime among the employed workforce, with about a quarter of both men and women
workers desiring more work hours. In spite of women's increased participation in paid employment and more liberal attitudes about gender roles, the traditional dichotomy between male "breadwinner" and
female "nurturer" still continues to animate desired participation in
both workplace and household spheres. The differences by union status are again quite strong, with non-unionized employees being about
twice as likely (23 percent) as unionized workers (12 percent) to be
employed part-time. The fact that most industrial workers are unionized men while most service workers are non-unionized women
largely explains the great difference between these sectors in the incidence of part-time work. Also, regardless of the lack of sex differences
in worktime preferences, unionized workers appear to be somewhat
less likely (22 percent) than nonunionized workers (30 percent) to
want more worktime.

Part-time work is somewhat less likely for those with university
degrees (14 percent) than those with lower educational attainments
(20 percent or more). But the class and gender analyses reveal a
much wider range of part-time underemployment rates than educational attainment does; male corporate executives, managers and
professional employees, as well as male unionized industrial workers, have much lower rates of part-time employment (less than 5
percent) than their educational attainments would predict, while
women generally and nonunionized female service workers in particular have much higher rates (over 40 percent). The interplay of
class and gender power is most evident in this dimension of underemployment.

Class and the Credential Gap

In addition to the continual flux regarded as normal in market
economies, other factors contribute to an ongoing *credential gap*. Young
job entrants often compete for and accept positions for which they are
overqualified, in the expectation that they will be able to climb career
ladders to more suitable jobs. Older workers can retain jobs for which
the formal entry requirements have increased, on the basis of their
experience and seniority. As documented in Chapter Two, educational entry requirements for jobs have increased rapidly. Employers often
use these educational entry requirements very flexibly. They have

clearly raised them in response to the increasing educational attainments of job market entrants. But they also use them in conjunction with other specific or intuitive criteria, and tend to avoid hiring highly overqualified applicants (Bills 1992, 79–92; Roizen and Jepson 1985). Nevertheless, with the cumulative expansion of formal schooling, a large supply of highly educated people among the unemployed and even larger numbers of employed people who cannot find jobs commensurate with their qualifications have become persistent features of the post-1970 era. This phenomenon has been more difficult for post-industrial and human capital theorists to rationalize in terms of market forces than either structural unemployment or involuntary part-time employment per se. The obvious and extensive underutilization of workers with advanced knowledge flies in face of their prevalent assumptions about the growing centrality of theoretical knowledge and "knowledge workers" in the production process, as well as the associated assumptions that both technological change and increased market competition lead to rapid skill upgrading of jobs.

In terms of class-specific differences, since the main criterion for entry into ownership positions is the possession of capital assets, knowledge credentials are generally a secondary consideration and rarely enforceable versus the power of wealth;[24] nevertheless, educational credentials have increasingly been used as a supplement to capital assets by executives to legitimate their exclusive control of corporate decisions. Small employers and the self-employed have been less able to control access to their markets by possession of capital assets and have remained relatively disorganized politically. So, small employers and the self-employed are more likely to perceive themselves as underemployed in terms of their entry credentials than corporate capitalists. Collins' (1979) credentialling argument at least implies that mobilized professional and managerial employees with specialized knowledge claims will generally be sufficiently successful in restricting access to educational credentials that there will be little difference between their actual attainments and the credential requirements they determine for future entry into their jobs. Semi-professional employees and supervisors tend to have less well defined knowledge claims or experiential knowledge bases in their jobs, so that they tend to meet the credential entry requirements of their jobs only moderately well. Most working class jobs, perhaps with the exception of a few traditional skilled crafts, are now generally subject to increased formal educational entry requirements imposed by employers; this may lead to both a high level of under-qualification as employers inflate entry credentials beyond previously hired workers' attainments, and a fairly high level of under-employment as prospective workers obtain ever higher formal attainments in pursuit of scarce good job offers. But, given the ease with which employers can inflate the requirements for entry credentials, especially for working class jobs, it is unlikely that credential underemployment will increase very rapidly.

As Table 5.4 suggests, the most notable class-specific finding concerning the credential gap is that it is fairly similar in most class groups. In virtually all class groups, including small employers and the self-employed for whom credential requirements are most arbitrary, a majority report that their educational attainments match their job entry requirements. The patterns of differences in credential underemployment are much as predicted, with one important

Table 5.4   Class Position by Credential Gap, Ontario Labour Force, 1984–1996

Class Position	% with higher credential than now required for job entry
Corporate executives	8
Small employers	21
Self-employed	25
Managers	10
Professionals	9
Semi-prof. employees	17
Supervisors	23
Service workers	
Skilled service	22
Other service	27
Industrial workers	
Skilled industrial	21
Other industrial	18
Total labour force	20
N	5000

Source: OISE Survey of Educational Issues Data Archive.

exception. As predicted, corporate executives do have significantly lower credential underemployment (8 percent) than small employers or the self-employed. Managers and professional employees also have similarly low credential underemployment, consistent with Collins' credential society perspective. All other employee classes have higher credential underemployment rates (17 percent or greater) that are about double those of executives and professional-managerial employees. But industrial and service workers do not have substantially higher credential underemployment rates that semi-professional and supervisory employees. The range of class differences in credential underemployment among these employee class groups is less than it is on most other dimensions of underemployment. This again underlines employers' flexible use of educational entry requirements for most of their employees in response to rapid increases in the educational attainments of prospective workers.

As detailed in Chapter Two, younger people are more likely to experience credential underemployment than older folks. Sex differences in the credential gap are generally insignificant. But visible minorities in all class positions are more likely to have excess credentials than those from other ethnic backgrounds, which confirms the persistence of race-related barriers to job entry.

Union status is insignificant in relation to the credential gap in all class positions, which is again indicative of employers' prerogative to alter entry credential requirements in conditions of a ready surplus of qualified job seekers. As long as employers retain this capacity to continually adjust entry credential requirements, the credential gap is likely to remain a relatively modest, if slowly increasing, underemployment problem.

Class and the Performance Gap

Both previous critical empirical research and the analysis in Chapter Two strongly suggest that there is a large and increasing *performance gap* in the workplaces of most advanced industrial market economies, in spite of gradual increases in technical skill requirements. The central congruent general prediction of both the neo-Marxist structural conflict theory of Carnoy and Levin (1985) and the neo-Weberian status competition theory of Collins (1979) is that the performance gap is likely to increase. In neo-Marxist terms this is because of the irresolvable contradiction between popular demand for more advanced education

and the more restrictive requirements of hierarchical capitalist production systems; in Collins' neo-Weberian terms, it is because more
and more specialized occupational groups try to impose elaborate credential regulations beyond the knowledge actually needed to do their
types of jobs. I concur with both of these general arguments.

In class-specific terms, any performance gap that might exist for
owners is likely to be quite small since business owners generally
directly control their own working conditions. Once again, any discrepancies between their performance capacities and their chances to
apply them are likely to be related to their enterprises' extent of control of market entry requirements, so corporate executives should
have the lowest performance underemployment rates and the self-
employed should have the highest among the owner classes. "Middle
class" employees, including managers, professionals, semi-professionals and supervisors, are likely to experience at least moderate
underemployment of their work-related knowledge, with the credentialized knowledge they have acquired to obtain their jobs in competitive labour markets sometimes exceeding what they actually need to
perform them. Industrial and service workers, however, are likely to
have considerably higher levels of performance underemployment.
With the growing surplus of qualified job seekers in contemporary
economies, workers generally have been unable either to effectively
contest employers' hiring prerogatives to select more highly qualified
applicants than jobs really need, or to prevent employers from keeping actual skill performance requirements substantially beneath
workers' own knowledge capacities. Indeed, performance underemployment may increase in many working class jobs at the same time
as the physical intensity of their workloads also increases.

The general Ontario profiles of performance underemployment by
class position are summarized in Table 5.5. These profiles rely on the
same four different estimates of the performance gap that were discussed in Chapter Two. As noted in Chapter Two, these measures
(Burris; Berg1; Berg5; Eckhaus) are successively less restrictive in the
formal educational levels they equate with the GED score requirements of jobs. But regardless of which of these sets of assumptions one
takes to be most plausible, the pattern of class differences in performance underemployment is very similar. As predicted, corporate executives have the lowest underemployment rates of all class groups;
small employers and the self-employed have medium underemployment rates consistent with their lesser control of market entry. Man-

Table 5.5 Class Position by Performance Gap,
Ontario Labour Force, 1984–1996

Class Position	% with more schooling than required for actual job performance			
	Burris	Berg5	Berg1	Eckhaus
Corporate executives*	1	5	17	17
Small employers	15	20	37	49
Self-employed	19	27	44	58
Managers	12	15	40	43
Professionals	12	35	50	50
Semi-prof. employees	11	19	37	43
Supervisors	8	9	35	53
Service workers				
Skilled service	36	52	72	91
Other service	32	47	65	84
Industrial workers				
Skilled industrial	27	40	56	82
Other industrial	33	43	63	83
Total labour force	22	33	52	67
N	5309	5309	5309	5309

*Special supplementary samples of corporate executives (N=727)

Source: OISE Survey of Educational Issues Data Archive.

agers, professionals, semi-professionals and supervisors exhibit similar medium levels of performance underemployment which are either slightly less than or overlap with the underemployment rates of small employers and the self-employed. Again as predicted and most significantly, *service and industrial workers of all skill levels consistently experience much higher levels of performance underemployment than all other class groups.* Whatever measure is used, those employed in working class jobs are at least 50 percent more likely than those in most other class positions to have educational credentials that exceed the skill requirements of their jobs.

Younger people tend to experience higher levels of performance underemployment; 29 percent of those aged 18 to 24 are overquali-fied for their jobs, compared to 15 percent of those over 55. Both trend analysis and cross-sectional comparisons of age cohorts suggest that differences in performance underemployment between the working class and other classes are widening over time. For example, we can compare professional employees and skilled industrial workers, the working class group that has historically had the greatest organiza-tional capacity to control their conditions of employment. While per-formance underemployment rates for professional employees remain fairly constant around 12 percent across age cohorts and over time, the rates for industrial workers increase from 13 percent among skilled industrial workers over 55 years of age to 36 percent among workers aged 25 to 34. *In contrast to post-industrial rhetoric about greater worker participation in the social division of labour, these findings indicate that the working class has been losing control over job performance require-ments rather than gaining it in recent generations.*

There are no discernible sex differences in performance underem-ployment, with the notable exception of corporate executives. Cor-porate executives and skilled industrial workers are the two class positions that have remained almost exclusive male preserves as women increased their participation very significantly in all other forms of employment. The few women who have made it into the skilled trades appear to have been treated fairly, at least in the sense of not having to obtain higher qualifications than male tradesper-sons. But women who have made it into the board room have gen-erally been extremely well qualified and remain much more likely (about 40 percent) to be underemployed than male executives. Visi-ble minorities are somewhat more likely (29 percent) to experience performance underemployment than other ethnic groups (about 20 percent), a difference that applies across all class positions.

Those who have higher educational attainments also tend to have higher rates of performance underemployment: 15 percent for school dropouts; 28 percent for high school graduates; 35 percent for com-munity college graduates; and 41 percent for university graduates. This confirms the general trend found in Chapter Two. That is, in contrast to the recent stability in the credential gap, the performance gap is increasing as aggregate educational attainments outpace the skill upgrading of jobs. Unions have not demonstrated any greater capacity to mediate performance requirements than entry require-ments; there are no significant differences between unionized and nonunionized workers in their high levels of performance underemployment.

Overall, the performance gap findings suggest that *the current organization of paid work wastes a substantial amount of peoples' work-related knowledge across the class structure.* Depending on the estimates used, the performance underemployment of professional employees varies from 12 percent to 50 percent; while Collins (1979) does not offer quantitative estimates, his case studies strongly suggest high levels of performance underemployment among professionals. But the present analysis indicates that there is an even greater waste of relevant knowledge in the working class, where the performance gap is now also increasing most rapidly.

Class and Subjective Underemployment

Finally, *subjective underemployment,* people's sense that their knowledge and skills are being wasted in their present employment situation, is likely to be influenced by their actual status on some of the preceding five dimensions, by the effectiveness of opposing ideological claims about the degree of authority and control respective classes have in the workplace, and by a host of other mediating socio-historical conditions. The following class-specific predictions are therefore very tentative.

Corporate executives are probably least likely to think of themselves as underemployed because their class position is the most powerful and exclusive, as well as most richly compensated. Other owners' perceptions of the extent of their use of their working knowledge is likely to vary with the extent to which they can control their firm's market performance, so the self-employed may more frequently think of themselves as underemployed than small employers will. Professionals and managers are likely to have relatively low perceptions of underemployment, either because they see themselves as collectively controlling their own knowledge base or because they have succeeded in a long and arduous formal training program for a "calling" which they take to define their work more than their everyday tasks. The perceptions of other employees are more difficult to predict. Semi-professional employees also have specialized knowledge bases but, with less discretionary control over the definition of their jobs, may be somewhat more likely than professionals and managers to see their actual job requirements as discrepant with these knowledge bases. Supervisors may or may not have specialized knowledge bases that are superior to the most skilled employees they supervise. But their experiential knowledge is typically substantial, and their sense of underemployment is likely to be contingent on the extent to which both of these forms of knowledge are called upon by their own superiors; in the prevalent North American organizational model, supervisors sense of underemployment may be fairly high. Workers may generally have an even greater sense that much of their really useful knowledge is being wasted in jobs which they have usually had little role in designing. But skilled industrial workers who have extensive specialized training for their trades may still define their work more in terms of their traditional trade than their actual job requirements, much like classical professionals.

As discussed in Chapter Two, I have identified three distinct aspects of subjective underemployment: perception of overqualification for current job; unfulfilled desire to use work skills that are not recognized in present job; and sense of entitlement to a better job. The three aspects are both conceptually and empirically distinct. The results for these three measures by class position are summarized in Table 5.6.

As predicted, corporate executives have the lowest levels of subjective underemployment on all measures, while small employers have consistently higher levels and the self-employed have even higher levels. But managers and professionals tend to have higher levels of subjective underemployment than predicted, generally comparable to those of semi-professionals. Supervisors have even higher levels of subjective underemployment which are largely indistinguishable from the high levels expressed by most working class groups.

A few distinctive findings within the working class are worthy of note. As predicted, skilled industrial workers very rarely (6 percent) feel overqualified for their jobs, probably because they identify most closely with their trade rather than current task requirements; conversely, they are far more likely (66 percent) than any other class group to feel they have skills that are untapped by their current job. Industrial workers in less skilled jobs express relatively low levels (24 percent) of desire to use unrecognized job skills, probably because of high levels of alienation from routinized work.

The generally high levels of subjective underemployment among the working class groups are mainly as predicted. But subjective underemployment is higher than predicted among professional-

Table 5.6 Class Position by Subjective Underemployment, Ontario Labour Force, 1994–1996

Class Position	% who feel overqualified for present job	% with skills untapped in present job	% who feel school entitles them to better job*	Ave. of columns 1, 2, 3
Corporate executives**	2	20	5	9
Small employers	14	32	29	25
Self-employed	19	38	41	33
Managers	14	37	27	26
Professionals	23	46	28	32
Semi-prof. employees	15	45	40	33
Supervisors	29	42	54	42
Service workers				
Skilled service	26	42	44	37
Other service	38	41	53	44
Industrial workers				
Skilled industrial	6	66	39	37
Other industrial	22	24	48	31
Total Labour Force	23	40	43	35
N	968	1280	2639	

*Data from 1986, 1988, 1990, 1992 as well as 1994–96.
**Special supplementary samples of corporate executives

Source: OISE Survey of Educational Issues Data Archive.

managerial employees, semi-professionals and supervisors. *While the sense of wastage of work-related knowledge is highest within the working class, it is also quite extensive across the rest of the class structure, with the exception of corporate executives.*

Feelings of overqualification for one's job are much more common among younger people in all class positions; while over 40 percent of those in employment who are aged 18 to 24 feel their qualifications exceed their job requirements, this sentiment drops to around 25 percent among those aged 25 to 34 and then declines regularly so that only

5 percent of those over 55 express this view. Women in most classes are not significantly more likely than men to perceive themselves to be overqualified for their jobs. School dropouts are generally less likely to feel overqualified (10 percent) than those at all higher educational attainment levels. Unionized employees may be slightly less likely to feel overqualified (15 percent) than nonunionized employees (25 percent). But the sense of overqualification is most concentrated among younger people in lower class positions, most notably majorities of those under 25 in less skilled working class jobs. Similar patterns occur on the other measures of subjective underemployment.

Those in visible minority groups — whether or not they feel overqualified — are more likely than whites to feel they are entitled to a better job, and more likely to think that they have skills that are wasted in their present jobs. Again these feelings of entitlement and wastage are greatest among visible minorities in lower class positions, especially feelings of entitlement to better jobs among visible minority service workers.

Prior U.S. case studies have suggested that low level clerical service workers have relatively high levels of subjective overqualification (B. Burris 1983a), a finding consistent with our finding of the highest levels of subjective overqualification among less skilled service workers. Lowe's (1992, 58) Canadian national survey in 1989 found very similar levels of subjective overqualification by occupational class as our more recent Ontario surveys; managerial and professional employees expressed substantially higher levels of overqualification than either service workers or blue collar workers. The related longitudinal surveys by Krahn and Lowe (1993) in Edmonton, Alberta, have found the highest levels of subjective overqualification among young university graduates who are service or blue collar workers, just as I have. Derber's (1978, 1979) studies of unemployed suburban Boston workers found similar levels of entitlement to a better job to those expressed by the unemployed in the present study. However, there is little evidence that the incidence of subjective underemployment on any of these measures has increased substantially among the lower classes over the past generation. For example, the measure for which we have the longest time series in the Ontario surveys, sense of entitlement to a better job, has been basically stable among both service workers and industrial workers over the past ten years. While some aspects of objective underemployment have certainly increased during this period, it may be that more educated workers have continued to orient toward trying to maintain their relative privileges within established work settings and labour markets, in part through the pursuit of even more credentials, rather than becoming more critical of established workplaces and other social institutions. As Beverly Burris (1983b, 108) concluded in the early 1980s:

> It appears, then, that new working class theory [and other approaches that expect objective underemployment to lead directly to political disaffection] has underestimated how the elitism and individualism of educated workers can counteract any tendencies towards radical discontent.

CONCLUDING REMARKS

The underlying dynamics of capitalist production — inter-firm competition, the struggles between owners and employees over profits and wages, and the consequent revisions of production techniques — continually lead to changes in the specific organization of paid work, and provoke workers to continually learn more in order to be able to adapt to these changes and keep their jobs or try to find new ones. This new and different job-related information is not necessarily more complex or more advanced knowledge; much of what is occurring is job enlargement with increasing numbers and intensity of tasks, rather than job enrichment using more comprehensive knowledge systems in more discretionary ways. The education-jobs gap is primarily related not to educational deficiencies but to "job churning." In particular, underemployment of highly qualified workers is a systemic problem which is far more than an issue of "frictional adjustment."

The analyses presented throughout this book suggest that there has been extensive and increasing underemployment of the working knowledge of many well-qualified people throughout the past generation, especially in North America. Most of the above posited predictions about the class distribution of underemployment have been tentatively confirmed. The class analysis indicates that most objective dimensions of underemployment are lowest among corporate owners and professional-managerial employees, and most prevalent among the working class. The working knowledge of the North American working class is definitely underused in contemporary workplaces. Additional analyses indicate that underemployment is often greatest among young people and visible minorities, and sometimes among women; all these factors tend to heighten class differences in underemployment.

Conversely, underemployment is generally lower among unionized workers than nonunion workers. All of these findings are consistent with a general conflict theory of underemployment of working knowledge that identifies the highest incidence with the least powerful social groups.

Further empirical research with different populations is clearly needed. But further studies in other times and places should keep in mind that these predictions refer to *relative* rather than absolute levels of *underemployment*. If the global capitalist economy enters another period of expansion, global levels of unemployment could fall and levels of underemployment on other dimensions could also fall because of enhanced bargaining power on the job for workers. In other words, underemployment is not a evolutionary phenomenon that irreversibly grows. It is continually subject to change on all dimensions through further contestation by various social groups. But as long as the underlying structure of power is grounded in capitalist property relations, working class people will remain most likely to experience objective underemployment.

A subjective sense of underemployment may be fairly widespread across the class structure in North America. Subjective underemployment tends to be somewhat higher among the working class than those in higher class positions, but less consistently than objective underemployment. The apparent stability of responses to questions of overqualification, job entitlement and untapped skills over the past generation in North America suggests that subjective underemployment has not been increasing in concert with increases in more objective measures of underemployment during this period.

The incidence of subjective underemployment is likely to be closely related to people's individual and collective sense of alternatives to overcome the education-jobs gap. Even if one is highly underemployed in objective terms, it may not be very useful to take critical action in response to this condition or even to recognize its existence, unless some *real vehicle* for practical effect is clearly available. Educational upgrading has been a practical individual response because it has improved relative chances of getting a decent job. But at the same time it has stimulated credential inflation and the impoverishment of relatively less credentialed workers who get squeezed out of the jobs race. Ultimately educational upgrading becomes a less and less viable means of coping with objective underemployment. But all subjective and objective aspects of the education-jobs gap continue to be negotiated social relationships, subject to collective actions that can close or expand the gap fairly quickly. As the value of individual educational upgrading depreciates, the attraction of more collective alternatives, particularly alternative ways of organizing work, could well be increasing. I will turn to an assessment of such alternatives and popular receptivity to them in the final chapter.

6

Bridging the Gap:
Prospects for Work Reorganization
in Advanced Capitalism

The future will be determined by whether people can confront capitalism's repetitive pathologies and organize a new system that genuinely merges markets with democracy.... The ownership of productive capital must be broadly shared in societies as the predicate for discovering genuine democracy and general social well-being. The industrial system must be reinvented to save the earth. The social values that are precious to most people must be freed from the confinements of [global capitalist private market] imperatives and allowed to find fuller expression. These ideas are not utopian platitudes but the hard, practical work of the future.

—Greider 1997, 469–70

I feel like an outcast in one of the world's wealthiest countries. I just can't get a job and I have nobody to really talk to. I wish I had more power to make things happen. I would create jobs for all people. Just because you are a nobody doesn't mean you can't become a somebody.... If I could be a genie or something, I would switch roles between an executive and a street kid. Let the executive panhandle, eat and sleep in shelters. Let's see how they would feel about that. If these executives were more in touch with people they would be able to help us more.

—Kris Riches, unemployed young male
high school graduate, 1997, SS5

INTRODUCTION

If underemployment of peoples' knowledge and skills in the legal labour market economy of advanced capitalist societies is as extensive as the prior analyses suggest, recommendations that stress the need for more and better education miss the point. Our primary emphasis should rather be on reorganizing work to enable more people to apply in legitimate and sustainable ways the knowledge and skills they already possess. In this final chapter, I will: (1) briefly examine past and possible future forms of work; (2) suggest that recognition of the importance of unpaid household and community work and informal learning can aid in bridging the gap between paid work and organized schooling and lead to a sustainable knowledge society; (3) explore work reorganization and underemployment under basic economic alternatives broadly identified as "shareholder capitalism," "stakeholder capitalism" and "economic democracy"; and (4) assess popular support for these alternatives, especially features of economic democracy (i.e. socialized ownership; worker self-management; reduced standard workweeks; green work) that can serve to close the education-jobs gap. Without *active popular support for economic alternatives related to more democratic visions of work organization*, little substantial reduction in current levels of underemployment is likely in the near future.

PAST AND FUTURE WORK

To live is also to act. Human beings are an active and creative species who express themselves through their labours, both in reaction to the external world and in action to change it. Through our actions and reactions we change both the external world and our own nature. In pre-industrial societies, most people *worked to live*. In hunter-gatherer societies, food production work typically took up 3 to 5 hours a day and most men spent the rest of their time in rest, sleep and other, often ritualized ceremonial activities; women's domestic work was never done but it was conducted at a slower pace than in modern times (Sahlins 1974). In feudal societies a few hundred years ago, serfs were tied to the land to produce for both their own subsistence and the conspicuous consumption of their lords. Their still ample free time appears to have been commonly used to rest and recuperate from these subsistence and tithing labours, and to engage in mainly ritualized cultural activities (Hill 1967).

Only with the emergence of industrial capitalism did most people begin to *live for their productive work*. As serfs were driven from the land and the factory production system developed, people became "free" to chose to work for the best employer they could find rather than endure severe poverty. The working day for hired industrial labourers lengthened immensely to consume most of the waking hours of men, women and even children. With the introduction of large-scale machinery, daily life became rigidly structured around "factory time."[1] The notion that humans are defined by their work, homo faber, effectively emerged with these harsh realities of nineteenth century capitalism. The subsequent struggles of organized workers in the context of increasingly efficient production technologies led to gradual reductions in the standard workweek for most wage earners through most of the past century. But most peoples' personal and household relations to paid work had become central to their personal identity. This is so both because the particular type of employment one was able to obtain came to largely determine the material conditions of the rest of one's life, and because our socialization through the family, church and school, as well as government policies and employment and welfare agencies, have continued to emphasize a necessary link between paid work, human dignity and the possibility of self-fulfillment. The need to work remains a central feature of most people's personal identity in advanced capitalist societies today.[2] Psychologists now find that most people want to work even when their subsistence is provided, because of three common motives:

> the desire for a feeling of competence, that is, the belief that when one acts the environment responds; the desire for self-esteem; and the desire for consistency, that is, a sense of continuity with past experience, and an integrated identity. (Langmore and Quiggin 1994, 10)

As an unemployed American worker put it shortly before he killed himself recently, "Working is breathing…. When you stop you die." (Cottle 1992, 16). Governments and their commissions are compelled to at least pay heavy lip service to the political reality of these popular desires:

> Work [today] plays a crucial and perhaps unparalleled psychological role in the formation of self-esteem, identity, and a sense of order. (U.S. Department of Health, Education and Welfare 1973, 4)

The most elementary distinction among different types of work is between production for *direct use*, barter and community exchange on the one hand, and production for *external exchange,* for money. People work to make something of benefit to themselves, their families and communities *or* they work to make money in return for making something for others. This basic distinction is only awkwardly projected onto world history because ever since people exchanged products with other peoples via trade, and sent significant amounts of their product out of the community, ever since they began to employ some general equivalent, some form of money, to expedite that external trade, then from that time on, *production for community use and production for exchange with others were combined* in a single economy.

The major impetus for development of long-distance trade came from European merchants who bought cheaply abroad and sold dearly at home to amass great wealth. Over the past five centuries the money economy has become increasingly dominant, the division of labour has increased greatly, and the proportion of all goods produced in a given locale that are consumed locally has steadily declined. The subsistence-based economy has been systematically displaced, its labour economically devalued. The relative value of subsistence work has been undermined and submerged. This process of displacement of subsistence work is not irreversible but it is ongoing.

Subsistence labour for direct use is still important, as is evident every time we prepare and then consume a home-cooked meal, for example. We still find it emotionally valuable to make time as a family, to cook a meal together and then sit down and eat it together. This commensality or mutually beneficial food production/consumption is universal to our species. But such integrative activities are becoming more and more "relatively inefficient" in the terms of the money economy. The more economic use of our time in these terms is to work overtime at the plant or office, then rush home with a take-out order. This may be economically enriching but spiritually impoverishing. The consequences of this private market-driven efficiency are increasing numbers of overworked and emotionally drained people, at the same time as there are increasing numbers of people who are underemployed and emotionally drained.

Can we shift the balance? Can we restore the value of production for community use and provide more meaningful work for the underemployed, while making production for profitable sale serve the local community in socially valuable ways, instead of simply supplying more and more relatively cheap commodities to private consumers while undermining community self-sufficiency?

None of us want to reject the benefits of external trade. I happen to love to eat bananas. It is impossible to grow them in the northerly locale where I live. Those in warmer climates may have developed tastes for wheat products or maple syrup which they cannot produce. By trading our comparative advantages we can diversify and enrich our respective modes of consumption, as well as remaining motivated to continue to enhance our specialized production knowledges to gain further comparative advantages. Just because I need money to buy bananas doesn't mean that I will leave my family and community for any opportunity to make the money to buy this lovely fruit, or any other bunch of commodities, however desirable. With our rich supply of talent and knowledge, we should be able to find ways to sustain our communities and produce enough surplus product to trade externally for other things we want.

The first step toward community sustainability is to recognize that work is always a dual activity. It creates an end product (a use-value) and it generates a human experience for the producers/reproducers. This duality applies to all work, to production for community use and to production for market sale. What sense we make of our work competence and contribution, and how our work is recognized by others are important to the formation of our identity.

Production for community use closes the field-to-table loop within the meaningful human circle, among the people we live with, know to meet, and care about. The two outcomes of work, the end-product and the experience, can be more readily integrated in these cases. In subsistence activities, people get to enjoy the fruits of their labour directly or they get to observe significant others doing so. There is a production-consumption feedback loop which makes work meaningful in an integrated way. We tend to take much more pride in things we or others around us have built than in things we have bought in impersonal market exchanges.

Where the product is put up for sale to anyone who wishes to purchase, this link is never made. The first purpose of production becomes making money. But since money cannot feed, clothe and shelter us, we must go to the market to purchase food, clothing and housing, then convert these consummables through unpaid domestic work. These two labours, paid employment and domestic labour, become separated in time and place under capitalist production.[3] Domestic work becomes subordinated to making money via wage work and efforts to combine and co-ordinate the two labours become increasingly vexed. At the same time, wage work becomes a means to an impersonal end, making money. It becomes alienating in terms of: (a) appropriation of one's labour power by employers and a struggle with employers over the distribution of earnings; (b) the end product being removed from the community and consumed anonymously; (c) workers' loss of control of the use of their working knowledge and competencies, with work assignments they may have mastered and enjoy being open to arbitrary change; and (d) lack of any necessary or consistent relation between the quality of one's work and the longevity of employment. Wage employment becomes determined by private market forces which appear remote and totally separated from subsistence labours.

As Chapter Three graphically illustrates, people generally would prefer to work, to secure their own livelihoods as an integral aspect of controlling their own destiny. If striving for self-determination can be posited as a near-universal, then the economic basis of that drive is to make ends meet, to produce the equivalent of one's own consumption, to be a contributor. Thus, not only is lack of employment soul-destroying in modern society, but those whose active labours are underused or unrecognized also feel wasted and demoralized.

We need to find better ways both to recognize subsistence work and to reconnect it with the money economy. In contemporary capitalist societies, work is generally divided into three fairly distinct spheres of life: paid work in the sphere of commodity exchange; domestic labour; and community volunteer work.

Paid work in the production, distribution and exchange of goods and service commodities is predominant. Most paid work in advanced capitalist states now involves legal activities that are recorded and taxed by governments. This work has been the focus of prior chapters. But a growing proportion of paid work is in activities beyond the grasp of governments in the so-called "underground economy."[4] There are trivial forms of monetary exchanges of goods and services that escape government detection, such as some flea markets and yard sales. The major underground economic activities include both "under the table" payments for legal labour such as residential construction, and production and sale of narcotic drugs, prostitution, some kinds of pornography and other illicit goods and services. Serious estimates of the extent of the underground economy have ranged from a few percentage points to over a third of the Gross Domestic Product (GDP) in advanced capitalist economies (Frey and Pommerehne 1984; P. Smith 1994).[5] Beyond anecdotal accounts, systematic studies of the organization and forms of labour in these areas, most notably organized crime and inner-city ghetto economies, have yet to be done. The central point here is that as long as underemployment in legitimate paid work increases, many people are likely to seek compensations for their underemployment through the underground economy (see Currie 1993).

Another form of directly compensated or "paid" labour still frequently conducted in household and community spheres is the production of goods and services for non-monetary exchange. Prior to the emergence of long-distance trading systems, barter between small commodity producers in local markets was a major means of acquiring all you needed to live. Barter systems have persisted within localities among friends and neighbors. Underemployment in wage work has rejuvenated barter activities and led to the development of more extensive organized forms, such as the Local Employment and Trading System (LETS) (Dobson 1993).

Paid work is hardly the only important form of human labour even in the most technologically advanced economies: domestic labour and community volunteer work both remain essential to the continuance of human life. Reproductive labour and household tasks have generally been performed mainly by women throughout history.[6] Recent estimates indicate that domestic cooking, cleaning, child care and other household tasks take up about as much of our total time as paid work (Statistics Canada 1997; Robinson and Godbey 1997). National accounting systems have completely ignored the value of these labours (Waring 1988). While there are now increased efforts to commodify domestic labours — for example, home cleaning companies and surrogate mothers — this work is now largely hidden in the household and greatly undervalued as merely "women's work." Women in dual-earner heterosexual households have recently had some marginal success in getting their male partners to share more equally in housework (Seccombe 1987; Statistics Canada 1997). But in societies that value paid work so highly and have now provided so much preparatory schooling for women, those confined purely to an unpaid domestic role have increasingly felt unable to use their capacities fully and exhibited a high incidence of depression (Sayers 1976, 12–13).

In addition, many people continue to produce goods and services for their own household use. Making your own home repairs and renovations, clothing and gifts, as well as food growing and preserving tend to see a resurgence as underemployment reduces incomes and provides the time.

The diverse activities involved in building communities and preserving ecosystems are certainly necessary forms of labour to sustain social life as well. Such labours as collecting resources for infirm people, leading children's clubs and teams, serving in community organizations, and participating in environmental cleanup programs are often called "volunteer work" and typically have been accorded little material reward. Community volunteer work may have declined as we have become more caught up in urbanized, commodified structures of activity. Recent estimates indicate that on average we now spend about one-twentieth as much time on community work as we do on household work (Statistics Canada 1997). I suspect that this estimate, based on a conventional time use survey, captures only a fraction of many people's socially useful community activities. In any case, the centrality of community volunteer work to a decent human existence becomes more evident when we experience periods of isolation through unemployment, graveyard shift schedules or other alienating social conditions. In Robert Putnam's (1995) graphic example, nobody wants to bowl alone. The necessity of community work for building a democratic and sustainable society is increasingly being recognized in research on "social capital" (Edwards and Foley 1997) and the "third sector" (Rifkin 1995). Such work is now taken up for diverse motives, including sense of family responsibility, civic duty, fear of extinction, and the pleasure of the activity itself. Whatever the motivation, those who engage extensively in such necessary labours have been unable to make their living in this way.

Overall estimates of the proportion of people's labour time that is devoted to work activities beyond paid work, and of the value that should be imputed to such work, vary immensely. Time estimates face the challenge of counting simultaneous and overlapping unpaid tasks without discrete start and stop times. Value estimates are even more problematic given the pervasive tendency in standard economic analyses to discount "external economies" and ignore unpaid household and community work, while at the same time adding nonproductive monetized activities such as the costs of auto accidents and oil spills into the GDP. Some recent serious estimates — using forgone earnings, opportunity cost and replacement cost methods — suggest that the monetary value of household labour is now between 30 and 50 percent of the GDP (Chandler 1994). If the same average value applied to community volunteer work, it would probably now amount to at very least about two percent of the GDP (P. Smith 1994). Whatever the actual magnitude of all this unpaid household and community work in contemporary societies, it is very extensive and vital to the survival of our species and — as long as we are allowed to be part of it — the global ecosystem.

The notion that we live by and need to identify ourselves in terms of our **paid** employment is increasingly revealed as a recent historical creation rather than an inherent part of our being. Not only does anthropological and historiographic research show that productive work was not as much of a preoccupation in earlier societies as it became in money market-driven ones. But, as machine-intensive production increases and the availability of decent paid jobs declines in advanced private market economies, the viability of a continuing connection between paid work and identity is being challenged, most prominently by the advocates of a leisure society.

Leisure society theorists of both post-industrial and neo-Marxist persuasions (Bell 1973; Gorz 1982, 1985) generally suggest that people's creative use of their free time will naturally blossom as they are released from the coercive need to work. Such arguments serve to point out that the work-identity relation is as subject to future variations as it has been to past ones. As a species, we have worked to live, then lived for our work. Perhaps in the distant future we could live without work as we presently understand it. But leisure society theorists have made two fatal errors.

First, they have equated work with paid employment or productive labour, and thereby at least imply that other waking activities are part of freely chosen leisure time. For those women engaged in the endless demands of childcare and associated domestic labour, and particularly for those who have added the double burden of dual-earner status, leisure time may still be quite elusive even in the most technologically advanced societies. Similarly, a significant portion of unpaid community labour is not freely chosen but remains necessary in order for social groups to reproduce themselves. Both reproductive domestic and community sustaining activities will require significant amounts of necessary labour time for the foreseeable future. In addition, as noted above, a wide array of economic activities transacted between households through barter or other cashless transactions remain largely invisible to leisure theorists and professional economists alike. To *ignore and undervalue* all this work as conventional paid work disappears is both to denigrate the women who continue to do so much of it, and to fail to identify these necessary labours as alternative sources of self-fulfilling work. These alternative forms of work could be redistributed as current forms of decent paid work decline and large numbers of underemployed people continue to feel the need to work.

Secondly, leisure society theorists have tended to treat our need for creative use of our actual free time as an inherent, ahistorical urge that will naturally fill up the day beyond our necessary labours. But the extensive active, free and creative use of non-work time by working people is largely a development of modern industrial society (Cunningham 1980). The devotion of non-work time to autonomous activities such as arts and crafts, hobbies, sports and recreation has grown very substantially since the eighteenth century in industrial societies. Of course, we still have many passive leisure pursuits too; TV watching has replaced many of the ritualized cultural diversions of the past and may have increased more rapidly than more creative non-work activities in recent decades (Robinson and Godbey 1997). But growth in a need for positive active use of non-work time has been historically *related* to the growth of the need to work. This relationship has tended to apply to individuals as well. Studies of unemployed people in the 1930s depression and in recent recessions have found that they often *decrease* their active leisure activities (see O'Brien 1986). But as Chapter Three documents, the urge to paid work remains very strong even among the chronically unemployed. In today's credential society, underemployed people are now devoting increasing amounts of their discretionary time to organized and informal learning activities with the objective of obtaining better paid work.

Rewarding work is now so important for most peoples' identities that when they don't have it for protracted periods, they do become depressed and less creative. Whatever the long-term future changes in work-identity relations, this is the reality that we must deal with for the foreseeable future. Most of us in advanced industrial societies now strongly feel a need to engage in some form of paid work in order to be at all happy. Even if all the hidden and undervalued forms of work could be instantly automated, we are not about to march gladly into a fully leisured society as passive consumers and captivated hobbyists. For a sense of self-esteem, continuity and competence, we still need to do work that is widely recognized by those around us. As economies dominated by production for external sale and private profit continue to convert previous subsistence labours into commodified ones, it is possible that there will eventually be less work of any necessary kind, paid or unpaid. But that may well make its distribution an even greater challenge and underemployment an even larger social problem than it is now.

BRIDGING THE EDUCATION-JOBS GAP

As Michael Polyani (1983, 23–24) has demonstrated generally with regard to the process of scientific discovery:

> We can have a tacit foreknowledge of yet undiscovered things.... Tacit knowledge is shown to account (1) for a valid knowledge of a problem, (2) for the scientist's capacity to pursue it, guided by a sense of approaching its solution, and (3) for a valid anticipation of the yet indeterminate implications of the discovery arrived at in the end.

We all have at least a tacit understanding that unpaid work activities and also informal learning constitute significant portions of our everyday lives. The central problem of this book is the underemployment of most people's knowledge and skills in paid jobs. My search for a solution to the problem of underemployment has been guided by a lifetime of experience and observation of the wasting of much of subordinate workers' knowledge in various paid workplaces (a sort of tacit knowledge of the waste of others' tacit knowledge), and by the anticipation that an effective resolution lay not in the pursuit of still more formal knowledge but the reorganization of work to permit the fuller use of existing knowledge.

The real contribution of Bowles and Gintis' (1976) correspondence principle was to observe the historical development of analogous organizational forms of the social relations of schooling and the social relations of capitalist production. But closing the education-jobs production gap requires recognition of other existing and emergent connections between learning and work. The optimal solution to the education-jobs gap lies in reconnecting schooling and jobs with those dimensions of work and learning that they have been separated from with the spread of industrial capitalism.

Figure 6.1 summarizes the general condition of learning-work relations in advanced capitalist societies at present. It also illustrates

Figure 6.1   Work and Learning Connections

A. *Current Connections*

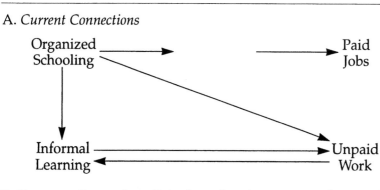

B. *Emergent Connections: Prior Learning Assessment and Recognition*

C. *Missing Links*

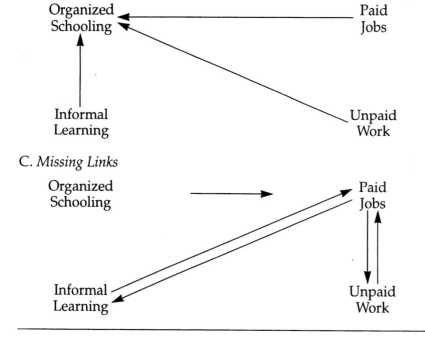

the generic ingredients of the solution to the gap, although only in terms of simple dichotomies. As Chapter One has shown, our preoccupation with organized schooling has ignored the hidden iceberg of informal learning. As the above account suggests, conventional economic analysis has largely ignored or devalued unpaid work. As Chapters Two through Five document, the link between organized schooling and paid jobs through competitive labour markets has become highly problematic.

However, the reciprocal links between informal learning and unpaid work have remained quite close. People in advanced capitalist societies face few constraints, besides their available time, to applying whatever they learn informally to any household and community work they do; they are free to seek new knowledge to aid in doing such unpaid work from many information sources, such as public libraries, self-help books, educational television, computer networks and friends and neighbors. People are also free to apply school knowledge as they wish in the spheres of informal learning and unpaid work. In liberal democratic states, most folks now take these connections to be self-evident.

There are also some emergent connections of work and learning. With growth of the availability of school offerings and of the popular belief in the necessity of school credentials, people have become increasingly predisposed to want to combine their extensive informal learning as well as their existing paid and unpaid work skills with further organized schooling. Adult educators have long argued for making organized schooling more accessible to mature learners on the basis of their life experience. But when "lockstep" enrollments of post-WWII baby boom cohorts began to decline, many school and college administrations became more receptive to the adult population as the only alternative source to refill their classrooms. In spite of the problems of overqualification of many workers for existing jobs, employers have become increasingly receptive to supporting job retraining and skill upgrading programs through organized schooling, as a means of enhancing the "intellectual capital" and competitive advantage of their enterprises (see Stewart 1997). During the past decade or so, there have been concerted initiatives to develop better institutional mechanisms to recognize and assess people's prior informal knowledge and paid and unpaid work skills, and to design further education programs that can build directly on existing tacit skills and knowledge.[7] But these very promising initiatives remain small and it is yet to be demonstrated whether they will have positive feedback effects, particularly in the sphere of paid work. In any case, overcoming the education-jobs gap between organized schooling and paid work will take a lot more than a few successful skill upgrading programs.

For most employable adults, the missing links all involve paid work. Besides the schooling-paid work gap documented extensively in prior chapters, there are major barriers between informal learning and paid work, and also between unpaid work and paid work. Most people receive few incentives to bring their wealth of informal learning to bear on their jobs. Certainly most of us have to continue to exercise our tacit knowledge on the job in order to do our jobs; formal job descriptions and specified technical skills are never enough (see Kusterer 1978; Hamper 1992). But, as every ethnography of paid work documents, few folks are inclined to hone these tacit skills off the job and most receive zero reward for bringing informal knowledge gained elsewhere to enrich or improve their paid jobs.[8]

The gap between paid and unpaid work is even greater. As the prior section suggests, the separation of wage work from all other forms of human work has been one of the signal achievements of capitalism. All other forms of work have been devalued and made largely invisible. If it isn't commodified, it doesn't count. Depending on our social location, we have tended to become either fixated on our paid work or alienated from it. The rich array of experiences we gain in our unpaid work and the continuing informal learning stimulated by these experiences are now largely divorced from our paid work. Our personal identities have become so tightly bound to our paid work statuses that most of us cannot even clearly see this disjuncture as a problem. We need the money and that's all there is.

In order for the education-jobs gap to be effectively resolved, or even significantly reduced, the missing links must be rejoined. If we can find ways of revaluing unpaid work and informal learning in relation to paid work, then the other current and emergent connections between work and learning will be immensely nourished. The only other gap, the underemployment of organized schooling in paid work which I have mainly focussed on in the prior analysis, could not be sustained under the pressure of all these other reciprocal interactions of work and learning. It boils down to the following if-then proposition:

(a) if I could combine my household and community work with my paid work; and

(b) if my informal learning relevant to both my paid work and unpaid work can be given further certification in organized schooling; and

(c) if all major interest groups agree on the merits of job upgrading school programs; then

(d) the redesign of paid jobs to respond to all of the experiential-ly-based work and learning demands flowing through orga-nized schooling would be unavoidable.

These are big "ifs."

Everything revolves around the reorganization of paid work. What-ever tacit knowledge we may have about the array of work and learn-ing relations, effective reconnections will require identification of *spe-cific economic alternatives* to the status quo and *political commitment* from many people. As we all know at least tacitly, and as Chapter Five shows, there are very powerful social forces interested in maintaining established disconnections and partial connections between work and learning. The next section addresses specific economic alternatives and their likely effects on education and learning. The final section exam-ines the question of the public will to close the education-jobs gap.

ECONOMIC ALTERNATIVES: SHAREHOLDER CAPITALISM, STAKEHOLDER CAPITALISM OR ECONOMIC DEMOCRACY

Alternative patterns of the social division of labour are not only required by our moral interests in human welfare but are fully com-patible with our economic interests in efficient production.... Experi-ments in job design have shown that there is usually a variety of effi-cient divisions of labour; the actually existing division of labour is almost never experimentally established, but is simply the product of customary rules of thumb. (Murphy 1993, 15, 165)

Contemporary economic thought suffers from a severe absence of vision. No analysis of the forms and dynamics of a social system is likely to be more than superficial if its historical specificity is not rec-ognized. But, as Heilbroner and Milberg (1995, 5–7) observe, there is rarely any reference in the prestigious journals of the economics pro-fession to the specifically capitalist nature of the system whose prop-erties are under examination. Modern economics emerged with the development of industrial capitalism. Its dominant mode of thought has been a preoccupation with individual transactions on commodi-ty markets, to such an extent that the profession — including human capital theorists — has become incapable of dealing with any social problem that cannot be easily translated into a narrow vision of mar-ginal utility based on commodified supply and demand.

As I have argued in Chapter Five, Marx's profound insight into capitalist production dynamics has endured. This is probably at least partly because his analysis speaks to a larger vision of human needs and our tacit sense of our exploitation and oppression under capitalism. But, as Heibroner and Milberg (1995, 99) point out, Marxism has been unable to provide an adequate alternative consensual base for economics, because of a widely imputed association of theoretical Marxism with Soviet regimes, hostility of the majority of social scientists to the radical views accurately associated with Marxian analysis, and the division of Marxist thought into fundamentalist and various analytic schools — as well as the fact that capitalism actually "delivered the goods" to a growing majority of the population in the post-WWII expansionary era.

The incapacity of conventional economics to address the myriad of contemporary social and environmental problems, and the emergence of social movements that focus on the specificity and urgency of these problems, have stimulated the development of a new paradigm that gives priority to human needs and the natural environment rather than marginal market utilities. This new paradigm, variously termed humanistic economics, participatory economics, green or moral economy, or political ecology, seriously questions both the standard capitalist model of organizing an economy which has been so naturalized by professional capitalist economists and the now departed standard socialist model. As Barbara Brandt (1995, 1) puts it:

> A new economics is emerging in the world today, an economics that more fully meets human needs, supports personal and community relationships, promotes justice and empowerment and is more respectful of the natural environment than our officially recognized economic systems.

This new paradigm represents a synthesis of socialist, ecological and feminist thought.[9] It challenges many of the precepts of both neo-classical economics and the entire evolutionary progress mode of thought — of which conventional versions of human capital theory remain one of the purest current expressions. More specifically, the new economics gives priority to the following:

- the principle of ecological sustainability over belief in the sacrosanctity of economic growth;

- community rights to sustainability over the inviolability of private business property rights;
- social justice for subordinated social groups over unconditional license for affluent individuals to do whatever they want;
- thorough democratization of all social relations rather than assuming the necessity of hierarchical authority structures; and
- the desirability of balance and synergy between all spheres of human life and the global ecosystem rather than seeing private market exchanges as the final arbiter.

The new economics is oriented to recognition of all forms of human labour, not just paid labour in commodity relations, and to the importance of meaningful work for all people to attain fulfillment. As Anne Else (1996, 157), a New Zealand practitioner of the new economics, declares in the context of discussing unpaid community work:

> The true meaning of 'work' is meaningful, purposeful activity. No matter what happens to jobs, there will be no shortage of work. The erosion of jobs can be seen as an extraordinary opportunity. We can finally get our priorities the right way round. Instead of being the poor relation of production for profit, genuinely human work may at last come into its own.

The new economics perspective is far from a unitary school of thought. Beyond the organizing principles just cited, there are many differences among adherents in terms of such issues as the actual role of private market forces, corporate enterprise and profit making in a future economy; means of political representation and the roles of government; and strategies and tactics for realizing the new economy. But, in association with this emergent paradigm, a number of specific features of work organization which loosely clustered together might be called "economic democracy" are gaining increased credibility. Some of these organizational features which could generate more inclusive forms of rewarding work and reduce some forms of underemployment are summarized in the right hand column of Figure 6.2.

Of course, as Figure 6.2 also suggests, there are other basic alternatives. The defenders of the existing capitalist economy are unlikely to accede meekly to the new economics of new social movements, any more than they have to prior challenges from the organized

Figure 6.2 Economic Alternatives: Shareholder Capitalism,
Stakeholder Capitalism or Economic Democracy

	Shareholder Capitalism	*Stakeholder Capitalism*	*Economic Democracy*
Ownership	People's Capitalism	Profit sharing	Socialized market
Labour Process	Re-engineering	Co-determination	Self-management
Work Redistribution	Flexible labour force	Reduced workweek	Full Employment
New Forms of Work	Workfare	Guaranteed income	Green work

labour, socialist and feminist movements. Some intellectual defenders of capitalist economics have offered creative alternatives of their own to rejuvenate the current economic system. The main difference is now between those who favour either "shareholder" or "stakeholder" versions of the future capitalist economy.

All three of these economic alternatives should be seen as *loosely related clusters of social tendencies* rather than coherently developed working models of work organization. These ideal types are rarely found in the real world. Each of the four dimensions of work organization is best regarded as a continuum of possible social relations. The options are only more or less closely approximated in actual countries, communities and workplaces.

My basic thesis is that economic alternatives that are based on greater genuine democratic participation in each of the dimensions of work organization will be associated with sustainable lower levels of underemployment on most dimensions. At an abstract philosophical level, the association between real democracy and the existence of universal rights and opportunities to use one's talents fully may be self-evident. But in practice there are many conflicts of interest between different social groups sharing espoused beliefs in democracy that may impede actual empowerment in formally democratic settings, as the class-centered analysis in Chapter Five suggests.[10] I will briefly summarize each of these three general economic alternatives in terms of their dominant relations in ownership of the workplace, social division of labour, distribution of paid work and associated prospects for new forms of work; I will also estimate the respective likely effects of each basic alternative on specific dimensions of underemployment.

Shareholder Capitalism

"Shareholder capitalism" is the new version of the familiar story outlined in Chapter Five.[11] The central objective remains the expanded accumulation of capital, more profits to be used for continuing business growth. Private markets rule social life. Since at least the 1880s, the owners of large pools of private capital assets have called on the small savings of non-owners to subsidize their expansion strategies. From the emergence of joint stock companies traded on local exchanges to the recent growth of mutual funds and employee share ownership plans (ESOPs), a slowly growing proportion of wage and salary earners has purchased nominal shares, cashed their dividends and regularly followed the stock market. Advocates of this diffused form of ownership of the stock of large corporations anticipate that eventually all citizens will have a piece of the action in a "people's capitalism" made up of affluent entrepreneurs (Kelso and Kelso 1986). But those who have even nominal individual stock ownership remain a small minority of the general population. The global integration of financial markets facilitated by electronic technologies leads to massive growth in the volume of stock transactions, and increasing numbers of investment capitalists and corporate raiders whose main interest is in making a paper profit and moving on to the next undervalued stock, indifferent to what happens to the workers left behind. In "people's capitalism" there is lots of capital but very few people benefit.

The labour process in shareholder capitalism is characterized by constant reorganization to ensure that all workers are maximizing their productivity for higher company profits. A prominent current example is American re-engineering of organizations (Hammer 1996). Employees are impelled by diverse means to devote themselves single-mindedly to the pursuit of excellence in terms of high output, high quality products. Everyone is expected to give up narrow job titles and focus on a process of continuous improvement. In Hammer's (1996, xv, 233) vision:

Before long it will be as quaint to speak of workers and managers and jobs as it already is to speak of knights and squires and quests. The radical transformation of work has ramifications far beyond the walls of the factory, the office, and the stock exchange. Business is the seed that forms the crystal that is our society. As the seed changes, so does the crystal. The process-centered organization is creating a new economy and a new world.... Process centering will repeat the history of all major advances of the last two hundred years: a brief period of dislocation followed by a new plateau of greater prosperity.

This rosy view of history and the future ignores both the fact that it was the work of serfs and other feudal labourers that permitted knights to go off on their quests, as well as the reality that periods of serious underemployment over the past two centuries have been far from brief.

A direct consequence of this capital-oriented labour process is the creation of a largely contingent labour force which must be prepared to move from job to job and place to place on brief notice. Aside from a diminishing core of "process managers," this flexible labour force becomes increasingly dependent on temporary employment, which some might see as a sort of mobile serfdom! Although the advocates of shareholder capitalism rarely talk about it beyond allusions to "brief dislocations," another consequence of this approach is the growth of substantial numbers of people who, whether on grounds of purportedly outmoded skill or resistant will, do not fit the process molds of restructuring corporations. In this neo-liberal world view, the able-bodied unemployed must abide the will of the private market. But various workfare and low wage employment subsidy programs may be established by deregulating state regimes to teach them sufficient discipline to compete effectively in the labour market (e.g. Phelps 1997).

The implications of shareholder capitalism for underemployment are still more of it. The private market-based determination of everything important ensures that university and college fees escalate and the talent use gap widens even more in favour of those from affluent families. Structural unemployment may fluctuate with the business cycle but is likely to continue an upward trend as firms eliminate "non-value-added work" and "dislocations" become more frequent. Extensive involuntary reduced employment is a systemic feature of the model. The credential gap probably increases in the short term as process managers pick and choose from a burgeoning contingent of highly educated applicants; in the longer term, the credential gap could decrease somewhat if market-based fee increases for higher education make credentials much scarcer, but people will still compete like crazy to get more credentials than employers can credibly require for entry into jobs of an increasingly generic process character. The performance gap may diminish marginally in the short term under re-engineering process compulsions for workers to apply more of their talents; but in the longer term it has always been more difficult to motivate employees to sustained application of their work knowledge without relations of trust. In this model, the continual anticipation of dislocation severely reduces trust.[12] Subjective underemployment is also likely to be extreme because continual reorganization undermines workers' sense of entitlement to a job and reduces the probability that they will retain a good job for very long before the next dislocation.

Stakeholder Capitalism

From the inception of industrial capitalism, there have been advo-cates of kinder regulatory provisions to take the edge off its crueler underlying dynamics, such as the legislative efforts of William Win-stanley and others in the early 1800s to get young children out of British factories. *"Stakeholder capitalism"* is based on compromises between capitalist interests and their most well-organized oppo-nents, and is characterized by management and regulation of the private market economy through joint committees and negotiated programs. The initiatives to develop this economic alternative come mainly from social democratic political parties, reform-oriented labour unions and some far-sighted capitalist thinkers.[13] The most politically successful recent version has been the electoral program of the British Labour Party under Tony Blair, which led to a land-slide victory in early 1997. The strong appeal of this stakeholder ver-sion is partly a reaction to the individualist excesses of shareholder capitalism under the prior Conservative regime (Hutton 1995). As Blair (1996, 291, 299–300) declared in pre-election speeches:

> I start from a simple belief that people are not separate economic actors competing in the market-place of life. They are citizens of a community. We are social beings, nurtured in families and communi-ties and human only because we develop the moral power of per-sonal responsibility for ourselves and each other. Britain is simply

stronger as a team than as a collection of selfish players.... The stake-holder economy is the key to preparing our people and business for vast economic and technological change. It is not about giving power to corporations or unions or interest groups. It is about giving power to you, the individual. It is about giving you the chances that help you to get on and so help Britain to get on too; a job, a skill, a home, an opportunity — a stake in the success we all want for Britain. We will fight for that stake, working with you, in partnership. The Tories fight only for the privileged few. We stand for the majority, the many.

In terms of ownership of the workplace, the most common mechanisms to give employees a stake in their company are preferred shares of company stock and profit-sharing schemes. These are most likely in industries where the production infrastructure is expensive and immobile and/or the enterprise is dependent on a labour force with quite specialized skills, such as integrated steel mills or computer companies. Various other bonus schemes for workers may also be used under the rubric of all members of the organization or community being "in it together" and needing to cooperate either for survival or to achieve greater wealth. Workers' pension funds may also be seen as part of the stakeholder model, if workers control the management of these funds and can decide for themselves where the funds will be invested.

In developed forms of stakeholder capitalism, the labour process typically involves some version of co-determination of work organization. The most fully elaborated example is the German Mitbestimmung model which entails the legal rights of all workers in larger firms to have a say in the design of their work through a works council that serves as an internal governance body, as well as substantial employee representation on company boards of directors (Knudsen 1994).

In terms of work redistribution, if unionized workers have a greater say in work organization, there is likely to be less intensive exploitation of core workers through overtime and less resort to the contingent labour force strategies preferred by shareholder capitalism. For example, the German metalworkers' union, after almost twenty years of struggle and negotiation, achieved a normal work-week of 35 hours for 40 hours pay in late 1995 (Slaughter 1995). Standard paid worktimes have contracted by around 40 percent over the past century in advanced capitalist societies, largely because organized workers' need to recuperate, do unpaid work and enjoy recreational time has corresponded with employers' interest in having refreshed and efficient workers handling increasingly expensive and high output production systems (Nyland 1989). But in capitalist economies, employers are also compelled to intensify production and lay off workers in order to pay their private shareholders' dividends and keep up with other firms that are doing the same. In the wake of such work intensification, large layoffs and mounting general unemployment, German metalworker leaders have recently announced that they will not seek to further shorten hours "for a long time," in spite of institutionalization of the co-determination model (Slaughter 1995).

Stakeholder capitalism regards the private market economy as in the public interest and remains oriented to continued capital accumulation and economic growth, including the production and consumption of an ever greater array of marketable commodities. Core workers in large firms may get a modest share of the profits. Some workers may have a say in the design and pace of their working conditions. But managerial prerogatives still essentially remain with executives and top managers. The commodity market orientation of the major players — corporate managers, labour union leaders and government officials — encourages little interest in recognition of other forms of previously unpaid work. But the persistence of substantial underemployment in this market model leads to initiatives to establish forms of guaranteed annual income or other direct subsidies from the state to ensure that many of the unemployed will continue to be part of the commodity consumption community.

Many dimensions of underemployment in stakeholder capitalism are generally somewhat lower than under the shareholder model. Regarding the talent use gap, Tony Blair (1996, 173) asserts with reference to British comprehensive schools:

> New Labour is committed to meritocracy. We believe that people should be able to rise by their talents, not by their birth or the advantages of privilege. We understand that people are not borne into equal circumstances, so one role of state education is to open up opportunities for all, regardless of their background.

While elected governments in stakeholder capitalism may be committed to closing the talent use gap, they have so far had very limited success in this regard. This is probably attributable to the fact that profit-sharing and co-determination schemes have had little positive impact to date beyond the paid workplace on the lives of the vast majority of people relative to the affluent minority.

Structural unemployment has generally been lower in such regimes than in shareholder-oriented regimes because the capital-labour compromise contains some form of a job security for productivity accord. This is especially clear if discouraged workers are considered (Therborn 1986). Involuntary reduced employment also tends to be less because the reduced workweek, overtime restrictions and more mandatory holidays create more full-time jobs. The credential gap may be smaller because workers have a greater role in selecting and training new entrants through apprenticeship schemes. The performance gap is also likely to be smaller because workers have a significant role in designing the performance requirements of their own jobs. Subjective underemployment may diminish because many workers have a sense of owning their jobs and having the discretion to use more of their knowledge and skill in reshaping them.

While there are examples of stakeholder organizations which have lasted for generations, stakeholder government institutions have been less enduring. The leading case is probably Swedish social democracy, which has recently experienced serious decline under the concerted attacks of Swedish and international capital (see Olsen 1992; Clement and Mahon 1994).

Economic Democracy

"Economic democracy" is the organization of production and consumption by the majority of the people for the majority. Popular efforts to create economic communities in which all members have a voice and a vote have occurred throughout the history of capitalism (Oved 1988). The Paris Commune, a two-month phenomenon in a city under siege in 1871, has continued to fascinate left intellectuals (Schulkind 1972). Of greater relevance are the *experiments* in economic democracy which have occurred throughout the past century and continue to be created in thousands of local instances around the world.[14] But these experiments have so far only touched a small minority of the population in any country. For ease of presentation, the primary empirical focus here will be on two of the experiments in economic democracy which have been sustained the longest and been subjected to the most critical research, the kib-

butzim movement in Israel and the Mondragon worker cooperatives in the Basque region of Spain.[15]

Economic organizations involving popular ownership are no
longer isolated. Most of these communitarian organizations within
capitalist economies have so far blended privately owned, cooperatively owned and state-sponsored economic resources. But the primary impulse of these diverse co-operative enterprises is to pre-
serve and nurture means of production that will ensure community
sustainability rather than profit maximization; they represent a
much larger part of the overall economy than is generally recognized.[16] In the U.S., there are now around 10,000 firms which are at
least partially worker-owned, a six-fold increase over the past twenty years, and they employ more Americans than belong to labour
unions (Blasi and Kruse 1990).

Economic democracy is based on socialized market models,
rather than the individualist private markets that have driven capitalism or the authoritarian central planning mechanisms that contributed to the downfall of Soviet style regimes. Socialized markets
presume that economic actors include communities as well as individuals, that social costs and benefits must be factored into economic decisions rather than regarded as externalities, and that workers,
consumers and public interest representatives should all have voice
and vote in these decisions. Ideally, the means of production are
owned either by the community or by the workers as a whole. The
value of the capital assets of a given organization cannot be sold off
for individual gain without authorization from relevant community
authorities, typically elected legislative bodies and democratically-
controlled banks or credit unions. New investments are preferably
generated by direct taxes on capital assets (thereby replacing the
capitalist economy's need for interest to stimulate investment
funds), and dispensed through a democratically adopted and regularly publicly reviewed investment plan.[17] Guild socialism in post-
WWI Britain developed elaborate conceptual models of producer-
consumer control which have inspired some later social ownership
fund initiatives (Livingstone 1983; Olsen 1992).

A crucial point here is that self-managed cooperatives are inherently less growth-oriented than capitalist firms which are compelled
by their shareholders to plough their profits back into expanded
production regardless of negative effects on subsistence of the workers. Some of the generated surplus tends to be used for member ben-

efits while the remaining portion is retained as *social earnings* which may be reinvested to improve production conditions or employment. This difference is generally regarded as an ecological strength and political weakness versus the ever-expanding capitalist production system (Schweikart 1993; Derber 1994). But as those experiencing underemployment know best, much capitalist growth has been illusory; most workers' standard of living has not increased in the past several generations and their meaningful work has decreased (Outhwaite 1992).

Work organizations consistent with the principles of economic democracy are managed by those who work in them. Such co-operative work organizations remain much rarer than general co-operatively owned enterprises.[18] The members are responsible for day-to-day operation, workplace organization, job design and techniques of production, production goals and distribution of net proceeds. Decisions in co-operative work organizations are supposed to be based on one person, one vote, although some decisions may be practically delegated to a workers' council (see Schweickart 1993). In practice to date there have been many problems in developing fully democratic workers' councils, particularly in worker co-operatives such as Mondragon in which top managers have been inclined to focus on capital investment strategies and workers remain divided among themselves on many economic and political issues (see Kasmir 1996). The survival of such worker co-operatives to date owes a great deal to pragmatic politics which continue to attempt to recognize workers' economic rights while adapting their social and technical division of labour sufficiently to sell their products in capitalist markets and acquire other needed, externally produced goods. As Don Jose Maria Arizmendiarrieta, founder of the Mondragon cooperatives, has stated:

> We are not working for chimerical ideals. We are realists. Conscious of what we can and cannot do.... Dedicated to changing those things we can and that we are in fact changing, we are conscious of the force that this movement produces. (Cited in Moye 1993, 270)

Initiatives toward self-managed production continue to emerge within capitalist economies. These initiatives have gone in divergent directions (Clark 1984) and industrial democracy remains more a de jure phenomenon than a real achievement in most countries (International Research Group 1993, 149). But self-management has been associated with innovative production techniques such as the movement toward human-centered design of production systems, and with more socially useful production objectives like the Corporate Plan of the Lucas aerospace workers (see Cooley 1987; Rauner and Ruth 1991). In sharp contrast to the Bolshevik revolutionaries who relied heavily on scientific management techniques in establishing Russian Soviet work organizations in the 1920s, those attempting to build worker cooperatives or other communitarian economic organizations today have a much wider array of socio-technical choices compatible with democratic process. The central unresolved question is whether the workers in the large private enterprises who continue to produce most of the goods and services will come to see the mutual benefit of not only reducing their paid work time through application of these new technological choices, but sharing this work with the subemployed (see Lichtenstein and Harris 1993).

Self-management combined with socialized ownership permits substantial reductions in total work time because human needs rather than profit maximization have priority in determining the scale and intensity of production. It is quite evident to anyone in the advanced industrial societies who cares to look carefully that, with a relatively small portion of our collective time, we can now produce all the food, clothing, shelter, energy, infrastructural and personal care services we need for secure survival. In fact, this has always been the case. Capitalism convinced us otherwise and has generated many material benefits, from air conditioning to zippers. Most of us still need meaningful and creative work. But when it comes down to a choice between earning more money to buy a bigger TV set or spending more time with our kids, most of us would now opt for the kids.

In contrast to capitalist production dynamics, the work organizations of economic democracy give a high priority to ensuring work for everyone. Paid work hours may not be any shorter because these work organizations must still compete in a capitalist trade environment. But productive labour time can be more closely and comfortably integrated with community life. For example, the responsibilities of domestic labours such as cooking and cleaning as well as child care have been eased by being communally shared in the kibbutz (see Ben-Peretz and Lavi 1982; Levitan, Oliver and Quarter 1998).

Various current thinkers envisage the end of work as we know it in industrial capitalism, often in vastly overstated terms compared to current levels and trends in actual paid employment. Rifkin's (1995) quickly celebrated solution to this problem is the greater organization of community volunteer work and the allocation of vouchers for labour in this "third sector." As capitalist production dynamics squeeze more and more labour time out of commodity production processes, the problem for both the shareholder and stakeholder versions of capitalism becomes how to retain the interest of the burgeoning numbers of underemployed people in pursuing contingent paid labour and how to get enough money to them to continue to buy the commodities produced by automated enterprises. Rifkin's vouchers offer to fill the work void and in the bargain ensure more contented consumers. Under capitalist logic, if you don't get paid for it, it doesn't count as work. The next step, unaddressed by Rifkin but previously proposed by some well-meaning feminists, is wages for housework (Dalla Costa 1975).

But, as the proponents of the new economics have recognized, there is no shortage of meaningful work, just commodified work. In an economic democracy organized around human needs rather than profits, the reproduction of households and the sustainability of communities are just as important as production of goods and services. The "green work" of domestic nurturing, community building and environmental stewardship receives recognition and priority time. The real democratic challenge is not to create more commodified work or consumer credits, but to distribute the necessary paid and unpaid work more equitably. The critical required change, which has only begun to be addressed even in the kibbutz and Mondragon, is for men to take a fair share of domestic labour so that women have fair opportunity to contribute in other spheres.[19]

Underemployment in economic democracy does not vanish entirely, but it can be substantially reduced on most dimensions from underemployment in either capitalist economic alternative.[20] The division of labour and wage inequalities are relatively limited within economic democracies and other community members cannot accumulate lavish wealth through appropriating the benefits of workers' labour time. So, the talent use gap is less, and ordinary workers' children have fairer opportunity to use their learning talents, particularly in work-study formats consistent with a polytechnic model (Leviatan 1982; Meek and Woodworth 1990).

Structural unemployment and involuntary reduced employment

can be minimized in such communities. The greater integration of money economy and subsistence labours encourages higher sustained worker motivation to contribute to the productive success of communal enterprise. Community ownership and democratically determined limits on wage differences mean that the benefits of productive labour are divided more equitably, surpluses are used primarily to maintain productive capacity and sustain the community, and there is increased incentive to share production work since "overtime" amounts to self-exploitation. Individual initiative and creativity can still be rewarded, just not with an excessive amount of money that serves to deprive others of their economic rights. Although the kibbutzim lose some highly qualified workers to the surrounding Israeli capitalist economy because of their relatively low egalitarian wages, everybody is expected and allowed to work (Rosner 1998). The Mondragon worker cooperatives have consistently had much lower unemployment rates than the surrounding Spanish economy, and recent corporate plans project sustained employment growth while most European enterprises continue to downsize.[21] However, both the kibbutzim and Mondragon have increasingly relied on temporary workers beyond their own members (Rosner 1998; Kasmir 1996).

Credential and performance gaps between schooling and paid work continue to exist in economic democracy. But they can be significantly diminished in comparison with capitalist enterprises because workers themselves are supposed to cooperatively determine the relevant entry criteria for their jobs and can design and redesign their jobs in accord with their own performance capacities and knowledge. The phenomenon of credential *underqualification*, which is endemic to capitalist labour markets because of employers' inflation of educational entry criteria to select among many competitors for diminishing numbers of subordinated operative jobs, becomes less likely. Performance underqualification may occasionally occur because production requirements continue to shift in response to changing environmental conditions, technological developments and human needs.

The continuing challenge is to respond to credential and performance underemployment of increasingly highly qualified people in the paid work that is supposed to be largely shared and rotated on egalitarian principles. But, as Gamson and Palgi (1982, 64–65) concluded in the most specific assessment of this problem on the kibbutz:

Even though highly educated members may not find their [paid] work as intrinsically challenging as they would ideally prefer, participation in determining the work process and investment decisions calls on complex judgements and group skills. In this way the desire for self-development can be harnessed to social reproduction. Participation in community life also requires qualities that are rarely exercised by other citizens. On a world-wide basis, research is needed on precisely how the work environment can provide opportunities for self-development, especially for highly educated workers, when the intrinsic nature of the [paid] work may not be especially challenging.... Settings such as the kibbutzim can be informative as they attempt to cope with this problem.

As kibbutz members have been increasingly enabled and encouraged to participate in advanced schooling away from the kibbutz, the problem of credential underemployment has persisted and led to substantial numbers of the "third generation" leaving the kibbutz for higher paying technically skilled jobs in the Israeli capitalist economy (Sheaffer and Helman 1994). In the Mondragon co-ops, with a more hierarchical job structure, well integrated technical training system and better job creation than the surrounding private enterprise economy, both credential and performance underemployment are likely to be lower and less vulnerable to envious comparisons with jobs in the private market economy (Kasmir 1996). Overall, the available empirical evidence indicates that underemployment is generally a less extensive and intense problem for those living in the still tiny number of experiments in economic democracy.

The primary reference for subjective underemployment in all current economic democracies is not the lack of internal opportunities. It is envious comparisons with more affluent individuals who perform similar occupations in a surrounding capitalist economy (Leviatan, Oliver and Quarter 1998). Within an economic democracy, subjective underemployment loses much of the objective structural basis it has in a capitalist economy because there is supposed to be greater scope for workers to apply their knowledge and skills in the planning and design of paid work and more integrative opportunities to use and be recognized for diverse skills in subsistence work. But occupational prestige differences certainly persist and, even among those who are highly committed to their community's particular brand of economic democracy, younger people with higher education may continue to feel underemployed in relation to the flattened job hierarchy (Adar 1982). Also, as the kibbutz "brain drain" illustrates, it is very difficult for those living in these communities to ignore the surrounding reality of capitalism either objectively or subjectively.

In assessing both the general performance of economic democracies and the existence of underemployment within them, it is important to keep in mind their current enclave status within capitalism. For example, neither the kibbutzim in Israel nor Mondagon and all the other producer cooperatives in Spain currently represent more than a few percentage points of the total employment in these respective countries. The general situation is analogous to the formative period of capitalism when it was largely limited to a small number of city-states within feudal Europe.

The tendencies within capitalist societies toward socialized ownership with the growth of worker-controlled pension funds, as well as toward other communitarian economic institutions and shorter normal workweeks could lead to rapid growth of economic democracy. I share David Schweickart's (1993, 292) assessment of the prospects for economic democracy:

> A powerful, committed, intelligent political movement would be necessary for a successful challenge to a ruling class as deeply entrenched as is the capitalist class in an advanced capitalist society. But it seems to me possible.

The most important point about the array of current experiments in economic democracy is that we now have a fairly clear available vision of a democratic alternative to the capitalist economy. There are growing numbers of sustained initiatives within many capitalist countries to test and develop this alternative mode of life. It is easy enough for more radical political movements and critical empirical researchers who look closely at the current tiny sustained experiments to find serious contradictions between their avowed and actual benefits for workers. For example, the Mondragon co-operatives have been severely criticised by some factions in the Basque independence movement because:

> Co-operative workers were isolated from the rest of the local working class and from the labour movement. They also charged that, as the regional economy became increasingly competitive, the co-operatives

became more like private firms; thus co-operators were subject to the same kind of exploitation as non-co-op workers.... Another criticism was that democratic organs in the co-operatives, especially the Social Council, were ineffective and unable to represent the workers. Finally, co-operative management was accused of being paternalistic and of using the ideology of co-operativism to exploit workers. (cited in Kasim 1996, 117).

As long as capitalist private market economies remain powerful and pervasive, there is imminent danger of any emergent progressive alternative being reincorporated or diverted. But basic alternative structures of workplace organization — worker ownership, self-management forums, member full employment — remain visible through such experiments even when they are attacked by those further to the left and subverted by capitalist-oriented management.

These three economic alternatives, shareholder and stakeholder versions of capitalism and economic democracy, represent distinguishable current tendencies in the relations between ownership of the major means of reproduction of material life and direct control of these reproduction processes themselves. But they are hardly mutually exclusive. Elements of co-determination keep popping up in the labour processes of shareholder capitalism. Self-management initiatives emerge within stakeholder capitalism. The transition from feudalism to capitalism in Western Europe occurred slowly over a period of several centuries with capitalism gradually taking over feudal forms of work organization as it found them. A transition from capitalism to any future mode of production is likely to be similarly incremental, however much advocates of the new economics wish for rapid transformation.

Any such transition within the liberal democracies of advanced capitalism is likely to be contingent on mobilizing popular support for change among the majority of citizens. There are substantial numbers of people involved in the environmental, feminist, antiracist and communitarian social movements as well as the labour movement who are advocating elements of the new economics while continuing to work within the capitalist economy. But no democratic movement can be successful without widespread support in the general population. So how much tacit popular support is there now for these different tendencies in relation to the education-jobs gap?

POPULAR SUPPORT FOR ECONOMIC SOLUTIONS
TO THE EDUCATION-JOBS GAP

Capitalism is the most prolific and adaptable economic system yet devised. Anyone who poses as its imminent gravedigger at the end of the 20th century is dreaming in multiple dimensions. Yet it is our dreams of overcoming underemployment and our visions of economic alternatives that can do so which will ultimately drive the action to transform this system and provide meaningful work and dignity for all. Some sense of the extent of popular support for social transformation may be drawn from public opinion surveys that address the central economic choices. Following the dimensions laid out in Figure 6.1, I will assess public preferences regarding ownership of workplaces, control of the labour process, and distribution of paid work, as well as support for new forms of work such as workfare and an equal role for men in housework. Finally, I will look closely at popular sentiments about basic causes and cures for the education-jobs gap, with special attention to the views of those living in the gap. The primary sources of data are our Ontario surveys and in-depth interviews which permit detailed analysis by all underemployment statuses as well as numerous other social factors; these are supplemented by other relevant U.S. and Canadian opinion surveys.

Ownership of Work Organizations

Popular support for the central principle of shareholder capitalism, the right of the owners of private property in the means of production to profit maximization, is alive and fairly well. Throughout most of the past generation, small majorities in most social groups have generally agreed that shareholders should be able to invest profits made with the labour of local workers wherever they think they can make the greatest profits (Livingstone 1987b). This has been an era of chronic high unemployment but also one in which capitalist leaders and their allies have sometimes successfully promoted fiscal restraint and the necessity for business enterprises to be free to compete effectively in continental and global commodity markets (see McBride and Shields 1997). However, as Table 6.1 shows, support for stakeholder models of economic ownership has also been very substantial during this period, sometimes stronger than for shareholder ver-

Table 6.1 Popular Support for Economic Ownership
Alternatives, Ontario Labour Force, 1980–1992

	Ownership Model*		
Year	*Shareholder Capitalism (%)*	*Stakeholder Capitalism (%)*	*Economic Democracy (%)*
1980	30	56	7
1982	53	33	8
1984	48	38	10
1986	52	30	13
1988	44	44	13
1990	39	46	14
1992	44	40	14

* Respondents were asked which of several specific models they would like to see as the dominant feature of the Canadian economy in the future. The options were: *shareholder capitalist* — "large private corporations operating with minimum interference by government or trade unions," and "small independent businesses operating under competitive free market conditions"; *stakeholder capitalist* — "privately owned enterprises regulated by government with government investment and joint partnership in important projects," and "economy managed through formal agreements between private business, labour and the government"; and *economic democracy* — "public ownership and state control of major sectors of the economy," and "direct worker control of major enterprises."

Source: OISE Survey of Educational Issues Data Archive.

sions. Political parties with neo-liberal shareholder agendas and social democratic stakeholder ones with more regulatory approaches have alternated in government through this period. The electoral changes have been roughly according to the swing voters who shift their support between the need for deregulation of private business enterprises to stimulate economic growth and the need for greater social welfare provisions to care for the poor. This flip flop pattern of electoral change between pro-capital and regulatory regimes has been commonplace in most advanced capitalist societies throughout most of this century (Esping-Anderson 1990; Pierson 1995).

Support for ownership models associated with economic democracy, including public ownership of major sectors or worker-owned cooperatives, has continued to come from small minorities of around ten percent, the largest numbers of whom have been in the working class. No reputable progressive party in North America currently judges it politically viable to promote public ownership of the means of production, so this aspect of the vision of economic democracy garners whatever support it gets largely through grassroots paid workplace and community experiences.

However, when private firms are making large profits but continue to lay off employees, as many have in the 1990s, popular support for unconditional private ownership rights plummets. A Canadian survey in March of 1996 (Southam News-Angus Reid 1996) found that over three-quarters of respondents said large companies should not be laying off while making high profits. A U.S. survey at the same time (Business Week/Harris Poll 1996, 65) found that 95 percent of Americans felt that U.S. corporations should have other purposes than shareholders' profits; "they also owe something to their workers, and they should sometimes sacrifice some profit for the sake of making things better for their workers and communities." Support for some version of employee control of capital investment generally increases in such circumstances (see Bowles, Gordon and Weisskopf 1990, 321).

Workplace Democratization

People generally have increasing access to relevant knowledge and information. They are regularly encouraged by the institutional forms of liberal democracy to participate as citizens. The prevalence of hierarchical authority structures and managerial prerogatives in paid workplaces which prohibit worker participation in significant firm decisions becomes more incongruous with its surrounding social context. Authoritarian management is becoming extremely difficult to maintain. As Table 6.2 shows, popular demand for a greater say in the running of their firms is now very widespread among most class positions. The only substantial support for continuing to run firms by the executive management model of shareholder capitalism is from corporate executives themselves. Among all other classes, only a small minority now support the hierarchical workplace run by top man-

Table 6.2 Popular Support for Workplace Democratization by Class Position, Ontario Labour Force, 1994

	Labour Process Model*		
Class Position	Shareholder capitalism (%)	Stakeholder capitalism (%)	Economic democracy (%)
Corporate executives	63	35	2
Small employers	22	55	20
Self-employed	8	62	29
Managers	9	64	26
Professionals	9	63	24
Semi-professional employees	8	66	23
Supervisors	5	64	31
Service workers			
Skilled service	8	75	17
Other service	3	64	31
Industrial workers			
Skilled industrial	2	65	28
Other industrial	5	58	34
Unemployed	5	75	20
Total labour force (N=712)	8	64	26

* The actual wording of the question was: "Which one of the following three options is closest to how you would like to see the economy organized?

- privately owned enterprises run by executive management (*shareholder capitalism*);
- privately owned enterprises run with employee participation in management (*stakeholder capitalism*);
- cooperative enterprises owned and managed by employees (*economic democracy*)."

Source: OISE Survey of Educational Issues Data Archive.

agement. About two-thirds would prefer a stakeholder model with substantial employee participation in running privately owned firms. Over a quarter in most class positions would like to see cooperative enterprises run by their employees. The popular demands for workplace democratization have become so strong that even the most established authoritarian managements now at least rhetorically recognize it (see Livingstone 1996c).

However, there is no deterministic relationship between economic development and democratic institutions. As Przeworski and Limongi (1997, 177) have recently concluded on the basis of extensive comparative historical analyses:

> The emergence of democracy is not a by-product of economic development. Democracy is or is not established by political actors pursuing their goals, and it can be initiated at any level of development. Only once it is established do economic constraints play a role: the chances for survival are greater when the country is richer. Yet ... if they succeed in generating development, democracy can survive even in the poorest nations.

The same observation applies to work organizations within advanced capitalist countries. The initiation and survival of workplace democracy is always contingent on the labour force acting on these expressed beliefs.

Over three-quarters of both the credentially underemployed and underqualified workers in our in-depth interviews expressed support for greater employee control in the workplace in order to allow them to make fuller use of their knowledge. In the words of a credentially underqualified middle-aged male supervisor:

> More worker control, most definitely. They know what is going on on the floor. Our engineers don't know what's going on. A lot of the stuff is trial and error and engineers don't like that. So, if you listen to the right employees, they have a lot to offer. We have consultants, too, but they are not good. They're just getting paid to make cuts.

Shorter Workweek

Proposals to redistribute paid work have been around since the inception of capitalist production disrupted the more balanced life rhythms of pre-capitalist economies. In one of the first post-WWII initiatives, the Canadian Labour Congress outlined its support for shorter worktime, including reduced hours, longer vacations, and early retirements, before the Royal Commission on Canada's Economic Prospects in 1956 (Riche 1990, 269–280). But such proposals gain more popular support when unemployment mounts, as happened in the early 1930s. Some of these proposals, such as the reduction of the normal workweek to 30 hours at full pay have recently found a serious place in some enterprises and on the general politi-

Table 6.3   Popular Support for Shorter Standard Workweek by Class Position, Ontario Labour Force, 1996

	Government should establish a shorter standard workweek and restrict overtime so that employers will need to hire additional employees.'		
Class Position	*Agree (%)*	*Disagree (%)*	*Can't say (%)*
Corporate executives	17	75	9
Small employers	53	46	1
Self-employed	62	29	9
Managers	59	39	2
Professional employees	57	35	8
Semi-professional employees	48	43	9
Supervisors	43	55	2
Service workers			
Skilled service	68	23	10
Other service	49	38	12
Industrial workers			
Skilled industrial	58	32	10
Other industrial	51	40	9
Unemployed	69	23	8
Total labour force (N=691)	53	38	9

Source: OISE Survey of Educational Issues Data Archive.

cal agenda in various countries, most notably France and Italy.[22] Almost certainly most of the unemployed will be enthusiastic supporters, given the associated prospect of more jobs and the still intimate connections between work, identity and dignity in private market-based societies.

In general, support for a shorter standard workweek appears to have increased in recent years. A 1985 survey (Benimadu 1987) found that over two-thirds of Canadians were opposed to a reduced workweek. As Table 6.3 shows, our 1996 Ontario survey found a small majority in favour of the concept of a shorter standard workweek.[23] Only corporate executives express really strong opposition to a shorter workweek among occupational classes, while the unemployed as well as skilled workers and professional-managerial employees are among the strongest supporters.

There is now a potentially strong alliance between many of the underemployed and those compelled to work overtime, the "job-hungry," and the "job-weary." As a recent Canadian survey confirms (Statistics Canada 1995b), the job-weary are typically professional, managerial and skilled trades workers with full-time, high seniority positions who are well paid and working long hours; they can afford a reduction of working time without jeopardizing their standard of living. Job-hungry folks are generally young, have little seniority or security; most of them want to work longer hours and cannot afford to work less.

But, as the same survey found, workers generally are personally less willing to work shorter hours for less pay than they were a decade earlier. In a tight labour market with diminishing numbers of good jobs, nobody wants to give up whatever competitive edge they think they might have on job security. Many of the job-insecure folks in our in-depth interviews with credentially underqualified workers expressed personal reluctance about the idea of a shorter normal workweek, because they saw such worktime reductions as threatening their already marginal earnings and making them more vulnerable to unemployment. An underqualified, middle-aged woman full-time service worker with little schooling put it most directly:

> No, I don't agree to a shorter normal workweek. There should be 40 hours so we can make enough to live. If there's overtime, then hire people. But don't take the hours away from us.

But many others, especially those in part-time and temporary jobs with less to lose, did find the idea of a shorter standard workweek very attractive. An underqualified young woman part-time service worker with a high school diploma told us:

> I would definitely support a shorter normal workweek if there is really work time sharing. It'll mean work for more people who have little or nothing now.

More concrete legislative programs for a reduced normal work-week could well now garner massive popular support, as happened in the early 1930s. It is instructive to remember that, in early 1933, the Black-Connery Thirty Hour Week Bill passed in the U.S. Senate with strong support both from organized labour and from more than half of industrial employers who had already reduced work hours to save jobs and promote consumer spending. Public enthusiasm became very widespread. But it was also short-lived. President Roosevelt, in consultation with Wall Street-dominated business advisors, blocked the bill and began to cobble together the public works and other government subsidies programs that became known as the New Deal. Roosevelt reportedly later regretted blocking this bill (Rifkin 1995, 29). Will elected politicians now listen to the people or to Wall Street?

New Forms of Work

Just as governments answered high unemployment in the 1930s with public works programs, they have tried to respond to contemporary conditions of underemployment with subsidies and legislative provisions to stimulate job creation (Phelps 1997). Some jurisdictions have created compulsory public works jobs at minimum wage for able bodied welfare recipients. The OECD Jobs Study (1994a, 48) has recommended setting low "training wage" levels to induce employers to supply more entry jobs. Such direct and indirect "workfare" strategies have evoked storms of protest led by critics who see them as merely another means of further cheapening wage labour. Public support for these low wage strategies for job creation in Ontario is summarized in Table 6.4.

There is little current public enthusiasm in Ontario for either version of workfare. Only a quarter of the current workforce express even modest support for either compulsory public works jobs or a lower training wage. There is majority opposition to compulsory

Table 6.4   Popular Support for Workfare by Class Position,
Ontario Labour Force, 1994–1996

	Workfare I* (% agree)	Workfare II** (% agree)	
Class Position	*96*	*94*	*96*
Corporate executives	25	65	49
Small employers	23	58	28
Self-employed	24	42	29
Managers	26	43	35
Professional employees	25	40	40
Semi-professional employees	26	40	26
Supervisors	34	38	30
Service workers			
Skilled service	35	25	19
Other service	26	33	25
Industrial workers			
Skilled industrial	5	40	20
Other industrial	15	23	15
Unemployed	28	45	29
Total labour force	25	39	27
N	691	745	691

* Respondents to the 1996 survey were asked whether they supported a program designed to get people off welfare and back to work
that stressed "community public works jobs at minimum wage."
** Respondents to the 1994 and 1996 surveys were asked to agree or
disagree with the statement: "The minimum wage for young people
should be lowered if this would create more jobs for youth."

Source: OISE Survey of Educational Issues Data Archive.

public works programs across virtually all social groups, from corporate executives who reject direct state intervention in the economy to
spokespersons for the poor who see mandatory workfare for welfare
recipients as associated with growing poverty, hunger and homeless-

ness (Kilpatrick 1997). After the training wage idea was publicly supported by the OECD in 1994, there was somewhat stronger initial support, particularly among large employers. Two years later, support had dwindled in all social groups. Opposition, especially among the groups most likely to have their wages directly affected — students and the working class — had become very strong (Livingstone, Hart and Davie 1997, 81). Voluntary low wage subsidies for the working poor have been found to have some positive effects for individuals (Heckman and Klenow 1997) and are somewhat more palatable in a democratic society. But the majority of employees are likely to continue to show little support for workfare options based on state subsidies while profits grow, unemployed competitors for their own jobs abound and their real wages fall. In the context of greater established social welfare entitlements, government "makework" projects no longer hold the popular appeal they did in the dirty thirties.

Many people feel that capitalism has essentially solved the "production problem" in terms of any reasonable notion of essential goods and services, and that we should become more concerned with the problem of fair distribution (e.g. Galbraith 1958). Advocates of the new economics argue that we should not continue to pay and make work for people to produce things that hurt other people or damage the environment. The growing disappearance of jobs that provide a living wage or adequate income for young couples to reproduce the social order (i.e. buy a home, have babies, plan a future life together) has provoked analysts of all stripes to propose versions of a guaranteed annual income.[24] Increasingly detailed proposals to combine guaranteed annual income with a reduced workweek continue to be generated (e.g. Reid 1995), but so far have elicited little popular support (Economic Council of Canada 1991). The fusion of personal identity with paid work in capitalist societies is still much too strong and the absence of plausible demonstration models too complete for most people to give such proposals to be paid not to work much credibility.

Recognition of domestic labour is quite another matter. Even with the disappearance of much paid work, we all have to do some housework. Popular support for women's right to paid work has increased greatly over the past two generations (Boyd 1984). Women are now being slowly accepted into even the most exclusionary male paid work preserves, like steel mills. Men's willingness to take up more "women's work" in the household has been much slower (Seccombe

1987; Statistics Canada 1997). But, as Table 6.5 summarizes, sentiments of support for greater equity in the performance of housework
are now very strong in both sexes, even among those men who are
most marginalized in their present jobs.

The major barriers to greater equity in the actual performance of
housework, as with "glass ceilings" in paid work, are persisting
deep-seated notions of inherent limits to the capacity of the opposite
sex to take full control of the work. The barriers are starting to fall.
As an underemployed woman service worker married to a steelworker says:

> Men are starting to realize that they can't just be the breadwinner and
> come home to a home-cooked meal and that's it. Women are working
> now and you can't do it that way. But there's still an awful lot of men
> that just don't want to change. Even my husband, he'll always say,
> "What is there to do?" And later on he'll say, "Why didn't you tell me
> you had all that stuff to do?" Well, you can hear me doing dishes,
> why don't you come in and help me. I hate to ask you to do every-
> thing. If I'm still working, you should still be working (Livingstone
> and Luxton 1996, 129).

Women continue to struggle for more equitable economic and

Table 6.5 Popular Support for Housework Equity,
Credentially Mismatched Labour Force, Ontario, 1995

	'Men should do more housework so their wives or partners can hold good jobs more easily' (% agree)		
Credential Gap	Men	Women	Total
Highly underemployed	92	70	79
Underemployed	83	81	82
Underqualified	71	90	83
Highly underqualified (N=136)	69	74	71

Source: Follow-up interview of credentially mismatched respondents to
Tenth OISE Survey of Educational Issues, February-March, 1995.

political power across the paid-unpaid work divide. Many are no longer willing to go back to full-time married homemaker roles. Men, on the other hand, have demonstrated very little inclination to give up full-time breadwinner status for temporary paid work, to say nothing of opting for full-time housework. No redistribution or flexible scheduling of employment is likely to diminish popular demands from both women and men for more meaningful paid work, unless such initiatives are associated with very substantial increases in income which ensure that their households can be sustained. This would be comparable to the effects of reduced normal workweek or guaranteed income proposals. The problem of underemployment in paid work can no longer easily be pushed back into the household.

Causes and Cures: "It's the Economy, Stupid!"

George Bush was the man who aspired to be the education president but he was the president who was responsible for neutralizing the Sandia Report which documented the waste of education in the U.S. economy more thoroughly than any prior study (Sandia Laboratories 1993; Tanner 1993). His campaign slogan, "It's the economy, stupid!," has much deeper popular resonance than the president's moving lips appeared to comprehend. It's the economy that is the major social problem, not education.

As prior chapters have documented, most people are preoccupied with making individual education and learning responses to the problem of the education-jobs gap. This is all they can see to do in the absence of seriously discussed economic alternatives in the mass media or general public sphere debate, and when more education still has significant marginal utility in getting or holding any job at all in the credential society. As the evidence in Chapters One and Three especially suggests, the strong popular demand for more access to advanced formal and further education is unlikely to diminish in the foreseeable future.

But most people know that education cannot solve the shortage of good jobs. The current views of the general public in Ontario about the causes and cures of unemployment are summarized in Table 6.6.

A growing majority believe that unemployment is basically caused by the economy itself rather than attributable to either the school system or people's lack of motivation. This is the majority attitude in virtually all social groups, and there is little real popular

Table 6.6   Perceived Causes and Preferred Cures for Youth
                 Unemployment, Ontario Population, 1994–1996

A. *Perceived Causes of Unemployment**

Which of the following do you think is the most important cause of unemployment among young people?

	94 (%)	96 (%)
The economy is not generating enough jobs	50	58
Schools are not preparing students well enough for jobs	21	20
Many young people do not want to work	25	18
Can't say	3	4
N	1070	1000

B. *Preferred Cures for Youth Unemployment***

If there are more university and college graduates than jobs that really need university and college education to do the work, do you think we should:

	94 (%)
Cut back on the number of people going to universities and colleges	8
Reorganized work so more people can use their university and college education	85
Can't say	7
N	136

Sources: * OISE Survey of Educational Issues Data Archive.
** Follow-up interview of credentially mismatched respondents to the Tenth OISE Survey of Educational Issues, February-March 1995.

inclination to blame the schools for the economy's problems. There is little reason to suspect that popular views are much different anywhere else in capitalist societies. A New York Times (1996, 309) survey recently found that majorities of those who had experienced layoffs or were worried about losing their jobs blamed the economic system for the loss of jobs in the U.S.

In terms of solutions for the credential gap, the vast majority feel strongly that access to advanced education credentials should not be limited. There is also widespread responsiveness to the idea of trying to reorganize work. As our in-depth interviews with those living in the education-jobs gap confirm, there is near unanimity of both the credentially underemployed and underqualified in reacting strongly against any challenge to the right to advanced education. Views on the need for workplace reorganization are more diverse.

The most common response is a spirited defence of the right to as much education as people can handle, whatever the economic conditions:

> You just cannot deny people's right to learn! Everybody has the right to learn and you cannot judge who can and cannot learn. (Underemployed young female service worker with a college certificate)

> You shouldn't tell a person they can't learn! Can't say, hey, you go to high school and that's it. That is wrong. A mind is a terrible thing to waste. (Underqualified middle aged male supervisor with some high school).

Some of the credentially mismatched continue to couple support for universal access to education with a belief that normal competitive market pressures or liberating private markets from government intervention will do all that's feasible to narrow the education-jobs gap:

> There's always going to be a gap. Somebody's going to be on the cutting edge and it'll be up to the rest of the people to catch up. How many people are good enough to get to the very top? The rest are going to be going into subsidiary positions where they will be overqualified. I'm sure it's worse now than it's ever been but that's life…. But no education is a waste. (Underemployed young male service worker with a B.A.)

Government should cut taxes so business will come back and there will be more work available. So many people are going back to school to upgrade right now, I'm worried there won't be enough good jobs. Computers are taking over a lot of things. But education is the key. Without it, people don't get anywhere. (Unemployed middle aged male service worker with some high school)

There should be less government intervention in the workplace. Private businesses need to develop their own reorganization strategies. I believe in free enterprise. Universities and businesses should be working more closely so kids know what business is looking for, so they know what the limitations are. But things will get better. (Underqualified older male professional with a high school diploma).

A few frankly admit that they can see no credible economic alternative to current conditions:

For the underemployed like me, there's nowhere to go in the job and the employer can't create a new position. I don't know how we could change workplace relations. There certainly should be better vocational counselling in the schools. But where do you start to change the workplace? I have no idea.... If I didn't have 2 degrees, I still wouldn't be happy in this job. But you can't stop people from learning more. And if they can't find a job where they can use all their skills, that's unfortunate, but that's life. (Underemployed young female service worker with a B.Ed. degree)

But at least a third of those living in the education-jobs gap express an explicit hope that more education may lead to some form of democratization of paid workplaces and help to narrow the gap by creating more decent jobs:

More education is never harmful. If people could work 3 or 4 days a week with an equal standard of living, people would be happier with positive results. (Underemployed middle aged male self-employed university graduate)

Education is never a waste. It's a real shame that you cannot use your education on the job. We should never hold people back from going to school. We've got to reorganize the workplace. (Underemployed young woman technician with a university degree)

We need to look into workplace changes more. Slow down computerization and save manual labour jobs. Those who are overqualified
should get what they demand, and those who are less qualified
should be helped to go back to school. *Get some serious leaders who are
for the people.* Everything comes back to the solidarity of working people. Let people interact, with the less qualified learning from the
overqualified. (Unemployed middle aged male service worker with
some high school) [emphasis added]

Some of those living in the education-jobs gap who are most critical of capitalism's economic imperatives express explicit hopes that
interactive educational and workplace reforms will lead to a more
human-centered system:

We need a society which puts human beings first, not money. The education system needs to be more geared to practicalities. Whatever you
learn you should be able to apply to your job. Learning on the job should
also be recognized as learning experience by educational institutions. It
works both ways. There should be an ongoing process of on-the-job and
in-school learning. Education-job gaps are bound to happen, because the
economy is changing and types of qualifications don't match, because
institutions of learning have different timetables and don't react so fast
to the market…. There needs to be more coordinated planning among
governments, schools/colleges and business. But businesses are not taking that initiative at all…. The people who control things need a massive
dose of education to bring them down to the human level as opposed to
a preoccupation with money. (Underemployed middle aged female service worker with a university degree)

The system is screwed up. I don't expect much change. The rich want
to stay rich, so you can't expect they're going to give up so easy. But
people are staying longer in school and more people are going back.
Maybe employees will be more able to have more say in workplace
changes. (Underqualified young female part-time service worker
with some high school)

Overall, there is serious public support for democratizing measures such as cooperative forms of ownership, workplace participation, shorter workweeks and gender equity in unpaid labour. People
in general are giving these these progressive economic alternatives
more serious consideration than the writings of professional economists. The elements of viable solutions to the education-jobs gap

exist in the tacit foreknowledge of the general public. Where are "the serious leaders who are for the people?"

CONCLUDING REMARKS

The shortage of adequate paid work is a far more profound problem than most political leaders are yet prepared to admit publicly. The real scope of underemployment continues to be underestimated because so much of it beyond official unemployment counts remains hidden in the underground economy, the household and prisons, among discouraged and involuntary part-time workers, and in the largely invisible credential and performance gaps. Most political leaders persist in focusing on enhancing a "training culture" as the primary policy response, when a continual learning culture is already thriving across the current and potential workforce. In collaboration with corporate business leaders, elected politicians continue to promote partnership programs to try to ensure that specific groups of potential workers obtain better employability skills.[25] Indeed, the focus on education and training solutions has continued to mount, to the level of colleges now offering warranties that include taking back their graduates from unhappy employers for retraining (Lewington 1994). Many educational reforms may be admirable in themselves. But they remain utterly incapable of resolving the problem of underemployment. Basically, most political leaders continue to be preoccupied with shuffling education and training deck chairs on increasingly computerized workships while the sea of underemployment mounts.

Will the popular support among both the employed and the growing ranks of the underemployed for progressive economic reforms, such as genuine workplace democratization and a reduced normal workweek, be taken up effectively in local, national and international initiatives by progressive political movements such as the advocates of the new economics and political ecology? Or can vested economic and political power hierarchies continue to promote the "more education as secular salvation" solution in conjunction with individual internalization of the blame for underemployment, fear of unemployment and a sense that there is no real economic alternative? The massive systemic extent of underemployment in all of its aspects must be widely recognized and the false claims for a "knowledge economy" full of "high performance," "learning organizations" must be directly confronted. Otherwise, the wastage of much of our work-related education and training, along with the relative withering of our collective opportunities to use this knowledge in any future workplaces, is likely to continue to grow.

The currently dominant technologically-driven forms of mass production and globally pervasive private markets are not inevitable. As Sabel and Zeitlin (1985, 176) have observed with regard to the origins of capitalist mass production systems:

> It is politics and not the immanent characteristics of the technologies which will decide how the new machines are designed. And, if that is so, then a deeper understanding of the historical alternatives ... is one way to ensure that current possibilities are not unwittingly dismissed as utopian simply because they did not win out in the past.

We have to grasp the present as part of history and recognize that economic and other institutions are nothing but sets of behavior patterns subject to transformation when we identify better alternatives and can convince enough others of their merits. Nelson Mandela, Richard Turner (1972) and many others exercised this form of "utopian" thought and action in leading South Africa to overcome apartheid during the past 30 years. Many American citizens exercised the same mode of thought and action in helping to end the Cold War in the 1980s (Cortright 1993). Underemployment is no less a threat to human fulfillment than racism or the arms race. In my view, economic democracy offers the only discernible alternative to this problem that is positively sustainable both within the advanced capitalist societies and in terms of their impact on the rest of the world.

Sooner or later, the growing gap between the ample rewards and secure lives of executives and top experts, and the wasted education and withered work of most of the population could provoke profound social upheaval. The result may be either the growth of versions of economic democracy, or a more authoritarian shareholder capitalist society run by a technocratic elite, or some other historic compromise. The findings of this book — particularly the evidence of widespread demand among an increasingly underemployed labour force for more opportunities to use their increasing knowledge in meaningful and rewarding work, and the popular sentiments of resistance to government moves to make advanced education less accessible — suggest that the political choices are right in front of us. What is your choice?

Endnotes

Introduction

1. Letter from American male university graduate to Ann Landers (1995).

2. Canadian aboriginal woman university graduate in her early 20s, interviewed in summer of 1994.

3. For one of the most graphic examples, see Secretary's Commission on Achieving Necessary Skills (1991).

4. For example, the last two U.S. presidents, George Bush and Bill Clinton, have both styled themselves to be "the education president" and put forward numerous plans and programs to make increased educational participation their number one priority, in order to ensure that Americans know all that they need to succeed in the "knowledge economy" of the 21st century.

5. See Lane (1991) for well-grounded documentation of the continuing centrality of work for human identity.

6. See, for example, Task Force on Education and Training (1989). Shortages of specific technical skills certainly occur in all private market-based economies. But to generalize from such occasional shortages in the context of widespread underemployment and unemployment of well qualified people is to commit a fallacy of composition error of logic.

7. At least since the creation of junior colleges early in the post-World War II expansionary era, some astute social scientists have comprehended this deferring aspect of most new government-sponsored training schemes in relation to the education-jobs gap. The sociologist Burton Clark (1962) quite aptly called it "the cooling out function."

8. It is relevant to note here that one of the most extensive assessments of the performance of the U.S. education system was conducted in 1990–91 by federal government researchers at the Sandia National Laboratories in New Mexico. The researchers found steady or slightly improving trends on nearly every measure. The report was finally published in 1993 (Sandia Laboratories 1993). But this was only after it had been deliberately withheld, subjected to extraordinary internal reviews and effectively neutralized by long delays, because its findings ran counter to President Bush's national agenda focussed on school reform (see Tanner 1993).

9. Some of the leading recent examples of this genre are Senge (1990),

Marshall and Tucker (1992), Wirth (1992), Berryman and Bailey (1992), Resnick and Witt (1996) and Stewart (1997).

10. The most sophisticated human capital theorists have nearly all worked in the U.S., where "overeducation" has been most pervasive. As influential exponents of their respective eras, see Schultz (1963), Freeman (1976), and Romer (1994). A fuller critique of human capital theories is offered in Chapter Four and in Livingstone (1997b).

11. For a detailed description of the research design, sample composition, types of questions and basic results, see Livingstone, Hart and Davie (1997).

12. For a more detailed analysis of the attitudes of corporate executives toward general educational policy options than is appropriate in this text, see Livingstone and Hart (forthcoming).

13. See especially the classification schemes and associated discussions of possible economic and educational reforms in Levin (1976, 1980) and Carnoy and Levin (1985). More recently, Levin has been centrally involved in some of the most promising experiments to close the talent use gap for economically disadvantaged youngsters in the U.S., the Accelerated Schools Project (see Hopfenberg and Levin et al. 1993).

Chapter 1

1. For one of the most extensive documentation efforts in the period prior to proliferation of computerized information technologies see Machlup (1962). Machlup also continued to assay the spread of institutionalized forms of information and knowledge in later works, including *Information through the Printed Word: The Dissemination of Scholarly, Scientific and Intellectual Knowledge, 1978–80, 4 volumes; and Knowledge, Its Creation, Distribution and Economic Significance,* 1980. See also Porat (1977).

2. Estimates of the growth of collective human knowledge have become increasingly difficult with the proliferation of new information technologies. Suggestions that recorded forms of knowledge are now doubling within very short time periods are seen as plausible by many observers, especially those enamored with these technologies. A representative example is provided by Lew Perlman (1992, 59): "[T]he sheer volume of available information being generated by the new technologies is exploding. Analysts estimate that the total volume of encoded information doubles at least every decade; in fast-paced fields, available information doubles every few years — or even months. One study cited by George Gilder even indicated that stored data would *double nineteen times* (in other words, would be over half a million times greater) by the year 2000. Indeed, rapid advances in science and technology have reduced the "half-life" of valid knowledge in many areas to as little as eighteen months."

3. For a useful overview of this preoccupation, see Beniger (1986). For a representative critique of schooling as "the channelling colony " in the "pyramidal state," see Raskin (1971).

4. These three types of learning have been most commonly distinguished by adult education researchers (see, for example, Selman and Dampier (1991, 11–12). Throughout the book I will generally use such terms as "adult courses" or "further education" rather than the somewhat confusing term "nonformal." In a strictly denotative sense, nonformal can also be taken to include informal. The critical distinction is whether the learning activity is organized under the authority of some institution (such as an adult course at a high school or a training program at a paid workplace) in which case it is *nonformal education,* or initiated and sustained by learners themselves (such as an individual who chooses to learn a computer language alone or a group who agree to learn such a language together outside any school or externally imposed program) in which case it is *informal learning.*

5. For a provocative critique of the limitations of modern schooling, see Illich (1971).

6. As Table 1.2 shows, France has achieved the next highest tertiary enrolment ratios among the OECD countries in these terms, reaching 40 percent in 1990 and 50 percent by 1993. For fuller discussion of the French case, see Baudelot and Establet (1989). Other analyses of the Japanese case indicate that tertiary enrolment ratios have continued to grow, with over 70 percent of students who complete upper secondary education now continuing to various forms of post-secondary schooling (Makino 1996). More cohort-specific measures of participation would be needed to take account of the effects of variations in the size of age cohorts, particularly baby boom and bust cycles. But the general trend to increasing tertiary level participation is clear enough.

7. This table, as well as many of the U.S. data tables presented later in the book, is based on the series of General Social Surveys conducted by the National Opinion Research Center (Davis and Smith 1994). The data file is distributed by the Roper Center for Public Opinion Research, University of Connecticut, Storrs, CT. The samples typically involve about 1000 respondents and are therefore subject to sampling error of 3 to 4 percent. Such sample surveys generally underrepresent those with less formal schooling somewhat but the upward trend in formal attainments is clear.

8. These data are drawn from the archive of the OISE Survey of Educational Issues. The OISE Survey, which began in 1978, remains the only regular, publicly disseminated survey of public attitudes toward educational policy issues in Canada (see Livingstone, Hart and Davie 1997). Each survey is based on a representative random sample of over 1000 Ontario adults as well as a supplementary sample of over 100 corporate executives.

This data set will be used extensively throughout the book. The sample data have been weighted to correct for underrepresentation on age, sex, and formal schooling criteria.

9. See OECD (1994b), especially Chapter Seven, "Skills and Competencies."

10. All of these survey findings are reported in detail in Livingstone, Hart and Davie (1995, 1997).

11. In addition to the time series on public support for education funding increases in the OISE/UT Survey, various other Canadian surveys have found strong majority support for increased education funding (see Hart and Livingstone 1998). Similar attitude patterns have been found during the 1990s in most of the G7 countries; see, for example, the 1990 finding of strong support for "much more" public spending on education in the U.S., Britain, Italy and West Germany (Taylor-Gooby 1993).

12. For a detailed account of Turner's plan and its influence see Powell (1918).

13. In addition to Burton Clark's (1962) original analysis of this "cooling out function" in California junior colleges of the 1950s, see Brint and Karabel (1989) on the subsequent development of U.S. community colleges.

14. For brief overviews and informative case studies of the British case, see Dale et al. (1990), Holland (1990) and Shilling (1989).

15. In a series of five separate surveys between 1978 and 1984 in Ontario, the general public clearly chose job training as its top priority from a long list of possible educational objectives. However, it should also be noted that corporate executives were distinct from all other social groups, in consistently giving much greater priority to the development of creativity and critical thinking skills (Livingstone, Hart and Davie 1985 31).

16. For representative accounts of these initiatives to strengthen the vocational training of youths in the U.S., see Farrar and Connolly (1991), Marschall (1990) and Spangenberg (1995). On adult vocational training, see McFarland (1996).

17. For the most extensive recent effort to compare employee training programs across the OECD countries, see OECD (1991b, 135–175).

18. For an overview of post-WWII changes in the general orientation, teaching methods and target groups of these programs, see Romiszowski (1990).

19. See Betcherman (1991, 1992) and Sharpe (1990). For a revealing case study of the substantive limits of Canadian job retraining programs, see Dunk and Nelson (1992). On U.S. underinvestment in employee training, see Bishop (1992).

20. Basil Bernstein's major work is his four volume series on class, codes and control. The most recent of these is Bernstein (1990). For a critical overview, see Sadovnik (1995). Among Pierre Bourdieu's prolific writings,

the most relevant ones dealing with cultural capital and available in English are Bourdieu and Passeron (1977 [1970]); Bourdieu and Passeron (1979 [1964]) and Bourdieu (1984 [1979]). For an overview of Bourdieu's engagement with his critics and admirers, see Bourdieu and Wacquant (1992).

21. For a brief overview of these variants of cultural deficit theories of learning, see Curtis, Livingstone and Smaller (1992, 16–18).

22. For an example of a general study that does focus on the creative cultural capacities of working class youths in relation to dominant cultural forms, see Willis (1990). For a more extensive critique of cultural deficit theories and the development of an alternative theoretical perspective on working class learning based on Vygotskian activity theory, see Livingstone et. al. (forthcoming).

23. For a brief review of innate difference theories of learning, see Curtis, Livingstone and Smaller (1992, 14–16). The most infamous recent instance, of course, is Herrnstein and Murray (1994). The legion of American critiques of this book are summarized in Jacoby and Glauberman (1995). Canadian critiques, including my own, appear in Cameron (1995).

24. A useful recent review of different philosophical approaches to the notion of informal learning and their political implications appears in Garrick (1996).

25. For studies on voluntary learning activities of economically disadvantaged urban adults, see Serre (1978), Booth (1979), Livingstone (1997a) and Livingstone et al. (forthcoming); on young and older school dropouts, see Virgin and McCatty (1976), as well as Armstrong (1971) and Brookfield (1982); on functional illiterates, see Eberle and Robinson (1980), Kratz (1980), and Johnson, Levine and Rosenthal (1977). For recent overviews of empirical research on adults' informal learning which focus on disadvantaged social groups, see Padberg (1991) and Adams et al (1997).

26. Personal communication from Allen Tough, April 26, 1994.

27. See, for example, Browne (1992). As he notes: "The richness of the popular culture study is too important to leave in the hands of the elite. Literacy means far more than they understand or care to admit…. As many people have come to recognize the potential breadth and depth of the term *literacy* today, the conventional narrow meaning has been relaxed and broadened to include various concepts associated with fluency in the various media of communication — verbal, visual, imitational and examples. New and future means of communication are questioning the dominance — or demonstrating the lack of dominance — of the printed word. Movies, television, photographs, billboards, pictures, music, fossils, graffiti, body language, sign language, sports and outdoor entertainment, each challenging the exclusive superiority of the print medium, represents a culture that to one degree or another requires its own expertise and literacy. Each opens up its own world. (109, 175–76)."

28. Consider, for example, Ben Hamper's (1992) autobiographical account of life on General Motors' Flint, Michigan assembly line in the late 1970s and early 1980s. This is a richly irreverent view of informal learning related to many aspects of the job, such as technical task mastery, job combining, safety issues, and relations with workmates and supervisors.

29. Interview with auto press operator, St. Catharines, Ontario, October 6, 1995. From Livingstone et al. (forthcoming).

30. Interview #3115, follow-up to 10th OISE Survey, February, 1995.

31. Matsushita statement quoted by Carre and Pearn (1992, 88). It may be of interest to note that Matsushita has been singularly unsuccessful in applying this mobilization strategy after taking over the American entertainment company, MCA, and recently divested its ownership of this company. For other management-centered views, see Mulder et al. (1990).

32. See also Jarvis (1992) for a review of the conventional wisdom in the adult education literature on managerial, professional and manual employees learning dispositions in relation to their jobs and, Merriam and Clark (1991) for an extensive and insightful profile of the general learning practices of a group of mainly professional employees over a twenty year time period.

33. See, for example Sharp, Hartwig and O'Leary (1989), Altenbaugh (1990), Simon (1990) and Welton (1987). On recent initiatives of the Canadian Auto Workers' (CAW) union (which succeeded the UAW in 1985) around paid educational leave, and a case study of associated nonformal and informal learning practices within the biggest industrial union local in the country, see Roth (1997).

34. For a general historical perspective on workers' thirst for really useful knowledge, see Johnson (1979). For recent general discussions of this common tendency, see especially Newman (1993) and Hart (1992).

35. Of course, recorded history has always been dominated by the accounts of writers from the more affluent classes with the time, energy and means to set down their reflections and interpretations. As (Moore 1966) has noted, this makes recorded history largely an intellectual conceit! The relatively small numbers of working class autobiographies over the past two centuries typically provide many suggestive indications of the informal learning practices of more disadvantaged people. For relevant nineteenth century working class autobiographies, see especially Burnett (1982), Burnett, Vincent and Mayall (1994), and Lane (1991).

36. Interview transcript provided by Robert Bowd, August, 1995.

37. For suggestive ethnographic studies, see Sacks and Remy (1984) and Westwood (1985).

38. See, for example, the recent best-seller by Senge (1990). The term "knowledge economy" was probably first coined by Machlup (1962).

39. See Vincent (1989) Courts (1992) and Street (1995) for informative

accounts of the political uses of illiteracy claims and actual conditions of popular literacy in earlier periods of industrial capitalist society.

40. For rich testimony from peasants themselves about changes in their modes of thought in the context of this transition from an oral to a print-dominated culture, see Luria (1976).

41. For sensitive accounts of the problems and accomplishments of print illiterates in the U. S., see Kozol (1985) and Rose (1990).

42. See Cuban (1986) and Noble (1991) for critical historical analyses of the bases for the emergence of these claims for imperative public invest-ment in new educational technologies to cope with imputed new econom-ic requirements.

43. Interview with assembler in auto parts plant, St. Catharines, Ontario, October 13, 1995.

Chapter 2

1. Sheak's (1994) article provides a useful brief overview of the develop-ment of the concept of subemployment, as well as his estimate of its extent in the U.S. between 1970 and 1992 which is cited at the end of the chapter. He focuses on four dimensions, namely the officially counted unemployed, those not in the labour force but who want a job now, the involuntary part-time employed, and full-time workers who have low earnings. Low earn-ings cut off points, such as the official poverty standards on which Sheak relies, are often arbitrary and fluctuate in relation to monetary factors that make trend comparisons even more arbitrary. The subsequent analyses in this book will not use earnings criteria. This is not intended to deny the fact that those who are subemployed on other criteria are often among the most materially impoverished people. Other, similarly arbitrary aggregate sta-tistical criteria have been used by researchers in the labour utilization tra-dition to identify underemployed people on educational attainment-per-formance requirement variables. These empirically-derived criteria will also not be considered here. For a general critique, see Halaby (1994).

2. It should be noted here that these generational comparisons have been constructed excluding anyone under 25 years of age, in order to generate comparisons of the last 3 generations of Americans who are now clearly old enough to have completed a first university degree. However, as Chap-ter One documents, younger people are now frequently "stopping out" and resuming formal schooling later, as well as generally participating more extensively in formal upgrading through continuing education pro-grams; so the attainments of this youngest age cohort will undoubtedly continue to increase in relation to the 2 older generations.

3. Major differences remain in the educational and occupational social-ization of boys and girls (Thorne 1994) and in their subsequent acceptance

into advanced natural science programs and careers (Hanson 1996).

4. These race-specific class origin differences in school attainments may underestimate the talent use gap for blacks since blacks have been much more likely than whites to be raised in poor single-parent female-headed households with less material resources to support higher educational aspirations than those containing male industrial workers.

5. The estimation process was as follows: the current U.S adult population over 25 is more than 150 million people; over 20 percent of this population, or 30 million, hold degrees; those in upper middle class (professional, managerial and employer-based) households comprise no more than 20 percent of the population; with completion rates of over 40 percent, those from upper middle class households constitute about a third of degree holders, whereas those from lower class origins, with completion rates averaging under 20 percent, constitute about two thirds of degree holders or 20 million people; if the lower class completion rate were equal to the upper middle class rate, the number of those from lower class origins with degrees would double to more than 20 million people. If blacks and Hispanics who constitute about 30 million of the over 25 population and have degree completion rates of less than half of whites are taken into account, equalizing their completion rates would add more than 5 million degree holders. Equalization of women's completion rates is now being approached in the most recent age cohorts, but the systemic discrimination against older women in higher education would add many additional millions to these estimates of the talent use gap. All figures have been drawn from the Statistical Abstract of the United States (1992).

6. The exception to the upward trend in long term unemployment has been Japan where the proportion circled around 15 percent between 1979 and the early 1990s (OECD 1994a, 12, 14). But it is possible that the exceptionally large numbers of discouraged workers found in recent Japanese surveys (Sorrentino 1993, 15–16) has also been increasing.

7. For example, it has been estimated that more than half a million unemployed working-age disabled people in Canada could perform regular jobs if they were allowed to retain some basic support services (e.g. for wheelchairs and therapy treatments) that would allow them to enter the workforce on an equitable basis, rather than losing such support services entirely (Fischer 1994).

8. Each OISE Survey from 1982 to 1996 asked respondents the following question: "What general educational requirement, apart from professional certification or licensing, is currently set for new applicants for the type of job you now hold or last held? If you are self-employed, what general educational requirement is set for your trade or profession?" The options were: 1 no specific requirement; 2 some high school; 3 completed high school; 4 some community college or other business/technical college; 5 communi-

ty college or other business/technical college certificate or diploma; 6 some university; 7 undergraduate university degree (e.g. B.A., B.Sc., LLB.); 8 some graduate university; 9 graduate university degree (e.g. M.A., Ph.D., MD.). While these Ontario surveys have been administered every second year, the findings have been aggregated in Table 2.5 for greater accuracy of estimation and ease of presentation.

9. For recent overviews, see Shelly (1992, 13–21), Holzer and Vroman (1993, 81, 112), and Livingstone (1994b).

10. This 1976 U.S. surplus education figure of over 40 percent included all respondents who had more *years of schooling* than their self-reports indicated were required to enter jobs like theirs. The later underemployment rates reported in this section are all based only on *credentials required and attained*; these measures do not take into account partial attainments, so those who have some university education and whose jobs only require a high school diploma for entry are not counted as underemployed. When these more inclusive surplus education estimates are made for the Ontario samples, the rate is also around 40 percent.

11. Throughout the text, "credentially underemployed" refers to people who have one credential higher than their job now requires for entry. The "highly underemployed" have two or more credentials beyond the current requirement. "Underqualified" people have the reverse conditions.

12. Prior to the development of the GED scale, there were other empirical efforts to assess the correspondence between job requirements and educational achievements. These studies, which began in the 1940s and included scholars such as H.M. Bell (1940), Seymour Harris (1949) and Lawrence Thomas (1956), are discussed in Berg (1970).

13. This finding of the relatively high underemployment of community college attendees and graduates is consistent with those of our Ontario surveys and the 1989 Canadian national survey. The argument that Burton Clark (1962) first suggested after the development of the first North American junior colleges in California — that these institutions were intended primarily to serve a "cooling out function" for a growing surplus of high school graduates — still may have some relevance.

14. See National Center on Education and the Economy (1990). Compare Hall and Carlton (1977) and the classic earlier study by Berg (1970).

15. For detailed information on these surveys, see Davis and Smith (1994) and Livingstone, Hart and Davie (1997), respectively.

16. The specific estimates of GED levels used by the NORC in all its national surveys between 1972 and 1990, were developed by Lloyd Temme (1975) using the 1967 Dictionary of Occupational titles and the April, 1971 Current Population Survey. Burris (1983) used the NORC 1977–78 survey and these GED scores. I have used the 1972–90 surveys and the same GED scores for the estimates of the U.S. performance gap in the present study.

17. I am indebted to the late Alf Hunter for his generous provision of this coding scheme prior to publication of his own findings and his untimely passing.

18. Halaby (1994) offers a critique of GED-based measures of skill mismatch. He also presents an analysis of skill mismatch based on an alternative self-report question from the 1973 and 1977 Quality of Employment Surveys in the U.S. These surveys found a skill underuse rate of about 30 percent of the workforce (52). We have replicated the same question in the 1994 and 1996 OISE surveys and found rates of just over 40 percent; see Livingstone, Hart and Davie (1997, 73).

19. See, for example, many of the autobiographical accounts of 19th century British industrial workers in the books of John Burnett and David Vincent.

20. This distribution of a sense of skill wastage may be contrasted with self-reports of the "usefulness" of one's schooling. Our Ontario surveys since 1978 have consistently found that about half the employed workforce have found their schooling to be only moderately useful at best for their jobs (Livingstone, Hart and Davie 1995, 26–27). But the more schooling people have, the more likely they are to rate it as "useful." In 1994, two-thirds of university graduates had found their schooling to be quite useful for their jobs, in contrast to less than 20 percent of high school dropouts; three-quarters of corporate executives found their schooling useful, as opposed to only one-quarter of industrial workers. There are also high correlations between perceived usefulness and income. Assessments of the usefulness of schooling are much more closely associated with the benefit of advanced credentials for getting a job with higher earnings than with the use of schooling for job performance. These patterns essentially replicate Rumberger's (1980) finding that college graduates could be overeducated but not experience a loss of relative income. Both sets of results tend to confirm Thurow's (1974) job competition model which posits that with credential inflation, the best-educated people still get both the best jobs and the highest wages.

21. More sensitive measures might detect such differences. There is a large research literature on the existence of "cultural capital" among families in more affluent social classes, which at least implies that there is likely to be less underemployment of their children because they can parlay this "capital" into both higher status educational programs and better jobs (e.g. Bourdieu 1984). But see the critical discussion of this perspective as a simplification of the relations of cultural power in Chapter Four.

22. See, for example, the research studies discussed in Barlow and Robertson (1994, 45–60).

23. Canada's leading business magazine, *Canadian Business*, provides a particularly absurd example of this evasive approach. In a recent cover article on credential underemployment, the authors first describe current con-

ditions, relying partly on some of my own research findings. They then conclude that because such entrepreneurs as Microsoft's Bill Gates have become successful without college degrees, the solution to inflated credentialism is to focus on performance skills. They conveniently ignore the fact that performance skill underemployment is actually much greater than the credential gap! See Taylor and McGugan (1995).

Chapter 3

1. Performance underemployed male store clerk in his late 30s with a Grade 9 education, interviewed in the follow-up to the 1994 OISE survey.

2. Detailed accounts of the sample designs, interview questions and preliminary findings for these surveys and case studies may be found in Livingstone, Hart and Davie (1997); and Livingstone (1992, 1994b, 1996a, 1996b).

3. The eligible sample was restricted to university and community college graduates who were underemployed on credential criteria (N=62) and those with high school diplomas or less who were underqualified for their jobs on credential criteria (N=74). All 136 eligible people responded to further semi-structured questions about their own learning and work experiences as well as offering more detailed views on education-jobs relations.

The restriction of the eligible sample to credentially underemployed respondents with post-secondary certification and credentially underqualified respondents with no more than a high school diploma was necessitated by cost constraints. This restriction ensured that we had a representative sample of those who were most likely to be credentially mismatched for their jobs. But it excludes roughly the same number of other respondents to the original 1994 general population survey who were also credentially mismatched, for example, underemployed high school graduates in jobs with no education entry requirement and underqualified community college graduates in jobs that now require a university degree for entry. The interview was administered by telephone by the Institute for Social Research at York University, between February 18 and March 12, 1995. The questions about learning practices were adapted and updated from the original interview schedule on self-directed learning projects developed by Allen Tough (1978, 1979). The interview schedule is available on request.

4. Given the general difficulty of identifying the populations of underemployed and underqualified people, the initial university placement office and adult basic education upgrading class interviews were based on selective samples which were chosen primarily on criteria of accessibility. These samples exclude the most extreme cases of both underemployment and underqualification. The underemployed interviewees were all fairly

recent graduates actively seeking better employment through the placement centre. The underqualified interviewees all had sufficient material resource support, motivation and basic education to qualify for upgrading programs. The findings of these preliminary interviews are reported in more detail in Livingstone (1994b; 1996b). There are substantial numbers of people living in more difficult conditions of chronic underqualification and underemployment. Our further research has attempted to address this limitation through interviews with clients of food banks, and with the 1995 follow-up survey to the 1994 OISE Survey of Educational Issues. The results of all of these inquiries are incorporated in this chapter.

5. Among the multitude of these studies, see for the U.S.: Stinchcombe (1964), Anyon (1980), Powers (1985), Steinitz and Solomon (1986), MacLeod (1987), Lareau (1989), and Weis (1990). For Canada, see: James (1990), Curtis, Livingstone and Smaller (1992), and Dei (1995). For the U.K., see Willis (1977), Shilling (1989), Holland (1990), and Mizra (1993).

6. Interview with a delegate to the Ontario Federation of Labour Conference, Toronto, November 30, 1988. Cited in Curtis, Livingstone and Smaller (1992, 6).

7. Jim Hughes, age 35, former welder and prospective X-ray technician, small town in Indiana, quoted in Maurer (1979, 39–43).

8. Denny Reid, age 43, former teacher and mechanic, in Vancouver, British Columbia, quoted in McKay (1983, 30).

9. Young unskilled man with two young children and a pregnant wife in Sunderland, United Kingdom, quoted in Seabrook (1982, 3).

10. All following quotes in this chapter are drawn from our Ontario in-depth interviews in 1994–5, unless otherwise indicated.

11. For a critical analysis of such claims, see Curtis, Livingstone and Smaller (1992).

12. See, for example, deRoche, Riley and Smith (1994). Consider also the cycling of young people between short-term training courses and temporary jobs, which has been more extensive to date in countries such as Great Britain where the normal school leaving age has been much earlier than in the U.S. and Canada (Bates et. al. 1984).

13. For a critical overview of this field of research, see Candy (1993). An extensive bibliography of current research on informal learning has been produced by Adams et al. (1997). This bibliography is accessible online at the Website of the National Research Network for New Approaches to Lifelong Learning (NALL): www.edu.oise.utoronto.ca/depts/sese/csew.

14. Many of the relevant empirical studies are identified in note 25 in Chapter One.

15. Willis' (1977) classic ethnographic study of this tendency traces the presumptive denial of mental aspects of manual labour among working class lads involved in rejecting an academic school culture and headed for

manual jobs, as the quote from Joey at the beginning of the chapter reflects.

16. For provocative discussions, see Foley (1987) as well as, more generally, Zolberg (1972, 183–207) and Scott (1990).

17. In an attempt to address this limitation, I have recently conducted a research project in cooperation with several labour educators and trade unions in the Toronto region. The project uses participatory action research methods, engaging with workers and members of their households to identify the scope and content of working class informal learning activities and develop more effective educational resource centers. See Livingstone et al. (forthcoming).

18. It should be noted here that further analysis of the follow-up sub-sample of underqualified non-college respondents has found that the small minority of the credentially underqualified who identify themselves as actually underqualified are spending much more time in work-related course studies than any other group, an average of about 150 hours per year.

Chapter 4

1. It is interesting to note that human capital theory is in accord with the Marxist labour theory of value on this recognition of labour as the primary source of wealth in capitalist society. From 18th century physiocrats who imputed primary value creating capacity to the land up to our contemporary econometricians, dominant economic theories have tended to diminish the role of labour in the creation of wealth. The limits of human capital theory, as will be illustrated in this chapter, are its fixation with individual market transactions and blindness of macro-level underemployment. In Marxist terms, human capital theory is preoccupied with *value creation* while ignoring *value realization*. That is, human capital theory insists on the importance of investment in education, the imparting of value to the future labourer, but does not directly address the fact that this embodied value must be harnessed in the production of goods or services by labour power in order for the human capital invested to be realized. It is precisely this failure of value realization that constitutes the education-jobs gap. I am indebted to Wally Seccombe for developing this comparison.

2. For my own early critique of the "post-industrial" perspective, Porter's rejoinder and my reply, see Livingstone (1972).

3. See Stehr (1994) for a recent revisionist overview of post-industrial/knowledge *society* theories which attempts to respond to some critiques and recuperate the concept by formulating an explicitly non-evolutionary version which stresses its theoretical elasticity and transitional character, and with decidedly less emphasis on economic aspects of social relations than its predecessors.

4. A prominent example of a post-modernist thinker who has self-consciously attempted to offer a macro-level explanation for contemporary social conditions is Francis Fukuyama (1991). For an overview of this genre of contemporary social theories, see Jencks (1989).

5. In addition to evolutionary explanations, other forms of explanation of social change and continuity that have been common in the social sciences at various times include functionalist, genetic, historicist (e.g. "great man" theories of history), and inter-group struggle theories. For useful accounts of the varieties of social explanation, see Robert R. Brown (1964) and Christopher Lloyd (1986).

6. Murphy (1993) has traced the development of the conflation of social and technical divisions of labour and the emergence of technological determinism in classical political economy, with particular attention to the influences of Smith and Karl Marx. Murphy also draws on Aristotle to distinguish natural, customary and stipulated or deliberately designed aspects of divisions of labour.

7. See also the discussion in Chapter Two of the performance gap, which is based on the same GED measures. The primary sources of the occupation-specific GED scores were Temme (1975) for the U.S. and Hunter (1986) for Canada.

8. While each individual job title has been given a whole number rating on both the GED and SVP scales by government analysts, the groupings of thousands of these titles into summary occupational classifications results in average scores which produce a continuous rather than a simple ordinal scale. The mid-point split procedure groups all scores up to 1.5 as 1, from 1.5 to 2.5 as 2 and so on, with scores over 5.5 up to the maximum of 6 grouped as 6. We have also analyzed the same data with a grouping that reduces all scores below any whole number to the lower skill level (e.g. 1.75 becomes 1) and an alternative grouping that raises all scores above any whole number to the higher skill level (e.g. 1.25 becomes 2). The trends in each case are very similar.

9. Both Eckhaus (1964, Table 3, 185) and Berg (1970, Table III-1, 46) apparently used median scores to produce their estimates of the distributions of GED skill levels in the U.S. labour force. Eckhaus used an earlier seven point scale which I have grouped downward for equivalence with the six point scale that has been used since the 1950s. Eckhaus also produced estimates for 1950 using the seven point scale. When they are regrouped downward, his 1950 estimates are fairly similar to those of Berg, but Berg's estimates are presented here because they rely on the now standard six point scale.

10. For more extensive accounts of historical and current trends in the class structures of the U.S. and Canada, see, for example: U.S. (Szymanski 1983; Kerbo 1983; Wright 1997); Canada (Ornstein 1983; Clement 1988; Livingstone and Mangan 1996).

11. Clement and Myles' (1994, 63–90) analysis confirms the stronger managerialist tendency of the U.S. class structure in comparison with Sweden, Norway and Finland with regard to the regulation of labour. They find a more mixed mode in Canada, with the largely American branch plant goods producing sectors having a similar proportion of employees with managerial authority to the U.S., while Canadian government and service sectors are closer to the Nordic model of less managers and greater worker consultation. It should be noted, however, that these comparative analyses are based primarily on survey respondents' self-reports all of which likely provide overestimates of many respondents' actual managerial authority.

12. Special tabulations of 1986 and 1991 Canada census as well as secondary analysis of the 1972–94 NORC U.S. data set (Davis and Smith 1994).

13. According to the OECD (1996d), CEO:factory worker wage ratios for some relevant countries were as follows: U.S. 120; Canada 36; UK 33; Germany 21; Japan 16.

Chapter 5

1. For an extensive critical overview of contemporary theories of the relations between educational systems and their societal contexts, which systematically relates specific theories of cultural and educational reproduction to their metatheoretical foundations and four basic theoretical paradigms (namely systemic functionalist, analytical neo-Weberian conflict, structuralist Marxist conflict and post-structuralist conflict theories), see Morrow and Torres (1995).

2. The following discussion of Marxist and Weberian class distinctions is largely based on Livingstone and Mangan (1996), especially Chapter One.

3. As noted in Chapter Four, human capital theory and the Marxist labour theory of value are in accord on the recognition of labour as the primary source of wealth in capitalist society. In contrast to human capital theory, Marxist economic theory does distinguish *value creation* from *value realization*. It therefore provides a ready basis to identify the failure of business enterprises to harness the embodied value of human capital in the production of goods and services, the education-jobs gap.

4. It should be noted here that Collins (1980) has elsewhere provided a systemization of Weber's theory of the development of capitalism. He has not, to my knowledge, linked this explicitly with his theory of credentialism. In any case, the rationalization imperative in both Weber's and Collins' theoretical perspectives predisposes them toward continuing attention to bureaucratic control of occupational systems, and relative inattention to issues of underemployment beyond the performance gap based on arbitrary rules.

5. U.S. empirical researchers using the labour utilization framework have documented greater underemployment among women than men (Lichter and Landry 1991; Mutchler 1987); among blacks and Hispanics than whites (Lichter 1988; Zhou 1993); and among black women than black men (Johnson and Herring 1993). As noted in Chapter Two, these studies have generally included more arbitrary low income criteria, as well as unemployment, involuntary reduced employment and credential gap criteria. Researchers in this tradition have made valuable contributions to identifying race and gender-based underemployment. They have paid relatively little attention to class differences in underemployment.

6. For grounded critiques of classical Marxism and synthetic general analyses along these lines, see for example Gramsci (1971), Mies (1986), Blackburn (1990), O'Brien (1981), Murphy (1993) and Seccombe and Livingstone (1996), respectively.

7. One feature of the economic reductionist tendencies in orthodox Marxist scholarship has been to overemphasize the moment in the capitalist production process involving the production of goods and services commodities. As Marx (1939, 89) recognized in his early unpublished writings, the production process incorporates at least four moments:

"In *production* the members of society appropriate (create and shape) the products of nature in accord with human needs; *distribution* determines the proportion in which the individual shares in the product; *exchange* delivers the particular products into which the individual desires to convert the proportion which distribution has assigned to him; and, finally, in *consumption*, the products become objects of gratification, of individual appropriation." As my colleague, Wally Seccombe (1992, 1993), has ably documented in his historical sociological account of the development of family/household/kinship forms in feudal and capitalist societies, the moment of consumption is simultaneously the moment of *reproduction of labour*. This expanded conception of modes of production and reproduction facilitates the recognition of the value of domestic labour which remained largely invisible in earlier Marxist economic analyses. The significance of an expanded conception of valued labour beyond currently paid work will be developed in Chapter Six.

8. Some current Marxist sociologists argue that "neo-Marxist" theory is distinguished by the de facto *denial* of all three assumptions (Levine and Lembecke 1987). While I have some sympathy with this argument, such "theological" discussions are beyond the scope of this study.

9. For a recent study which reviews various Marxist as well as Weberian theories of class structure and class consciousness, identifies mediated forms of class, gender and race consciousness, and examines their current expressions in a cross-class survey and a case study of steelworkers and

their partners, see Livingstone and Mangan (1996).

10. For lucid accounts of Marx's general method of dialectical inquiry, in contrast to the ahistorical conceptualizations of "orthodox" Marxisms, see Sayer (1987) and Ollman (1993). See also Smith's (1987) development of a closely related method of feminist sociological inquiry.

11. See Marx (1867, Volume 1) for his own most fully developed and documented analysis of these relationships, as well as part III of the posthumous Volume 3 on the tendency of the rate of profit to fall.

12. This accelerated continuity thesis of current capitalist production is more fully developed with detailed documentation in relation to the global and Canadian steel industries in Livingstone (1993, 1996c).

13. Most research on changes in the capitalist labour process since Braverman (1974) has focused on forms of management control (e.g. Edwards, 1979) or issues of deskilling and reskilling (e.g. Wood, 1989) in and of themselves. The *contingent* character of these specific relations in association with enterprise profitability prospects has very frequently been ignored, as is well documented by Cohen's (1987) critical review.

14. For a general critique of the "post-industrial society" thesis which stresses its mystifying infatuation with new information technologies and its obscuring of underlying social relations of capitalist production, see Robins and Webster (1988). For a general critique of the more recent but related "flexible specialization" thesis, see Williams et al. (1987). Critical discussions of the extensiveness of a "Fordist" regime or mode of development, and hence of the inadequacy of the concept of "post-Fordism," may be found in Foster (1988) and Brenner and Glick (1991).

15. For a general analysis of retraining tendencies in mature industries, see Streeck (1989). A representative case study of an extensive retraining scheme in the British auto industry may be found in Beattie (1997).

16. A more detailed and fully documented development of this assessment of neo-Marxist theories of education with greater attention to both the critics of the correspondence thesis and the general limitations of these theories to date may be found in Livingstone (1995c).

17. For insightful critical overviews, see Liston (1988) and Moore (1988). The significance of Althusser's (1971) conceptual work on education as an "ideological state apparatus" should also be noted here, especially in terms of its explicit challenge to the base/superstructure perspective. As Moore (1988, 65–71) argues, in spite of Althusser's more nuanced original model of social totality, he reached a similarly flawed conclusion about the correspondent reproduction of capitalist social relations of and in production through the educational reproduction of labour power.

18. Liston (1988) has offered a book-length critique of explanatory failings of this general body of scholarship which he variously terms "radical," "Marxist" and "neo-Marxist." He includes Bowles and Gintis, Carnoy and

Levin, Hogan and Willis, as well as myself, within this tradition (15). In the terms of Figure 5.1, Liston omits class hegemony theorists, who have attended to historically-specific conflicts between class forces over educational policies. He also generously omits any direct criticism of my own contested subordination perspective and juxtaposes my early research to Bowles and Gintis documentary research as "a seminal empirical study" (167). Other critics have not been so kind! In any event, as I have noted elsewhere (Livingstone (1995c), I agree with the thrust of his general critique of the failure of much of the writing in this genre to use explicit explanatory forms of social theory or to subject arguments to evidentiary tests. The various theories of a "knowledge economy" have been prone to a similar facile functionalism, as I have tried to demonstrate in Chapter Four.

19. See Weiler (1988, 1–25) for a broader discussion of distinctions between critical and traditional educational theories focused on either reproduction of existing social structures or production of knowledge by agents, but which tends to conflate the differential emphases of these theories on consensus or conflict; and Morrow and Torres (1995) for a more extensive exposition of most major current types of reproduction theories in terms of both structure/agency and consensus/conflict emphases. Both accounts are primarily interested in cultural reproduction and devote very little attention to capitalist production dynamics in relation to education.

20. See especially their own accounts of their adult education experiences in McIlroy and Westwood (1993) and Thompson (1968).

21. For documentation of education downsizing initiatives in the U.S., U.K. and Canada since the 1970s, as well as the strong corporate support for and popular reactions against such reforms, see Pierson (1994) and Livingstone and Hart (forthcoming).

22. This theoretical perspective on education-work relations is most decidedly not, as Rikowski (1996, 435) erroneously claims, an attempt:

"to go back and rescue the old reproduction paradigm, and in doing so ... attempting to bring an old discredited educational Marxist tradition back to life.... New directions ... will be smothered by attempts (as in Livingstone ...) to resuscitate the old reproductionist perspective."

It should be clear to the reader that I view Bowles and Gintis' as well as Althusser's reproductionist perspectives as provocative but fundamentally flawed. In fact, my theoretical intent is to help to resuscitate the much older tradition of recognition of the *contradictory relations* between the multifaceted development of labourers and the rigid capitalist forms of divisions of labour that Marx observed. Generations of educational Marxist scholars who have focused on superstructural analyses have served to smother this older tradition. While Rikowski himself claims to have developed a Marxist theory of the social production of labour-power, nowhere in his own extensive overview of Marxist educational theory since 1976 does he intimate any recognition of these contradictory relations or of the associated social problem of underemployment.

23. The percentage differences reported in the following discussion are generally both consistent with the predicted directions and statistically significant at the .05 level of confidence. Further empirical tests using these class distinctions with other data sources are necessary to confirm these results.

24. Some successful businessmen without high formal educational credentials continue to be celebrated as "self-made men" (e.g. Taylor and McGugan 1995), although in more muted ways than in earlier, less highly schooled periods.

Chapter 6

1. A classic analysis of this process may be found in E.P. Thompson (1967).

2. For a brief but insightful analysis of the historical creation of the need to work becoming part of our current human nature, see S. Sayer (1987, 17–26).

3. I am indebted to Wally Seccombe for developing this distinction based on his analysis of the separation of subsistence labour in unpaid domestic work from labour in production for sale during the past millennium. See Seccombe (1992, 1993).

4. Illegal and nonlegal exchanges of goods and services in contemporary market economies have been given many labels over the past 50 years, such as: the "black market," "irregular economy," "subeconomy," "social economy," "hidden economy," "informal economy," "informal sector," "informal markets," "second economy," or "concealed economy." The preoccupation in most of the research literature has been with illegal monetary exchanges which escape government taxation. For an insightful summary and critique of this literature, see Wiegard (1992).

5. In the so-called "underdeveloped" countries, the vast majority of the rural population often continues to live in a subsistence economy with very little monetary exchange. In urban areas, employment in the underground economy is commonly estimated at around a third of the economically active population (see Portes 1996).

6. For a brilliant feminist analysis of the reproductive labour of bearing and caring for children, in terms analogous to Marx's analysis of productive labour, see O'Brien (1980); on domestic labour generally, see Luxton (1980).

7. This initiative goes by different names in different countries and has been variously taken up by educational institutions, governments, employ-

ers and organized labour. In Canada, it has been known as prior learning assessment and more recently as Prior Learning Assessment and Recognition (PLAR). For a preliminary bibliography on PLAR, see Vanstone (1998), available at website http://edu.oise.utoronto.ca/depts/sese/csew. Some of the most effective reconnections with organized schooling have been joint management-labour union initiatives to develop technical skills upgrading programs in close collaboration with community colleges, such as the recent efforts by the Canadian Steel Trade and Employment Congress (CSTEC).

8. The Working Class Learning Strategies project, which I have conducted with the aid of three labour union educators (Mike Hersh, D'Arcy Martin and Jennifer Stephen) at five unionized work sites in the Greater Toronto Area over the past four years, has discovered a massive amount of informal learning among unionized workers with diverse amounts of organized schooling. Most workers have been permitted to use very little of their newly acquired knowledge in their jobs. See Livingstone et al. (forthcoming).

9. For very readable introductions to this "new economics" see Daly and Cobb (1989); Nozick (1992); Brandt (1995); and Henderson (1996). A brief overview of the common vision in this literature may be found in Gonick (1995).

10. For a well grounded and informative analysis of the general problems involved in achieving democratic participation in contemporary societies, see Pateman (1970).

11. This is the dominant and still expanding global economic model. For an optimistic assessment of its future prospects, see the Special Issue of *Business Week* (November 18, 1994) on 21st Century Capitalism which identifies four different faces — consumer capitalism, producer capitalism, family capitalism and frontier capitalism (19) — as prevalent in different countries. For critical recent overviews from U.S. perspectives, see Thurow (1996), Greider (1997) and Harrison (1997).

12. Management consultants periodically rediscover the importance of trust in workers' relationships with their employers. Elton Mayo's human relations theory in the 1930s, Douglas McGregor's Theory Y in the 1960s and Edwards Deming's (1986) ideas on worker commitment as the key to quality improvement all rework the same basic insight, and encourage greater worker participation in the technical task decisions of the labour process. Over the past century, cooperative approaches to industrial relations have gone back and forth in popularity with more coercive approaches like scientific management and re-engineering. However, both approaches permit workers no significant role in management decisions and are generally compatible with other aspects of the shareholder capitalism model. For a general historical overview of these respective approach-

es, see Clegg and Dunkerley (1980).

13. Variants of the stakeholder alternative have frequently been promoted by diverse humanitarians. The most prominent advocates throughout the past century have been social democratic parties. Critics on the right have been concerned about a regulatory state undermining market dynamics and social welfare provisions in particular destroying the will to perform hired labour (see Friedman 1962). Critics on the left have worried about the limitations of regulatory state regimes' reforms and corporatist accords to offers sustained address to human needs in relation to the power of capitalists. For a trenchant critique of social democratic regimes and corporatism generally, see Panitch (1976).

14. For overviews of worker ownership and self-management, see King and van de Vall (1978); Holmstrom (1989); and Benello (1992).

15. For detailed accounts of the continuing development of these particular initiatives in cooperative work organization, see Whyte and Whyte (1991), Kasmir (1996) and MacLeod (1997) on Mondragon worker co-operatives; and Palgi (1998) and Rosner (1998) on the kibbutzim movement. My personal experience has included working and learning on the kibbutz of Givet Hayam Meuhaud in late 1963.

It should be noted that Mondragon is a series of interrelated workers' co-operatives based originally on a Catholic priest's interpretation of Robert Owen's ideas of industrial democracy and operating in extensive interaction with the capitalist civil society in the Basque region of Spain. The kibbutzim movement had its origins in Zionist socialism and built largely self-contained co-operative communities, many on the rural borders of Israel, prior to independence in 1948. While both deserve to be called emerging economic democracies, their origins, development strategies and community inclusiveness have been quite different. In my view, sustained experiments in economic democracy owe much more to their founders' and some continuing active members' deep sense of commitment to principles of democracy and social justice than to any particular associated religious or nationalist ideology. The founders of the American and French republics in the period of the emergence of industrial capitalism were not all of a single religious faith or nationalist zeal, but they were similarly united in their anti-monarchist commitment to constitute a new social order based on principles of greater liberty and equality.

16. The actual extensiveness of community-owned, non-profit and cooperative work organizations in most capitalist societies has typically been seriously underestimated even by most advocates of economic democracy. For an informative account including a number of case studies, see Quarter (1992).

17. For a well-documented account of ownership relations and investment processes in currently viable versions of economic democracy, as well

as insightful comparisons with variants of capitalism and other types of socialized economies, see Schweickart (1993). For a critical account of the limits of popular control of Mondragon's community banking system, see Axworthy (1985).

18. My colleague Jack Quarter estimates that there are now about 300 worker-run co-operatives in Canada and even less in the U.S. Personal communication, January 7, 1998.

19. For an in-depth analysis of the recent restructuring of paid work and domestic and community work and renegotiation of gender roles in an advanced capitalist setting among working class households, see Corman, Luxton, Livingstone and Seccombe (forthcoming). Patriarchal structures of work and training have persisted in communitarian economies but have become somewhat less pronounced than in capitalist societies. See Hacker (1989) and Adar (1998).

20. This assessment is based both on the inherent design principles of the organization of work in economic democracy and on the available empirical research on learning and work relations in the kibbutz (see Quarter 1982; Leviatan, Oliver and Quarter 1998) and Mondragon (see Whyte and Whyte 1988; Meek and Woodworth 1990; Kasmir 1996).

21. Personal communication from Greg MacLeod, February 17, 1998. According to MacLeod, the current plan calls for an increased employment level of 20 percent over the next few years. See also MacLeod (1997). However, in the past, such rapid growth has not always been in the interest of the existing Mondragon workers and the surrounding community (Kasmir 1996).

22. The most notable Canadian example is probably the Advisory Group on Working Time and the Distribution of Work (1994). For general recent reviews of distributional alternatives, see Hinrichs, Roche and Sirianni (eds.) (1991); Offe and Heinze (1992); Pixley (1993); and Rifkin (1995). In late 1997, the French and Italian governments both announced the reduction of the standard workweek to 35 hours, to be implemented over the next few years (see Hayden 1997).

23. U.S. studies have found increasing majority willingness to forego income for more free time among the employed workforce. See Rifkin (1995, 233–35).

24. For representative capital-oriented proposals, see Milton Friedman's (1962) negative income tax scheme; a well-developed labour-oriented plan may be found in Gorz (1985).

25. For analyses of some of the most widely heralded North American examples, see Farrar and Connolly (1991) on the Boston Compact, Spangenburg (1995) on the Rochester School-to-Work Programs and Bellissimo (1997) on the Toronto Learning Partnership.

Glossary of Acronyms

CSEW	Centre for Study of Education and Work, SESE at OISE/UT
DOT	Dictionary of Occupational Titles, U.S. Census
ESOPs	Employee Share Ownership Plans
G7	Group of 7 largest OECD economies (Canada, France, Germany, Italy, Japan, United Kingdom, United States)
GDP	Gross Domestic Product
GED	General Educational Development Scale
IALS	First International Adult Literacy Survey, conducted in Fall 1994 (including Canada, Germany, Netherlands, Poland, Sweden, Switzerland, United States)
ISR	Institute for Social Research, York University
NALL	SSHRC Research Network on New Approaches to Lifelong Learning, OISE/UT
NORC	National Opinion Research Center, University of Chicago
OECD	Organization for Economic Co-operation and Development
OISE/UT	Ontario Institute for Studies in Education of the University of Toronto
PLAR	Prior Learning Assessment and Recognition
SESE	Department of Sociology and Equity Studies in Education, OISE/UT
SSHRC	Social Sciences and Humanities Research Council of Canada
SVP	Specific Vocational Preparation Scale
UNESCO	United Nations Educational, Scientific and Cultural Organization

Bibliography

Abbas, J. (2003). *Disability and the Dimensions of Work*. M.A. Thesis, University of Toronto.

Abercrombie, N. and J. Urry. (1983). "Capital, Labour and the Middle Classes," in T.B. Bottomore and M.J. Mulkay (eds.) *Controversies in Sociology*, Issue No. 15.

Adams, M. et al. (1997). "Preliminary Bibliography of the Research Network for New Approaches to Lifelong Learning (NALL)." Toronto: Centre for the Study of Education and Work, OISE/UT.

Adar, G. (1982). "Occupational Prestige in the Kibbutz," *Interchange* 13, 1: 45-54.

Adar, G. (1998). "Women in the Changing Kibbutz," in U. Leviatan, H. Oliver and J. Quarter (eds.) *Crisis in the Israeli Kibbutz: The Challenge of Changing Times*. Westport, CT: Praeger/ Greenwood.

Adler, P. (1993). "The 'Learning Bureaucracy': New United Motor Manufacturing, Inc," *Research in Organizational Behavior* 15: 111-194.

Advisory Committee on the Changing Workplace. (1997). *Collective Reflection on the Changing Workplace*. Ottawa: Human Resources Development Canada.

Advisory Group on Working Time and the Distribution of Work. (1994). *Report of the Advisory Group on Working Time and the Distribution of Work*. Ottawa: Minister of Supply and Services, (December).

Altenbaugh, R. (1990). *Education for Struggle: The American Labor Colleges of the 1920s and the 1930s*. Philadelphia: Temple University Press

Althusser, L. (1971). "Ideology and Ideological State Apparatuses," in *Lenin and Philosophy and Other Essays*. New York: Monthly Review Press.

Antikainen, A., et al. (1996). *Living in a Learning Society: Life Histories, Identities and Education*. London: Palmer Press.

Anyon, J. (1980). "Social Class and the Hidden Curriculum of Work," *Journal of Education* 162: 67-92.

Apple, M. (1986). *Teachers and Texts: A Political Economy of Class and Gender Relations in Education*. New York: Routledge and Kegan Paul.

Armstrong, D. (1971). "Adult Learners of Low Educational Attainment The Self-Concepts, Backgrounds, and Educative Behavior of Average and High-Learning Adults of Low Educational Attainment." Ph.D. dissertation, University of Toronto.

Armstrong, P. and H. Armstrong. (1994). *The Double Ghetto: Canadian Women and Their Segregated Work*. Toronto: McClelland and Stewart.

Aronowitz, S. (1973). *False Promises: The Shaping of American Working Class Consciousness*. New York: McGraw-Hill.

Axworthy, C. (1985). *Worker Co-operation in Mondragon, the U.K. and France*. Saskatoon: Centre for the Study of Co-operatives, University of Saskatchewan.

Baer, D. and R. Lambert. (1982). Education and support for dominant ideology. *Canadian Review of Sociology and Anthropology* 19, 2: 173-195.

Bahktin, M.M. (1981). *The Dialogical Imagination*. Austin: University of Texas Press.

Bakke, E.W. (1940). *Citizens Without Work*. New Haven: Yale University Press.

Barlow, M. and H-I. Robertson. (1994). *Class Warfare: The Assault on Canada's Schools*. Toronto: Key Porter Books.

Barrett, S. (2001). "Integrating Hidden Unemployment into Measures of Labour Market Health." Paper presented at the 8th National Unemployment Conference, Department of Education, Training and Youth Affairs, Southern Cross University.

Batenburg, R. & de Witte, M. (2001). Underemployment in the Netherlands: How the Dutch 'Poldermodel' Failed to Close the Education-Jobs Gap. *Work, Employment and Society, 15* (1), 73-94.

Bates, I. et al. (eds.). (1984). *Schooling for the Dole: The New Vocationalism*. London: Macmillan.

Baudelot, C. and R. Establet. (1989). *Le Niveau Monte*. Paris: Editions du seuil.

Beattie, A. (1997). *Working People and Lifelong Learning*. Leicester: National Institute of Adult Continuing Education.

Beck, U. (1992). *Risk Society: Towards a New Modernity*. London: Sage.

Becker, G. (1964). *Human Capital: A Theoretical and Empirical Analysis, with Special Reference to Education*. New York: National Bureau of Economic Research.

Becker, G. (1993). *Human Capital*. (Third Edition). Chicago: University of Chicago Press.

Becker, G. (1996). "Human Capital: One Investment Where America is Way Ahead," *Business Week* (March 11).

Beirne, M. and H. Ramsay (eds.). (1992). *Information Technology and Workplace Democracy*. London: Routledge.

Bell, D. (1964). "The Post-Industrial Society," in E. Ginzberg (ed.) Technology and Social Change. New York: Columbia University Press, 44-59.

Bell, D. (1973). *The Coming of Post-Industrial Society*. New York: Basic Books.

Bell, H.M. (1940). *Matching Youth and Jobs*. Washington: American Council on Education.

Bell, I., Houston, N., & Heyes, R. (1997). Workless Households, Unemployment and Economic Inactivity. *Labour Market Trends, 105* (9), 339-345.

Bellissimo, D. (1997). "Business/Education Partnerships: Real Partnerships, Real Results?" M.Ed. thesis, University of Toronto.

Benello, C.G. (1992). *From the Ground Up: Essays on Grassroots and Workplace Democracy*. Boston: South End Press.

Ben-Peretz, M. and Z. Lavi. (1982). "Interaction Between the Kibbutz Community and the School," *Interchange* 13, 1: 55-67.

Bengtsson, I. (1993). "Labour Markets of the Future: The Challenge to Educational Policy Makers," *European Journal of Education* 28, 2.

Beniger, I.R. (1986). *The Control Revolution: Technological and Economic Origins of the Information Society*. Cambridge, MS: Harvard University Press.

Benimadhu, P. (1987). *Hours of Work: Trends and Attitudes in Canada*. Ottawa: Conference Board of Canada.

Bennet, K. (1994). "Recent Information on Training," *Perspectives on Labour and Income* 6, 1.

Bercuson, D. et al. (1984). *The Great Brain Robbery: Canada's Universities on the Road to Ruin*. Toronto: McClelland and Stewart.

Bereiter, C. and M. Engelmann. (1966). *Teaching Disadvantaged Children in the Preschool*. Engelwood Cliffs, NJ: Prentice-Hall.

Berg, I. (1970). *Education and Jobs: The Great Training Robbery.* New York: Praeger.

Berg, I. (2003). *Education and Jobs: The Great Training Robbery.* Clinton Corners, N.Y.: Percheron Press/Elliot Werner Publications. [Unabridged republication of 1970 edition with a new introduction].

Berggren, C. (1992). *Alternatives to Lean Production: Work and Organization in the Swedish Auto Industry.* Ithaca, NY: ILR Press.

Berggren, C. (1994). "NUMMI vs. Uddevala," *Sloan Management Review* 35, 2 (Winter): 37-45.

Berliner, D. and B. Biddle. (1995). *The Manufactured Crisis: Myths, Fraud, and the Attack on America's Schools.* Reading, Mass.: Addison-Wesley.

Berliner, D. and B. Biddle. (1996). "Making Molehills Out of Molehills: Reply to Lawrence Stedman's Review of The Manufactured Crisis," *Education Policy Analysis Archives* 4, 3 (February).

Bernstein, B. (1965). "A Socio-Linguistic Approach to Social Learning," in J. Gould (ed.) *Penguin Survey of the Social Sciences.* Harmondsworth: Penguin.

Bernstein, B. (1990). *The Structuring of Pedagogic Discourse.* London: Routledge.

Bernstein, B. (1996). *Pedagogy, Symbolic Control and Identity.* London: Taylor and Francis.

Berryman, S.E. and T.R. Bailey. (1992). *The Double Helix of Education and the Economy.* New York: The Institution on Education and the Economy.

Betcherman, G. (1992). "Are Canadian Firms Underinvesting in Training?" *Canadian Business Economics* 1, 1 (Fall): 25-33.

Betcherman, G., K. Newton and I. Godin. (1990). *Two Steps Forward: Human-Resource Management in a High-Tech World.* Ottawa: Ministry of Supply and Services.

Betcherman, G. et al. (1994). *The Canadian Workplace in Transition.* Kingston: IRC Press.

Betcherman, G., N. Leckie and K. McMullen. (1997). *Developing Skills in the Canadian Workplace: The Results of the Ekos Workplace Training Survey.* Ottawa: Canadian Policy Research Networks.

Biddle, B.J. (ed.) (2001). *Social Class, Poverty and Education: Policy and Practice.* New York: Routledge Falmer.

Bills, D. (1992). "The Mutability of Educational Credentials as Hiring Criteria: How Employers Evaluate Atypically Highly Credentialed Job Candidates," *Work and Occupations* 19, 1 (February)

Bishop, I. (1992). "The French Mandate to Spend on Training: A Model for the United States." Center on the Educational Quality of the Workforce, Cornell University.

Blackburn, R. I. (1990). The Vampire of Reason: An Essay in the Philosophy of History. London: Verso.

Blair, T. (1996). *New Britain: My Vision of a Young Country.* London: Fourth Estate.

Blasi, I. and D. Kruse. (1990) *New Owners.* New York: Harper Collins.

Bloom, A. (1987). *The Closing of the American Mind.* New York: Simon and Schuster.

Bloom, M. and Grant, M. (2002). *Brain Gain: The Economic Benefits of Recognizing Learning and Learning Credentials in Canada.* Ottawa: The Conference Board of Canada.

Bluestone, B. & Rose, S. (1997). Overworked and Underemployed. *American Prospect, 8* (31), 58-69.

Booth, N. (1979). "Information Resource Utilization and the Learning Efforts of Low-Income Urban Adults." Ph.D. dissertation, University of Maryland.

Boothby, D. (1993). "Schooling, Literacy and the Labour Market: Towards a 'Literacy Shortage'?" *Canadian Public Policy* 19, 1: 29-35.

Boothby, D. (1999). *Literacy Skills, the Knowledge Content of Occupations and Occupational Mismatch.* Catalogue no. W99-3E. Ottawa: Applied Research Branch, Human Resources Development Canada.

Borgen, W., N. Amundson and H. Harder. (1988). "The Experience of Underemployment," *Journal of Employment Counselling* 25: 149-59.

Borghans, L. & de Grip, A. (eds.). (2000). *The Overeducated Worker? The Economics of Skill Utilization.* Cheltenham, UK/Northampton: European Low-wage Employment Research Network and Edward Elgar.

Boudon, R., et al. (ed.) (1997). *The Classical Tradition in Sociology: The European Tradition.* Thousand Oaks: Sage.

Bourdieu, P. (1984 [1979]). *Distinction: A Social Critique of the Judgement of Taste.* Cambridge: Harvard University Press.

Bourdieu, P. (1988 [1984]). *Homo Academicus.* Stanford: Stanford University Press.

Bourdieu, P. (1993). *La misere du monde.* Paris: Seuil

Bourdieu, P. and I-C. Passeron. (1977 [1970]). *Reproduction in Education, Society and Culture.* London: Sage.

Bourdieu, P. and I-C. Passeron. (1979 [1964]). *The Inheritors: French Students and Their Relation to Culture.* Chicago: University of Chicago Press.

Bourdieu, P. and L.J.D. Wacquant. (1992). *An Invitation to Reflexive Sociology.* Chicago: University of Chicago Press.

Bowen, H.R. (1973). "Manpower Management and Higher Education," *Educational Record,* 54, 1: 5-14.

Bowles, S. and H. Gintis. (1976). *Schooling in Capitalist America: Educational Reform and the Contradictions of Economic Life.* New York: Basic Books.

Bowles, S. and H. Gintis. (1988). "Schooling in Capitalist America: Reply to Our Critics," in M. Cole (ed.) *Bowles and Gintis Revisited.* London: Falmer Press, 235-45.

Bowles, S. & H. Gintis. (2001). Schooling in Capitalist America Revisited. *Sociology of Education* 75 (1), 1-18.

Bowles, S., D. Gordon and T. Weisskopf. (1990). *After the Wasteland: A Democratic Economics for the Year 2000.* Armonk, NY: M.E. Sharpe.

Bracey; G. (1997). *The Truth About America's Schools: The Bracey Reports,* 1991-97. Bloomington, IN: Phi Delta Kappan Educational Foundation.

Brandt, B. (1995). *Whole Life Economics, Revaluing Daily Life.* Philadelphia: New Society Publishers.

Braverman, H. (1974). *Labor and Monopoly Capital.* New York: New York Monthly Review Press.

Brenner, R. and M. Glick. (1991). "The Regulation Approach: Theory and History," *New Left Review* 188 July/August): 45-119.

Brint, S. and J. Karabel. (1989). *The Diverted Dream: Community Colleges and the Promise of Educational Opportunities in America.* New York: Oxford University Press.

Brockett, R. and R. Hiemstra. (1991). *Self-Direction in Adult Education: Perspectives on Theory, Research and Practice.* New York: Routledge.

Brookfield, S. (1981). "The Adult Education Learning Iceberg," *Adult Education* (UK) 54, 2: 110-118.

Brookfield, S. (1982). "Successful Independent Learning of Adults of Low Educational Attainment in Britain: A Parallel Educational Universe." Proceedings of 23rd Annual Adult Educational Research Conference, University of Nebraska, April, 1982, 48-53.

Brosio, R. (1991). "Capital's Domination of the Quotidian: The Unbalanced Teeter-totter," *Discourse* 12, 1, (October): 85-99.

Brown, C., M. Reich and D. Stem. (1990). *Skill and Security and Evolving Employment Systems: Observations from Case Studies.* Berkeley: University of California.

Brown, D.K. (1995). *Degrees of Control: A Sociology of Educational Expansion and Occupational Credentialism.* New York: Teachers College Press.

Brown, P. (1992). "Education, the Free Market and Post-Communist Reconstruction," *British Journal of Sociology of Education* 13, 3: 285-305.

Brown, P. and H. Lauder. (1992). "Education, Economy; and Society: An Introduction to a New Agenda," in Brown and Lauder (eds.) *Education for Economic Survival: From Fordism to Post-Fordism?* London: Routledge, 1-44.

Brown, R.R. (1964). *Explanation in Social Science*. Chicago: Aldine.

Browne, K. (1981). "Schooling, Capitalism and the Mental/Manual Division of Labour," *Sociological Review* 29, 3: 445-73.

Browne, R.C. (1992). *The Many Tongues of Literacy*. Bowling Green, OH: Bowling Green University Popular Press, 127, 179.

Burke, M & Shields, J. (1999). *The Job Poor Recovery: Social Cohesion and the Canadian Labour Market*. A Research Report of the Ryerson Reporting Network, Ryerson Polytechnic University.

Burnett, J. (1982). *Destiny Obscure: Autobiographies of Childhood, Education and Family from the 1820s to the 1920s*. London: Allen Lane.

Burnett, J. (1994). *Idle Hands: The Experience of Unemployment, 1790-1990*. London: Routledge.

Burnett, J., D. Vincent and D. Mayall. (1984). *The Autobiography of the Working Class: An Annotated Critical Bibliography*. Brighton: Harvester.

Burris, B.H. (1983a). *No Room at the Top: Underemployment and Alienation in the Corporation*. New York: Praeger.

Burris, B.H. (1983b). "The Human Effects of Underemployment," *Social Problems* 31, 11 (October): 96-110.

Burris, V. (1983). "The Social and Political Consequences of Overeducation," *American Sociological Review* 48, 4: 454-467.

Business Week. Special Issue on Human Capital. (1988). "Needed: Human Capital," *Business Week* (September 19): 100-141.

Business Week-Harris Poll. (1996). "America, Land of the Shaken," *Business Week* (March 11): 64-65.

Cain, G. (1986). "The Challenge of Segmented Labor Market Theories to Orthodox Theory: A Survey," *Journal of Economic Literature* 14: 1215-1257.

Cameron, J. (ed.). (1995). "Special Issue: Canadian Perspectives on the Bell Curve," *Alberta Journal Educational Research* XLI, (September): 3.

Canadian Labour Congress. (2002). Part-time work. Ottawa: CLC. Retrieved May 03 2003 from http://action.web.ca/home/clcpolcy/attach/fs6.pdf

Candy, P. (1993). *Self-Direction for Lifelong Learning: A Comprehensive Guide to Theory and Practice*. San Francisco: Jossey-Bass.

Cappelli, P. (1993). " Are Skill Requirements Rising? Evidence From Production and Clerical Jobs," *Industrial and Labor Relations Review* 46, 3.

Carey, E. (1996). "Flex time helps more beat those 9 to 5 blues," *The Toronto Star.* (December 17): A3.

Carey, E. (1997). "No time to relax? Not so, they say," *The Toronto Star*. (May 19): A1, 18.

Carnegie Commission on Higher Education. (1973). *College Graduates and Jobs, Adjusting to a New Labor Market Situation*. New York: McGraw-Hill.

Carnoy, M. and H. Levin. (1985). *Schooling and Work in the Democratic State*. Stanford: Stanford University Press.

Carre, P. and M. Pearn. (1992). *L'autoformation dans l'enterprise*. Paris: editions entente.

Carrick, R. (1996). "Jobless rate understated, bank reports," *The Toronto Star*. (May 10): E3.

Carter, J. (1997). "Post-Fordism and the Theorisation of Educational Change: What's in a Name?" *British Journal of Sociology of Education* 18, 1: 45-61.

Carter, R. (1985). *Capitalism, Class Conflict and the New Middle Class.* London: Routledge and Kegan Paul.

Centre for Contemporary Cultural Studies. (1981). *Unpopular Education: Schooling and Social Democracy in England since 1944.* London: Hitchinson.

Centre for Contemporary Cultural Studies. (1991). *Education Limited: Schooling, Training and the New Right in England Since 1979.* London: Unwin Hyman.

Center for Workforce Development. (1998). *The Teaching Firm: Where Productive Work and Learning Converge.* Newton, Mass.: Education Development Center.

Chandler, A. (1990). *Scale and Scope: The Dynamics of Industrial Capitalism.* Cambridge: Harvard University Press.

Chandler, W. (1992). "The Value of Household Work in Canada, 1992," *National Income and Expenditure Accounts, Fourth Quarter 1993.* Statistics Canada Catalogue 13-001, April 1994.

Clark, B. (1962). *The Open Door College: A Case Study.* New York: McGraw-Hill.

Clarke, T. (1984). " Alternative Modes of Co-operative production," *Economic and Industrial Democracy* 5, 1: 97-129.

Clegg, S. and D. Dunkerley. (1984). *Organization, Class and Control.* London: Routledge and Kegan Paul.

Clement, W. (1974). *The Canadian Corporate Elite.* Toronto: McClelland and Stewart.

Clement, W. (1988). *The Challenge of Class Analysis.* Ottawa: Carleton University Press.

Clement, W. and R. Mahon (eds.). (1994). *Swedish Social Democracy: A Model in Transition.* Toronto: Canadian Scholars' Press.

Clement, W. and J. Myles. (1994). *Relations of Ruling: Class and Gender in Postindustrial Societies.* Montreal: McGill-Queen's University Press.

Clogg, C. (1979). *Measuring Underemployment: Demographic Indicators for the United States.* New York: Academic Press.

Cohen, G. (1991). "Then and Now: The Changing face of Unemployment," *Perspectives* (Statistics Canada) (Spring: 37-45).

Cohen, M.S., & Zaidi, M.A. (2002). *Global Skill Shortages.* Cheltenham, UK: Edward Elgar.

Cohen, S. (1987). " A Labour Process to Nowhere?" *New Left Review* 165, (September/October): 34-50.

Cole, E. (1976). "The Experience of Illiteracy." Ph.D. dissertation. Union Springs Graduate School, Yellow Springs, Ohio.

Coleman, J.S. (1966). *The Equality of Educational Opportunities.* Washington, DC: U.S. Office of Education.

Coles, M. (ed.). (1988). *Bowles and Gintis Revisited.* New York: Falmer Press.

Collins, R. (1979). *The Credential Society: An Historical Sociology of Education and Stratification.* New York: Academic Press.

Collins, R. (1980). "Weber's Last Theory of Capitalism: A Systemization," *American Sociological Review* 45 (December): 925-42.

Connell, R.W. et al. (1982). *Making the Difference: Schools, Families and Social Division.* Sydney: Allen and Unwin.

Connell, R.W. (1997). "Why is Classical Theory Classical?" *American Journal of Sociology* 102, 6: 1511-57.

Cookson, P. and C.H. Persell. (1985). *Preparing for Power: America's Elite Boarding Schools.* New York: Basic Books.

Cooley, M. (1987). *Architect or Bee? The Human Price of Technology.* London: Hogarth Press.

Coombs, P.H. (1985). *The World Educational Crisis in Education: The View from the Eighties.* New York: Oxford University Press.

Corman, J., M. Luxton, D.W. Livingstone and W. Seccombe. (forthcoming). *Working Class Families in Hard Times*. Toronto: University of Toronto Press.

Corrigan, P.R.D. (1987). "In/Forming Schooling," in D.W. Livingstone (ed.) *Critical Pedagogy and Cultural Power*. South Hadley, MA: Bergin and Garvey, 17-40.

Cortright, D. (1993). *Peace Works*. Boulder: Westview Press.

Cottle, T. (1992). "When You Stop You Die," *Commonweal* June): 16.

Courts, P. (1992). *Literacy and Empowerment: The Meaning Makers*. Toronto: OISE Press.

Crane, D. (1995). "New style of boss for changing times," *The Toronto Star* (August 13): D2.

Creese, G., N. Guppy and M. Meissner. (1991). *Ups and Downs on the Ladder of Success: Social Mobility in Canada* Ottawa: Statistics Canada.

Crompton, R. (1993). *Class and Stratification: An Introduction to Current Debates*. Oxford: Polity Press.

Crompton, S. (1992). "Studying on the Job," *Perspectives on Labour and Income* 4, 2 (Summer): 30-8

Crompton, S. (1994). "Employer-Supported Training ¾ It Varies by Occupation," *Perspectives on Labour and Income* 6, 1, (Spring): 9-17.

Cuban, L. (1986). *Teachers and Machines: The Classroom Use of Technology Since 1920*. New York: Teachers' College Press.

Cunningham, H. (1980). *Leisure in the Industrial Revolution*. London: Croom Helm.

Currie, E. (1993). *Reckoning: Drugs, The Cities and The American Future*. New York: Hill and Wong.

Curti, M. (1935). *The Social Ideas of American Educators*. Paterson, NJ: Littlefield, Adams and Company.

Curtis, B. (1984). "Capitalist Development and Educational Reform: Comparative Material from England, Ireland and Upper Canada to 1850," *Theory and Society* 13: 41-68.

Curtis, B., D.W. Livingstone and H. Smaller. (1992). *Stacking the Deck: The Streaming of Working Class Kids in Ontario Schools*. Toronto: Our Schools/Our Selves Educational Foundation.

Daily Bread Food Bank. (1994) *Daily Bread Food Bank 1994 Spring Summary*. Toronto: Daily Bread Food Bank.

Dale, R. (1990). "Regulation Theory, Settlements and Education Policy." Paper presented to Conference on Education Policy; Massey University, July.

Dale, R. (1992). "Recovering from a Pyrrhic Victory? Quality, Relevance and Impact in the Sociology of Education," in M. Arnot and L. Barton (eds.) *Voicing Concerns: Sociological Perspectives of Contemporary Education Reforms*. Wallingford, OX: Triangle Books, 201-217.

Dale, R. et al. (1990). *The TVEI Story: Policy, Practice and Preparation for Work*. Milton Keynes: Open University Press.

Dalla Costa, M. (1975). *Women and the Subversion of the Community*. New York: Falling Wall Press.

Daly, H. and J. Cobb. (1989). *For the Common Good: Redirecting the Economy Toward Community, the Environment and a Sustainable Future*. Boston: Beacon Press.

Daly, M., Buchel, F., & Duncan, G. (2000). Premiums and Penalties for Surplus and Deficit Education: Evidence From the United States and Germany. *Economics of Education, 19* (2), 169-178.

Dar, Y. (1998). "The Changing Identity of Kibbutz Education," in U. Leviatan, H. Oliver and J. Quarter (eds.) *Crisis in the Israeli Kibbutz: The Challenge of Changing Times*. Westport, CT.: Praeger/Greenwood.

Darrah, C. (1992). "Workplace Skills in Context," *Human Organization* 51, 3: 264-273.

Darrah, C. (1995). "Workplace Training, Workplace Learning: A Case Study," *Human Organization* 54, 1: 31-41.

Davin, A. (1996). *Growing Up Poor: Home, School and Street in London 1870-1914*. London: Rivers Oram Press.

Davis, J.A. and T.W. Smith. (1994). *General Social Surveys 1972-1994*. Chicago: National Opinion Research Center.

Davis, J. and M. Stack. (1992). "Knowledge in Production," *Race and Class* 34,3: 1-14.

Davis, J.A., Smith, T.W., & Marsden, P.V. (2003). *General Social Surveys, 1972-2002:* [Cumulative file] [Computer file]. ICPSR version. Chicago, IL: National Opinion Research Center [producer], Storrs, CT: Roper Center for Public Opinion Research, University of Connecticut/Ann Arbor, MI: Inter-university Consortium for Political and Social Research [distributors].

Dawson, P. and J. Webb. (1989). "New Production Arrangements: The Totally Flexible Cage?" *Work, Employment and Society* 3, 2, June): 221-238.

Dei, G. et al. (1995). *Drop Out or Push Out? The Dynamics of Black Students' Disengagement from School*. Toronto: Department of Sociology in Education, OISE, October.

Deming, W.E. (1986). *Out of the Crisis*. Cambridge: Massachusetts Institute of Technology.

Dennison, J. and G. Jones. (1995). *Challenge and Opportunity: Canada's Community Colleges at the Crossroads*. Vancouver: UBC Press.

Derber, C. (1978). "Unemployment and the Entitled Worker," *Social Problems* 26, 1.

Derber, C. (1979). "Underemployment and the American Dream ¾ 'Underemployment Consciousness' and Radicalism Among Young Workers," *Sociological Inquiry*, 49, 4: 37-44.

Derber, C. (1994). "Communitarian Economics: Criticisms and Suggestions from the Left," *The Responsive Community* 4, 4: 29-42.

Derber, C., W. Schwartz and Y. Magrass. (1990). *Power in the Highest Degree: Professionals and the Rise of a New Mandarin Order*. New York: Oxford University Press.

deRoche, J., B. Riley and G. Smith. (1994). "Job Dislocation and Retraining: The Case of Sydney Steel," *Making Waves* 5, 4 (Winter): 12-3.

Devereaux, M. (1985). *One in Every Five: A Survey of Adult Education in Canada*. Ottawa: Statistics Canada and Education Support Section, Secretary of State.

Diamond, D. and H. Bedrosion. (1970). *Hiring Standards and Performance*. (U.S. Department of Labor, Manpower Research Monograph No. 18). Washington: U.S. Government Printing Office.

DiFazio, W. (1999). [Review of The Education-Jobs Gap]. *American Journal of Sociology*, *105* (3), 904-906.

Dimaris, S. (1997). "It's hard dealing with that constant, 'No, no, no,'" *The Toronto Star*. December 6: SS6.

Dobson, R. (1993). *Bringing the Economy Home from the Market*. Montreal: Black Rose.

Doray, P. and L. Paris. (1995). *La participation des adultes a l'education au Quebec en 1991*. Montreal: Institut Canadien d'Education des Adultes.

Dore, R. and M. Sako. (1989). *How the Japanese Learn to Work*. London: Routledge.

Drolet, M. and R. Morissette. (1997). *Working More? Working Less? What Do Canadian Workers Prefer?* Research Paper Series: Analytical Studies Branch. No. 104 - Ottawa: Statistics Canada.

Douthwaite, R. (1992). *The Growth Illusion*. Devon: Resurgence Press.

Drucker, P. (1954). *The Practice of Management*. New York: Harper.

Duncan, G.J. and S. Hoffman. (1978). "The Economic Value of Surplus Education," in G. Duncan and J. Morgan (eds.) *Five Thousand American Families-Patterns of Economic Progress*. (Volume 6). Michigan: ISR Survey Research Center, Institute for Social Research.

Dunk, T. and R. Nelson. (1992). "Release, Retrain, Readjust: The Three R's of the New Economic Reality in Resource Hinterlands." Paper presented at annual meetings of the Canadian Sociology and Anthropology Association, University of Prince Edward Island, June.

Eberle, A. and S. Robinson. (1980). *The Adult Illiterate Speaks Out.* Washington, D.C.: National Institute of Education.

Eckaus, R.S. (1964). "Economic Criteria for Education and Training, " *The Review of Economics and Statistics* 46, 1: 181-190.

Economic Council of Canada. (1990). *Good Jobs, Bad Jobs: Employment in the Service Economy.* Ottawa: Canadian Government Publishing Centre.

Economic Council of Canada. (1991). *Income Maintenance, Work Effort and the Canadian Mincome Experiment.* Ottawa: Minister of Supply and Services.

Education Support Branch. Human Resources Development Canada. (1994). *Profile of Post-Secondary Education in Canada.* Ottawa: Minister of Supply and Services.

Edwards, B. and M.W. Foley. (1997). "Social Capital, Civil Society, and Contemporary Democracy," *American Behavioral Scientist* [Special Issue] 40, 5 (March/April).

Edwards, R. (1972). "Alienation and Inequality: Capitalist Relations of Production in a Bureaucratic Enterprise." Ph.D. dissertation, Harvard University.

Edwards, R. (1979). *Contested Terrain: The Transformation of the Workplace in the Twentieth Century.* New York: Basic Books.

Edwards, R.E. and J. Hughes. (1995). "Surf's Up! Seven Percent of Canadians Currently Use the Internet." *The Gallup Poll.* August 3.

Ehrenreich, B. (1989). *Fear of Falling: The Inner Life of the Middle Class.* New York: Pantheon.

Ekos Research Associates. (1993). *Reskilling Society (Phase I): Industrial Perspectives. The National Survey of Employers on Training and Development Issues.* Hull, Que.: Human Resources Development Canada.

Eleen, J. (1995). "Freight Trains and Memory Lanes," *Our Times* 14, 4: 24-27.

Else, A. 1996. *False Economy.* North Shore City: Tandem Press.

Esping-Andersen, G (ed.). (1993). *Changing Classes: Stratification and Mobility in Post-Industrial Societies.* London: Sage.

Esping-Anderson, G (1993). *The Three Worlds of Welfare Capitalism.* Princeton: Princeton University Press.

European Commission. (2001). *Underemployment Trends in the European Union.* Brussels: ECOTEC Research and Consulting. Retrieved May 25, 2003 from <http://www.eu-employment-observatory.net/ersep/trd30_uk/>

Evans, R.I. (1973). *Jean Piaget: The Man and His Ideas.* New York.

Evans, T. (1988). *A Gender Agenda: A Sociological Study of Teachers, Parents and Pupils in Their Primary Schools.* Sydney, Allen and Unwin.

Evenson, B. (1996). "Report sketches changing face of work world," *The Toronto Star.* (March 13): B2.

Farrar, E. and C. Connolly. (1991). "Improving Middle Schools in Boston: A Report on Boston Compact and School District Initiatives," *Educational Policy* 5, 1: 4-28.

Feldman, D.C. (1996). The Nature, Antecedents and Consequences of Underemployment. *Journal of Management, 22*(3), 385-407.

Ferguson, D. (1995). "Wage gap widened in '80s, StatsCan finds," *The Toronto Star.* July 27): C1.

Ferguson, J. (1994). "Biologist, 28, fears her dreams are lost," *The Toronto Star.* (March 27): D5.

Fine, S.A. (1968). "The Use of the Dictionary of Occupational Titles as a Source of Estimates of Education and Training Requirements," *The Journal of Human Resources* 3, 3: 363-375.

Fischer, D. (1994). "Disabled are overlooked," *The Calgary Herald.* June 14): A9.

Fisher, D. and K. Rubenson. (1992). "Polarization and Bifurcation in Work and Adult Education: Participation in Adult Education in British Columbia," *Policy Explorations.* Occasional Papers of the Centre for Policy Studies in Education, University of British Columbia, 6, 3: 9.

Foley, G. (1987). " Adult Education for the Long Haul." Paper presented at the 27th National Conference of the Australian Association of Adult Education, Sydney (September).

Foster, J.B. (1988). "The Fetish of Fordism," *Monthly Review* 39, 10, (March)

Fowler, B. (1977). *Pierre Bourdieu and Cultural Theory: Critical Investigations.* London: Sage.

Freeman, R. (1976). *The Overeducated American.* New York: Academic Press.

Freidman, M. (1962). *Capitalism and Freedom.* Chicago: University of Chicago Press.

Freire, P. (1970). *The Pedagogy of the Oppressed.* New York: Herder and Herder.

Freire, P. (1994). *The Pedagogy of Hope.* New York: Herder and Herder.

Frennette, M. (2001). Overqualified? Recent Graduates, Employer Needs. *Perspectives on Labour and Income 13* (1), 45-53.

Frey, B. and W. Pommerehne. (1984). "The Hidden Economy: State and Prospects for Measurement," *Review of Income and Wealth* 1 (March): 1-23.

Friedman, A. (1977). *Industry and Labour: Class Struggle at Work and Monopoly Capitalism.* London: Macmillan.

Friedson, E. (1973). "Professionalization and the Organization of Middle-Class Labour in Post-Industrial Society," in P. Holmes (ed.) *Professionalization and Social Change.* Keele: University of Kent, 47-59.

Fryer, D. (1992). "Psychological or Material Deprivation: Why Does Unemployment Have Mental Health Consequences?" in E. McLaughlin (ed) *Understanding Unemployment.* London: Routledge, 103-125.

Fryer, D. and R. Payne. (1986). "Being Unemployed: a Review of the Literature on the Psychological Experience of Unemployment," in C.L. Coopier and I.T. Robertson (eds.) *International Review of Industrial and Organizational Psychology.* New York: Wiley, 235-78.

Fukuyama, F. (1993). *The End of History and the Last Man.* New York: Maxwell.

Galbraith, I. (1958). *The Affluent Society.* New York: American Library.

Gait, V. and M. Cernetig. (1997). "Two schools, worlds apart." *The Globe and Mail.* (April 26): A1, 12.

Gamson, Z. and M. Palgi. (1982) "The 'Over-Educated' Kibbutz: Shifting Relations Between Social Reproduction and Individual Development on the Kibbutz," *Interchange* 13, 1: 55-67

Garrick, J. (1996). "Informal Learning: Some Underlying Philosophies." *Canadian Journal for the Study of Adult Education.* 10, 1: 21-46.

Gaskell, J. (1992). *Gender Matters from School to Work.* Toronto: OISE Press.

German Ministry of Education. (1993). *Berichtssystem Weiterbildung 1991.* Bonn: Helmut Kuwan.

Gephart, M.A. (1995). "The Road to High Performance," *Training and Development* 49, 6: 30-44.

Gibb-Clark, M. (1997). "About 12% of Jobs Temporary, StatsCan Finds," *The Globe and Mail.* (September 11): 84.

Gintis, H. and S. Bowles. (1981). "Contradiction and Reproduction in Educational Theory;" in R. Dale et al. (eds.) *Education and the State.* (Volume 1). Lewes: Falmer Press.

Giroux, H. (1981). *Ideology, Culture and the Process of Schooling.* London: Falmer Press.

Gittleman, M.B. and D. R. Howell. (1995). "Changes in the Structure and Quality of Jobs in the United States: Effects by Race and Gender, 1973-1990," *Industrial and Labor Relations Review*, 48, 3.

Gonick, C. (1995). "Exploring a New Vision," *Canadian Dimension* 29, 4: 46-47.

Gonzales, G. (1982). *Progressive Education; A Marxist Interpretation.* Minneapolis: Marxist Educational Press.

Goodall, A. (1994). "Two Decades of Change: College Postsecondary Enrolments, 1971 to 1991," *Education Quarterly Review* 1, 2: 41-56.

Gordon, D.M., R. Edwards and M. Reich. (1982). *Segmented Work, Divided Workers: The Historical Transformation of Labor in the United States.* Cambridge: Cambridge University Press.

Gordon, J. (1993). "Into the Dark: Rough Ride Ahead for American Workers," *Training* 30, 7 July): 21-9.

Gorelick, S. (1977). "Undermining Hierarchy: Problems of Schooling in Capitalist America," *Monthly Review* 29, 5: 20-36.

Gorz, A. (1982). *Farewell to the Working Class: An Essay on Post-Industrial Socialism.* Boston: South End Press.

Gorz, A. (1985). *Paths to Paradise: On the Liberation from Work.* London: Pluto Press.

Gradler, G.C. and K.E. Schrammel. (1994). "The 1992-2005 Job Outlook in Brief," *Occupational Outlook Quarterly* (Spring): 2-45.

Graff, H.J. (1981). *Literacy and Social Development in the West.* Cambridge: Cambridge University Press.

Graff, H.J. (1987). *The Labyrinths of Literacy: Reflections on Literacy Past and Present.* Philadelphia: Palmer Press.

Gramsci, A. (1971). *Selections from the Prison Notebooks.* New York: International Publishers.

Green, F., McIntosh, S., & Vignoles, A. (1999). *Overeducation and Skills—Clarifying the Concepts.* London: Centre for Economic Performance, London School of Economics.

Greider, W. (1997). *One World, Ready or Not: The Manic Logic of Global Capitalism.* New York: Simon and Schuster.

Groot, W. & Maassen van den Brink, H. (2000). Overeducation in the Labor Market: A Meta-analysis. *Economics of Education Review, 19* (2), 149-158.

Hacker, Sally. (1989). *Pleasure, Power and Technology: Some Tales of Gender, Engineering, and the Cooperative Workplace.* Boston: Unwin Hyman.

Halaby, C.N. (1994). "Overeducation and Skill Mismatch," *Sociology of Education* 67, 1 January): 47-59.

Hall, 0. and R. Carlton. (1977). *Basic Skills at School and Work.* Toronto: Ontario Economic Council.

Halsey, A.H. (1980). *Origins and Destinations: Family, Class and Education in Modern Britain.* London: Oxford University Press.

Hammer, M. (1996). *Beyond Reengineering: How the Process-Centered Organization is Changing Our Work and Our Lives.* New York: Harper Business.

Hamper, B. (1992). *Rivethead; Tales from the Assembly Line.* New York: Warner Books.

Handel, M. (2000a). *Is There a Skill Crisis? Trends in Job Skill Requirements, Technology and Wage Inequality in the U.S.* Working Paper No. 295. Annandale-on-Hudson, NY: Jerome Levy Economics Institute, Bard College.

Handel, M. (2000b). *Trends in Direct Measures of Job Skill Requirements.* Working Paper No. 301. Annandale-on-Hudson, NY: Jerome Levy Economics Institute, Bard College.

Handel, M. (Forthcoming). Skills Mismatch in the Labour Market. *Annual Review of Sociology* (2003). Retrieved May 25, 2003 from <http://www.ssc.wisc.edu/cde/demsem/ARS_final_h.pdf>

Handelman, S. (1996). "The Downsizing of America: Economic Insecurity Fuels Class Warfare," *Ottawa Citizen.* (April 6): B3.

Hansenne, M. (1995). *Promoting Employment; International Labour Conference 82ⁿᵈ Session*. Geneva: International Labour Office.

Hanson, S. (1996). *Lost Talent: Women in the Sciences*. Philadelphia: Temple University Press.

Harper, D. (1987). *Working Knowledge: Skill and Community in a Small Shop*. Chicago: University of Chicago Press.

Harris, L. (1991). *An Assessment of American Education: The View of Employers, Higher Educators, Recent Students and Their Parents*. New York: Lou Harris and Associates Information Services, (September).

Harris, S. (1949). *The Market for College Graduates*. Cambridge: Harvard University Press.

Harrison, B. 1997. *Lean and Mean*. New York: The Guilford Press.

Hart, D. and D.W. Livingstone. (1998). "The 'Crisis' of Confidence in Schools and the Neo-Conservative Agenda: Diverging Opinions of Corporate Executives and the General Public," *Alberta Journal of Educational Research* 43, 1.

Hart, M.U. (1992). *Working and Educating for Life: Feminist and International Perspectives on Adult Education*. New York: Routledge.

Hart, P.E. (1990). "Types of Structural Unemployment in the United Kingdom," *International Labour Review* 129, 2: 213-228.

Hartog, J. (2000). Over-education and Earnings: Where Are We, Where Should We Go? *Economics of Education Review, 19* (2), 131-147.

Hartsock, N. (1983). *Money, Sex and Power: Toward a Feminist Historical Materialism*. New York: Longman.

Hauser, R. (1974). "The Measurement of Labor Utilization," *Malayan Economic Review* 19: 1-17.

Havelock, E. (1976). *Origins of Western Literacy*. Toronto: OISE Press.

Hay, J. (2000). A Profile of Underemployed University Graduates. Unpublished paper, Centre for Education Statistics, Statistics Canada.

Hayden, A. (1997). "35-Hour Workweek Shakes Europe," *Better Times* 5 (November): 1, 7-8.

Hayden, A. (1999). *Sharing the Work, Sparing the Planet: Work Time, Consumption & Ecology*. Toronto: Between the Lines.

Hayes, P. (1993). "Marx's Analysis of the French Class Structure," *Theory and Society* 22: 99-123.

Hecker, D. (1992). "Reconciling Conflicting Data on Jobs for College Graduates," *Monthly Labour Review* July)

Hecker, D. (2001). Occupational Employment Projections to 2010. *Monthly Labor Review, 124* (11), 57-84.

Heckman, J. (1994). "Is Job Training Oversold?" *The Public Interest* (Spring): 91-115.

Heckman, J. and P. Klenow. (1997). "Is There Underinvestment in Human Capital?" Unpublished paper, Center for Social Program Evaluation, University of Chicago, October.

Heilbroner, R. and W. Milberg. (1995). *The Crisis of Vision in Modern Economic Thought*. Cambridge: Cambridge University Press.

Henderson, H. (1996). *Building a Win-Win World: Life Beyond Global Economic Warfare*. San Francisco: Berrett-Koehler.

Henry, F. and E. Ginzberg. (1985). *Who Gets the Work: A Test of Racial Discrimination in Employment*. Toronto: The Urban Alliance on Race Relations and the Social Planning Council of Metropolitan Toronto.

Herbert, B. (1997). " A Workers' Rebellion," *The Globe and Mail*. (August 12): B2.

Herrnstein, R. and C. Murray. (1994). *The Bell Curve: Intelligence and Class Structure in American Life*. New York: Free Press.

Hickox, M. and R. Moore. (1992). "Education and Post-Fordism: A New Correspondence?," in P. Brown and H. Lauder (eds.) *Education for Economic Survival: From Fordism to Post-Fordism?* London: Routledge, 95-116.

Hiemstra, R. (1976). *Lifelong Learning.* Lincoln: Professional Educators Publications.

Hill, C. (1967). *Reformation to Industrial Revolution: A Social and Economic History of Britain, 1530-1780.* London: Weidenfeld and Nicolson.

Hinrichs, K., W. Roche and C. Sirianni (eds.). (1991). *Working Time in Transition: The Political Economy of Working Hours in Transition.* Philadelphia: Temple University Press.

Hirsch, D. (1992). *Schools and Business: A New Partnership.* Paris: OECD.

Hirsch, E.D. (1988). *Cultural Literacy: What Every American Needs to Know.* New York: Vintage Books.

Hiscott, R. (2000). [Review of The Education-Jobs Gap]. *Canadian Review of Sociology and Anthropology, 37,* (2), 239-242.

Hobsbawm, E. (1994). *The Age of Extremes: A History of the World, 1914-1991.* New York: Pantheon.

Hogan, D. (1979). "Capitalism, Liberalism and Schooling," *Theory and Society* 8, 3: 387-413.

Hogan, D. (1985). *Class and Reform.* Philadelphia: University of Pennsylvania Press.

Holland, R. (1990). *The Long Transition: Class, Culture and Youth Training.* London: Macmillan.

Holmstrom, M. (1989). *Industrial Democracy in Italy: Workers Co-ops and the Self-Management Debate.* Brookfield: Avebury.

Holzer, H.J. (1996). *What Employers Want: Job Prospects for Less-Educated Workers.* New York: Russell Sage Foundation.

Holzer, H.J. and W. Vroman. (1993). "Mismatches and the Urban Labor Market," in G.E. Peterson and W. Vroman (eds.) *Urban Labor Markets and Job Opportunity.* Washington, D.C.: The Urban Institute Press, 81-112.

Hopfenberg, W., H. Levin et al. (1993). *The Accelerated Schools Resource Guide.* San Francisco: Jossey-Bass.

Horowitz, M. and I. Herrnstadt. (1966). "Changes in Skill Requirements of Occupations in Selected Industries," in *National Commission on Technology, Automation and Economic Progress.* (Appendix, Volume 2 of *Technology and the American Economy.*) Washington, DC: Government Printing Office, 223-87.

Howell, D.R. and E.N. Wolff. (1991). "Trends in the Growth and Distribution of Skills in the U.S. Workplace, 1960-1985," *Industrial and Labor Relations Review* 44, 3: 486-502.

Hunter, A. (1988). "Formal Education and Initial Employment: Unravelling the Relationships Between Schooling and Skills Over Time," *American Sociological Review* 53, 5: 753-765.

Hunter, A. and M. Manley:.(1986). "On the Task Content of Work," *Canadian Review of Sociology and Anthropology* 23,1: 47-71.

Hutton, W. (1995). *The State We're In.* London: Jonathan Cape.

Illich, I. (1971). *Deschooling Society.* New York: Harper and Row.

International Labour Office. (1998). *Resolution Concerning the Measurement of Underemployment and Inadequate Employment Situations.* Sixteenth International Conference of Labour Statisticians, Geneva, 6-15 October, 1998. Geneva: ILO.

International Labour Office. (2003). *Global Employment Trends.* Geneva: ILO.

International Labor Organization. (1995). *World Employment (1995).* Geneva: ILO.

International Research Group. (1993). *Industrial Democracy in Europe Revisited.* New York: Oxford University Press.

Israelson, D. (1996). "Corporate backfiring, " *The Toronto Star.* (June 2): F1.

Jackson, N. (ed.). (1992). *Training for What? Labour Perspectives on Skill Training.* Toronto: Our Schools/Ourselves Education Foundation.

Jacoby, R. and N. Glauberman (eds.). (1995). *The Bell Curve Debate.* New York: Times Books.

Jarvis, P. (1992). *Paradoxes of Learning: On Becoming an Individual in Society.* San Francisco: Jossey-Bass, 177-194.

James, C.E. (1990). *Making It: Black Youth, Racism and Career Aspirations in a Big City.* Oakville: Mosaic Press.

Japanese Ministry of Education. (1994). *Educational Policy in Japan 1994.* Tokyo: Ministry of Education.

Jencks, C. (1989). *What is Post-Modernism?* Third Edition. London: Academy Editions.

Jensen, A.R. (1969). "How Much Can We Boost I.Q. and Scholastic Achievement?" *Harvard Educational Review* 39, 1: 1-123.

Johnson, G.J. and C.O. Herring. (1993). "Underemployment Among Black Americans," *The Western Journal of Black Studies* 17, 3 (Fall): 126-134.

Johnson, R. (1979). "Really Useful Knowledge: Radical Education and Working Class Culture," in J. Clarke et al. (eds.) *Working Class Culture.* London: Hutchinson.

Johnson, V., H. Levine and E. Rosenthal. (1977). "Learning Projects of Unemployed Adults in New Jersey." Unpublished paper, Educational Advancement Project, Rutgers Labor Education Center, New Brunswick, N.J.

Johnston, B.J. (1993). "The Transformation of Work and Educational Reform Policy," *American Educational Research Journal* 30, 1 (Spring) 39-65.

Johnson, W.R., Morrow, P.C., & Johnson, G.J. (2002). An Evaluation of a Perceived Overqualification Scale Across Work Settings. *The Journal of Psychology, 136* (4), 425-441.

Jolin, M. (1987). "The Occupational 'Mismatching' Problem Re-examined: 'Overeducation,' Financial Satisfaction, and Community Participation in Rhode Island." Ph.D. dissertation, Brown University.

Jordan, B. et al. (1992). *Trapped in Poverty? Labour Market Decisions in Low-Income Households.* London, UK: Routledge.

Jowell, R., I. Curtice, A. Park, L. Brook and K. Thomson. (1996). *British Social Attitudes The 13ᵗʰ Report.* Cambridge: Great Britain at the University Press.

Kamata, S. (1983). *Japan in the Passing Lane: An Insider's Account of Life in a Japanese Auto Factory.* Boston: George Allen & Unwin.

Kasmir, S. (1996). *The Myth of Mondragon: Co-operatives, Politics and Working Class Life in a Basque Town.* Albany, NY: SUNY Press.

Kastner, S. (1996). "It's getting a lot richer at the top," *The Toronto Star.* July 20): A10.

Katz, M. (1971). *Class, Bureaucracy and Schools.* New York: Praeger.

Katz, M. (ed.). (1993). *The 'Underclass' Debate.* Princeton, NJ: Princeton University Press.

Katznelson, I. and M. Weir. (1985). *Schooling for All.* New York: Basic Books.

Katznelson, I. et al. (1982). "Public Schooling and Working Class Formation: The Case of the United States," *American Journal of Education* 90, 2: 111-143.

Kelly, K., Howatson-Leo, L., & Clark, W. (Winter, 1997). "I feel overqualified for my job...". *Canadian Social Trends, 47,* 11-16.

Kelso, L.O. and P.H. Kelso. (1986). *Democracy and Economic Power: Extending the ESOP Revolution.* Cambridge: Ballinger Publishing Company.

Kelvin, P. and J.E. Jarrett. (1985). *Unemployment: Its Social Psychological Effects.* New York: Cambridge University Press.

Kerbo, H.R. (1983). *Social Stratification and Inequality: Class Conflict in the United States.* New York: McGraw-Hill.

Kettle, J. (1995). "Kettle's future," *The Globe and Mail*. (October 13): B7.

Keung, N. (1997). "Facing a life of dead-end jobs." *The Toronto Star*. July 27): A10.

Kilpatrick, K. (1997). "Churches want forced workfare abolished," *The Toronto Star*. (December 22): A7.

Kinchloe, J. (1995). *Toil and Trouble: Good Work, Smart Workers, and the Integration of Academic and Vocational Education*. New York: Peter Lang Publishing.

Kinchloe, J., S. Steinberg and A. Gresson. (1996). *Measured Lies: The Bell Curve Examined*. Toronto: OISE Press.

King, C.D. and van de Vall, M. (1978). *Models of Industrial Democracy: Consultation, Co-determination and Workers' Manager*. New York: Mouton Publishers.

King, T. & Bannon, E. (2002). *At What Cost? The Price That Working Students Pay for a College Education*. Washington, D.C.: The State PIRGs' Higher Education Project.

Knel-Paz, B. (1995). "Was George Orwell Wrong?" *Dissent* (Spring): 267-69.

Knoke, D. and A. Kalleberg. (1995). "Job Training in U.S. Organizations," *American Sociological Review* 59, 4: 541 [537-546].

Knowles, M. (1970). *The Modern Practice of Adult Education: Andragogy versus Pedagogy*. Chicago: Follett.

Knudsen, H. (1994). *Employee Participation in Europe*. London: Sage.

Kochan, T.A. and M. Useem (eds.). (1992). *Transforming Organizations*. New York: Oxford University Press.

Kohlberg, L. (1981). *The Meaning and Measurement of Moral Development*. Worcester, Mass.: Clark University Press.

Kozol, J. (1985). *Illiterate America*. New York: Plume.

Kozol, J. (1991). *Savage Inequalities: Children in America's Schools*. New York: Crown Publishers.

Krahn, H. (1992). *Quality of Work in the Service Sector*. General Social Survey Analysis Series, Catalogue II-612E, No 6. Ottawa: Statistics Canada.

Krahn, H. (1997) "On the Permanence of Human Capital: Use it or Lose it," *Policy Options* 18, 6: 17-21.

Krahn, H. and G. Lowe. (1993). *The School-to-Work Transition in Edmonton: Final Research Report*. Edmonton, AB.: Population Research Laboratory; Department of Sociology, University of Alberta.

Krahn, H. & Lowe, G. (1998). *Literacy Utilization in Canadian Workplaces*. Ottawa: Statistics Canada.

Kruger, J. & Dunning, D. (1999). Unskilled and Unaware of it: How Difficulties in Recognizing One's Own Incompetence Lead to Inflated Self-assessments. *Journal of Personality and Social Psychiatry. 77* (6), 1121-1134.

Kumar, K. (1995). *From Post-Industrial to Post-Modern Society: New Theories of the Contemporary World*. Oxford: Blackwell.

Kumazawa, M. (1996). *Portraits of the Japanese Workplace: Labor Movements, Workers, and Managers*. Boulder, CO: Westview Press.

Kusterer, K. (1978). *Know How on the Job: The Important Working Knowledge of "Unskilled" Workers*. Boulder: Westview Press.

Lacharite, J. (2002). Sustained and Growing Underemployment in Australia and Canada: The Truth Behind Government Employment Figures. *Journal of Australian Studies, 14*, 243-252.

Lakey, J. (1996). "Well-educated on Welfare: Survey," *The Toronto Star*. (October 30): A3.

Landers, A. (1995). "Reader says job woes fault of corporations," *The Toronto Star*. July 23): E3.

Lane, R. (1991). *The Market Experience*. Cambridge: Cambridge University Press

Langmore, J. and J. Quiggan. (1994). *Work for All: Full Employment in the Nineties*. Melbourne: Melbourne University Press.

Lareau, A. (1989). *Home Advantage: Social Class and Parental Intervention in Elementary Education*. New York: Palmer Press.

Latouche, S. (1993). *In the Wake of the Affluent Society: An Exploration of Post-Development*. London: Zed Books Ltd.

Lavoie, M. & Roy, R. (1998). *Employment in the Knowledge-based Economy: A Growth Accounting Exercise for Canada*. Ottawa: Applied Research Branch, Human Resources Canada.

Lawler, E., S. Mohrman and G. Ledford. (1992). *Employee Involvement and Total Quality Management: Practices and Results In Fortune 1000 Companies*. San Francisco: Jossey-Bass.

Lazonick, W. (1991). *Business Organization and the Myth of the Market Economy*. New York: Cambridge University Press.

Leckie, N. (1996). *On Skill Requirements Trends in Canada, 1971-1991*. Research report for Human Resources Canada and Canadian Policy Research Networks.

Leean, C. and B. Sisco. (1981). *Learning Projects and Self-Planned Learning Efforts Among Undereducated Adults in Rural Vermont*. Washington, D.C.: National Institute of Education.

Lester, B.Y. & McCain, R.A. (2001). An Equity-based Redefinition of Underemployment and Unemployment and Some Measurements. *Review of Social Economy, 59* (2), 133-159.

Leviatan, U. (1982). "Higher Education in the Israeli Kibbutz: Revolution and Effect," *Interchange* 13, 1: 68-82.

Leviatan, U., H. Oliver and J. Quarter (eds.). (1988). *Crisis in the Israeli Kibbutz: The Challenge of Changing Times*. Westport, CT: Praeger/Greenwood.

Levin, H. (1976). " A Taxonomy of Educational Reforms for Changes in the Nature of Work," in M. Carnoy and H. Levin (eds.) *The Limits of Educational Reform*. London: Longman.

Levin, H. (1980). "Workplace Democracy and Educational Planning," in M. Carnoy, H. Levin and K. King (eds.) *Education, Work and Employment-II*. Paris: UNESCO

Levin, H. and R. Rumberger. (1989). "Education, Work and Employment: Present Issues and Future Challenges in Developed Countries," in F. Caillods (ed.) *The Prospects for Educational Planning*. Paris: UNESCO, 209-243.

Levine, R. and J. Lembcke. (1987). "Introduction: Marxism, Neo-Marxism, and U.S. Sociology," in Levine and Lembcke (eds.) *Recapturing Marxism: An Appraisal of Recent Trends in Sociological Theory*. New York: Praeger, 1-12.

Levitas, M. (1974). *Marxist Perspectives in the Sociology of Education*. London: Routledge and Kegan Paul.

Lewington, J. (1994). "Nova Scotia plans to offer warranties on grads," *The Globe and Mail*. (February 3): A1. 1

Li, P. (1988). *Ethnic Inequality in a Class Society*. Toronto: Wall and Thompson.

Lichtenstein, N. and H.J. Harris. (1993). *Industrial Democracy in America: The Ambiguous Promise*. New York: Cambridge University Press.

Lichter, D.T. (1988). "Racial Differences in Underemployment in American Cities," *American Journal of Sociology* 93: (January): 771-792.

Lichter, D.T. and D.J. Landry. (1991). "Labor Force Transitions and Underemployment: The Stratification of Male and Female Workers," *Research in Social Stratification and Mobility* 10: 63-87.

Liston, D. (1988). *Capitalist Schools: Explanation and Ethics in Radical Studies of Schooling*. New York: Routledge.

Livingstone, D.W. (1972). "Inventing the Future: Anti-Historicist Reflections on Towards 2000." *Interchange*. 3, 4: 111-123.

Livingstone, D.W. (1983). *Class, Ideologies and Educational Futures*. London and Philadelphia: Palmer Press.

Livingstone, D.W. (1985a). "Class, Educational Ideologies, and Mass Opinion in Capitalist Crisis: A Canadian Perspective," *Sociology of Education* 58, 1: 3-20.

Livingstone, D.W. (1985b). *Social Crisis and Schooling*. Toronto: Garamond Press.

Livingstone, D.W. (ed.). (1987a). *Critical Pedagogy and Cultural Power*. New York: Bergin and Garvey.

Livingstone, D. W. (1987b). "Job Skills and Schooling, " *Canadian Journal of Education* 12, 1: 1-30.

Livingstone, D.W. (1987c). "Class Politics, Class Consciousness and Political Party Preference in Hard Times," in R. Argue, C. Gannage and D.W. Livingstone (eds.) *Working People and Hard Times*. Toronto: Garamond Press, 179-193.

Livingstone, D.W. (1992). "Lifelong Learning and Chronic Underemployment Exploring the Contradiction." In P. Anisef and P. Axelrod (eds.), *Transitions: Schooling and Employment in Canadian Society*. Toronto: Thompson Educational Publishing, 113-125.

Livingstone, D.W. (1993). "Working at Stelco: 'Re-Tayloring' Production Relations in the Eighties," in J. Corman et al. *Recasting Steel Labour: The Stelco Story*. Halifax: Fernwood Publishing, 13-53.

Livingstone, D.W. (1994a)."Searching for Missing Links: Neo-Marxist Theories of Education," in L. Erwin and D. MacLennan (eds.) *Canadian Sociology of Education*. Toronto: Copp Clark Longman, 55-82.

Livingstone, D.W. (1994b). "Living in the Education-Jobs Gap." Paper presented at the annual meetings of the Canadian Sociology and Anthropology Association. Calgary: University of Alberta, June).

Livingstone, D.W. (1995a). "The Uses of Computer Literacy." *Orbit* 26, 2: 36-40.

Livingstone, D.W. (1995b). "For Whom the Bell Curve Toils," *Alberta Journal of Educational Research* XLI, 3: 335-341.

Livingstone, D.W. (1995c). "Searching for Missing Links: Neo-Marxist Theories of Education," *British Journal of Sociology of Education* 16, 1: 53-73.

Livingstone, D. W. (1996a). "Wasted Education and Withered Work: Reversing the 'Post-Industrial' Education-Jobs Optic," in T. Dunk, S. McBride and R. Nelson (eds.) *The Training Trap: Ideology, Training and the Labour Market*. Halifax: Fernwood Publishing, 73-100.

Livingstone, D.W. (1996b). "Post-Industrial Dynamics: Economic Restructuring, Underemployment, and Lifelong Learning in the Information Age." 27th Annual Sorokin Lecture, Saskatoon: University of Saskatchewan.

Livingstone, D.W. (1996c). "Steel Work: Recasting the Core Workforce at Hilton Works, 1981-96." Final Report of the Workplace Change Section of the Steelworker Families Project, Toronto: Department of Sociology and Equity Studies in Education.

Livingstone, D.W. (1997a). "Living in the Credential Gap: Responses to Underemployment and Underqualification," in A. Duffy, D. Glenday and N. Pupo (eds.) *Good Jobs, Bad Jobs, No Jobs: The Transformation of Work in the 21st Century*. Toronto: Harcourt Brace.

Livingstone, D.W. (1997b). "The Limits of Human Capital Theory: Expanding Knowledge, Informal Learning and Underemployment," *Policy Options* 18, 6: 9-13.

Livingstone, D.W. (1997c). "Computer Literacy, the 'Knowledge Economy' and Information Control: Micro Myths and Macro Choices," in M. Moll (ed.) *Tech High: Globalization and the Future of Canadian Education*. Ottawa: Canadian Centre for Policy Alternatives, 99-116.

Livingstone, D.W. (2001). *Basic Patterns of Work and Learning in Canada: Findings of the 1998 NALL Survey of Informal Learning and Related Statistics Canada surveys.* NALL Working Paper 33-2001. Retrieved May 25, 2003 from <www.nall.ca>

Livingstone, D.W. (2002). *Working and Learning in the Information Age.* Ottawa: Canadian Policy Research Network. Retrieved May 25, 2003 <http://www.cprn.com/docs/work/wlia_e.pdf>

Livingstone, D.W. (2003). Informal Learning: Conceptual Distinctions and Preliminary Findings, in Z. Bekerman, N. Burbules and D. Silberman (eds.). *Learning in Hidden Places: The Informal Education Reader.* Berlin: Peter Lang.

Livingstone, D.W. and D. Hart. (forthcoming). "Where the Buck Stops: Class Differences in Support for Education," *Journal of Educational Policy.*

Livingstone, D.W., D. Hart and L.E. Davie. (1985). Public Attitudes Toward Education in Ontario; Fifth OISE Survey. Toronto: OISE Press.

Livingstone, D.W., D. Hart and L.E. Davie. (1993). *Public Attitudes Toward Education in Ontario (1992): Ninth OISE Survey.* Toronto: OISE Press.

Livingstone, D.W., D. Hart and L.E. Davie. (1995). *Public Attitudes Toward Education in Ontario (1994): Tenth OISE Survey.* Toronto: OISE Press.

Livingstone, D.W., D. Hart and L.E. Davie. (1997). *Public Attitudes Toward Education in Ontario (1996): The Eleventh OISE/UT Survey.* Toronto: University of Toronto Press.

Livingstone, D.W. and M. Luxton. (1996). "Gender Consciousness at Work: Modification of the Male Breadwinner Norm," in D.W. Livingstone and J.M. Mangan (eds.) *Recast Dreams: Class and Gender Consciousness in Steeltown.* Toronto: Garamond Press, 100-129.

Livingstone, D.W. & P. Sawchuk. (2003). *Hidden Knowledge: Organized Labour in the Information Age.* Toronto: Garamond Press and Lanham, MD: Rowman & Littlefield.

Livingstone, D.W. & Stowe, S. (2003). Class and University Education: Intergenerational Patterns, in A. Scott and J. Freeman-Moir (eds.) *Yesterday's Dreams: International and Critical Perspectives on Education and Social Class.* Auckland: Canterbury University Press.

Livingstone, D.W. et al. (forthcoming). *Working Class Learning: Final Report of the Working Class Learning Strategies Project.* Toronto: Department of Sociology and Equity Studies in Education, OISE/UT.

Lloyd, C. (1986). *Explanation in Social History.* New York: Blackwell.

Loveman, G.W. and C. Tilly. (1988). "Good Jobs or Bad Jobs? Evaluating the American Job Creation Experience" *International Labour Review* 127, 5: 593-611.

Lovett, T., C. Clarke and A. Kilmurray. (1983). *Adult Education and Community Action.* London: Croom Helm.

Lowe, G. (1992). Human Resource Challenges of Education, Computers and Retirement. Ottawa: Statistics Canada.

Lowe, G. (1996). "The Use of Computers in the Canadian Workplace." Paper prepared for Information Technology Innovation, Industry Canada, March 31.

Lowe, G. et al. (1986). "Class, Labour Market and Educational Influences on Young People's Explanations of Unemployment." Paper presented at the XI World Congress of Sociology, New Delhi, India (August 19).

Lowe, G. (2000). *The Quality of Work: A People-centred Agenda.* Don Mills: Oxford University Press.

Lowe, G. & Schellenberg, G. (2001). *What's a Good Job: The Importance of Employment Relationships.* Ottawa: Canadian Policy Research Network.

Lucas, R.E. (1988). "On the Mechanics of Economic Development," *Journal of Monetary Economics* 22: .3-42.

Lucas, S. (1999). *Tracking Inequality: Stratification and Mobility in American High Schools.* New York: Teachers College Press.

Luria, A.R. (1981). *Cognitive Development: Its Cultural and Social Foundations.* Cambridge: Harvard University Press.

Luttrell, W. (1992). "Working-Class Women's Ways of Knowing: Effects of Gender, Race and Class," in J. Wrigley (ed.). *Education and Gender Equality.* London: Palmer.

Luxton, M. (1980). *More Than A Labour of Love.* Toronto: Women's Press.

Machlup, P. (1962). *The Production and Distribution of Knowledge in the United States.* Princeton: Princeton University Press.

Machlup, P. (1978-80). *Information through the Printed Word: The Dissemination of Scholarly, Scientific and Intellectual Knowledge.* (4 Volumes). New York: Praeger.

Machlup, P. (1980). *Knowledge, Its Creation, Distribution and Economic Significance.* Princeton: Princeton University Press.

MacLeod, G. (1997). *From Mondragon to America.* Sydney, NS: University College of Cape Breton Press.

MacLeod, J. (1987). *Ain't No Makin' It: Aspirations and Attainment in a Low-Income Neighbourhood.* Boulder, CO.: Westview Press.

Madamba, A.B. (1998). *Underemployment Among Asians in the United States; Asian Indian, Filipino, and Vietnamese Workers.* New York: Garland Publishing, Inc.

Makino, A. (1996). "The Theoretical Problem of Recent Educational Reform in Japan: The Collapse of the Framework." Unpublished paper, Nagoya University.

Mallet, S. (1975). *The New Working Class.* Nottingham, UK: Spokesman Books.

Mann, M. (1995). "Sources of Variation in Working Class Movements in Twentieth Century Europe" *New Left Review* 212: 14-54.

Manpower Report of the President. (1967). Washington, D.C.: Government Printing Office.

Marable, M. (1985). *Black American Politics.* London: Verso.

Marschall, D. (1990). *Upgrading America's Workforce through Participation and Structured Work-based Learning: UCLP Research Report.* Washington, D.C.: Human Resources Development Institute, 21.

Marshall, G. (1997). *Repositioning Class: Social Inequality in Industrial Societies.* London: Sage.

Marshall, K. (2000). Part-time by Choice. *Perspectives on Labour and Income The Online Edition, 1* (2), 20-27. Retrieved May 25, 2003 from Statistic Canada Web site <http://www.statcan.ca>

Marshall, R. and M. Tucker. (1994). *Thinking for a Living: Education and the Wealth of Nations.* New York: Basic Books.

Martin, D. (1995). *Thinking Union: Activism and Education in Canada's Labour Movement.* Toronto: Between the Lines.

Martin, P. (1994). "Martin's tightrope walk," *The Toronto Star.* (November 20): A8.

Marx, K. (1967 [1867]). *Capital.* (Volumes 1 and 3). New York: International publishers.

Marx, K. (1973 [1939]. *Grundrisse: Foundations of the Critique of Political Economy.* Harmondsworth, UK: Penguin Books.

Marx, K. and F. Engels. (1970). *The German Ideology, Part One.* New York: International Publishers.

Masatoshi, N., K. Koji, S. Hiroshi (eds.). (1994). *The State of Continuing Education in Japan.* Tokyo: Research Institute of Educational Systems, Nyhon University.

Masuda, Y. (ed.). (1992). *Human-Centred Systems in the Global Economy.* Berlin: Springer-Verlag.

Maurer, H. (1979). *Not Working.* New York: Plume.

Maurice, M., F. Sellier and J. Silvestre. (1986). *The Social Foundations of Industrial Power.* Cambridge: MIT Press.

McBride, S. (1992). *Not Working: State, Unemployment, and Neo-Conservatism in Canada.* Toronto: University of Toronto Press.

McBride, S. and J. Shields. (1997). *Dismantling the Canadian State.* Toronto: Garamond Press.

McChesney, R. (1999). *Rich Media, Poor Democracy.* New York: The New Press.

McDade, K.(1988). *Barriers to Recognition of the Credentials of Immigrants to Canada.* Ottawa: Institute for Research on Public Policy.

McDowell, R. (1991). *The Flow of Graduates from Higher Education and Their Entry into Working Life.* Ottawa: Research and Information on Education Directorate, Secretary of State.

McFarland, L. (1996). "Continuing Vocational Training in the Unites States," in I. Brandsma, F. Kessler and J. Munch (eds.) *Continuing Vocational Training: Europe, Japan and the United States.* Utrecht: Uitgeverij LEMMA BV; 335-60.

McIlroy, J. and S. Westwood (eds.). (1993). *Border Country: Raymond Williams in Adult Education.* Leicester: National Institute of Adult Continuing Education.

McKay, S. (1983). "Out of Work," *Maclean's* 96, 13 (March 28): 30-38.

McLaughlin, E. (1992). "Towards Active Labour Market Policies: An Overview," in E. McLaughlin (ed.) *Understanding Unemployment.* London: Routledge, 1-22.

Meek, C. and W. Woodworth. (1990). "Technical Training and Enterprise: Mondragon's Educational System and Its Implications for Other Cooperatives," *Economic and Industrial Democracy* 11, 4 (November): 505-27.

Menzies, H. (1996). *Whose Brave New World?: The Information Highway and the New Economy.* Toronto: Between the Lines.

Merriam, S. and R.M. Caffarella. (1991). *Learning in Adulthood: A Comparative Guide.* San Francisco: Jossey-Bass.

Merriam, S. and M.C. Clark. (1991). *Lifelines: Patterns of Work, Love and Learning in Adulthood.* San Francisco: Jossey-Bass.

Metcalf, H. (1992). "Hidden Unemployment and the Labour Market," in E. McLaughlin (ed.) *Understanding Unemployment.* London: Routledge, 160-180.

Mies, M. (1986). *Patriarchy and Accumulation on a World Scale: Woman in the International Division of Labour.* London: Zed Books.

Milani, B. (2000). *Designing the Green Economy: The Postindustrial Alternative to Corporate Globalization.* Lanham, MD: Rowman & Littlefield.

Miles, A. (1996). *Integrative Feminisms.* New York: Routledge.

Mishel, L., J. Bernstein and J. Schmitt. (1997). *The State of Working America: 1996-1997.* Armonk: M.E. Sharpe.

Mishel, L. and R. Teixeira. (1991). *The Myth of the Coming Labor Shortage: Jobs, Skills, and Incomes of America's Workforce 2000.* Washington, D.C.: Economic Policy Institute.

Mirza, H.S. (1993). *Young, Female and Black.* London: Routledge.

Mitchell, W. & Carlson, E. (2000). Beyond the Unemployment Rate: Labour Underutilisation and Underemployment in Australia and the USA. Working Paper # 00-06. Callaghan, NSW: Centre of Full Employment and Equity, University of Newcastle.

Mohammed, K. (1997). "Why didn't somebody set me straight?" *The Toronto Star.* (December 6): 553-4.

Mohanty, C. (1997). "Women Workers and Capitalist Scripts: Ideologies of Domination, Common Interests, and the Politics of Solidarity," in M. Alexander and C. Mohanty (eds.) *Feminist Genealogies, Colonial Legacies, Democratic Futures.* London: Routledge, 3-29.

Molander, B. (1992). "Tacit Knowledge and Silenced Knowledge: Fundamental Problems and Controversies," in B. Goranzon and M. Florin (eds.) *Skill and Education: Reflection and Experience.* London: Springer-Verlag.

Moll, L. (ed.). (1990). *Vygotsky and Education: Instructional Implications of Sociohistorical Psychology*. Cambridge: Cambridge University Press.

Mondragon. Website address: <webmaster@mondragon.mcc.es> email: <info@mondragon.mcc.es>.

Moore, B. (1966). *Social Origins of Dictatorship and Democracy: Lord and Peasant in the Making of the Modern World*. Boston: Beacon.

Moore, R. (1988). "The Correspondence Principle and the Marxist Sociology of Education," in M. Cole (ed.) *Bowles and Gintis Revisited*. London: Falmer Press, 51-85.

Morissette, R., J. Myles and G. Picot. (1993). "What is Happening to Earnings Inequality in Canada?" *Analytical Studies Branch: Research Paper Series No. 60*. Ottawa: Statistics Canada.

Morrow, R.A. and C.A. Torres. (1995). *Social Theory and Education: A Critique of Theories of Social and Cultural Reproduction*. Albany: State University of New York.

Moye, A.M. (1993). "Mondragon: Adapting Co-operative Structures to Meet the Demands of a Changing Environment," *Economic and Industrial Democracy* 14,2: 251-276.

Mulder, M. et al. (eds.) (1990). *Strategic Human Resource Development*. Amsterdam: Swets and Zeitlinger.

Mullaby, S. (1994). "A Survey on Japan," *Economist* 332 (July 9): 3-18.

Murphy, J.B. (1993). *The Moral Economy of Labour: Aristotelian Themes in Economic Theory*. New Haven: Yale University Press.

Murphy, R. (1979). *Sociological Theories of Education*. Toronto: McGraw-Hill Ryerson Limited.

Murphy, R. (1988). *Social Closure: The Theory of Monopolization and Exclusion*. Oxford: Clarendon Press.

Musgrove, F. (1979). *School and the Social Order*. Chichester: Wiley.

Musgrove, F.W. (1999). [Review of The Education-Jobs Gap]. *Choice. 36*, (6), 1104-1105.

Myles, J. (1988). "The Expanding Middle: Some Canadian Evidence on the Deskilling Debate," *The Canadian Review of Sociology and Anthropology* 25: 335-64.

Myles, J. & Fawcett, G. (1990). *Job Skills and the Service Economy*. Working Paper No. 4. Ottawa: Economic Council of Canada.

NALL. Website address: http://edu.oise.utoronto.ca/depts/sese/csew.

National Advisory Commission on Civil Disorders. (1968). *Report of the National Advisory Commission on Civil Disorders*. New York: Bantam Books.

National Advisory Panel on Skill Development Leave. (1984). *Learning for Life: Overcoming the Separation of Work and Learning*. Ottawa: Minister of Employment and Immigration.

National Center on Education and the Economy. (1990). *America's Choice: High Skills or Low Wages*. Washington, D.C.: NCEE.

National Center on the Educational Quality of the Workforce. (1995). *First Findings from the EQW National; Employer Survey*. Philadelphia: National Center on the Educational Quality of the Workforce.

National Jobs for All Coalition. (2003). *April 2003 Unemployment Data*. Retrieved May 25, 2003 from <www.njfac.org/jobnews.html>

New York Times. (1996). *The Downsizing of America*. New York: Random House.

Newman, F. and L. Holzman. (1993). *Lev Vygotsky: Revolutionary Scientist*. New York: Routledge.

Newman, M. (1993). *The Third Contract: Theory and Practice in Trade Union Training*. Sydney: Stewart Victor Publishing. .

Newton, K. et al. (1992). *Education and Training in Canada*. Ottawa: Canadian Communication Group.

Nisbet, R. (1970). *Social Change and History: Aspects of the Western Theory of Development.* New York: Oxford University Press.

Noble, David. (1998). "Digital Diploma Mills: The Automation of Higher Education." *Monthly Review* 49,9: 38-52.

Noble, Doug. (1991). *The Classroom Arsenal: Military Research, Information Technology and Public Education.* New York: Palmer Press.

Noreau, N. (2000). *Longitudinal Aspects of Involuntary Part-time Employment.* (Catalogue no. 75F002MIE-00003). Ottawa: Statistics Canada.

Nozick, M. (1992). *No Place Like Home: Building Sustainable Communities.* Ottawa: Canadian Council on Social Development.

Nyhan, B. (1991). *Developing People's Ability to Learn: A European Perspective on Self Learning Competency and Technological Change.* Brussels: European Interuniversity Press.

Nyland, C. (1989). *Reduced Worktime and the Management of Production.* Cambridge: Cambridge University Press.

Oakes, J. (1985). *Keeping Track: How Schools Structure Inequality.* New Haven: Yale University Press.

O'Brien, G.E. (1986). *Psychology of Work and Unemployment.* New York: John Wiley.

O'Brien, M. (1981). *The Politics of Reproduction.* Boston: Routledge and Kegan Paul.

O'Toole, J. (1975). "The Reserve Army of the Underemployed: I - The World of Work, and II- The Role of Education" *Change,* (May/June): 26-33,60-3.

O'Toole, J. (1977). *Work, Learning, and the American Future.* San Francisco: Jossey-Bass.

Odrich, B. (1997). *Japan in the 1990s: Facing Higher Unemployment in Japan.* Website Address: <http://www.nkk.co.jp/nkknews/36-6/japan.htm>.

OECD. (1983). "Education and Work: The Views of the Young," *OECD Observer* 118 (September).

OECD. (1989a). *Educational Attainment and the Labour Force Employment Outlook.* Paris: OECD.

OECD. (1989b). *OECD Employment Outlook.* Paris: OECD

OECD. (1991a). *Further Education and Training of the Labour Force in OECD Countries: Evidence and Issues.* Paris: OECD.

OECD. (1991b). "Enterprise-related Training," *OECD Employment Outlook 1991.* Paris: OECD.

OECD. (1993a). *Industry Training in Australia, Sweden and the United States.* Paris: OECD.

OECD. (1993b). *Education at a Glance - OECD Indicators.* Paris: OECD.

OECD. (1994a). *The OECD Job Study: Facts, Analysis, Strategies.* Paris: OECD.

OECD. (1994b). *The OECD Job Study: Evidence and Explanations, Part I - Labour Market Trends and Underlying Forces of Change.* Paris: OECD.

OECD. (1994c). *The OECD Jobs Study: Evidence and Explanations, Part II – The Adjustment Potential of the Labour Market.* Paris: OECD.

OECD. (1994d). *OECD Societies in Transition: The Future of Work and Leisure.* Paris: OECD.

OECD. (1996a). *The OECD Jobs Strategy: Enhancing the Effectiveness of Active Labour Market Policies.* Paris: OECD.

OECD. (1996b). *The OECD Jobs Strategy: Technology, Productivity and Job Creation, Vol. 1 - Highlights.* Paris: OECD.

OECD. (1996c). *The OECD Jobs Strategy: Technology, Productivity and Job Creation, Vol. 2 - Analytical Report.* Paris: OECD.

OECD. (1996d). *Lifelong Learning for All: Meeting of the Education Committee at Ministerial Level.* Paris: OECD.

Offe, C. and R.G. Heinze. (1992). *Beyond Employment: Time, Work and the Informal Economy.* Cambridge: Polity Press.

Office of Technology Assessment. (1983). *Automation and the Workplace.* Washington, D.C.: OTA.

Okano, K. (1993). *School to Work Transition in Japan: An Ethnographic Study.* Philadelphia: Multilingual Matters

Ollman, B. (1993). *Dialectical Investigations.* New York: Routledge.

Olsen, G.M. (1992). *The Struggle for Economic Democracy in Sweden.* Brookfield: Ashgate Publishing Company.

Ontario Royal Commission on Learning. (1994). *For the Love of Learning.* (Volume 4). Toronto: Queen's Printer.

Oosterbeek, H. (2000) Introduction to Special Issue on Overschooling. *Economics of Education Review, 19* (2), 129-130.

Ornstein, M.D. (1983). "The Development of Class Canada," in J.P. Grayson (ed.) *Introduction to Sociology: An Alternate Approach.* Toronto, ON: Gage Publishing, 216-259:

Osberg, L. (1993). "Social policy and macro policy in a federal state" *Canadian Business Economics* 2,1 (Fall): 39-40.

Osberg, L., F. Wien and J. Grude. (1995). *Vanishing Jobs: Canada's Changing Workplaces.* Toronto: Lorimer.

Osterman, P. (1994). "How Common is Workplace Reform and Who Adopts It?" *Industrial and Labor Relations Review* 47, 2 January): 173-88.

Oved, Y. (1988). *Two Hundred Years of American Communes.* New Brunswick, NJ: Transaction Books.

Padberg, L. (1991). *A Study of the Organization of Learning Projects of Adults of Low Formal Educational Attainment.* Ph.D. dissertation, University of Missouri –Kansas City.

Palgi, M. (1998). "Organization in Kibbutz Industry," in U. Leviatan, H. Oliver and J. Quarter (eds.) *Crisis in the Israeli Kibbutz: The Challenge of Changing Times.* Westport, CT: Praeger/ Greenwood.

Parenti, M. (1996). *Dirty Truths.* San Francisco: City Lights Books.

Panitch, L. (1986). *Working Class Politics in Crisis: Essays on Labour and the State.* London: Verso.

Parker, M. and J. Slaughter. (1994). *Working Smart: A Union Guide to Participation Programs and Reengineering.* Detroit: Labor Notes.

Parker, R. [Review of The Education-Jobs Gap]. *Contemporary Sociology, 28* (4), 429-430.

Pateman, C. (1970). *Participation and Democratic Theory.* Cambridge: University Press.

Perlman, L.J. (1992). *School's Out: Hyperlearning, the New Technology, and the End of Education.* New York: William Morrow.

Penland, P. (1977). *Self-Planned Learning in America.* Pittsburgh: University of Pittsburgh.

Perkins, H. (1996). *The Third Revolution: Professional Elites and the Modern World.* London: Routledge.

Peters, J.M., Johnson and P. Lazzara. (1981). "Adult Problem Solving and Learning." Paper presented at 62nd annual conference of the American Educational Research Association, Los Angeles, April.

Peters, L. and R. Hull. (1969). *The Peter Principle.* New York: Morrow.

Phelps, E. (1997). *Rewarding Work: How to Restore Participation Support to Free Enterprise.* Cambridge, MA: Harvard University Press.

Phillips, P. (2000). [Review of The Education-Jobs Gap]. *Socialist Studies, 59,* 63-69.

Piaget, Jean. (1929) *The Child's Conception of the World.* New York: Harcourt Brace.

Pierson, P. (1995). *Dismantling the Welfare State?* Cambridge: Cambridge University Press.

Pixley, J. (1993). *Citizenship and Employment: Investigating Post-Industrial Options.* Cambridge: Cambridge University Press.

Pollert, A. (ed.). (1991). *Farewell to Flexibility?* Oxford: Blackwell Business.

Polanyi, M. (1983). *The Tacit Dimension.* Gloucester: Peter Smith.

Porat, M.U. (1977). *The Information Economy.* Washington, D.C.: U.S. Department of Commerce, Office of Telecommunications.

Porter, J. (1961). *The Vertical Mosaic.* Toronto: University of Toronto Press.

Porter, J. et al. (1971). *Towards 2000: The Future of Post-Secondary Education in Ontario.* Toronto: McClelland and Stewart.

Portes, A. (1996). "The Informal Economy: Perspectives from Latin America," in S. Pozo (ed.). *Exploring the Underground Economy.* Kalamazoo: W.E. Upjohn Institute for Employment Research.

Powell, B.E. (1918). *The Moment of Industrial Education and the Establishment of the University, 1840-1870.* Urbana, IL.: University of Illinois Press.

Powers, B.A. (1985). "Resistance in Britain and California: High School Students Poised at the Brink of Work," *Humboldt Journal of Social Relations* 12, 2: 115-142.

Pratt, Courtney. (1997). "Business Accountability: Shareholders, Stakeholders or Society?" Address to the Canadian Club of Toronto, September 29.

Pringle, R. (1989). *Secretaries Talk: Sexuality, Power and Work.* London: Verso.

Przeworski, A. and F. Limongi. (1997). "Modernization: Theories and Facts," *World Politics* 49 January): 155-83.

Putnam, R. (1995). "Bowling Alone: America's Declining Social Capital," *Journal of Democracy* 6, 1: 65-78.

Quarter, J. (1982). Special Issue on Kibbutz Education. *Interchange* 13, 1.

Quarter, J. (1992). *Canada's Social Economy: Co-operatives, Non-Profits, and Other community Enterprises.* Toronto: Lorimer.

Rachel, L. (1987). "Assessing the Extent and the Political Implications of Underemployment Among College Graduates." Ph.D. dissertation, University of Colorado.

Raskin, M. (1971). *Being and Doing.* Boston: Beacon Press.

Rauner, F. and K. Ruth. (1991). *The Prospects of Anthropocentric Production Systems: A World of Comparison of Production Models.* Brussels: Forecasting and Assessment in Science and Technology Programme, Commission of the European Communities.

Reich, R. (1991). *The Work of Nations: Preparing Ourselves for 21ˢᵗ Century Capitalism.* New York: Vintage.

Reid, D. (1995). *Work and Leisure in the 21st Century: From Production to Citizenship.* Toronto: Wall and Emerson.

Resnick, L.B. and J.G. Wirt (eds.). (1996). *Linking School and Work: Roles for Standards and Assessment.* San Francisco: Jossey-Bass Inc.

Reynolds, J. (2003). When Too Much is Not Enough: Overwork and Underwork in the United States and Abroad. Retrieved May 25, 2003 from <http://www.arches.uga.edu/~jeremyr/profdocs/cnhours.pdf>

Riche, N. (1990). "Proposals for Future Public Policy on Technological Impacts on Unemployment and the Labour Force," in S. Bennett (ed.) *Technology and Work in Canada.* Lewiston, N.Y.: Edwin Mellon Press, 269-80.

Riches, K. (1997). "I have nobody to talk to." *The Toronto Star.* (December 6): 555.

Richta, R. et al. (1969). *Civilization at the Crossroads.* White Plains, NY: International Arts and Sciences Press.

Rifkin, J. (1995). *The End of Work: The Decline of the Global Labor Force and the Dawn of the Post-Market Era.* New York: Tarcher/Putnam.

Rikowski, G. (1996). "Left Alone: End Time for Marxist Educational Theory?" *British Journal of Sociology of Education* 17, 4: 415-451.

Robins, K. and F. Webster. (1988). "Athens without Slaves...or Slaves Without Athens? The Neurosis of Technology," *Science and Culture* 3.

Robinson, D. (April 13, 1999). Nice Work—If You Can Get It. *Behind the Numbers: Economic Facts, Figures and Analysis, 1* (1). 1-2.

Robinson, J. and G. Godbey. (1997). *Time for Life: The Surprising Ways Americans Use Their Time*. University Park, PA: Pennsylvania State University Press.

Roizen, J. and M. Jepson. (1985). *Degrees for Jobs: Employer Expectations of Higher Education*. Guildford, Surrey: SRHE and NFER-NELSON.

Romer, P. (1994). "Economic Growth and Investment in Children," *Daedalus* 123 (Fall).

Rojo, O. (1995). "Survey finds employment relationship alters slowly," *The Toronto Star*. (November 6): C3.

Romiszowski, A. (1990). "Trends in Corporate Training and Development," in M. Mulder et al. (eds.) *Strategic Human Resource Development*. Amsterdam: Swets and Zeitlinger, 17-48.

Rosdolsky, R. (1977). *The Making of Marx's Capital*. London: Pluto Press.

Rose, M. (1990). *Lives on the Boundary*. New York: Penguin.

Rosner, M. (1998). "Work in the Kibbutz," in U. Leviatan, H. Oliver and J. Quarter (eds.) *Crisis in the Israeli Kibbutz: The Challenge of Changing Times*. Westport, CT.: Praeger / Greenwood.

Ross, R. and K. Trachte. (1990). *Global Capitalism: The New Leviathan*. Albany: State University of New York Press.

Roth, R.N. (1997). "Kitchen Economics for the Family: Paid Education Leave and The Canadian Autoworkers Union." M.A. thesis, University of Toronto.

Rothstein, R. (2002). Out of Balance: Our Understanding of How Schools Affect Society and How Society Affects Schools. 30th Anniversary Conference, Traditions of Scholarship in Education. Spencer Foundation.

Rubenson, K. and J.D. Willms. (1993). *Human Resource Development in British Columbia: An Analysis of the 1992 Adult Education and Training Survey*. Vancouver, B.C.: Centre for Policy Studies in Education.

Rubin, B. (1972). "Marxism and Education -Radical Thought and Educational Theory in the (1930)s" *Science and Society* 36,2.

Rubin, L. (1994). *Families on the Fault Line: America's Working Class Speaks About the Family, the Economy, Race, and Ethnicity*. New York: Harper Collins Publishers.

Rumberger, R. (1980). *Overeducation in the U.S. Labor Market*. New York: Praeger.

Rumberger, R. (1984). "The Growing Imbalance Between Education and Work," *Phi Delata Kappan* 65: 342-346.

Ryan, J. and C. Sackrey. (1984) *Strangers in Paradise: Academics from the Working Class*. Lanham: University Press of America.

Sabel, C. and J. Zeitlin. (1985) "Historical Alternatives to Mass Production: Politics, Markets and Technology in Nineteenth Century Industrialization," *Past and Present* 108: 133-76.

Sacks, K. (1989). "Toward a Unified Theory of Class, Race, and Gender," *American Ethnologist* 16, 3 (August): 534-550.

Sacks, K. and D. Remy. (1984). *My Troubles Are Going to Have Troubles with Me: Everyday Trials and Triumphs of Women Workers*. Rutgers, N.J.: Rutgers University Press.

Sadovnik, A.R. (ed.). (1995). *Knowledge and Pedagogy: The Sociology of Basil Bernstein*. Norwood, N.J.: Ablex Publishing.

Said, E. (1978). *Orientalism*. New York: Random House.

Sandia Laboratories. (1993). "Perspectives on Education in America," *Journal of Educational Research* 86,5: 259-310.

Sargent, N. (1991). *Learning and 'Leisure': A Study of Adult Participation in Learning and Its Policy Implications*. Leicester: National Institute of Adult Continuing Education.

Sarup, M. (1978). *Marxism and Education*. London: Routledge and Kegan Paul.

Sarup, M. (1982). *Education, State and Crisis: A Marxist Perspective*. London: Routledge and Kegan Paul.

Savage, M. et at. (1992). *Property, Bureaucracy and Culture: Middle-Class Formation in Contemporary Britain*. London: Routledge.

Sawchuk, P. (1996). "Working Class Informal Learning and Computer Literacy." M.A. thesis, University of Toronto.

Sayer, D. (1987). *The Violence of Abstraction: The Analytic Foundations of Historical Materialism*. Oxford: Basil Blackwell.

Sayers, J. (1976). " A Woman's Work..." *Social Work Today* 8: 12-13.

Sayers, S. (1987). "The Need to Work," *Radical Philosophy* 46 (Summer): 17-26.

Schiff, M. and R. Lewontin. (1986). *Education and Class: The Irrelevance of I.Q.* Genetic Studies. New York: Oxford University Press.

Schor, J. (1991). *The Overworked American: The Unexpected Decline of Leisure*. New York: Basic Books.

Schulkind, E. 1972. *The Paris Commune: The View from the Left*. London: Cape.

Schultz, T.W. (1963). *The Economic Value of Education*. New York: Columbia University Press.

Schweickart, D. (1993). *Against Capitalism*. Cambridge: Cambridge University Press.

Scott, J.C. (1990). *Domination and the Arts of Resistance: Hidden Transcripts*. New Haven: Yale University Press.

Scoville, J.G. (1966). "Education and Training Requirements for Occupations," *The Review of Economics and Statistics* 48, 1: 387-394.

Seabrook, J. (1992). *Unemployment*. London: Quartet Books.

Seccombe, W. (1987). "Helping Her Out: The Participation of Husbands in Domestic Labor When Wives Go Out to Work." Unpublished paper, Steelworker Families Project. I

Seccombe, W. (1992). *A Millennium of Family Change: Feudalism to Capitalism in Northwestern Europe*. London, New York: Verso.

Seccombe, W. (1993). *Weathering the Storm: Working-Class Families from the Industrial Revolution to the Fertility Decline*. London, New York: Verso.

Seccombe, W. and D.W. Livingstone. (1996). "Down-to-Earth People": Revising a Materialist Understanding of Group Consciousness," in D.W. Livingstone and M. Mangan (eds.) *Recast Dreams: Class and Gender Consciousness in Steeltown*. Toronto: Garamond, 131-194.

Secretary's Commission on Achieving Necessary Skills. (1991). *What Work Requires of Schools: A SCANS Report for AMERICA 2000*. Washington, D.C.: U.S. Department of Labor, (June).

Selman, G. and P. Dampier. (1991). *The Foundations of Adult Education in Canada*. Toronto: Thompson Educational Publishing.

Senge, P. (1990). *The Fifth Discipline: The Art and Practice of the Learning Organization*. New York: Doubleday.

Serre, F. (1978). "The Importance of Learning Alone: A Study of Self-Planned Learning Projects" *Adult Learning* 3, 2: 16-20.

Servan-Schreiber, J.J. (1971). *The American Challenge*. New York: Avon.

Shapiro, S. (1990). *Between Capitalism and Democracy: Educational Policy and the Crisis of the Welfare State*. New York: Bergin and Garvey.

Sharp, R. (ed.). (1986). *Capitalist Crisis and Schooling: Comparative Studies in the Politics of Education*. Melbourne: Macmillan.

Sharp, R. et al. (1989). "Independent Working Class Education: A Repressed Historical Alternative," *Discourse: The Australian Journal of Education Studies* 10, 1 (October): 1-26.

Sharpe, A. (1990). "Training the Workforce: A Challenge Facing Canada in the '90s" *Perspectives on Labour and Income* (Winter): 21-31.

Sharpe, A. (1993). "The Rise of Unemployment in Ontario." Paper presented at the conference *Unemployment: What is to be Done?* Laurentian University, March 26-27.

Shavit, Y. and H.P. Blossfield (eds.). (1993). *Persistent Barriers: Changes in Educational Opportunities in Thirteen Countries*. Boulder, CO: Westview Press.

Sheaffer, Z. and A. Helman. (1994). "Brain Drain: The Israeli Kibbutz Experience," *The British Academy of Management*. Lancaster University, September 12-14.

Sheak, R. (1994). "The Chronic Jobs' Problem in the United States: No End in Sight" *Free Inquiry in Creative Sociology* 22, 1: 23-32.

Shelley, K.J. (1992). "The Future of Jobs for College Graduates," *Monthly Labor Review* (July): 13-21.

Shilling, C. (1989). *Schooling for Work in Capitalist Britain*. New York: The Falmer Press.

Simon, B. (1974). *Studies in the History of Education*. (3 Volumes). London: Lawrence and Wishart.

Simon, B. (ed.). (1990). *The Search for Enlightenment: The Working Class and Adult Education in the Twentieth Century*. London: Lawrence and Wishart.

Simon, B. (1991). *Education and the Social Order, 1940-1990*. London: Lawrence and Wishart.

Sinclair, U. (1923). *The Goose-Step: A Study of American Education*. Pasadena, CA: The Author.

Sirianni, C. (1987). "Economies of Time in Social Theory: Three Approaches Compared," *Current Perspectives in Social Theory* 8: 161-195.

Sisco, B. (1983). "The Undereducated: Myth or Reality," *Lifelong Learning: The Adult Years* 6, 8: 14-15, 24, 26.

Sissons, L. (1990). "Trade Union Education and Democracy," in H. Lauder and C. Wylie (eds.) *Towards Successful Schooling*. London: Palmer Press, 209-18.

Sklar, H. (1995). *Jobs, Income, and Work: Ruinous Trends, Urgent Alternatives*. Philadelphia: Community Relations Division of the American Friends Service Committee.

Slaughter, J. (1995). "Germany: Short Work Week Saves Jobs But Brings Problems, Too," *Labor Notes* 196 (July): 7, 13.

Smith, D.E. (1987). *The Everyday World as Problematic: A Feminist Sociology*. Toronto: University of Toronto Press.

Smith, D.E. (1990). "Women's Work as Mothers; A New Look at the Relation of Class, Family and School Achievement," in F. Forman (ed.) *Feminism and Education: A Canadian Perspective*. Toronto: OISE Press, 219-246.

Smith, D.E. and G. Smith. (1990). "Re-organizing the Job Skills Training Relation: From 'Human Capital' to 'Human Resources,'" in J. Muller (ed.) *Education for Work/Education as Work: Canada's Changing Community Colleges*. Toronto: Garamond Press.

Smith, H. (1986). "Overeducation and Underemployment: An Agnostic View," *Sociology of Education* 59 (April): 85-99.

Smith, M.R. (2001). Technological Change, the Demand for Skills and the Adequacy of Their Supply. *Canadian Public Policy, 27* (1), 1-22.

Smith, P. (1994). "Assessing the Size of the Underground Economy: The Statistics Canada Perspective," *Canadian Economic Observer*. Statistics Canada Catalogue 11-010, May.

Smith, V. (1994). "Braverman's Legacy: The Labor Process Tradition at 20," *Work and Occupations* 21, 4: 403-442.

326 *Bibliography*

Sobel, R. (1989). *The White Collar Working Class: From Structure to Politics.* New York: Praeger.

Sorokin, P. (1937-1941). *Social and Cultural Dynamics: A Study of Change in Major Systems of Art, Truth, Ethics, Law and Social Relationships.* (4 Volumes). Boston: Porter Sargent.

Sorokin, P. (1943). *Sociocultural Causality, Space, Time.* Durham: Duke University Press.

Sorokin P. (1957). *Social and Cultural Dynamics.* Revised and abridged. Boston: Porter Sargent.

Sorrentino, C. (1993). "International Comparisons of Unemployment Indicators," *Monthly Labor Review* (March): 3-24.

Sorrentino, C. (2000). "International Unemployment Rates: How Comparable Are They?" *Monthly Labour Review, 123* (6), 3-20.

Southam News-Angus Reid Poll. (1996). "Poll reveals angers at profits, layoffs." *The Toronto Star.* (March 29): El.

Spagenburg, C. (1995). *Implementing a School-to-Work Transition System: A Rochester, New York, Case Study.* Rochester: National Center on Education and the Economy.

Spencer, P. (1996). "Reactions to a Flexible Labour Market," in R. Jowell et al. (eds.) *British Social Attitudes: The 13th Report.* Cambridge: Dartmouth.

Spender, D. (1980). *Man Made Language.* London: Pandora.

Spenner, K. (1983). "Deciphering Prometheus: Temporal Change in the Skill Level of Work," *American Sociological Review* 48, 6 (December): 824-837.

Spenner, K. (1985). "The Upgrading and Downgrading of Occupations: Issues, Evidence, and Implications for Education," *Review of Educational Research* 55, 2 (Summer).

Staines, G. and R. Quinn. (1979). "American Workers Evaluate the Quality of Their Jobs," *Monthly Labor Review* 102, 1: 3-12.

Standing, G. (1983). "The Notion of Structural Unemployment," *International Labour Review* 122, 2: 137-53.

Stasz, C. et al. (1996). *Workplace Skills in Practice: Case Studies of Technical Work.* Berkeley: National Center for Research in Vocational Education.

Statistics Canada. (1993). *The Labour Force.* Ottawa: Statistics Canada.

Statistics Canada. (1995a). *1991 Adult Education and Training Survey.* Ottawa: Employment and Immigration Canada.

Statistics Canada. (1995b). *As Time Goes By...Time Use of Canadians.* General Social Survey. Ottawa: Statistics Canada.

Statistics Canada. (1995c). *Women in Canada: A Statistical Report.* Ottawa: Statistics Canada.

Statistics Canada and OECD. (1995). *Literacy, Economy and Society: Results of the First International Adult Literacy Survey.* Ottawa: Statistics Canada.

Statistics Canada. (1996). *Reading the Future: A Portrait of Literacy in Canada.* Ottawa: National Literacy Secretariat, Human Resource Development Canada and Statistics Canada.

Statistics Canada and the Council of Ministers of Education Canada (2000). *Education Indicators in Canada.* Report of the Pan-Canadian Education Indicators Program 1999. Canadian Education Statistics Council. Ottawa : Statistics Canada.

Stehr, N. (1994). *Knowledge Societies.* London: Sage Publications Ltd.

Steinberg, R. (1989). *Job Training for Women: The Promise and Limits of Public Policies.* Women in the Political Economy. Philadelphia: Temple University Press, 1989.

Steinitz, V.A. and E.R. Solomon. (1986). *Starting Out: Class and Community in the Lives of Working-Class Youth.* Philadelphia: Temple University Press.

Steven, R. (1983). *Classes in Contemporary Japan.* Cambridge: Cambridge University Press.

Stevenson, H.W. and J.W. Stigler. (1987). *The Learning Gap: Why Our Schools Are Failing and What We Can Learn from Japanese and Chinese Education.* New York: Touchstone.

Stewart, T.A. (1997). *Intellectual Capital: The New Wealth of Organizations.* New York: Doubleday/Currency.

Stiglitz, J. (1975). The Theory of Screening, Education, and the Distribution of Income. *American Economic Review, 65* (3), 283-300.

Stiglitz, J. (2002). *Globalization and its Discontents.* New York: Norton.

Stinchcombe, A. (1964). *Rebellion in a High School.* Chicago: Quadrangle Books.

Storper, M. and R. Walker. (1989). *The Capitalist Imperative.* Oxford: Blackwell.

Stratton, L.S. (1996). "Are 'Involuntary' Part-Time Workers Indeed Involuntary?" *Industrial and Labor Relations Review* 49, 3: 522-536.

Streeck, W. (1989). "Skills and the Limits of Neo-Liberalism: The Enterprise of the Future as a Place of Learning," *Work, Employment and Society* 3, 1.

Street, B. (1995). *Social Literacies: Critical Approaches to Literacy in Development, Ethnography and Education.* London: Longman.

Struthers, J. (1983). *No Fault of Their Own: Unemployment and the Canadian Welfare State 1914-1941.* Toronto: University of Toronto Press.

Swift, J. (1995). *Wheel of Fortune: Work and Life in the Age of Falling Expectations.* Toronto: Between the Lines.

Syzmanski, A. (1983). *Class Structure: A Critical Perspective.* New York: Praeger.

Tanner, D. (1993). "A Nation 'Truly' at Risk," *Phi Delta Kappan.* December.

Tanner, J., G. Lowe and H. Krahn. (1984). "Youth Unemployment and Moral Panics," *Perception* 7, 5.

Task Force on Education and Training. (1989). *Putting Business into Training: A Guide to Investing in People.* Ottawa: Canadian Chamber of Commerce.

Taylor, P. and I. McGugan. (1995). "Devoured by Degrees," *Canadian Business* 68, 9 (September): 26-36.

Taylor-Gooby, P. (1993). "What Citizens Want from the State," in R. Jowell et al. (eds.) *International Social Attitudes: The 10th BSA Report,* Aldershot: Dartmouth Publishing, 81-101.

Technomania. (1995). [Special Issue]. *Newsweek* (February 27): 53.

Temme, L. (1975). *Occupation: Meanings and Measures.* Washington, D.C.: Bureau of Social Science Research.

Tharp, R. and R. Gallimore. (1989). *Rousing Minds to Life: Teaching, Learning and Schooling in Social Context.* Cambridge University Press.

Thompson, E.P. (1967). *The Making of the English Working Class.* Harmondsworth: Penguin.

Thompson, E.P. (1968). *Education and Experience.* Leeds: Leeds University Press.

Theobald, Steven. (1997a). "Out of school, out of work," *The Toronto Star.* (May 28): C1-2.

Theobald, Steven. (1997b). "Canadians burning the midnight oil-for free," *The Toronto Star.* (July 15): A1.

Therborn, G. (1986). *Why are Some People More Unemployed than Others?* London: Verso.

Thomas, L. (1956). *The Occupational Structure and Education.* Englewood Cliffs: Prentice Hall.

Thorne, B. (1993). *Gender Play: Girls and Boys in School.* New Brunswick, NJ: Rutgers University Press.

Thurow, L. (1974). "Measuring the Economic Benefits of Education," in M. Gordon (ed.) *Higher Education and the Labor Market.* New York: McGraw-Hill, 373-418.

Thurow, L.C. (1996). *The Future of Capitalism: How Today's Economic Forces Shape Tomorrow's World.* New York: Penguin Books.

Tilly; C. (1996). *Half a Job: Bad and Good Part-Time Jobs in a Changing Labor Market.* Philadelphia: Temple University Press.

Tilly, C. (1998). Part-time Work: A Mobilizing Issue. *New Politics,* 6 (4), 19-26.

Timmermann, D. (1995). "Human Capital Theory and the Individualization Theorem," in G. Neubauer and K. Hurrelmann (eds.) *Individualization in Childhood and Adolescence.* Berlin: Walter de Gruyter, 223-245.

Tough, A. (1971). *The Adult's Learning Projects.* Toronto: OISE Press.

Tough, A. (1978). "Major Learning Efforts: Recent Research and Future Directions," *Adult Education* (U.S.) 28, 4: 252.

Tough, Allen. (1979). *The Adult's Learning Projects: A Fresh Approach to Theory and Practice in Adult Learning,* (second edition). Toronto: OISE Press.

Touraine, A. (1971). *The Post-Industrial Society: Tomorrow's Social History: Classes, Conflicts and Culture in the Programmed Society.* NY: Random House

Tuijnman, A.C. (1989). *Recurrent Education, Earnings and Well-being: A Fifty-Year Longitudinal Study of a Cohort of Swedish Men.* Stockholm: Almqvist and Wiksell.

Tuijnman, A.C. (1991). "Lifelong Education: A Test of the Accumulation Hypothesis," *International Journal of Lifelong Education* 10, 4: 275-285. I

Tuijnman, A.C. (1992). "The Expansion of Adult Education and Training in Europe: Trends and Issues" *International Review of Education* 38, 6: 673-692.

Turner, R. (1980). *The Eye of the Needle: Towards Participatory Democracy in South Africa.* Johannesburg: Raven Press.

UNESCO. (1965). UNESCO *Statistical Yearbook.* Paris: UNESCO.

UNESCO. (1975). UNESCO *Statistical Yearbook.* Paris: UNESCO.

UNESCO. (1985). UNESCO *Statistical Yearbook.* Paris: UNESCO.

UNESCO. (1995). UNESCO *Statistical Yearbook.* Paris: UNESCO.

U.S. Bureau of the Census. (1982). *Statistical Abstract of the United States: 1982-83.* Washington, DC: U.S. Government Printing Office.

U.S. Department of Labor, Bureau of Labor Statistics. (1985). *How Workers Get Their Training.* Washington, DC: U.S. Government Printing Office.

U.S. Bureau of the Census. (1992). *Statistical Abstract of the United States: 1992.* Washington, DC: U.S. Government Printing Office.

U.S. Department of Education. (1996). *Condition of Education.* Washington, DC: U.S. Government Printing Office.

U.S. Department of Labor. (1991). *Dictionary of Occupational Titles. Volume II. Glossary. Appendixes. Indexes.* Lanham, MD: Bernan Press.

U.S. Department of Labor. (1993). *High Performance Work Practices and Firm Performance.* Chicago: U.S. Department of Labor.

U.S. Department of Labor, Bureau of Labor Statistics. (1994). *Employer-Provided Formal Training.* Washington, DC: U .5. Department of Labor.

U.S. Department of Labor, Bureau of Labor Statistics. (1996). *The 1995 Survey of Employer-Provided Training.* Washington, DC: U.S. Department of Labor.

U.S. Department of Labor, Employment and Training. (1989). *Work-Based Learning: Training American Workers.* Washington, DC: U.S. Government Printing Office, ED323365.

U.S. Department of Labor. (2003). *Labor Force Statistics From the Current Population Survey.* Retrieved May 25, 2003 from Bureau of Labor Statistics Web site <http://www.bls.gov/data/home.htm>.

United Nations. (1961). *United Nations Statistical Yearbook.* New York: United Nations.

Usalcas, J., & Bowlby, G. (1999). Supplementary Measures of Unemployment. *Canadian Economic Observer.* Retrieved May 25, 2003 from Statistics Canada Web site <http://www.statcan.ca/english /ads/11-010-XPB/pdf/oct99.pdf>.

Van de Meer, P. & Batenburg, R. (2002). Overeducation in the Netherlands: New Trends, Old Problems. Paper presented at the International Conference 'Overeducation in Europe: What Do We Know?' at Maastricht University, Berlin, November 22-23.

Van Osch, J. (1997). "Contracts are the curse of today's society," *The Toronto Star*. (December 6): 554-5.

Vanstone, S. (1998). *Publications and Resources far Prior Learning Assessment and Recognition*. Toronto: Centre for the Study of Education and Work, OISE/UT.

Verret, M. (1982). *Le travail ouvrier*. Paris: A. Colin.

Vincent, D. (1989). *Literacy and Popular Culture: England 1750-1914*. Cambridge, UK: Cambridge Press.

Vincent, D. (1991). *Poor Citizens: The State and the Poor in Twentieth Century Britain*. New York: Longman.

Virgin, A.E. and C. McCatty. (1976). "High School Dropouts: Characteristics of Their Post-School Learning and Their Perceptions of Why They Left." Report to North York Board of Education.

Vygotsky, L. (1962 [1934]). *Thought and Language*. Cambridge: MIT Press.

Vygotsky, L. (1978). *Mind in Society*. Cambridge: Harvard University Press.

Walker, J.C. (1988). *Louts and Legends: Male Youth Culture in an Inner City School*. Sydney: Allen and Unwin.

Walker, P. (ed.). (1978). *Between Labor and Capital*. Montreal: Black Rose Books.

Wallerstein, I. (1991). *Unthinking Social Science: The Limits of Nineteenth-Century Paradigms*. Cambridge: Polity Press.

Ward, K. and R. Taylor (eds.). (1986). *Adult Education and the Working Class*. London: Croom Helm.

Waring, M. (1988). *If Woman Counted: A New Feminist Economics*. San Francisco: Harper and Row.

Weber, M. (1968 [1928]). *Economy and Society*. New York: Bedminister Press.

Weick, K. (1976). "Educational Organizations as Loosely Coupled Systems" *Administrative Science Quarterly* (March): 1-19.

Weiler, K. (1988). *Women Teaching for Change; Gender, Class and Power*. South Hadley, MA: Bergin and Garvey.

Weir, M. (1992). *Politics and Jobs: The Boundaries of Employment Policy in the United States*. Princeton: Princeton University Press.

Weis, L. (1990). *Working Class Without Work: High School Students in a De-Industrializing Economy*. New York: Routledge.

Weisman, J. (1993). "Skills in the Schools: Now It's Business' Turn," *Phi Delta Kappan* 74, 5 (January): 367-69.

Wells, D. (1993). "Are Strong Unions Compatible with the New Model of Human Resource Management?" *Industrial Relations* 48, 1: 56-85

Welton, M. (ed.). (1987). *Knowledge for the People: The Struggle for Adult Learning in English-Speaking Canada*. Toronto: OISE Press.

Westwood, S. (1985). *All Day, Every Day: Factory and Family in the Making of Women's Lives*. London: Pluto Press.

Wexler, P. et al. (1992). *Becoming Somebody: Toward a Social Psychology of School*. Washington, DC: Palmer Press.

White, B. (1988). *Hard Bargains: My Life on the Line*. Toronto: McClelland and Stewart, 46-47.

Whyte, W. and K. King Whyte. (1991). *Making Mondragon*. Ithaca, NY: ILR Press.

Wiegand, B. (1992). *Off the Books: A Theory and Critique of the Underground Economy.* New York: General Hall.

Wilkinson, D. (2001). [Review of The Education-Jobs Gap]. *Our Schools; Our Selves, 62,* 148-156.

Williams, K. et al. (1987). "The End of Mass Production?" *Economy and Society* 16, 3 (August).

Williams, R. (1961). *The Long Revolution.* Westport: Greenwood Press.

Willis, P. (1977). *Learning to Labour: How Working Class Kids Get Working Class Jobs.* Pamborough: Saxon House.

Willis, P. (1990). *Common Culture: Symbolic Work at Play in Everyday Cultures of the Young.* Boulder: Westview Press.

Wilson, G. (1989). "Getting an Education the Hard Way;" in J. Davis et al. (eds.) *It's Our Own Education: Labour, Public Education and Skills Training.* Toronto: Our Schools/Our Selves Education Foundation, 9-18.

Wirth, A.G. (1992). *Education and Work for the Year 2000: Choices We Face.* San Francisco: Jossey-Bass Publishers.

Witte, J. (1999). [Review of The Education-Jobs Gap]. *Work and Occupations, 26*(4), 540-542.

Witter, S. (1991). "Canada's Occupational Training Programs: Three Decades of Deficiencies" *Canadian Vocational Journal* 26, 1 (Spring): 20-5.

Wolff, E.N. (2000). Technology and the Demand for Skills, in L. Borghans & A. de Grip (eds.) *The Overeducated Worker? The Economics of Skill Utilization.* Cheltenham, UK: Edward Elgar. pp. 27-56.

Wolfle, D. (1971) *The Uses of Talent.* Princeton: Princeton University Press.

Wood, S. (ed.). (1989). *The Transformation of Work: Skill, Flexibility and the Labour Process.* London: Unwin Hyman Ltd.

World Bank. (1997). *World Development Report: The State in a Changing World.* Oxford: Oxford University Press.

Wotherspoon, T. (ed.). (1991). *Hitting the Books: The Politics of Educational Retrenchment.* Toronto: Garamond Press.

Wotherspoon, T. (1999). Insightful Analysis Explodes the Education-Job Gap Myth. *CAUT Bulletin, 46*(11), 7-8.

Wright, E.O. (1980). "Class and Occupation," *Politics and Society.*

Wright, E.O. (1980). *Classes.* London: Verso.

Wright, E.O. (1997). *Class Counts: Comparative Studies in Class Analysis.* Cambridge: Cambridge University Press.

Wrigley, J. (1982). *Class Politics and Public Schools: Chicago, 1900-1950.* New Brunswick, N.J.: Rutgers University Press .

Zhou, M. (1993). "Underemployment and Economic Disparities Among Minority Groups," *Population Research and Policy Review* 12: 139-157.

Zolberg, A. (1972). "Moments of madness," *Politics and Society* 2, 2.

Index

If you have enjoyed reading this book, you will be interested in the following recently published Garamond Press titles:

Pat and Hugh Armstrong et al
MEDICAL ALERT: New Work Organizations in Health Care

William K. Carroll ed.
ORGANIZING DISSENT: Contemporary Social Movements in Theory and Practise, (second, revised edt.)

Catherine Cavanaugh and Jeremy Mouat, eds.
MAKING WESTERN CANADA: Historical Essays

Patricia Cormack, ed.
MANIFESTOS AND DECLARATIONS OF THE 20TH CENTURY

Tania Das Gupta
RACISM AND PAID WORK

Robert Hackett and Yuezhi Zhao
SUSTAINING DEMOCRACY? Journalism and the Politics of Objectivity

Steven Langdon
GLOBAL POVERTY, DEMOCRACY & NORTH-SOUTH CHANGE

David W. Livingstone and J. Marshall Mangan
RECAST DREAMS: Class and Gender Consciousness in Steeltown

John McMurty
UNEQUAL FREEDOMS
The Global Market as an Ethical System

Sylvia O'Meara and Doug West, eds.
FROM OUR EYES: Learning from Indigenous Peoples

Chris Schenk and John Anderson, eds.
RE-SHAPING WORK: Union Responses to Technological Change

Please contact us if you would like to receive a catalogue or more information:

Garamond Press, 67 Mowat Ave., Suite 144, Toronto, On. M6K 3E3
Phone 416-516-2709, fax 416-516-0571, e-mail Garamond@web.net
http://www.garamond.ca/garamond/